The Everyday Life of Global Finance: Saving and Borrowing in Anglo-America

£1

The Everyday Life of Global Finance: Saving and Borrowing in Anglo-America

Paul Langley

OXFORD
UNIVERSITY PRESS

OXFORD

UNIVERSITY PRESS

Great Clarendon Street, Oxford OX2 6DP
United Kingdom

Oxford University Press is a department of the University of Oxford.
It furthers the University's objective of excellence in research, scholarship,
and education by publishing worldwide. Oxford is a registered trade mark of
Oxford University Press in the UK and in certain other countries

© Paul Langley, 2008

The moral rights of the author have been asserted

First published 2008
First published in paperback 2010
Reprinted 2013

Published in the United States of America by Oxford University Press
198 Madison Avenue, New York, NY 10016, United States of America

British Library Cataloguing in Publication Data
Data available

Library of Congress Cataloging in Publication Data
Data available

ISBN 978-0-19-957396-7

For my girls—Lou and Grace

Preface

The routines and rhythms of saving and borrowing in the United States of America (US) and United Kingdom (UK) have fundamentally changed in the last three decades or so. Through the ownership of shares and contributions to pension plans and mutual funds, the savings of a much greater number of individuals and households are now bound-up with the capital markets. Many savers have, in short, become financial investors. At the same time, the boom in borrowing to fund the purchase of homes and consumer goods and services of all kinds has also been closely tied to developments in the capital markets. The ever-increasing future obligations of growing numbers of mortgagors, credit card holders, and instalment plan borrowers now directly provide for the payment of interest and principal on securities issued by their lenders. In meeting their obligations, American mortgagors are, for example, often unwittingly ensuring that the wheels of the mortgage-backed securities market continue to turn, a bond market even larger than that for US federal government debt. The focus of this book, then, is on the unprecedented relationships between everyday saving and borrowing in Anglo-America, on the one hand, and the capital markets that we tend to know as 'global finance', on the other.

My first motivation in the pages that follow is to begin to reveal and elucidate these unparalleled relationships. This, in itself, marks a departure from the vast majority of existing social scientific enquiry into contemporary finance. Social scientists of finance have almost exclusively concerned themselves with 'global finance', that is, with the changes in the capital markets that tend to be viewed as defining contemporary finance. The transformations of finance appear as 'out there somewhere', as separate and differentiated from 'real' socio-economic life. In this book, in contrast, I seek to break the hold of global finance on the research imaginations of social scientists of finance. It is certainly not the case that we should forget global finance, far from it. In recent times, the capital markets of Wall Street, the City of London, Chicago, and so on have witnessed profound and ongoing changes which have reverberated and resonated across the globe. But, as this book will show, the apparently extra-ordinary transformations of global finance are intimately related to transformations in seemingly mundane everyday saving and borrowing.

My first motivation leads, therefore, to the intuitive claim that, in understanding contemporary finance, we need to take seriously the changes in Anglo-American everyday saving and borrowing that have forged tight relationships with the capital markets. There is a danger that simply revealing the relationships between Anglo-American everyday saving and borrowing and the capital markets will not, however, prompt a (re)valuing of their place in contemporary finance. In presenting much of the research contained in this book to academics across the social sciences over the last few years, I have become acutely aware of this hazard. More often than not, sympathetic and supporting discussants and questioners have suggested that, when all is said and done, 'small' or 'local' changes in US and UK finance are taking place in the face of 'bigger' or 'global' forces. My various notes from these presentations are replete with lines of interrogation that have led to questions that have, for example, taken the following forms: 'As the power of Wall Street, the City, the International Monetary Fund (IMF), and World Bank extends globally and looms large in the management strategies of even the largest corporations, is it any wonder that finance capital also penetrates deep into society and economy at home?'; 'It is the major banks and finance houses that are driving and selling the transformations in everyday saving and borrowing, right?'; 'So, your central argument is that the financialization of economies includes households and not just firms—surely there is no surprise there?'; and 'Should we not speak of "global finance in everyday life", and thereby recognize the secondary importance of the latter?'

As this questioning serves to highlight, it is clearly insufficient to claim, on the basis of empirical research and intuitive assertion alone, that Anglo-American everyday saving and borrowing should be (re)valued in our understanding of contemporary finance. My second motivation in this book, therefore, is to turn many of the usual assumptions that are shared by social scientists about what matters in contemporary finance, about the spaces, practices and subjects of global finance, inside out and on their head. By calling this book *The Everyday Life of Global Finance* I have sought to signal an ontological move that elevates the status of everyday life. For me, everyday life has to come first. The category of everyday life does not just provoke a concern with that which is neglected in the vast majority of accounts of contemporary finance, that is, with the mundane routines of saving and borrowing. It also directs us to view transformations in those routines as crucial to the constitution and contestation of contemporary finance. The category of everyday life frames what we might interrogate, and what we come to regard as significant in contemporary finance.

The diverse and often contradictory literature on everyday life does not provide, however, a straightforward or satisfactory line of sight through which we might pursue our focus here. Finance has not been of particular interest to scholars of everyday life who tend to be preoccupied with issues of production, work, family, leisure, and consumption. Few specific clues are available as to how it is that transformed practices of saving and borrowing, so closely intertwined with the capital markets, have become prosaic and ordinary for so many. My first and second motivations in this book necessarily lead, then, to a third motivation: to draw from and contribute to recent conceptual debates amongst social scientists of finance in order to reveal and (re)value transformations in everyday saving and borrowing in our understanding of contemporary finance.

A growing body of research by sociologists, geographers, anthropologists, and heterodox economists—widely known as 'the social studies of finance'—already suggests that the concept of 'financial networks' provides a means of decentring finance.[1] Related enquiry into the scientific, rational, and calculative representations and performances of modern finance also suggests that, in order to interrogate financial power, we should not think only of finance capital, the major states, or the instrumental rationality of money. Present within the social studies of finance is, therefore, a kernel of conceptual work that, with development and innovation, provides a basis from which to begin to explore the transformations in everyday saving and borrowing without assuming that 'small' or 'local' changes have, at their centre, 'big' or 'global' forces. At the same time, several contributors to international political economy (IPE) are currently questioning the conceptual apparatus that tends to prevail in the study of finance within that field. This questioning has been prompted, at least in part, by a growing awareness of the importance of societal incorporation to framing the contours of contemporary finance. In sum, there would seem at present to be conceptual openings that, if explored, provide us with a route into our subject matter. This route holds

---

[1] For details of the interdisciplinary Social Studies of Finance academic network based at the University of Edinburgh, see http://www.sociology.ed.ac.uk/finance/

the potential to not only enable analysis of the transformations in everyday finance that have forged close relationships with the capital markets, but to follow through on our ontological move and take everyday life seriously in our understanding of contemporary finance.

In this book, my motivations to push back the boundaries of social scientific enquiry into contemporary finance, both empirically and conceptually, are, however, also joined by an additional and fourth motivation. Scholars of everyday life typically hold normative and political positions that oppose, in broad terms, the transformations in the mundane and ordinary routines that are their focus. For Henri Lefebvre, for instance, the point was to provide a critique of the ways in which modernity and capitalism had come to penetrate everyday life, and to reflect upon the political possibilities for contestation and change. I continue in this spirit in this book. Specifically, I seek to open up and (re)politicize the scientific and calculative representations and performances through which financial power operates, and to draw out multiple modes of dissent that question and challenge the everyday life of global finance. This, then, is my fourth and final motivation in the pages that follow.

My main motivations in writing this book were, of course, far from clear at the outset of the project some five years ago. Over that period, a large number of people and institutions have provided intellectual support, empirical insights, and financial resources, and have thus contributed to helping me to understand what it was I was trying to achieve. Indeed, it is perhaps only fitting that I have accumulated a large number of debts to a wide range of people and institutions in completing a book on saving and borrowing.

The research and writing of this book would not have been possible without the support of my colleagues at Northumbria University. Keith Shaw, Rosie Cunningham, and Lynn Dobbs have all helped with workload planning, financial support for conference attendance and fieldwork research, and by making possible a period of sabbatical leave in late 2006. Mary Mellor also read and commented on parts of the manuscript. I am also particularly pleased to say that, in September 2006, Ralph Chima was awarded a Doctoral Scholarship by Northumbria University. I would like to thank Ralph for our conversations on financialization and subprime borrowing which have contributed to shaping several chapters of this book.

The fieldwork that has contributed towards this book included interviews with bankers, regulators, asset managers, consultants, actuaries, government officials, and trade unionists. A total of fifty-one interviews were completed in London in September 2003 and January 2005, and New York and Washington, DC, in May 2005. Confidentiality prevents me from naming the individuals and institutions concerned but, without them, this book would not have been possible. In addition, the three non-participant observation studies that I undertook of the workplace training delivered by pension plan administrators in various parts of the UK in late 2004 were essential to forming my thoughts on the differences between defined-benefit and defined-contribution occupational pensions. Financial support for my fieldwork came from a Northumbria University Small Research Grant, and the British Academy (SG-37817).

Many of the ideas and much of the research contained in this book first appeared as papers presented at conferences and workshops: British International Studies Association annual conference (2004, 2005, and 2006); International Studies Association annual convention (2004 and 2006); Cultures of Money, University of Amsterdam (2005); Department of Politics Seminar Series, University of Bristol (2005); After De-regulation: The Financial System in the Twenty-First Century, University of Sussex (2005); Think Tank on Housing Wealth, Durham University (2007); International Working Group on Financialization, London (2007); Reconstructing International Political Economy, University of Sheffield (2007); and Cultural Political Economy, University of Ottawa (2007). I would like to thank all who invited me to participate in these events, acted as discussants, and asked thought-provoking and probing questions. Particular thanks to Rob Aitken, Karyn Ball, Jacquie Best, Mark Blyth, Tony Cutler, Matt Davies, Ewald Engelen, Julie Froud, Andrew Gamble, Randy Germain, Joyce Goggin, Adam Harmes, John Hobson, Sukhdev Johal, Donald MacKenzie, Johnna Montgomerie, Matt Patterson, Len Seabrooke, Tim Sinclair, Susanne Soederberg, Susan J. Smith, Andrew Sturdy, Marcus Taylor, Adam Tickell, Barbara Waine, William Walters, Matt Watson, Karel Williams, and Andrew Wyatt. Special thanks to Marieke de Goede. Marieke has not only commented on many of my conference papers and presentations, but has also carefully read the manuscript of this book and provided many points of useful criticism. Artist Kate Bingaman-Burt also very kindly supplied a 'Credit Card Drawing' from her 'Obsessive Consumption' project for inclusion in Chapter 9.

This book also builds on previously published journal articles and edited volume chapters: 'In the eye of the "perfect storm": the final salary pension crisis and financialisation of Anglo-American capitalism', *New Political Economy*, 9(4) (2004): 539–58; 'The everyday life of global finance: A neglected 'level' of governance', in Andrew Baker, David Hudson, and

Richard Woodward (eds.), *Governing Financial Globalisation: The Political Economy of Multi-Level Governance*, London: Routledge, 2004, 85–101; 'The making of investor subjects in Anglo-American pensions', *Environment and Planning D: Society and Space*, 24(6) (2006): 919–34; 'Securitising suburbia: The transformation of Anglo-American mortgage finance', *Competition & Change*, 10(3) (2006): 283–99; 'The uncertain subjects of Anglo-American financialisation', *Cultural Critique*, 65 (Winter, 2007): 66–91; and 'Global finance, Anglo-American mass investment, and everyday investor subjects', in John A. Hobson and Leonard Seabrooke (eds.), *Everyday International Political Economy*. Cambridge: Cambridge University Press, 2007. In all cases, the editors and anonymous reviewers who commented on my submissions certainly pushed me to tighten-up my arguments in the course of publication, so I would like to express my gratitude to them. The author would like to thank the following for permission to reproduce copyright material: Cambridge University Press; Maney Publishing Ltd.; Pion Ltd; Taylor and Francis; and University of Minnesota Press. Crown copyright material is reproduced under Class Licence Number CP01P0000148 with the permission of OPSI and the Queen's Printer for Scotland.

Gordon Clark at Oxford and David Musson at Oxford University Press have shown great enthusiasm for this project and have offered excellent advice. Efficient and friendly support with the technicalities of manuscript preparation was provided by Matthew Derbyshire. In commenting on the original book proposal and introductory chapter, three anonymous reviewers also helped to bring form to the project.

My final acknowledgements are to my daughter Grace, and to my wife Lou. Grace emerged into the world while this book was in its early stages, and has enriched my life more than I could have ever imagined. I would guess that fathers are always likely to say that about their children, but Grace has been special from the start. Lou has supported me in innumerable ways, from her knowledge of political economy, geography, and social theory, to her constant love, patience, and encouragement. Lou is my soul mate in everyday life.

PL

Contents

List of Abbreviations

ABCUL	Association of British Credit Unions Ltd.
ABI	Association of British Insurers
ABS	asset-backed securities
AFFIL	Americans For Fairness in Lending
AFL-CIO	American Federation of Labor-Congress of Industrial Organizations
ANT	actor-network theory
APR	annual percentage rate
ARM	adjustable rate mortgage
BIT	Building Investment Trust
BRIC	Brazil, Russia, India, and China
BSP	basic state pension
CalPERS	California Public Employee Retirement System
CalSTRS	California State Teachers Retirement System
CARDs	certificates for amortizing revolving debts
CARs	certificates for automobile receivables
CBO	collateralized bond obligation
CD	certificate of deposit
CDO	collateralized debt obligation
CDS	credit default swap
CRA	Community Reinvestment Act
CSR	corporate social responsibility
CUNA	Credit Union National Association
DB	defined-benefit
DC	defined-contribution
DoL	Department of Labor
DSS	Department of Social Security

DTI	Department of Trade and Industry
DVA	Department of Veterans Affairs
DWP	Department of Work and Pensions
ECB	European Central Bank
ERISA	Employee Retirement Income Security Act
ETIs	economically targeted investments
EU	European Union
FHA	Federal Housing Association
FICO	Fair Isaac Corporation
FLEC	Financial Literacy and Education Commission
FRS17	Financial Reporting Standard 17
FSA	Financial Services Authority
G-7	Group of 7
GDP	gross domestic product
GSE	government-sponsored enterprise
HIT	Housing Investment Trust
ICI	Investment Company Institute
IFIs	international financial institutions
IMF	International Monetary Fund
IPE	international political economy
IPO	initial public offering
IRA	Individual Retirement Account
IRS	Internal Revenue Service
ISA	Individual Savings Account
IVA	Individual Voluntary Agreement
LETS	Local Exchange Trading System
LIGs	lower-income groupings
M&A	merger and acquisition
MBS	mortgage-backed securities
MPC	Monetary Policy Committee
NASDAQ	National Association of Securities Dealers Automated Quotation
NAV	net asset value
NGO	non-governmental organization
NYSE	New York Stock Exchange

List of Abbreviations

OECD	Organization for Economic Cooperation and Development
OFT	Office of Fair Trading
PAYGO	pay-as-you-go
PBGC	Pensions Benefit Guaranty Corporation
PCI	Permissible Countries Index
PEP	Personal Equity Plan
PFEG	Personal Finance Education Group
PIN	personal identification number
PPF	Pensions Protection Fund
ROCE	return on capital employed
SAVER	Savings Are Vital to Everyone's Retirement
SEC	Securities and Exchange Commission
SERPS	State Earnings Related Pension Scheme
SIA	Securities Industry Association
SIPP	self-invested personal pension
SIV	structured investment vehicle
S&Ls	savings and loans
S&P	Standard & Poors Ratings Group
SPV	special purchase vehicle
SRI	socially responsible investment
SSA	Social Security Administration
T-bills	US Treasury bills
T-bonds	US Treasury bonds
TESSA	Tax-Exempt Saving Scheme
TUC	Trades Union Congress
UK	United Kingdom
US	United States of America

Introduction

In living rooms all across America, where cultural wars ultimately get settled, the verdict about the Street has been revised.... The well-springs of opposition seem to have dried up; not only in the political world, but more intimately too: in what people think about the relationship between God and Mammon, in the way our literary and cinematic fictions and daily newspapers assume a stance of fateful inevitability about the reign of the free market.... Delusional or not, for the moment at least Wall Street's promise of emancipation, of 'Every Man a Speculator', has taken hold. The old Wall Street is dead. Long live Wall Street!

(Steve Fraser, *Wall Street: A Cultural History*, 2005: xviii)

In his remarkable survey of 200 years of the cultural history of Wall Street, of the Street's representation by American novelists, playwrights, theologians, artists, poets, politicians, film-makers, academics, cartoonists, and journalists, Steve Fraser's view is that something fundamental has changed. There have, of course, long been images of Wall Street as a realm of heroic figures, entrepreneurial genius, and of rags-to-riches and derring-do. These have nevertheless always competed in the popular imagination with Wall Street's villainous and inscrutable gamblers, with robber barons living lavishly off the blood, sweat, and tears of others. While the cultural history of Wall Street is thus marked by 'deep ambivalence' (p. xvi), it is clear that 'the verdict has usually been negative' (p. xvii). As Fraser observes, 'Even as its power and cultural weight grew, those who applauded it and placed hope in its impressive if inscrutable undertakings found themselves on the defensive' (p. xvii). What has changed in the contemporary period, then, such that Wall Street's 'promise of emancipation' has come to hold sway?

1

It is the seemingly realistic possibility of 'the democratization of finance' (p. 324) that, for Fraser, holds the key to understanding why the 'old Wall Street is dead'. There was, of course, a previous period during which Wall Street 'shed the moral stigma that had shadowed it for generations' (p. xiv). During the late 1920s, through to the Crash of 1929, 'the stock market became the horizonless terrain on which millions of people spied a future of limitless good times for all' (p. 324). In the current period, however, from the early 1980s at least, the image of a 'shareholder nation' appears to have greater credence (pp. 506–43). There has indeed been an unprecedented stepwise growth in popular involvement in the financial markets, a development that others have also cast as 'the democratization of finance' (Erturk et al. 2007; Friedman 2000; Grant 1992; Gross 2000; Nocera 1994). By way of general illustration, at the time of the Wall Street Crash, only 3 per cent of US households held a stake in the stock market (Bygrave 1998). By 2001, often as a consequence of contributions to occupational and personal pension plans and mutual funds, 51.9 per cent of US households owned a slice (however meagre) of the stock market, up from 25 per cent as recently as 1987 (ICI and SIA 2005; Reuters 2003).

Although the power and legitimacy of modern finance has long turned on its representation as a highly technical and rational domain (de Goede 2005b), in the contemporary period 'the most sophisticated mathematical thinking and technological wizardry created a reassuring sense of the market's safety and predictability' (Fraser 2005: 510). A range of new medias—'how to . . . ' personal finance guides, regular special sections in newspapers, dedicated magazines, websites, and cable television stations—also all further the message of financial democratization. At the same time, the Wall Street villains of the 1980s—for example, the character of Gordon Gekko in Oliver Stone's movie Wall Street— have faded from the collective memory. They have become overshadowed by new heroes with a common touch, such as the investment gurus Warren Buffet of Berkshire Hathaway, and Peter Lynch who managed Fidelity's Magellan mutual fund (pp. 516–18). And, through the 1990s at least, the stock market experienced the long bull run associated with the so-called 'new economy' and 'dot.com boom', generating massive returns for investors who believed in the 'promise of emancipation'.

It is the unprecedented relationships that have developed between society and the financial markets in the contemporary period—the processes of change that Fraser, with considerable scepticism, refers to as 'the democratization of finance'—which form the focus of this book. Although we will acknowledge the long lineage of many recent developments in the chapters that follow, we will nevertheless take largely as given the argument that current relationships between 'Main Street' and Wall Street are exceptional. It is only over the last quarter of a century or so that stock market investment has become somewhat ordinary and mundane, very much embedded in everyday life. But, what transformations have taken place in routine saving practices in order that more extensive investment relationships have been forged? How are these relationships produced and consolidated, and in what ways do they contain their own vulnerabilities and contradictions? Do these new relationships signal a genuine and inclusive 'democratization' where the financial markets are made to work for all, or does investment in the financial markets remain out of reach for many? What are the implications of these relationships for our understanding of finance more broadly, and for political action that, once again, might serve to place Wall Street's financial markets 'on the defensive'?

It would be tempting, perhaps, to consider these and other questions solely with reference to transformations in saving practices, and to the emergence of mass financial market investment. Yet, the unprecedented relationships between society and the financial markets that prevail in the contemporary period have also arisen through transformations in borrowing practices, particularly those related to consumption and home ownership. Although popular media coverage of the recent crisis of sub-prime mortgage-backed securities has shed considerable light on these relationships (see Conclusion), the majority of mortgagors, credit card holders, and other borrowers seem unaware that claims on their future repayments, and the risks on their non-payment, are presently packaged and traded in the capital markets. But, if we are to truly examine 'the democratization of finance', the manner and terms upon which credit is made available to individuals and households through the capital markets is a central issue. Recent decades have witnessed an explosion in the scale of household borrowing across the industrialized societies as part of what Clayton (2000) terms 'the global debt bomb', and it is in the US and also the UK that this expansion is most pronounced and sustained. What is much less clear, however, is what transformations have taken place to create new and booming forms of routine borrowing that are closely bound up with the capital markets? How are these transformations in borrowing fashioned and to what extent are they laden with tensions? Furthermore, although the transformation and boom in borrowing appears to embrace ever-greater numbers of individuals and households, why is this not leading to an overturning of hierarchies and to equal access to credit for all?

The critical questions that we might ask about 'the democratization of finance' are, then, pertinent to contemporary transformations underway in both saving and borrowing. As such, the main body of this book is divided into two broadly equal Parts concerned, respectively, with saving and borrowing. Across both Parts of the book, we will also extend our enquiry into 'the democratization of finance' beyond Main Street and Wall Street, and consider the similarly unparalleled relationships that have developed in the UK between society and the financial markets. It is certainly not my methodological intention in this respect to undertake a formal and symmetrical comparative analysis. Comparative political economists typically emphasize the similarities between US and UK financial arrangements, stressing that their well-developed capital markets distinguish them from the bank-based arrangements that prevail in Germany, for example (e.g. Zysman 1983). Daniel Verdier (2002), in contrast, stresses the historical differences between US and UK finance. Compared to the UK, he characterizes US finance in terms of decentralization, that is, strong local state institutions and empowered local banks are present that veto the monopoly and centralization tendencies of finance. Verdier's intervention reminds us that there are important historical differences between finance in the US and the UK, disparities that have not completely evaporated in recent times. The degree to which the City of London centralizes UK financial arrangements is, for instance, certainly not matched by Wall Street in the US. But, the decentralized institutional arrangements in US finance have been eroded significantly over the last three decades or so. As Verdier himself observes, for example, legal restrictions on inter-state banking and requirements that commercial and investment banking remain compartmentalized have been swept away, while the absence of centralized state power has served only to slow or 'muffle' the 'big bang' process of securities market deregulation in the US (pp. 177–82).

For us, then, drawing a clear boundary around and between the practices of saving and borrowing in the US and the UK would be both problematic and unhelpful. Indeed, following Gamble (2003), we will talk of 'Anglo-America' in order to stress the distinctive and largely mutual trajectory of change in the US and the UK. In doing so, we will bring together apparently isolated and seemingly negligible moments and manifestations of the transformations underway on both sides of the Atlantic.

This will provide for both greater illustration and a deeper appreciation of processes of change. As Jamie Peck (2001) notes with regard to the methodological problems of exploring unprecedented developments that are 'in motion', the moments and manifestations that we highlight may, in retrospect, not be fully representative exemplars, but are certainly 'suggestive episodes in an on-going process' (p. 7). Put differently, in the terms of Nikolas Rose (1999), we seek to offer a 'history of the present' in Anglo-American finance, an enquiry that pays 'attention to the humble, the mundane, the little shifts in our ways of thinking and understanding, the small and contingent struggles, tensions and negotiations' (p. 11). This 'is not merely because of a general prejudice that one will learn more about our present and its past by studying the minor and everyday texts and practices'. It is also because it may well only be 'after the event', so to speak, that historians and social scientists may come to fully appreciate the contours and repercussions of 'the democratization of finance'.

Global Finance

The transformations in saving and borrowing that are producing close interconnections between Anglo-American society and the financial markets have, to date, received relatively little attention in the social sciences. For the vast majority of social scientists of finance, it is the emergence of 'global finance' and significant changes in the capital markets that tend to be viewed as the defining characteristic of our age. Global finance has been subjected to considerable debate and scrutiny in the social sciences, and I do not intend to offer an exhaustive summary of these debates here. Rather, what is notable for us are the ways in which global finance holds a tight and somewhat suffocating grip on research agendas and, therefore, on social scientists' understandings of contemporary finance. At worst, the unprecedented relationships between Anglo-American society and the financial markets become neglected in the face of global finance and are, in effect, written out of contemporary finance. At best, even when transformations in everyday saving and borrowing are addressed, they tend to remain of secondary importance to apparently more pervasive forces at work in the realm of global finance. Two sets of literature are particularly illustrative of these tendencies.

First, geographers, sociologists, anthropologists, and others working within the social studies of finance typically target the assumption that contemporary finance is marked by the emergence of a smooth, seamless, and genuinely integrated twenty-four hour global marketplace for capital. This assumption, especially prevalent amongst practitioners, policy makers, orthodox economists, and journalists, lies at the heart of the common sense representation of global finance as 'spaceless' and 'timeless' as it follows the sun from East to West (Langley 2002). For the social studies of finance, however, global finance remains firmly grounded in the principal financial centres that include London, New York, and Chicago (Carruthers 1996; Leyshon and Thrift 1997; MacKenzie 2006; Sassen 1999). The careful ethnographic enquiry favoured by the social studies of finance informs and illustrates the socially and spatially embedded nature of financial markets (Abolafia 1996; Fligstein 2001; Knorr Cetina and Preda 2005; MacKenzie 2006; Maurer 1999; McDowell 1997). Distinct cultural rituals, rules, and symbols; relationships of trust, friendship, and cooperation; the acceptance of models, formulas, and calculations; and trading floors of computer screens, interlinked by high-technology communication channels, are all shown to provide the architecture of the financial markets.

While standing as a significant corrective to popular assumptions about 'spaceless' and 'timeless' global finance, the social studies of finance also highlights the delimiting consequences that follow from the language that social scientists usually deploy to depict finance. It is common for scholars to describe finance in terms of 'system', 'flows', 'movements', and 'circulation', often in conjunction with prefixes such as 'global', 'capital', or 'cross-border' (e.g. Appadurai 1996; Clark 2005; Harvey 1999; LiPuma and Lee 2004). Such terms position the financial economy 'out there somewhere', a system of movements and circulations that are above and beyond and differentiated from society in general, and the 'real' economy in particular. From here, it is only a short step to claims made, for example, by Fredric Jameson (1998), that finance capital is both 'deterritorialized' and 'dematerialized' in contemporary times. But, as Rob Aitken (2005) puts it, talk of 'flows' leads to the 'diagramming' of finance and capital 'in terms of macro-structural forces or episodes of change' (p. 336). The result of such 'diagramming' are disembedded and disembodied accounts of finance, that is, accounts which neglect the very features of financial markets that are rightly emphasized by the social studies of finance.

Although the situated and embodied analyses of financial markets offered by contributors to the social studies of finance are certainly apposite, they nonetheless remain broadly united by a concern with what we usually know as 'global finance'. With the notable exception of Alex Preda's (2001, 2005) work on 'popular investment' which we discuss in detail in Chapter 2, very little is done to explicitly re-orientate enquiry beyond global finance, beyond professional, expert, and elite networks of knowledge and technology situated in specific centres. While finance becomes understood as grounded in the tight social networks of Wall Street, the City, and so on—and not a mass of flows 'out there somewhere'—the social studies of finance has, with some irony, tended to continue to divorce finance from society at large. Now, I do not deny the significance of changes in the capital markets in the pages that follow, and this is reflected in the inclusion of 'global finance' in the title of this book. But, just as the story of contemporary finance is not a tale of what is happening 'out there somewhere', it is also not enough to chronicle developments in the market and social networks of New York and London. Understanding finance in the current period requires that we explore the intersection between changes in the capital markets, on the one hand, and transformations in everyday spaces, practices and identities, on the other.

A second set of literature, from the field of international political economy (IPE), also illustrates the grip of global finance on social scientist's research imagination, and how this has considerable implications for our ability to take 'the democratization of finance' seriously in our understanding of contemporary finance. The principal contribution of the IPE literature is to challenge the prevailing assumption—again, an assumption shared by practitioners, policy makers, orthodox economists, and journalists alike—that the emergence and consolidation of global finance is inextricably linked to the triumph and spread of universal market rationality. This assumption informs, for example, representations of the so-called 'disintermediation' of finance. Here the assumed efficiencies of markets in the allocation of capital and distribution of risk prevail over intermediated forms of finance, that is, where banks act as the 'go betweens' of saving and investment and hold risk on their balance sheets (French and Leyshon 2004). For IPE scholars, however, it is the politics of institutions and collective interests, and not market rationality and technological innovation, which is held to be pivotal to explaining the course taken by global disintermediated finance.

Scholars such as Susan Strange (1986, 1998), Eric Helleiner (1994), and Randall Germain (1997), for instance, stress that the initial emergence of global finance in the London-centred off-shore Euromarkets of the 1960s required the tacit support of the UK and US governments.

The subsequent development of global finance is similarly interpreted as hinging on liberalization and deregulatory decisions taken by the key states, and on the market-reinforcing governance supplied by a complex mix of state institutions, regional and international organizations, and private authorities such as credit rating agencies (Best 2005; Blyth 2002; Pauly 1997; Porter 2005, Sinclair 2005; Soederberg 2004, 2006*b*). Decisions to liberalize and deregulate financial markets are shown to be grounded in competitive pressures on the state to attract mobile capital flows and, therefore, are not simply the outcome of the power and preferences of domestic financial interests (Vogel 1996). The governance arrangements that have evolved somewhat fitfully in response to periodic crises in global finance—for example, the so-called 'new international financial architecture' which emerged in the wake of the Asian crisis of 1997–8—are similarly shown to be the result of the interplay of institutions and competing collective interests (see Langley 2004).

IPE enquiry into global finance has for the most part, then, simply disregarded the interconnections that have taken hold between Anglo-American society and the capital markets. On the rare occasions when society does appear in the accounts of contemporary finance offered by IPE scholars, it tends to be reduced to a range of sectional collective interests that impact upon state-market relations. For example, in his account of the persistence of diverse national institutional and regulatory arrangements, Daniel Verdier (2002) argues that divergence reflects different state strategies for arbitrating re-distributional conflicts. Here the centralizing tendencies and interests of major banks are pitched against the demands for decentralization of local banks, firms, and borrowers, such that 'Many of the financial regulatory issues that have agitated financial systems during the past century and a half are reducible to a competition for market share between center and periphery' (p. 33). Not dissimilarly, when Mosley (2003) argues that the capital market openness and integration of global finance 'does not necessitate the death of social democratic welfare states' (p. 2), a key question becomes how the 'significant degree of policy autonomy' retained by governments is shaped by 'domestic distributional considerations' (p. 3).

A recent wave of IPE enquiry has, however, begun to loosen the straightjacket-like grip of global finance on scholars' research imaginations. Three contributions are especially notable. First, for Leonard Seabrooke (2006), 'who has access to credit, who can hold property, and who pays what kinds of taxes' matters because 'People in lower-income groupings' (what he calls 'LIGs') can, with 'state support', 'provide a potentially rich source of public and private capital to a financial system' (p. 1). It follows that 'if the state intervenes positively on behalf of LIGs, it can generate a social source of financial power by broadening and deepening the domestic pool of capital, which then bolsters the state's influence in the international financial order' (p. 2). He calls this 'the ideal-typical pocketbook-to-global finance scenario' (p. 17). 'Conversely, if the state intervenes against the interests of LIGs, it permits room for a "rentier shift" spurred on by economic elites' that 'diminishes the state's international influence' (p. 2). Seabrooke explores these scenarios with reference to England and Germany in the late nineteenth and early twentieth centuries, and the US and Japan in the final decades of the twentieth century. In contrast to the other cases he examines, what distinguishes US power in contemporary finance for Seabrooke is, therefore, the legitimacy that arises from its relatively deep and broad domestic pool of capital. Such legitimacy is, in turn, not the direct consequence of rational decisions by US state managers to buttress their power on the international stage, but an indirect consequence of contestation over financial reform between LIGs and rentiers at home.

Second, for Matthew Watson (2007), the study of intensified cross-border and cross-asset market capital mobility has become more pressing in the contemporary period because of a 'socialization' of finance in the US and UK that is driven primarily by transformations in everyday saving. As Watson suggests, individuals and households are now much more likely to have their living standards ruined by sudden and volatile movements of capital. As he puts it, 'the process of financial socialisation has deepened the impression that more is now at stake than ever before when the pricing structure of financial markets looks likely to break down' (p. 3). Although Watson's principal focus is upon the strategies of financial market traders that propel price determination, he regards the unprecedented relationships that have come to prevail between society and the markets as a key condition for the emergence of contemporary finance. Alongside the deregulatory decisions of government elites which are usually emphasized by IPE writers, Watson argues that financial markets' 'current operating logic is entirely dependent on societal inculcation of a particular understanding of risk and uncertainty' (p. 13). For Watson, then, developments in contemporary finance are grounded, in the terms of Ulrich Beck (1992), in the move from an 'industrial society' to a 'risk society'.

Third, Rob Aitken (2007) interrogates the troublesome representation of 'finance capital' as a material given and all-encompassing global force.

In contrast, he offers a genealogical and cultural analysis that decentres finance capital, viewing it as situated and performed in everyday spaces. Aitken's focus is upon what he calls the 'popular finance' of the last 150 years or so in the US, that is, the programmes of a diverse range of organizations (e.g. banks, the New York Stock Exchange, state agencies) that have sought to incorporate large sections of society into private market spaces and forms of self-government. Especially significant for Aitken are the advertising, advice, marketing materials, and promotional literatures that target savers and investors and which visualize and rationalize their performances. Ultimately, Aitken demystifies finance capital, thereby opening it up to a mode of critique that stresses complexity, ambiguity, and already-existing opportunities for political agency.

While this book is in part a contribution to this current wave of scholarship in the IPE of global finance, it also differs in crucial respects. Societal relationships with the financial markets are important for Seabrooke (2006) only in so far as they have consequences for a state's 'international financial capability', that is, 'the capacity to draw credit from and increase the generation of credit to the international financial order, as well as influencing this order's regulatory and normative structure' (p. 2). For him, 'analyzing small dynamics' is justified in terms of seeking 'to answer the big question of how states create financial power' (p. 3). Meanwhile, while Watson (2007) emphasizes that 'financial markets are culturally constructed', this construction is understood primarily as directed through public policies of 'new constitutionalism' which protect financial asset values and ensure 'government complicity in preserving the existing structure and stratifications of society' (pp. 19–20; cf. Gill 2003). Locked into markets of mobile capital and serving the collective interests of financiers, a restructured state is thus central to a 'contemporary society...controlled by a commercial rationality' (Watson 2007: 35). For us, in contrast to both Seabrooke and Watson, how the mundane and routine practices of saving and borrowing are themselves of great constitutive significance in contemporary finance—and not largely derivative of apparently 'bigger' forces of state power, or ultimately reducible to state-based legitimation of speculative forms of 'risky' accumulation and the sectional collective interests that they benefit—is precisely the question at hand.

Rob Aitken's (2007) *Performing Capital* certainly begins to address this question. Indeed, we will pick up on the notions of 'finance capital' and 'performativity' in Chapter 1. In addition, throughout this book, we will share with Aitken a desire to both decentre contemporary finance in a manner that brings everyday finance to the fore, and link the changing relationships between society and the financial markets to shifting assemblages of (neo)liberal government and self-discipline. However, for us, the interconnections between society and the capital markets which have become established over the last 30 years or so are unprecedented in their scope and pervasiveness. They encompass both the US and UK, and have been produced not simply through transformations in everyday saving and what it means to be a saver, but also through situated, embedded and embodied transformations in everyday borrowing. Apprehending these transformations and their constitutive significance in contemporary finance requires that we tease-out and sharpen-up key conceptual themes, and broaden our empirical remit. Furthermore, while Aitken is concerned to bring that which might be regarded as 'merely cultural' to the analysis of finance capital (cf. Butler 1998), for us, setting greater store by the routines of everyday life is what matters as we seek understanding of contemporary finance.

Everyday Life

According to the vast majority of social scientists, then, prosaic practices of saving and borrowing are deemed to be of marginal or secondary importance to understanding contemporary finance. However, that which may appear at the margins is not necessarily of marginal significance. It may actually be crucial to the constitution of social relations. As such, it is certainly our intention in the pages that follow to concentrate on, elucidate, and raise critical questions about the often neglected 'democratization of finance'. But, at the same time, I want to go further and (re)value the unprecedented relationships between society and the capital markets in our understanding of contemporary finance. As will be suggested in Chapter 1, this requires that we think carefully about hierarchical dichotomies such as 'big' and 'small' and 'global' and 'local', and pay closer attention to how we might conceive of financial power. It also requires, I would contend, that we recognize the potential of 'everyday life' to re-orientate our understanding of contemporary finance.

Re-valuing 'the democratization of finance' in our understanding of contemporary finance challenges us to, so to speak, turn the usual assumptions about the spaces, practices, and subjects of finance inside out and on their head. In confronting this challenge, using everyday life merely as a descriptive label, and not as a conceptual category, would seriously undercut its analytical and political potential (Davies 2006a). As an essay by Briys and de Varenne (2000) of Deutsche Bank illustrates, it is possible to describe, in positive terms, the consequences of financial markets for everyday life in a manner that does not disrupt the seemingly all-powerful reach of the former over the latter. But, as a conceptual category, everyday life implies an ontological commitment to dispute boundaries, to question the limits to enquiry which arise from the exclusion and marginalization of those spaces, practices, and subjects that are typically bracketed out (Featherstone 1992). For example, for Henri Lefebvre (1991), one of the principal theorists of everyday life, it is 'in a sense residual, defined by "what is left over" after all distinct, superior, specialized, structured activities have been singled out by analysis' (p. 97). For us, while contemporary finance is undoubtedly produced in important ways in the 'specialized' activities of Wall Street and the City that are 'singled out by [existing] analysis', it is nevertheless performed, experienced, lived, and given meaning in the routine practices of saving and borrowing. Anglo-American everyday savers and borrowers are, to draw on a phrase from another leading theorist of everyday life Michel de Certeau (1988), the 'unrecognized producers' of finance (p. xviii).

So, questioning the boundaries that lead to the representation of everyday life as 'residual' also produces a move to restore the routines and rhythms of everyday life to significance in social enquiry. In Lefebvre's terms (1991), 'Everyday life is profoundly related to *all* activities, and encompasses them with all their difference and conflicts; it is their meeting place, their bond, their common ground' (p. 97 *original emphasis*). It follows that, in giving everyday life its proper and prominent place in our understanding of contemporary finance, we should be careful to acknowledge the coexistence of commonality and difference that renders everyday life far from self-evident (Highmore 2002). When we invoke the category of everyday life here in relation to contemporary finance, then, we 'summon-up a specific everyday' and 'call a group of people together so as to recognize a shared everyday life' (p. 2). Those who we bring together by exploring their common practices and experiences— what de Certeau (1988: xi) calls 'modes of operation or schemata of action'—include, for example, mutual fund investors, credit card holders, and mortgagors in the US and UK. In doing so, however, we necessarily encounter stark inequalities, and individuals and households who are marginalized from, for example, occupational pension saving.

When we come upon the inequalities of 'the democratization of finance' in the chapters that follow, patterns and experiences of inequality will not be explored purely with reference to income groupings, or through simple prior assumptions about collective (class) interests. Our analysis will differ considerably, therefore, from that of Joseph Nocera (1994), for example. For Nocera, the 'money revolution', as a 'force for good' that advances 'financial democracy', is a story of 'how the middle class joined the money class', of how 'we've finally gotten a piece of the action' (p. 11). Now, particularly in terms of saving, there is certainly a sense in which the common experiences that we summon up in this book are the preserve of the Anglo-American middle-classes. However, if the category of everyday life is to reveal common experiences and the inequalities that they necessarily entail, we 'need to put on hold the *automatic* explanatory value placed on accepted cultural differences' (Highmore 2002: 2 *original emphasis*). Sensitivity is required to the ways in which categories of saver or borrower are designated, and to the manner in which common experiences of saving and borrowing are formed. How is it, for example, that mortgagors come to be differentiated, and differentiate themselves, from those who are marginalized in mortgage finance? Income and class are likely to be far from the only determinants in everyday experiences of financial inequality and, especially in terms of borrowing, representations of an increasingly 'included' middle-class and an 'excluded' poor and low-income other may well be highly problematic.

The category of everyday life also brings normative and political concerns to our analysis. While everyday life is marked by the coexistence of commonality and difference, theorists of everyday life almost universally recognize its colonization and homogenization. For example, Lefebvre's purpose is precisely to provide a *critique* of the ways in which, as he saw it, forces of capitalism and modernity create the routines and rhythms of everyday life in a 'bureaucratic society of controlled consumption' (see Davies 2006a). Meanwhile, de Certeau (1988) suggests that it is the production and reproduction of consumerist society, turning on the regularized performance of the use of consumer products in everyday practices, which should be questioned. In this vein, Arlie Russell Hochschild (2003) has more recently asked how we might resist the penetration of 'intimate life' by forces of commericalization and commodification. For us, it follows that we retain a healthy normative suspicion of the relationships between Anglo-American society and the financial markets that have been built up in recent times. As Warren and Warren Tyagi (2004) put it in their critical discussion of the campaigns of advocacy groups to advance financial inclusion and access to credit as of right: 'The dream of the democratization of credit was to use credit as a vehicle to expand home ownership, to launch businesses, and ultimately help to build wealth in neighbourhoods that are short on it. The point was not to bombard families with more credit than they could possibly afford or to flood the market with complicated loans . . . ' (p. 151). While many individuals and households undoubtedly gain from recently formed relationships with the capital markets, the material effects of these relationships are also highly divisive and, at points of crisis in particular, can be disastrous for those involved.

The persistence of difference in everyday life also begins to hint at its political possibilities. As Michael Gardiner (2004) argues in defence of Lefebvre, the critique of everyday life should not obscure the extent to which the routine and the creative, the trivial and the extraordinary, necessarily co-exist in everyday life. There remains scope, therefore, for politics in everyday life (de Certeau 1988; Kerkvliet 2005; Scott 1985). As Kerkvliet (2005) describes it, 'everyday politics . . . occurs where people live and work and involves people embracing, adjusting to, or contesting norms and rules' (p. 22). It 'includes quiet, mundane, and subtle expressions and acts that indirectly and for the most part privately endorse, modify or resist prevailing procedures, rules, regulations, or order', 'involves little or no organization', and 'features the activities of individuals and small groups as they make a living, raise their families, wrestle with daily problems, and deal with others like themselves' (p. 22). For us, the category of everyday life thus opens up new avenues for enquiry into the politics of contemporary finance. It encourages us to elaborate the conceptual theme of financial dissent in Chapter 1, and to explicitly address the (re)politicization of everyday saving and borrowing in Chapters 5 and 9, respectively. Although the politics that we focus on includes purposeful political critique and organized programmes of action that we typically recognize as 'resistance', we also consider financial dissent that is multiple, agnostic, and falls short of coherent and openly declared resistance.

Overview

I have begun here to by pointing out the relative neglect of 'the democratization of finance' in social scientist's understandings of contemporary finance, and by asserting the relevance and prominence of everyday life. But, how is the everyday life of global finance assembled? What has made possible the transformations in saving and borrowing that have forged close relationships between Anglo-American society, on the one hand, and the global financial markets, on the other? As Chapter 1 notes at the outset, if we are to address these questions, it is clearly inadequate to conceive of saving and borrowing as quantitative aggregates or rates. Such conceptions of saving and borrowing prevail in mainstream economics and amongst policy-makers in Anglo-America. Although providing insights into the scale of everyday financial practices, quantitative conceptions of saving and borrowing necessarily prevent consideration of qualitative transformations in the form that they take. Thus, considerable conceptual work is required if we are to address the everyday life of global finance, and Chapter 1 sets out four key conceptual themes that inform our subsequent analysis: financial networks, financial power, financial identity, and financial dissent. These themes are elaborated and explored across the subsequent chapters as they become manifest in our analysis of saving and borrowing respectively. We also return to these themes by way of Conclusion to the book, reflecting on their relevance to the current crisis in US sub-prime mortgage networks.

Arising out of an engagement with the actor-network theory associated primarily with Bruno Latour and Michel Callon, the conceptual theme of financial networks is already present within the social studies of finance. Yet, its capacity to inform enquiry into changing relationships between society and the financial markets remains under-theorized and largely unexplored. As developed in Chapter 1, the concept of financial networks leads to the decentring of contemporary finance. Multiple and relatively discrete everyday networks of saving and borrowing, and the transformations that create overlaps and intersections with the networks of the capital markets, become the focus for our enquiry. The making and re-making of market networks of saving and borrowing is held to turn on specific calculative tools and performances of 'risk': that is, the devices and techniques through which the future uncertainties of saving and borrowing are measured and managed as 'risks' in the present.

By drawing on Michel Foucault's work on power-knowledge and 'governmentality', the conceptual theme of financial power is advanced in order to make explicit the power relations and politics at work in the constitution of calculative market networks of saving and borrowing. The conception of financial power that is developed contrasts with the prevailing approaches in the social sciences that usually either simply assume the rationality of monetary and financial relations, or suggest that power as a material resource is wielded in a constraining fashion by finance capital as an economic group and class interest. Our focus becomes the materialization of transformations in networks that are understood to hinge on: the re-articulation and performance of calculations that, as techniques of truth, de-politicize and legitimate everyday finance as rational and scientific; and neo-liberal governmental rationalities and programmes which feature and prompt those calculative technologies. In short, the conceptual themes of financial networks and financial power inform an embedded and situated analysis of transformations in everyday saving and borrowing.

Furthermore, our concern with the theme of financial identity in Chapter 1 also leads us to consider the embodiment of qualitative transformations in everyday saving and borrowing. I suggest that different forms of saving and borrowing necessitate the assembly of various everyday financial subject positions and the self-disciplines that they entail. Everyday financial subject positions are summoned up through both the calculative performances of a particular network of saving or borrowing, and through neo-liberal governmental programmes that stress new self-disciplines in the name of individual freedom and security. In Chapter 8, for example, transformations in credit card networks are shown to be embodied through the calling up of 'the revolver', a subject for whom the self-disciplines of thrift and prudence have given way to the meeting, management, and manipulation of extended borrowing obligations. However, as Chapter 1 proposes, the performance of everyday subject positions, such as that of the revolver, are always perilous and beset with tensions and contradictions. This renders processes of identification problematic and uncertain.

The development of our final conceptual theme—financial dissent— informs the view that the politics of the everyday life of global finance is both multiple and ambiguous. As Chapter 1 suggests, social scientists of finance typically seek to reveal the 'truth' of the 'realities' of contemporary finance. They also tend to assume that financial power is distinct from resistance, that the regulatory authority of public institutions provides the means through which a coherent alternative to the prevailing order can be established, and that resistance can only hope to achieve this alternative if it takes collective and organized forms. In contrast, Chapter 1 begins to set out our concern to open up the scientific, technical, and thoroughly de-politicized performances of finance to critical scrutiny. It also proposes an analysis that recognizes that dissent is always ambiguous and compromised in one way or another, and that multiple modes of dissent are present in the everyday life of global finance that do not take collective, organized, and public forms.

Following our opening chapter, the book is divided into two equal Parts concerned, respectively, with saving and borrowing. Each Part consists of four chapters. Chapter 2 opens Part I by asking how contemporary everyday investment, understood as a set of qualitatively distinct networks, both differs from, and comes to be positively differentiated from, other forms of saving. Considerable overlaps with the networks of the capital markets, the indirect ownership of securities through occupational and personal pension funds and mutual funds, and specific calculative technologies of risk are shown to characterize networks of everyday investment. The tools and devices which construct risk as an opportunity to be embraced are held to be pivotal in the differentiation of investment, over and above thrifty deposit saving and insurance, as the most rational form of saving. The partial displacement of networks of thrift and insurance by those of investment is linked to the move from liberal to neo-liberal government in the early 1980s, but, with particular reference to mutual fund networks, it is also shown that technological developments had already begun to establish the relative rationality of practices of everyday investment.

Building on Chapter 2, Chapter 3 argues that the partial displacement of insurance by investment in pensions saving has been carried forward through three concurrent processes: neo-liberal governmental programmes that individualize responsibility and risk in pensions; the re-articulation of the calculative technologies at play in final salary pension schemes leading to greater stock market investment; and the drift from final salary to money purchase pensions and equity-based mutual funds. In Chapter 4, we consider the embodiment of transformations in Anglo-American saving, and address the making of everyday investor subjects with particular reference to the pension guides produced by state agencies on both sides of the Atlantic. Investment is conceived of as a contingent and contradictory technology of the self under neo-liberalism, and the subject position of the investor shown to be not simply occupied and performed by individuals in an unproblematic manner. Finally, Part I of the book closes with a chapter devoted to dissent in everyday investment. Dissent in everyday investment does feature collective, organized, and public campaigns for a return to the technologies and performances of thrift and insurance (e.g. state-based pensions). But, my focus in

Chapter 5 is on socially responsible investment as a mode of dissent that includes both 'pension fund socialism', that is, the targeted investments and collective shareholder activism of US multi-employer and public pension schemes, and 'ethical investment' by individuals in mutual fund networks. SRI provides unconventional discourses on investment and seeks to script, induce, and embody alternative approaches to investment, but is nonetheless ambiguous and compromised.

In Chapter 6, the opening chapter of Part II, we begin our exploration of contemporary transformations in everyday borrowing. On the savings side, the well-established and embedded networks of thrift and insurance have been partially displaced by newly predominant networks of everyday investment. On the borrowing side, however, as Chapter 6 shows, transformations have produced an intensification and boom in reasonably entrenched borrowing and mortgage networks, facilitated by significant innovations such as the development of credit card networks which are constituted through the calculative technologies of revolving credit, credit rating and scoring, and payment and authorization systems. Chapter 6 also suggests that close interconnections between mortgage and consumer credit networks, on the one hand, and the networks of the capital markets, on the other, have materialized through new calculative devices and performances which figure the uncertainties of future repayments by everyday borrowers as 'default risks'. Such technologies make possible the issue and trading of default risk-related instruments in the capital markets, and create confidence and legitimacy in the boom in mortgage and consumer lending.

Chapter 7 concentrates on issues of financial inequality in booming everyday borrowing. With particular reference to so-called 'sub-prime' borrowers within mortgage and consumer credit networks, I show how the dynamics of inequality increasingly turn on market segmentation and differentiation strategies. An expanding number of individuals and households may indeed be incorporated within borrowing networks that are tightly connected with the networks of the capital markets, but calculative technologies of 'risk-based pricing' ensure that those designated as sub-prime pay considerably more interest on their borrowings. Chapter 8 furthers our conceptual theme of financial identity by focusing on the embodiment of the borrowing boom, and the re-making of mortgagors and credit card borrowers in particular. It shows how the transformation and boom in borrowing entails the assembly of new financial subjects— what I call 'the revolver' in credit card networks, and 'the leveraged investor' in mortgage networks—who routinely perform changed forms of financial self-discipline. But, as I also make plain, the displacement of disciplines of prudence and thrift by the responsible meeting, management, and manipulation of ever-greater obligations is disrupted by significant tensions and contradictions. As with Part I, Part II of the book draws to a close with a chapter dedicated to the theme of financial dissent. Although the boom in consumer borrowing has generated calls for a return to the values of thrift and prudence, and also collective campaigns for the regulation of so-called 'predatory lending', we focus in Chapter 9 on additional modes of financial dissent. Specifically, we concentrate on the capacity of the work of artists to disturb entrenched meanings of borrowing and lending in ways that do not resort to religious condemnation, and upon attempts to provide alternative sources of borrowing through credit union networks. Again, the presence and possibilities of multiple modes of financial dissent in the everyday life of global finance is thus emphasized, but dissent is shown to be problematic.

1

Networks, Power, Identity, and Dissent

Introduction: 'The Great Thrift Shift'

In September 2005, *The Economist* magazine saw fit to devote its annual survey of the world economy to what it calls 'the great thrift shift'. The survey's cover page—a see-saw balanced precariously on a globe, a large and swollen piggy bank on the right-hand side weighing down a much smaller piggy bank replete with the Stars and Stripes on the left-hand side—graphically illustrates its concerns. 'The geography of thrift' has, according to the survey, been transformed in recent years (*The Economist* 2005c: 4). American households in particular are saving less and spending and borrowing more, while their counterparts in Asia, oil-producing countries, and especially China continue to save prodigiously. As the survey reminds us, 'According to the economics textbooks, saving and investment are always equal.... Saving and investment are two sides of the same coin' (p. 5). While a discrepancy may emerge between saving and investment levels in particular national economies, such as that which prevails in the US at present, cross-border capital flows ensure that saving and investment are always in balance globally. Yet, according to the magazine, today's persistent and growing global imbalance is 'excessive and dangerous' (p. 28). 'Too much foreign money is bad for America's economy' (p. 25), and it needs 'to reduce its domestic distortions' (p. 26). Household net worth as a percentage of disposable income has increased in the US considerably since 1990, but 'Americans have given up saving out of current income altogether' (p. 26). By July 2005, the household saving rate had fallen to −0.6 per cent, the lowest on record.

'Saving' is represented in the survey as the quantitative aggregate outcome of the financial decisions taken by households and, to a lesser extent, by firms and governments. 'Investment', meanwhile, is the preserve of firms, such that the collective level of investment is determined by company spending decisions. What matters for *The Economist* is 'explaining what drives saving' (p. 8), and 'convincing the American people to save more' (p. 28). This representation of saving and the concerns that follow are grounded in 'the economics textbooks' and the perspective of liberal economics. As Nigel Dodd's discussion of *The Wealth of Nations* makes plain, saving is regarded by Adam Smith and his fellow liberal economists as 'rational from both the individual and collective point of view' (Dodd 1994: 11). For Smith, individuals who do not save are guilty of 'prodigality and misconduct', while saving collectively provides the basis for investment and economic growth as 'capitals are increased by parsimony' (p. 10).

The static and fixed representation of saving as a quantitative aggregate and rate that is the outcome of rational household decisions is largely mirrored by orthodox representations of borrowing. Consider, for example, the Federal Reserve's calculations for the so-called 'household debt service ratio'. Aggregate figures for outstanding repayment obligations arising from households' decisions on mortgages, loans, and other unsecured debt, on the one hand, are set against figures for disposable income, on the other. Fluctuations over time in the resulting percentage thus give an indication as to whether the 'average' US household is borrowing more or less relative to its disposable income. For example, the boom in borrowing over recent decades, alongside incomes that are highly polarized and relatively stagnant overall (Henwood 2003: 84–90), can be seen in the US debt service ratio, which increased from 10.58 per cent in the last quarter of 1980 to 13.75 per cent in the third quarter of 2005.[1] To explain the increase in this ratio, policy makers have recently tended to reduce households, again in quantitative and aggregate terms, to a balance sheet (e.g. Aizcorbe, Kennickell, and Moore 2003; Bank of England 2006a; Greenspan 2004; Joint Economic Committee 2004). Here total collective household 'assets' (income and other sources of wealth) are weighted-up against total collective household borrowing as 'liabilities', and the increase on the 'liabilities' side becomes justified in the context of the price appreciation of financial and residential housing 'assets' in particular.

The prevailing representation of saving and borrowing as quantitative aggregates and rates may well give us some indication of the scale of recent developments in Anglo-American finance, but what is significant

---

[1] See http://www.federalreserve.gov/releases/housedebt/default.htm

for us is that it shrouds and obscures qualitative transformations in the forms taken by saving and borrowing. In the 28-page great thrift survey of *The Economist* (2005c), for example, the contemporary transformation of US saving and rise of mass financial market investment is not mentioned once. As in 'the economics textbooks', saving cannot, by definition, be investment. It is not surprising, therefore, that in trying to explain why US households' saving habits have changed in recent decades, the survey states that this is 'a question about human behaviour which economists cannot answer with total confidence' (p. 8; see Campbell 2006). Conceiving of saving and borrowing as quantitative aggregates and rates is certainly inadequate for our purposes here. As I set out in the Introduction, 'the democratization of finance' which is our focus turns precisely on qualitative transformations in everyday saving and borrowing routines that forge close relationships between the society and the financial markets. So, how might we conceive of contemporary finance in such a way as to understand these transformations, their vulnerabilities, and contestation?

In this chapter, I want to set out four key conceptual themes that, informing our subsequent analysis, provide us with the tools by which we begin to address this question. To be clear, I am not proposing and elaborating a 'theoretical framework' or 'methodology'—that is, a set of rigid propositions to be 'applied', 'tested', and 'proved'—either in the following chapters or in subsequent research. Rather, as Nikolas Rose (1999) has it, 'concepts are more important for what they do than for what they mean. Their value lies in the way in which they are able to provide a purchase for critical thought upon particular problems in the present' (p. 9). I have chosen to talk of conceptual themes precisely to emphasize the way in which concepts remain dynamic throughout our engagement with 'the democratization of finance' in the chapters that follow. I will draw, primarily, on actor-network theory (ANT), aspects of the scholarship of Michel Foucault, and insights from writers of everyday life, but seek an 'inventive and empirical' relation to this work (Rose 1999: 5). Our key conceptual themes are financial networks, financial power, financial identity, and financial dissent.

Financial Networks

The concept of financial networks—as it is utilized by several contributors to the social studies of finance (Leyshon 2000; Leyshon and Thrift 1997;

MacKenzie 2006; Pollard 2001) and further developed here—is grounded primarily in ANT associated primarily with social theorists Bruno Latour (1987, 1993, 1999) and Michel Callon (1986, 1998, 1999, 2005). Perhaps the most distinctive feature of ANT is its focus both on human and non-human actors or 'actants' (Law 1999: 4). Actors are necessarily situated and assembled within networks or 'actor-worlds' (Callon 1986) which produce the capacity to act and give meaning to action, while action or practice forges a network and keeps it in dynamic motion as a relatively stable form. To paraphrase from the discussion by Kendall (2004) of the contrasting use of the network concept in the work of Castells (1996) and Latour, the point is not to start from the assumption that the power of capital is in place at the centre of the financial system, and to attempt to study the networks, nodes, and performances (e.g. everyday saving) that comprise and contribute to this system. Rather, financial networks are, at once, integrated and stable, and decentred and dynamic.

Although ANT is already reasonably well established in the social studies of finance, its potential to enable the analysis of changing relationships between the society and the financial markets remains under-theorized and largely unexplored. Two potential lines of enquiry would seem especially apposite in this regard. First, recourse to ANT makes it possible for us to begin to decentre finance, to map transformations in multiple and relatively discrete financial networks that extend across manifold spaces. There is no singular 'global financial system', then, but a web of diverse networks of finance, each 'made up of human bodies but also of prostheses, tools, equipment, technical devices, algorithms, etc.' (Callon 2005: 4). While more or less distinct, financial networks are nevertheless dynamic and 'overlap and intersect' (Pollard 2001: 393 original emphasis). Not only is it the case that some financial networks are 'closely correlated' and some 'have remarkably little to do with each other' (Thrift and Leyshon 1999: 162–3), but also that the interconnections between financial networks change over time.

The decentring of finance through the concept of financial networks is, therefore, significant in furthering our concern to bring everyday spaces, practices, and subjects to prominence in our understanding of contemporary finance. As we distinguish between different financial networks, pre-existing categories of scale created for the measurement of space, such as 'global' or 'local', should not be used as a gauge against which networks might be mapped or judged (Kendall 2004: 69). Scalar differences are not pre-given, and often implicit representations of space and scale have important implications. Forces designated as 'global' always and necessarily appear as 'bigger' and likely to triumph over 'smaller' and 'local' routines. Put differently, the temptation to simply explain developments within 'small' everyday networks in terms of an apparently 'bigger picture' of 'the financial system' should be avoided. As Latour (in Bingham and Thrift 2000: 286) has it, 'A giant in a story is not a bigger character than a dwarf.' There is not some kind of process of 'globalization' at work which transforms Anglo-American saving and borrowing. It is not the case, for example, that stock market investment networks are 'global', and networks of commercial bank deposit accounts remain 'local'. Rather, what is significant is whether financial networks are 'more or less long and more or less connected' (Latour 1993: 122). 'Big does not mean "really" big or "overall" or "overarching", but connected, blind, local, mediated, related' (Latour 1999: 18). Thus, we can begin to distinguish the shorter and relatively disconnected networks of saving in deposit accounts, for example, from the bigger and longer networks of investment which are closely interconnected with the networks of the capital markets. Transformations in saving and borrowing networks that entail their lengthening, overlap, and intersection with the various networks of the capital markets are simultaneously 'global' and 'local', and can be explored without inscribing the hierarchical assumptions that follow from these categories.

A second line of enquiry, informed by ANT and the concept of financial networks, is especially significant as we seek to understand the differentiated constitution of relatively discrete market networks of saving and borrowing. From the perspective of the anthropology of organized market networks offered by Michel Callon (1998, 1999), it is rational calculation and calculative performances that can be seen as giving meaning to saving and borrowing practices, and to constituting market networks of saving and borrowing in action. For Callon, 'economics, in the broad sense of the term, performs, shapes and formats the economy, rather than observing how it functions' (1998: 2), and the performativity of economics turns on the 'configuration' and 'formatting' of the calculative, rational, and egoistic figure of *homo economicus* (1998: 22–3; 1999: 186). Calculating in market networks of saving and borrowing is necessarily 'a complex collective practice' (1998: 4). 'If agents can calculate their decisions, it is because they are entangled in a web of relations and connections' (1999: 185). As such, 'calculating tools' and 'technical devices' specific to more or less discrete market networks 'constitute spaces of calculability and define the way that calculation is made up' (1998: 23–6). Calculative performances thus draw boundaries between that which is taken into account as significant or insignificant and literally what counts, in saving and borrowing.

That calculation and calculative tools provide a key entry point into economic and financial life for ANT follows from its initial development in the social studies of science (Callon 1986; Latour 1987) and its ethnomethodological commitment not to 'claim to explain the actors' behaviour and reasons, but only to find the procedures which render actors able to negotiate their ways through one another's world-building activity' (Latour 1999: 21). Those drawing on ANT to explore accountancy, for example, are thus concerned with providing an account of the calculative practices within which economic reason is instantiated. As Miller (2004) puts it, accounting 'links agents and activities into a functioning calculative network' (p. 181). Accounting networks depoliticize market practices, framing 'a particular way of understanding, representing and acting upon events' (p. 187) that is 'set apart from political interests and disputes, above the world of intrigue, and beyond debate' (p. 181). By extension, organized market networks of everyday saving and borrowing materialize through the performance of calculations that provide for the apparently optimal and politically unquestionable means of storing and spending wealth into the future.

An exploration of the significance of calculative tools and performances in the constitution of relatively discrete market networks of saving and borrowing will, given its focus, contrast with the ways in which 'performativity' has tended to be explored in the social studies of finance. The term performativity is widely regarded to have been coined by philosopher J. L. Austin. For Austin, language does not describe an already present world, but helps to bring into being that of which it speaks. A 'performative utterance' is thus one that 'makes itself true' (Austin in MacKenzie 2004: 305), often through ongoing and repeated iterations. When appearing in Callon's work on market networks and Donald MacKenzie's related research into financial networks (MacKenzie 2004, 2006), the notion of performativity has thus turned attention to the ways in which particular branches, sub-fields, and models of economics do not describe economies, but are intrinsic to the constitution of that which they purport to describe. For MacKenzie (2006), financial models become 'an engine, not a camera' in derivative markets when they appear to ring true in their own terms. Reaching out to the calculative performances of everyday saving and borrowing networks will require, however, that we pay less attention to branches and models of economics, and instead foreground our enquiry in the specific tools and devices through which practices and identities are performed.

So, what calculative tools and performances feature in the materialization of relatively discrete market networks of saving and borrowing? Although it is hard to generalize in this respect, tools and performances that rationally figure and manage future risks are pivotal. The charging and payment of rates of interest, an elemental feature of market networks of saving and borrowing, is derived, for example, from risk calculations about the future prospects of returns or the likelihood of default. However, if we are to recognize the significance of risk calculations in the constitution of market networks of saving and borrowing, what precisely do we mean by 'risk'? 'Risk' within financial networks is a category of understanding, not an intuition or sensibility. It is not, furthermore, a condition of our times in a realist sense, what Beck (1992) famously characterized as the uninsurable 'risk society'. Revealing in this regard is the extension of Beck's work by Matthew Watson (2007) to address what he calls 'the financial risk society' (p. 62). The upshot of this view of 'risk' is the impression of a new set of real dangers that, multiplied through market innovation and increased speculative trading, create 'a critical mass of financial market risks that outgrow the protective capacity of coping mechanisms developed by industrial society' (p. 29). Yet, such a take on risk in financial networks misses the manner in which the category of 'risk' itself makes possible market innovation and trading and, for that matter, the charging of interest in everyday saving and borrowing. As Mitchell Dean (1999: 177) puts it,

There is no such thing as risk in reality.... Risk is a way—or rather, a set of different ways—of ordering reality, of rendering it into a calculable form. It is a way of representing events in a certain form so that they might be made governable in particular ways, with particular techniques and for particular goals.

Informing this view of risk is a critical reading of Frank Knight's classic investigation of indeterminacy (Knight 1921). Thus, the category of 'risk' can be seen as distinct from uncertainty, the former as the statistical and predictive calculation of the future and the latter as non-calculable future volatilities that are beyond prediction (Reddy 1996). As Timothy Mitchell's research into the technological constitution of economic networks suggests more broadly (Mitchell 2002), calculative devices that seek to count and account for economies always fall short of fully containing the complexities of economic life. Tools, devices, and techniques of risk, such as insurance and actuarialism, provide a means in the present of calculating and feigning control over an uncertain future.

If we understand the constitution of market networks of saving and borrowing in this way, how do well-established networks of saving and borrowing, embedded and embodied in the routines of everyday life, become transformed or displaced by alternative and/or additional networks? The so-called 'new accounting history' (Napier 2006), which draws on ANT but also takes much of its inspiration from Foucault, is especially insightful here. The new accounting history regards accounting 'as a subset of a broader category of calculation' (Napier 2006: 457; cf. Miller and Napier 1993), and traces the genealogies of 'particular accountings' (p. 460) as they emerge, consolidate, and, in some instances, disappear. As such, Miller (1998: 175) characterizes the broad historical development of accounting thus: 'Existing practices are criticised. Claims are advanced that other practices not only remedy these defects, but go substantially beyond them, offer something more, something different, something better.' By implication, the materialization of saving and borrowing networks becomes a dynamic process, entailing the reconfiguration and possible displacement of previously ascendant means of calculative saving and borrowing. The future retains irreducible uncertainties, and contradictions and tensions emerge in technologies of risk. To return to Callon (1998), calculative tools are 'open, reconfigurable and, moreover, constantly reconfigured' (p. 26).

Financial Power

How customary market networks of saving and borrowing are produced, transformed, and displaced is also, necessarily, a question of financial power. As it is developed here, the conceptual theme of financial power leads us to make explicit the power relations and politics at play as market networks are constituted through calculation and calculative tools. Pivotal to our conception of financial power is Michel Foucault's work on power/knowledge (Foucault 1980), and the extension of this work with reference to modern finance by Marieke de Goede (2005b). De Goede describes finance as 'a discursive domain made possible through performative practices' (p. 7), and unequivocally reminds us that the production of 'truth' in modern finance tends to exclude alternative conditions of possibility. Finance becomes a virtuous domain that acquires 'a logic of calculability and an appearance of scientific objectivity that places its fundamental assumptions...beyond discussion and debate' (p. 3). Depoliticizing techniques of truth—and, particularly, what we have termed calculative tools—are crucial to power relations and the materialization of modern finance. Techniques of truth license and privilege certain rational practices over seemingly irrational and/or illegal alternatives.

The Foucauldian-inspired literature on 'governmentality' (e.g. Barry, Osborne, and Rose 1996; Burchell, Gordon, and Miller 1991; Dean 1999; Foucault 1979; Rose 1990), meanwhile, draws our attention to the ways in which the calculative tools that feature in the constitution of saving and borrowing networks are also imbricated and deployed as apparatus in liberal governmental rationalities and programmes. For Foucault (1979), the concept of governmentality distanced him from Marxist theories of ideology, specifically the work of Althusser, and provided a means of understanding the operation of power in modern liberal society. Governmental modes of power forge control through a logic of calculation, circulation, and self-discipline, and are therefore distinguishable from modes of power that operate primarily through exclusion, like territorial sovereignty, and also those associated with division and surveillance. While wary of a simple periodization, Foucault suggests that governmental forms of power emerged in the eighteenth and nineteenth centuries, becoming highly developed and persistent in liberal orders. As he described it, governmentality is 'the ensemble formed by the institutions, procedures, analyses and reflections, the calculations and tactics, that allow the exercise of this very specific albeit complex form of power, which has as its target population' (p. 20). What he also calls 'the art of government' and 'the conduct of conduct' does not simply refer to the institutions, individuals, and groups that hold authority, but also includes those calculative technologies and expertise that are authorized within and through the population and which rationalize the exercise of power.

The place in liberal government of the calculative tools of saving and borrowing is closely bound up with their role in figuring uncertainty as 'risk'. As Dean (1999) emphasizes, the significance of calculative technologies to liberal government stems in large part from multiple and ongoing attempts to 'find a mode of government able to offer an assurance of the life of the population' and, in particular, to 'control the risks to a population' (p. 176). In this sense, 'risk' is 'a component of diverse forms of calculative rationality for governing the conduct of individuals, collectivities and populations' (p. 197). Various calculative technologies, for example, insurance in its many and varied forms, are 'technologies of risk' in liberal government (Ewald 1991: 197; Knights and Vurdubakis 1993). Furthermore, the importance attached to technologies of risk by contributors to the governmentality literature has led them to characterize the contemporary neoliberal period in terms of the reworking of risk. The reach of governmental technologies of risk has expanded into diverse fields of social life including, for example, those of public health and the environment (Kemshall 2002), while a subtle re-articulation of technologies of risk also supports the individualization of responsibility for welfare and security (Peters 2001). For us, the suggestion is that understanding the power relations that produce transformations in saving and borrowing requires that we consider reconfigurations in calculation arising, at once, from both dynamic financial networks and shifting governmental programmes.

It is important to stress that the conceptual theme of financial power, as developed in this book, stands in contrast with the perspectives on financial power that prevail in the social sciences. Two broad perspectives are intelligible. First, drawing primarily on Weber (1978), Simmel (1990), and Bell (1976), financial power is associated with the immutable advance of modernity and, in particular, with the inherent instrumental rationality that is assumed to be carried forward by the spread of modern monetary and financial relations. We encounter this perspective in the pages that follow in the sociological literature on consumer credit in particular (see Chapters 6 and 8). Here the rationalities of consumer credit relations bring a semblance of order to the irrational self-gratification of consumption, and thereby prevent consumerism from spiralling out of control (e.g. Calder 1999; Klein 1999; Ritzer 1995, 2001). In our terms, however, the rationalities of modern finance should be subjected to critical examination. Interrogating the power relations at work in finance is essential to its (re)politicization. Although the defining feature of modern finance is indeed an apparent scientific rationality, this representation of the 'truth' about finance is constantly made, negotiated, remade, and contested across more-or-less discrete networks (de Goede 2005b). Transformations in networks of saving and borrowing that forge seemingly rational financial practices and close relationships with the capital markets are made possible through calculative tools and performances, and are simultaneously the subject of considerable dissent.

A second perspective on financial power—framed by the Marxist (e.g. Hilferding 2005) and Keynesian (Keynes 1961) traditions of political economy, and by radical liberals and social democrats writing early in the twentieth century (Hobson 1988; Schumpeter 1983; Tawney 1982)—is also well established in the social sciences. Those who take this perspective are united in their opposition to the *rentier* economy of value-skimming that develops when finance capital is left unrestrained. Particularly pertinent for us is the influence of this second perspective on financial power within the literature on so-called 'financialization'. Financialization has become something of a buzzword for social scientists of finance in recent times, a notion used most commonly to describe processes of change that signal the growing power of finance capital. In quantitative terms, financialization describes the increasingly important role of speculative financial accumulation relative to the performance of other sectors in the economy (e.g. Arrighi 1994; Blackburn 2006b; Brenner 2002; Henwood 2003; Krippner 2005). A critique is offered here of disintermediation, and the assumption that markets are the most efficient means of allocating capital and distributing risk. The suggestion is that capital markets are dominated by secondary trading that does not support the formation of productive capital, but merely facilitates the transfer of ownership claims and risks. For Henwood (2003), for instance, 'the point about financialization' is that 'layers of claims have been piled on layers of claims, most of them furiously traded'. In qualitative terms, meanwhile, financialization denotes a shift in the parameters through which shareholders judge the performance of corporations (e.g. Aglietta and Rebérioux 2005; Cutler and Waine 2001; Froud et al. 2006; Lazonick and O'Sullivan 2000). Here the fetishes of 'shareholder value' and 'good corporate governance'—and associated corporate practices of boosting share prices, distributing dividends, share buybacks, share option schemes for managers, downsizing, subcontracting, off-shoring, and the sale and leaseback of plant and equipment—are important indicators that finance capital now calls the tune.

This second perspective on financial power, prevailing in the social sciences and currently finding expression within the literature on financialization, is problematic in crucial respects. For us, questions of financial power cannot be reduced to the material resources and rent-seeking ownership claims of finance capital as a specific economic group and class interest. While it is not in doubt that financial power is hierarchical, and that a massive increase in the trading of ownership claims and risks has taken place, power relations nonetheless operate in a productive as opposed to constraining manner. Power is also decentred and does not emanate from a single locus. Put differently, financial power is not a force that operates 'from the outside' on everyday saving and borrowing, but is necessarily present 'on the inside' of everyday networks. Consider, for example, research by scholars of financialization that includes households' pension and mutual fund investments within accounts of the processes of change (Boyer 2000; Froud, Johal, and Williams 2002). Froud, Johal, and Williams (2002) 'hypothesize two generic types of capitalism: coupon pool capitalism and productionism', and argue that financialized or 'coupon pool capitalism' is 'constituted when...the capital market moves from *intermediation* to *regulation* of firm and household behaviour' (p. 126 *original emphasis*). While they are careful to state that financialization does not create 'a kind of univocal logic as the power of the capital market inevitably overcomes all resistances' (p. 133), Froud, Johal, and Williams argue that 'the coupon pool has already been constituted as a regulatory institution' (p. 134). Such 'regulation' appears to operate in somewhat mechanical terms through the potential and actual returns provided by the capital markets on household saving. Indeed, in a later paper that builds on their notion of the coupon pool, the same group of authors (Erturk et al. 2007) focus on the discrepancies between 'what is promised and what can be delivered' to households. Thus, although Froud and her co-authors take issues of representation and knowledge seriously in their account of contemporary financial power, they nonetheless give the impression that everyday financial transformations are derivative of, and are ideologically legitimated by, power that resides 'outside' of everyday life and in the hands of financial capital as an identifiable collective interest. Certain representations of finance are indeed extremely profitable, but finance is not a pre-existing material reality that is legitimated through ideological representation.

Financial Identity

Questions of financial identity are explored almost exclusively in the social sciences in relation to the clearly delineated group of professionals who are employed as financiers. Attention concentrates, for instance, on what it means to be a financial market trader (Knorr, Cetina, and Bruegger 2004), the agency of hedge funds (Hardie and MacKenzie 2006), the 'gentlemanly capitalists' of the City of London (Augar 2000; Cain and Hopkins 1986), and the gendering of elite financial identities more broadly (McDowell 1997). Given that the unprecedented relationships between Anglo-American society and the capital markets mean that, in many ways, large numbers of us are now financiers, this focus on elite professionals is even more problematic than previously. Put differently, and to paraphrase from Featherstone's work on 'everyday life' and what he calls 'heroic life', finance is no longer the exclusive domain of the heroic life characterized by 'extraordinary deeds, virtuosity, courage, endurance and the capacity to attain distinction' (Featherstone 1992: 160). Rather, what we have in the contemporary period is a 'heroic society', where 'the heroic person is one who excels at the performance of a necessary role' (p. 168). The third key conceptual theme that I develop here is, then, financial identity or, more specifically, the embodiment of transformations in saving and borrowing through the making of everyday financial subjects.

The tendency for social scientists to focus solely on the professional financier would appear to be a consequence of how economic identities are understood more broadly. For mainstream liberal economics, economic identity is, of course, simply not an issue. All economic agents are necessarily rational utility maximizers, *homo oeconomicus*. This conception of economic agency is at work in economists' models of the financial markets, and provokes wide-ranging criticism from, for instance, 'behavioural' accounts of finance that emphasize the collective psychology of markets (e.g. Shiller 2001), and the social studies of finance (e.g. MacKenzie 2006). While essential, the targeting and critique of economists' assumptions about agency and the market models that follow has an unwanted side effect: the parameters for enquiry into financial identity are often narrowed down to professional market participants.

At the same time, delimiting consequences follow from the two principal competing ontological starting points that, across the social sciences, tend to frame consideration of questions of economic identity. For the Marxist tradition, an individual's economic identity as, for example, a 'worker', 'manager', or 'banker', necessarily and always arises from his or her place in the capitalist relations of production. So, for David Harvey (1999), workers cannot, by definition, be financiers because, unlike the latter, they do not rely solely on returns from investment for their material well-being. The development and questioning of the Marxist tradition has led some to explore important modifications in what it means to be a 'worker' as capitalism moves into a new phase (Boltanski and Chiapello 2006; du Gay 1996; Lui 2004; Sennett 2005). While this has prompted some important insights into the entrepreneurial, mobile, and flexible qualities of the economic subjects summoned up in the course of restructuring, there nevertheless remains an implicit assumption that production and work are of primary importance in questions of economic identity. A strong challenge to this assumption is made by those who see the emergence of a consumerist society as necessitating an ontological move towards the privileging of consumptive relations (see Clarke, Doel, and Housinaux 2003). Here individual identities tend to be viewed as defined not only through the consumption of goods, but as expressed and communicated through consumption choices. Yet, both of these onto-logical starting points leave little room for raising questions of financial identity, as economic identities as either workers or consumers are some-what fixed and singular. The everyday financial subject positions that we wish to explore are dynamic and multiple—including, for example, 'investors' and 'mortgagors'—and also coexist with economic and non-economic subject positions such as 'worker', 'consumer', 'father', and 'mother'.

As with our conceptual theme of financial power, then, we develop the theme of financial identity through recourse to the work of Fou-cault. For the Marxist tradition, and especially for the Critical Theory of Horkheimer, Marcuse, and Habermas, it is the repression of subjec-tivity which provides evidence of domination and the rationale for cri-tique. For Foucault, however, subjectivity in liberal societies is fabricated through entanglements in the circulations of power/knowledge (Miller 1987). There are, nevertheless, potential pitfalls in understanding the embodiment of transformations in saving and borrowing by drawing on the conceptual tools of Foucault. As critics suggest more broadly, there is a danger that 'disciplinary power' is explored not 'as a ten-dency within modern forms of social control', but as 'a fully installed monolithic force which saturates all social relations' (McNay 1994: 104). The result, as Stuart Hall (1996) puts it, is that 'discursive subject posi-tions become *a priori* categories which individuals seem to occupy in an unproblematic fashion' (p. 10). It would, indeed, seem fair to level such criticisms at Foucault's *Discipline and Punish* and the vast array of social scientific research that has followed from it (Foucault 1977). Here the Panoptican appears as 'a giant lighthouse shining its beams of dis-ciplining light into every nook and cranny, allowing nobody to escape the "normalising" gaze nor from the imperative that they themselves should interiorise that gaze' (Sharp et al. 2000: 15). But, I would argue, such criticisms can be less easily directed towards Foucault's later work on governmentality and *The History of Sexuality* (Foucault 1976, 1979, 1984).

The notion of governmentality prompts scrutiny of (neo)liberal programmes of government as they feature the government of the self by the self, a focus on the points 'where programmes for the administration of others intersect with techniques for the administration of ourselves' (Rose 1999: 5). As proponents claim, governmentality thus informs an embodied analysis of the economy that ascribes analytical significance to the making and performance of various economic subject positions (e.g. Gibson-Graham 2006; Larner and Le Heron 2002). In terms of enquiry into everyday financial identities, it is perhaps no surprise that research informed by the category of governmentality already addresses the assembly of 'investor subjects' (Aitken 2003, 2005, 2007; Martin 2002), 'suburban subjects' (Grey 1997), and the mobilization of financial self-discipline more broadly (Knights 1997b; Knights and Vurdubakis 1993). Stress is placed on the ways in which the making of financial subjects plays on central features of liberal subjectivity, namely freedom and security. For Martin (2002: 3), for instance, there is currently an 'invitation to live by finance', where finance 'presents itself . . . as a means for the acquisition of the self . . . a proposal for how to get ahead'. Such 'invitations' are not only made by finance 'itself' through advertising campaigns and the like, but often feature state regulatory and policy initiatives as previous welfare and insurance commitments wane (Aitken 2007; O'Malley 2004).

What interests me, in particular, is how the assembly of the 'entrepreneurial self' (Amoore 2004; Higgins 2001; O'Malley 2000), as a signature of neoliberal government, extends to the making of contemporary financial subjects in terms of both saving and borrowing. Yet, enquiry into entrepreneurial financial subjects and their new self-disciplines is not straightforward. What is striking about governmentality research to date is the manner in which the embodiment of financial transformations and self-disciplines appears to proceed relatively smoothly. Put differently, the performance of everyday financial identities and calculative self-disciplines appears as a somewhat mechanical process that is far from precarious. Governmentality would seem, therefore, to lead to a similar account of everyday financial identities to that offered from a range of other vantage points, whether post-Keynesian (Froud, Johal, and Williams 2002), regulationist (Boyer 2000), Gramscian (Harmes 2001a), or derived from Pierre Bourdieu (Aldridge 1998). The category of governmentality would appear not to challenge the impression that the subject position of the investor, for example, is performed in a relatively unproblematic fashion as the processes of financialization and neoliberalization march on. Everyday financial subjects continue to appear as artefacts of, and not architects in, transformations. This is problematic because, as Stuart Hall (1996) has it, 'identification is a construction, a process never completed' (p. 2), and we need to pay 'attention to what might in any way interrupt, prevent or disturb the smooth insertion of individuals into...subject positions' (p. 11).

In the remainder of this book, therefore, I pursue a Foucauldian approach that explicitly does not collapse into the Foucault of *Discipline and Punish* and cast everyday financial subjects as 'docile bodies'. The concept of governmentality has the potential to enable an analysis that views subjects' perceived financial self-interests as discursively framed and manifest in their reflective, intentional, and aspirational practices; and highlights the contingency, contradictions, tensions, and ambiguities present in the making of new forms of financial self-discipline. Echoing Judith Butler's work on performativity and subjectivity (Butler 1997), while repetitious calculative performances are the reiteration of the norms of calculative subject positions and self-disciplines, such performances are precarious and retain considerable scope for politics. Devices and technologies of calculation present in financial networks and wider governmental programmes certainly serve to summon up and authorize particular entrepreneurial financial subject positions and forms of self-discipline, but the performance of these remains contingent, contradictory, and uncertain.

Financial Dissent

The final conceptual theme that I develop here and in the pages that follow is financial dissent. Social scientists of finance tend to mirror broader tendencies that are currently present across the social sciences whereby, as Louise Amoore (2006) argues by drawing on Foucault (1976: 96), the hunt for 'resistance' becomes the 'curious and politically problematic search for a great refusal'. Nikolas Rose (1999) suggests that these tendencies have their roots in Marxist and critical theory which created

those binary divisions that have structured our political thinking and our theorizing about the political for so long: domination and emancipation; power and resistance; strategy and tactics...Each such binary suggests a principle of division between those political, technical and ethical strategies that have made up our present and those that have opposed them. (p. 277)

In terms of research into finance specifically, the pursuit of a great refusal is manifest in three main predispositions which I will seek to overcome in order that we might begin to explore the presence, practicalities, possibilities, and problematics of dissent in the everyday life of global finance.

First, social scientists of finance typically give the impression that what are needed are 'truthful' accounts that reveal the 'real' material horrors that are obscured from the view of the subordinated. For example, Susan Strange (1986, 1998) devoted two influential books, and much of her career as a leading scholar of international political economy (IPE), to the study of finance. For her, the ultimate beneficiary of unequal and volatile globalizing finance is always the US and, in particular, Wall Street's financiers. Against what she called 'dismal fatalism', the first step towards change or 'treatment' for Strange is a 'diagnosis' that exposes 'the madness' of contemporary finance (1998: 179, 1). It is in the name of 'ordinary people who have never been asked if they wanted to gamble their jobs, their savings, their income in this casino form of capitalism', therefore, that academics have a duty to examine the prospects 'for making money sane again' (1998: 3). Not dissimilarly, Adam Harmes's neo-Gramscian account of the advance of 'mass investment culture' seeks to expose who really benefits from these developments (Harmes 2001*a*). In his terms, mass investment has 'played a critical role in strengthening the hegemonic dominance of finance capital—linking the perceived interests of tens of millions of workers to its own by embedding "investor practices" in their everyday lives and offering them the appearance of a stake in the neo-liberal order' (p. 103). Individuals are necessarily deceived by the 'appearance of a stake' that is offered to them, and it is the responsibility of scholars to stress the ideological nature of the new investment culture.

Implicit in my previous remarks about financial power is, however, a contrasting view about the political purpose of research. Our task is not to reveal 'the madness' of some fundamental material financial 'reality' in the service of those currently duped by the prevailing ideology. This is what Foucault (1976) terms the 'repressive hypothesis' of power, whereby power dominates people, but the truth sets them free. Although it is important to recognize the great profits and advantages accumulated by Wall Street's financiers from transformations in everyday saving and borrowing, our task is nonetheless to open up the highly technical and thoroughly depoliticized performances of finance to critical scrutiny because it is precisely this which is central to the exercise of power (de Goede 2005*b*). The possibilities of dissent require acts of (re)politicization. To this end, by elevating the ontological status of everyday, and by interrogating the calculative technologies at work in saving and borrowing networks, we go some way in this book to making the seemingly extraordinary world of 'global finance' ordinary and open to debate.

Second, social scientists of finance tend to draw a clear and dichotomous dividing line between power and resistance. The constraining 'power over' that is wielded by and in the interests of finance capital is pitched clearly and unambiguously against the interests and deeds of 'resistors against'. The key task for resistance becomes making use of the regulatory authority of state and interstate institutions in order that finance capital is bought under control. For instance, among political economists, calls for a 'new Bretton Woods' in global finance—a social democratic and 'global Keynesian' agenda for change that, echoing the immediate post-war decades, features the use of capital controls, transaction taxes, and so on—are quite common. These calls are often made in the name of 'the people', 'labour', and 'communities' that the singular and clearly identifiable enemy of global finance is assumed to work against (Bello, Bullard, and Malhotra 2000: xii; Desai and Said 2001: 51).

However, and again, a contrasting view is implicit in the approach to financial power that we have begun to develop here. Power relations are always present, such that domination and resistance are dyadic and cannot be completely separated or autonomous. It is the case, then, that 'our present has arisen as much from the logics of contestation as from any imperatives of control' (Rose 1999: 277). On the one hand, while webs of power can never be escaped, power relations are incomplete, fragile, vulnerable, and contradictory. On the other hand, given that power has to be exercised and realized in resistance itself, resistance is also ambiguous and is always, at least in part, compromised in one way or another. Social scientists of finance who continue to search for unequivocally oppositional resistance and autonomous alternatives will necessarily be disappointed as harmony and resolution are impossible. My development of the conceptual theme of 'financial dissent', as opposed to the more established 'financial resistance', is, then, in part an attempt to move towards a political analysis that does not work through the simplifying and false dichotomy of power/resistance.

Third, social scientists of finance usually leave us in little doubt that dissent must take particular collective, public, and organized forms. For example, geographer Susan Roberts (1998) offers an interesting comparison of 'political geographies of dissent' in trade and finance, and argues that, relative to trade, 'there is so little fuss made about the secretive crystallizations of power and governance in the financial world' (p. 129). Yet, this view rests upon a particular and narrow understanding of what counts as resistance, namely 'a type of politics' that takes a 'trans-local' form (p. 119). This, of course, is the post-Marxist politics of social movements and especially non-governmental organizations (NGOs) which is typically understood to take place in the realm of 'global civil society'. Reaching more positive conclusions than those of Roberts, others also explore civil society campaigns to make the international financial institutions (IFIs), especially the International Monetary Fund (IMF) and World Bank, more transparent and accountable (e.g. Desai and Said 2001; O'Brien et al. 2000; Scholte and Schnabel 2002). Whether these collective and organized forms of resistance can be said to be more or less effective, however, misses the point. As de Goede (2005a) puts it, it is as if 'nothing short of broad-based and internally consistent global movements seem to be able to challenge the power of financial institutions' (p. 379). Amidst the many ambiguities of civil society resistance, it is important to note the ways in which other modes of dissent become sidelined by a civil society discourse that privileges a politics which is collective and organized (Amoore and Langley 2004).

While the conceptual theme of financial dissent somewhat pessimistically alerts us to the suppression and uncertainty of oppositional politics, then, it also rather optimistically suggests that greater credence should be given to many modes financial dissent. To return to Foucault (1976: 96), what interests us is 'a plurality of resistances' that may be 'possible, necessary, improbable', 'spontaneous, savage, solitary, concerted', and 'quick to compromise, interested, or sacrificial'. Given the manner in which the pursuit of a great refusal manifests itself in predispositions for collective and organized resistance that campaigns for state-based regulatory authority over markets, the development of the conceptual theme of financial dissent in the remainder of this book will precisely seek to emphasize this 'plurality' by concentrating on modes of dissent which largely eschew the state. We are interested, for example, in what Kerkvliet (2005) terms 'everyday politics', and in the representational politics of art, poetry, and comedy that de Goede (2005a) characterizes as the 'carnival of money'.

Aside from simply highlighting multiple modes of dissent that are typically neglected by social scientists of finance, our focus on dissent that does not rest on state control from without is also a response to a wider set of issues. As Roland Bleiker (2000) argues in relation to his own research into 'popular dissent', the state tends to legitimate certain forms of politics and delegitimize others, and these exclusions are significant to the exercise of power. Related, in Andrew Barry's terms (2002), the procedural and technical politics of democratic states—such as party conferences, parliamentary debates, public demonstrations, and electoral registers—play a critical role in making politics possible. But, they are simultaneously 'anti-political' if the essence of 'the political' is taken to be persisting disagreements, and 'political action' is taken to be that which 'opens up the possibility for disagreement' (p. 270; also Rose 1991). Furthermore, as Gibson-Graham (1996, 2006) remind us, feminist interventions since the 1960s challenge and disrupt the seemingly concrete boundaries between the public and the private, the political and the personal. New forms of ethical and identity politics have also emerged that transcend these realms, further questioning settled assumptions about politics as collective and organized public action. The result is certainly not unambiguous and uncompromised dissent—there are no 'true' modes of dissent, only those that are more-or-less politicizing and problematic. Nonetheless, it is precisely these interventions and new forms of politics that have stoked embodied activism and emplaced experimentations within economies, activism and experimentations that include the socially responsible investment and credit unions that we concentrate in Chapters 5 and 9, respectively.

Concluding Remarks

The transformation or 'great thrift shift' in Anglo-American saving and borrowing that is explored, respectively, in the subsequent parts of this book is certainly not simply a quantitative story of less saving and more borrowing. Rather, developing the conceptual themes of financial networks, financial power, financial identity, and financial dissent, we will begin to offer an analysis of the qualitative changes in the forms taken by saving and borrowing practices which produce close relationships between society and the financial markets. Indeed, how individuals and households in the US and UK have come to save less and borrow more is intimately bound up with these new forms of saving and borrowing. The conceptual theme of financial networks directs us, in the first instance, to consider multiple and relatively discrete calculative networks of saving and borrowing, their length, degrees of interconnection, and materialization through calculative tools and performances of risk. The making and remaking of saving and borrowing networks, following from the conceptual theme of financial power, involves both the dynamic interplay of technology and people within networks and the shifting place of technologies of risk in (neo)liberal government. As our conceptual theme of financial identity suggests, transformations in Anglo-American saving and borrowing also entail the assembly and performance of various everyday financial subject positions and self-disciplines. But, that said, these subject positions are precarious and beset with tensions and contradictions. Finally, informed by the theme of financial dissent, oppositional politics turns on the re-politicization of apparently optimal and unquestionable calculative performances of saving and borrowing, and on multiple and ambiguous forms of politics that are not limited to collective, organized, and public resistance. In sum, the everyday life of global finance is embedded in transformed networks of saving and borrowing that overlap with the networks of capital markets; situated in the operation of technological, moral, and political power relations; embodied in new and uncertain financial subjects and their self-disciplines; and marked by manifold but problematic practices of dissent.

Part I

Saving

2

From Thrift and Insurance to Everyday Investment

Introduction: 'Irrational Exuberance'?

One evening in Washington in December 1996, Alan Greenspan, then Chairman of the Federal Reserve, gave an after dinner speech to the American Enterprise Institute entitled 'The Challenge of Central Banking in a Democratic Society'. While the event and the speech were largely unremarkable, fairly typical of the activities and views of the world's most high profile central banker, fourteen pages into the speech Greenspan (1996) asked the following rhetorical question: 'But how do we know when irrational exuberance has unduly escalated asset values, which then become subject to unexpected and prolonged contractions as they have in Japan over the past decade?' The Tokyo stock market, which was open as Greenspan delivered the speech, was rocked by his words. Widespread selling ensued that led the Nikkei index to close down 3.2 per cent on the day's trading (Shiller 2001: 3). Similarly sharp falls beset the Hong Kong, Frankfurt, London, and New York exchanges into the next day, as traders reacted to Greenspan's question and took it to imply that he felt that stocks were overvalued. The Dow Jones index had soared nearly 25 per cent during the first eleven months of 1996, and that on the heels of a 33 per cent rise in 1995.

It was not just the reaction of the stock markets, and the media coverage that it provoked, which has ensured that 'irrational exuberance' has become Greenspan's most famous phrase. 'Irrational exuberance' certainly captured the mood of the times. 'Bulls' and 'bears' debated whether 'objective' analysis of the 'underlying market fundamentals' indicated that share prices truly reflected the future prospects of cutting edge hi-tech and dot.com companies in the so-called 'new economy'. The valuation of stock prices thus became intertwined with disputes over whether there was indeed a new economic era, a fundamental break from the past in which innovations in information and communications technology, highly skilled entrepreneurship, and venture capital heralded the death of the business cycle and limitless future growth (Henwood 2003; Thrift 2001: 414–18). Investors who were 'bullish' on the new economy certainly held sway during the late 1990s. For example, in March 2000, nine new economy stocks, including Freeserve and Psion, were added to the FTSE 100 index of leading UK shares because the market capitalization of these firms had grown to outstrip that of the 'old economy' stocks that they replaced. Similarly, in the US, the National Association of Securities Dealers Automated Quotation (NASDAQ) index—which includes the listings of many new economy stocks—soared by 500 per cent between the beginning of 1999 and March 2000. Although it captured the mood of the times, however, the lasting currency of the notion of 'irrational exuberance' turns on Greenspan's apparent foresight: the new economy bubble did indeed burst in the first few months of the new millennium.

As Nigel Thrift (2001) observes, while the new economy was a passing moment, it nevertheless produced a range of important legacies. These include, for example, its lasting imprint on corporate organizational cultures (Feng et al. 2001), and the persistence of 'brand equity', that is, the value that investors factor into the stock price of well-known and reputable corporations (Henwood 2003: 18–19). A further legacy that I want to concentrate on here is the manner in which the collapse of the new economy bubble catapulted 'irrational exuberance' to new heights as an explanatory touchstone in contemporary finance. Significant in this regard is the manner in which Greenspan's notion plays to, revives, and rearticulates a long-standing and diverse tradition of thought that, including Keynes, Schumpeter, and Hyman Minsky among many others, stresses the herd-like, self-fulfilling, and crisis-ridden nature of financial market speculation. Indeed, popular academics and financiers-turned-authors writing within this tradition were also vocal in the late 1990s, warning of the likely collapse of the new economy bubble. For example, in an interview in *Challenge* magazine, Charles P. Kindleberger (1997) reiterated his well-worn view that financial markets are, from time to time, gripped by a 'mania' or 'speculative excess' that, more often than not, leads to 'distress' and ultimately 'panic' and 'crash' (Kindleberger 1978). Similarly, in *Devil Take the Hindmost*, a book named as one of the top five business books of 1999 by *Money* magazine, Edward

Chancellor (1999) set out to show that there was nothing new in the speculation of the 1990s. Chancellor explicitly echoed Charles MacKay's *Extraordinary Popular Delusions and the Madness of Crowds* which, written in 1841, provided an account of the Dutch tulip mania and the Mississippi and South Sea bubbles. The seeming explanatory power of Greenspan's notion of 'irrational exuberance' was capped, however, by the publication of Robert J. Shiller's book (2001) of the same name at the very point that the US and UK stock markets peaked early in the new millennium.

Two days prior to Greenspan's speech of 5 December 1996, Shiller, a professor of economics from Yale University, had testified to the Federal Reserve Board and eaten lunch with Greenspan. Not only did his book reinforce the traditional suspicion that speculative manias can beset financial markets, but Shiller's deployment of the methods of psychology as the basis for what is known as 'behavioural finance' gave the notion of 'irrational exuberance' greater credence. 'Irrational exuberance' took on an air of scientific legitimacy as a means of interpreting developments in contemporary finance. As Adam Tickell (2003: 120) summarizes, the upshot of economists' work in behavioural finance has been to show that 'even the most sophisticated and professional financial traders make illusory correlations, believe that unusual and unsustainable trends are likely to last indefinitely, and place too much emphasis on recent events'. Thus for Shiller (2001), the doyen of behavioural finance, stock market prices during the 1990s reflected investor sentiment and herding tendencies rather than market fundamentals. Contrary to mainstream liberal economics and the models often employed by professional financial market practitioners, market actors and market prices can be far from rational. As Shiller (2001) puts it,

the price level is driven to a certain extent by a self-fulfilling prophecy based on similar hunches held by a vast cross section of large and small investors and reinforced by news media that are often content to ratify this investor-induced conventional wisdom.... At present there is a whiff of extravagant expectation, if not irrational exuberance, in the air. People are optimistic about the stock market. There is a lack of sobriety about its downside and the consequences that would ensue as a result (pp. xxxvii–xxxviii)

There is no doubt that Shiller's ultimate concern is with the determination of stock market prices. Nevertheless, by elevating the importance of 'similar hunches' and 'extravagant expectations', and by refusing to distinguish between the judgements of 'large' or 'professional' and 'small' or 'non-professional' investors (p. 18), Shiller gives some insights into why 'irrational exuberance' has become the common sense explanation of that which concerns us in this chapter and the subsequent chapters in Part I: the transformation of saving and the emergence, on an unprecedented scale, of mass financial market investment in Anglo-American society.

During what Frank (2000) calls 'the people's market of the 1990s' in the US, increasing numbers of individuals and households invested in the financial markets year-on-year, continually pushing mass investment to exceptional levels. Between 1990 and the turn of the new millennium, the number of US households with a stake in the stock market roughly doubled. While this 'democratization of finance' was highly unequal—largely the preserve of what Froud et al. (2001) call 'the fortunate 40 per cent', that is, the top two quintiles of households by income who account for 90 per cent of all savings by value in the US, and around 80 per cent in the UK (pp. 72–4)—it nevertheless forged extensive relationships between society and the capital markets in general, and the equities markets in particular. For Shiller (2001), this is explained by various 'structural factors' which, conspiring together, create both the popular perception that investment in an ever-rising financial market is the way ahead, and 'cause the market to behave so differently from other times' (p. 17). In his terms, 'These factors make up the *skin* of the bubble, ... *factors that have an effect on the market that is not warranted by rational analysis of economic fundamentals*' (p. 18, *original emphasis*). One such factor, for example, is occupational pension saving. Here the tendency for workers to save for their retirement through equity investment is viewed as a consequence of 'the interest value or curiosity value of stocks, not any kind of rational decision-making process' (p. 34). This 'encourages investors to want to buy more of them than they otherwise would. And this seemingly unconscious interest has helped bid up the price of the stock market' (pp. 34–5).

If we were to accept the explanation of mass investment proffered by the notion of 'irrational exuberance', then we are dealing with an aberrational moment during which an unhealthy market psychology has taken hold and speculation is simply too good to resist. Mass investment is therefore necessarily irrational and extraordinary, a deviation from the norm of household saving. However, in this chapter, I want to begin to turn the 'irrational exuberance' explanation of the transformation of Anglo-American saving on its head. Whether saving in the form of financial market investment, or for that matter the determination of stock prices, can be said in a realist sense to be rational or otherwise is something of a red-herring. Rather, as I will argue here, contemporary financial market investment practices are not the consequence of the grip of some collective and irrational psychology, but are made possible precisely because, in relative and emphatic terms, investment appears as the most rational form of saving.

We begin by asking, then, how everyday investment, understood as a set of qualitatively distinct financial networks, both differs from, and has come to be positively differentiated from, other forms of saving. This leads us to highlight that the multiple networks of everyday investment are marked by: their close interconnections with the networks of the capital markets; the significant presence of occupational and personal pension fund and mutual fund networks which provide individuals with an investment stake in the markets without direct ownership; and a contingent nexus of specific calculative tools and technologies of risk. It is these tools and devices that are essential to the differentiation of everyday investment from thrifty saving and insurance, and, therefore, to the ways in which the practices of investment are represented, in relative and affirmative terms, as the most rational form of saving. While thrift and insurance calculate and manage risk as a possible hindrance, danger, or loss to be minimized, risk is represented through the calculations of everyday investment as an incentive or opportunity to be grasped.

The second part of the chapter shows that the partial displacement of networks of thrift and insurance by networks of everyday investment both preceded the 'irrational exuberance' of the new economy bubble of the 1990s, and has continued to flourish into the new millennium after the bursting of the bubble. It also suggests that, while the technologies of investment form part of the apparatus of neo-liberal government and are promoted in a disciplinary manner across governmental programmes, to date the rise of everyday investment to the early 1980s would be to disregard sedimented technological developments that had already begun to establish the relative rationality of performances of everyday investment. This is illustrated in the final part of the chapter where we focus in detail on the production of mutual fund networks. One of the principal networks of everyday investment, mutual funds took hold in the face of the well-established and embedded networks of thrifty deposit account saving.

Networks of Everyday Investment

As we seek to understand the transformation of Anglo-American saving and the rise of mass investment, how investment networks differ, and come to be positively differentiated from, other market networks of saving are clearly significant questions. From within the social studies of finance, Alex Preda's enquiry (2001, 2005) into the French and English 'popular investment' networks of the mid-nineteenth century provides an insightful starting point. For Preda (2001), what is notable about popular investment in railways stocks during this period is that, for the first time, finance moved 'beyond the limits of a single marketplace' and became 'a network of economic exchanges over a large territory, with a homogenous, integrated structure' (p. 208; see, also, Chancellor 1999: 122–51; Fraser 2005: 99–102). The emergence of these initial networks thus sheds considerable light on how, more broadly, integrated but decentred networks of investment are manufactured and sustained in the face of prevailing practices. As Preda has it:

> The presence of relatively large numbers of individuals willing to invest in stocks and bonds requires not only economic capabilities (a financial surplus) or a common institutional and legal framework but also a certain shared attitude with respect to financial markets, specific knowledge about financial products (available at the same time in different places), a common way of talking about financial markets and products, and a shared framework in which such individuals can make sense of financial operations with respect to their lives (p. 210).

For Preda, railway stock investment hinges on the availability of standardized price lists, financial charts, investment brochures, and advice manuals that, taken together, inculcate the 'attitudes', 'knowledge', and so on of popular investment networks. These publications and their widespread distribution are central in demarcating investment from gambling in the popular imagination, thereby re-casting the investor as the dispassionate, calm, observant, and calculated 'investor-scientist' (2005: 152). As such, they constituted 'the ground for the expansion of financial investing', and 'transformed financial investing into a socially desirable activity' (2001: 205).

As we seek to characterize contemporary Anglo-American mass investment networks, a reading of Preda's work yields three pertinent insights. First, contemporary investment networks extend 'over a large territory' and, relative to networks of deposit account saving, are bigger, longer, and closely interconnected with the capital markets. Networks of investment extend across everyday spaces such as the home, high street, and work-place and into the dealing rooms and trading floors of Wall Street, the City, and financial centres the world-over. Compare, for example, the common practice of making a deposit at a branch of a thrift institution in the US or building society in the UK, and investing, from the com-fort of a living room in Newcastle-upon-Tyne in the north of England, in an East Asian stock mutual fund offered by an online brokerage firm.

Second, as we distinguish between networks of saving and investment in the contemporary context, it becomes apparent that it is insufficient to simply demarcate a singular investment network. In the railway invest-ment networks of the mid-nineteenth century, investment took the form of the direct ownership and trading of a very specific stock market instru-ment by a small number of wealthy individuals. Across contemporary Anglo-American investment networks, in contrast, investment takes the form of direct and indirect ownership and trading of a vast array of financial market instruments by large sections of the population. What we will call networks of everyday investment—as distinct from the 'pop-ular' investment networks of the mid-nineteenth century—are multiple, overlapping, and embedded in various ways in the mundane routines of life.

It is only once we recognize this multiplicity of networks that we can begin to grasp a somewhat paradoxical trend that is significant in everyday investment. On the one hand, the rise to predominance of investment as a form of saving has ensured that many more individuals and households hold a stake in the capital markets than at any time previously. Yet, on the other hand, the share of the stock market that is actually owned by individuals has fallen. To be clear, everyday investment has done little to challenge the privileged place of the wealthy in the direct ownership of equities. The richest 10 per cent of US households in 1995, for instance, held nearly 90 per cent by value of directly owned stock (Henwood 1997: 66). But, everyday investment has slowly but surely created new patterns in the ownership of financial market instruments (especially equities), with an increasing proportion of the total by value held by pension and mutual funds (Ghilarducci 1992; Harmes 1998; IMF 1995; Useem 1996). For example, in the UK, two-thirds of registered company shares were owned directly by individuals in the late 1950s. By the end of the 1970s, the proportion of the equity market owned by individuals was less than one-third (Martin 1999: 264–6), falling further to one-fifth by the beginning of the 1990s (Froud et al. 2001: 77). Although the decline in direct ownership of equities in the US has not been as stark as in Britain—households owned 83 per cent of corporate stock in 1966, 50 per cent by 1990, and 41 per cent in 1994 (Froud et al. 2001: 77)—everyday investment has similarly been associated with a pronounced and sustained increase in institutional ownership. Despite the rise of online brokerage accounts and the so-called 'day trader' (see Chapter 4), the new economy did little to challenge this trend towards the indirect owner-ship of equities. Indeed, Kindleberger (1997) describes the new economy as a 'mutual funds mania'. In short, institutionalized funds are crucial in networks of everyday investment, and contributions to pension and mutual funds are, in de Certeau's (1988: xi) terms, the main 'mode of operation'.

Third, Preda's work also suggests that the differentiation of everyday investment from other forms of saving turns on how its relative merits come to be represented. For us, the contemporary equivalent of mid-nineteenth-century price lists, charts, brochures, and manuals is a contin-gent nexus of specific and discrete calculative tools of risk. It is these tools and devices that are pivotal to the inculcation of the 'shared attitudes', 'specific knowledge', and so on which feature in the materialization of contemporary networks of everyday investment, and which establish and reproduce investment as the 'socially desirable' form of saving. Now, 'risk' is a ubiquitous category in finance. Yet, different saving networks entail different means of calculating and managing risk, of folding future uncer-tainties into the present. In broad terms, risk is calculated and managed either as a future danger, harm, or possibility that requires prudence in the present, or as a future opportunity that can be grasped through investment in the present.

The differentiation of everyday investment from other market forms of saving in terms 'risk' is essential, then, to the ways in which it comes to be represented, in relative and positive terms, as the most rational form of saving. How, precisely, does this differentiation through the calculation and management of risk operate in relation to established saving networks? Let us begin by reflecting on the insurance networks that developed throughout the nineteenth and twentieth centuries across friendly societies, state, and market institutions (Defert 1991; Ewald 1991; Knights and Vurdubakis 1993). Insurance creates a diverse range of pos-sible future individual misfortunes and experiences (e.g. industrial acci-dents, unemployment, sickness, poverty, old age, premature death) as risks. Via statistically and probability-based actuarialism, insurance pools such risks as capital, at once spreading them across time and collective populations, and promising to protect the individual through payouts in return for saving contributions in the form of premiums. As such, the promise of security and freedom in a precarious and uncertain future that is made by insurance rests upon 'financial self-discipline' in the present—that is, 'a form of discipline grounded on a social ethic which has economic rationality, planning and foresight, prudence, and social and moral responsibility among its cardinal virtues' (Knights and Vurdubakis 1993: 734). Consider, by way of illustration, the names given to the first British insurance companies: Provident, Prudential, and Equitable Life.

The performance of saving and financial self-discipline through the calculative technologies of insurance (i.e. the regular payment of premiums) has many parallels with thrifty saving (i.e. regular contributions to deposit accounts). As Pat O'Malley (2004) has it, in the performance of both insurance and thrift as 'more or less interchangeable forms of prudence', 'financial resources are set aside in order to provide for the effects of future harms' (p. 23). Thrift, 'Like insurance risk... converts harms into capital' and 'spreads the harms over time in the form of regular contributions to savings' (p. 23). O'Malley also notes an important difference between thrift and insurance: 'Unlike insurance, it [thrift] is not based on the probabilistic calculation of hazards, but on foresight—that is, on a prediction based on common sense knowledge of empirical frequencies. It works with possibilities rather than precise probabilities' (p. 23). Despite this difference, the similarities between thrift and insurance are such that, with particular reference to the UK, O'Malley is able to trace the ways in which both are legally and morally differentiated from speculation and gambling from the late eighteenth century onwards (pp. 95–115).

While O'Malley's work on the parallels between thrift and insurance is consummate, it is nevertheless worth noting that the calculative practices of thrifty saving may not, necessarily and always, be performed to provide for the effects of future harms. It is certainly the case that late nineteenth-century manifestations of thrift in Anglo-America, grounded in the Puritan canon, 'drew a link between thrift and self-denial, a virtue that took on major proportions in the character building of the era' (Calder 1999: 90). Saving and the popular doctrines of 'living within your means' were entwined with abstaining from luxuries, pleasures, and especially the lure of credit. Indeed, as Calder (1999) shows, since the late nineteenth century, innovations and increases in consumer credit tend to be associated with moral panic over the erosion of thrift. That said, thrifty saving is not always grounded in self-denial and a fear of the future. For example, in an illustrative paper on the promotion of bank saving in Finnish magazine articles and advertisements during the 1950s, Lehtonen and Pantzar (2002) document the representation of saving as part of 'a general model of the good life, structured by the ethos of thrift... in which the practices of saving and the ideals of restraint led to consumer activities' (p. 211). Thus, the financial self-discipline of careful, frugal, and self-reliant deposit saving is shown in this instance to 'create and enable corresponding forms of pleasure' (p. 212).

Despite the differences between thrift and insurance, there is certainly little doubt that both appear, together and independently, as the antithesis of everyday investment. Thrift and investment, for example, constitute specific spaces of calculability, and their calculations of risk are made up in quite different ways. Thrift is manifest not only in self-denial and provision for the future, but that provision is necessarily prudent and 'risk-averse'. Deposits in a bank account are, after all, typically made on the understanding that savings cannot be 'lost' (apart from to inflation) and that returns (interest payments) are guaranteed. The most basic calculations at work in everyday investment networks, in contrast, establish a relationship between risk and reward. Risk and reward become inseparable, two sides of the same coin—that is, the risk/reward trade-off. For contributors to a publication from the Investment Company Institute (ICI), then, an industry association representing US mutual fund providers and asset managers, 'demand for equity investments has risen... as more households have increased their risk tolerance and recognized the return potential of these securities' (Holden et al. 2005: 17). Indeed, financial advisers and financial guides and planners of all kinds often begin by asking would-be investors to consider their so-called 'attitudes', 'aptitudes', or 'appetites' for risk. The assertion that risk premiums are present assumes that most savers are risk adverse, and the implication is always that those investors who are willing to take greater risks will be those who, on average, receive the greater rewards.

Insurance, like thrift, is also poles apart from investment in terms of the manner in which 'risk' is represented. This is not to deny that there are also important similarities between insurance and investment networks— both hold out the prospect of individual security by constructing the uncertain future as a set of calculable and manageable risks; and both also rely on expertise, that is, 'the social authority ascribed to particular agents' and 'forms of judgment on the basis of their claims to possess specialized truths and rare powers' (Miller and Rose 1990: 2). Yet, whereas 'risk' is cast as a possible hindrance, danger, or loss to be shared collectively and therefore minimized in insurance networks, in networks of investment 'risk' appears as an incentive to be calculated and grasped by the individual. To be clear, the challenge posed to insurance by investment is not simply a rediscovery and celebration of uncertainty as the necessary context for entrepreneurial activity (Bernstein 1996; Knight 1921). Rather, actuarial technologies of risk tame collective chances, while investment technologies of risk actually license the calculative taking of chance by the individual.

The 'New Economy' and Neo-Liberalism

Making plain how investment comes to differentiated, in relative and certain terms, from other forms of saving is the first step to turning the 'irrational exuberance' explanation of Anglo-American everyday investment on its head. The expansion of investment as the socially desirable form of saving is made possible by its representation as the rational form saving. Significant here is a reworking and re-reckoning of 'risk', which is viewed positively in networks of everyday investment, and negatively in networks of thrift and insurance. It follows, therefore, that the transformation of Anglo-American saving entails the partial displacement of networks of thrift and insurance by networks of everyday investment.

The partial displacement of thrift and insurance by everyday investment was well underway before the so-called 'new economy' of the 1990s, and has continued subsequently. That said, the 1990s was certainly a period of intense change in Anglo-American saving practices. For example, according to the Federal Reserve Board's Survey of Consumer Finances, by 1998 stocks, mutual funds, and tax-favoured retirement accounts accounted for 71.3 per cent of the value of all US families' financial assets, up from 48.4 per cent in 1989. During the same nine-year period, the share of the value of all US families' financial assets accounted for by deposit accounts and certificates of deposit (CDs) fell from 29.3 per cent to 15.7 per cent (Kennickell, Starr-McCluer, and Surette 2000: 8). The 'new economy' was indeed 'an attempt at mass motivation', and proved successful at creating 'a new kind of market culture' (Thrift 2001: 414). But, the everyday investment that flowered throughout the 1990s, and during the new economy of the last years of the decade in particular, only served to accelerate and deepen a reasonably well-entrenched tendency. Financial market investment was coming to appear, relative to thrift and insurance, as the most rational form of saving prior to the 1990s.

Furthermore, if 'irrational exuberance' and the new economy were the whole story when it comes to everyday investment, then it would be fair to expect investment to have collapsed with the bursting of the bubble. Contrary to 'irrational exuberance', everyday investment has persisted into the new millennium. In the five-year period after the new economy, 7.1 million US households came to own equities for the first time, taking the total number of US households owning equities, whether directly or through a pension or mutual fund, to nearly 57 million (ICI and SIA 2005). The terms 'saving' and 'investment' continue to be used interchangeably in popular parlance, and that saving should take the form of financial market investment goes largely unquestioned. For example, in January 2004, American's poured $40.8 billion into mutual funds, the third highest monthly growth since 1992 (Fuerbringer 2004). Everyday investors during this period were certainly undeterred by the investigations, led by New York Attorney General Eliot Spitzer, into improper trading by asset managers at the height of the bubble. Indeed, everyday investment after the new economy was perhaps all the more remarkable because 2001 and 2002 witnessed the largest corporate bankruptcies in US history—Enron and WorldCom (Aglietta and Rebérioux 2005; Fusaro and Miller 2002). The bankruptcies led to the serious questioning of 'cowboy capitalism' by politicians and the media. This stemmed, in large part, from the standing of Enron in particular as the 'model corporation' in the US, 'one which had adopted all the management norms in vogue at the time: the creation of shareholder value, permanent re-engineering, e-business, derivatives trading, and so on' (Aglietta and Rebérioux 2005: 224; also Henwood 2003: 32–6). Once the crisis broke, the constant representation of Enron by policy-makers and the media as an aberrational 'bad apple' beset by auditing misdemeanours, accounting failures, and the greed of its executives—plus the apparent quick-fix re-regulation of the Sarbanes–Oxley Act which reinforced shareholder sovereignty and tightened-up the monitoring of corporations—were successful in ensuring that Enron, WorldCom, and the end of the new economy proved to be just a stutter in the on-going growth of everyday investment.

So, was their a key point at which the questioning of the previously embedded and predominant saving networks of thrift and insurance began to reach a crescendo, a period in which the apparent rationality of practices of everyday investment began to take hold? Drawing on the notion of governmentality, there are certainly grounds to suggest that the partial displacement of thrift and insurance by everyday investment could be dated to the early 1980s and the move to neo-liberal government. Insurance is imbricated in and was deployed across the liberal governmental rationalities and programmes of the nineteenth and twentieth centuries (Defert 1991; Ewald 1991; Knights and Vurdubakis 1993; O'Malley 2004: 116–34). In contrast, the defining feature of neo-liberalism as a governmental rationality is a move 'to render the social domain economic and to link a reduction in (welfare) state services and security systems to the increasingly call for "personal responsibility" and "self-care"' (Lemke 2001: 203). Neo-liberal programmes of 'personal responsibility' thus involve not only the extension of market technologies of risk into domains where state-based welfare and insurance previously prevailed, but also turn on the re-articulation of market technologies of risk in the name of individualized 'self-care' and 'security' (Peters 2001; Rose 1999: 159). Therefore, as O'Malley (2004) puts it, 'If "thrift" gives way to "investment", it is in part because risk is itself being more positively evaluated in contemporary liberal political rationality' (p. 131). Similarly, in Baker and Simon's terms (2002), what is at work here is 'embracing risk', that is, the 'historic shift of investment risk from broad pools (the classic structure of risk spreading through insurance) to individual (middle class) consumers and employees in return for the possibility of greater return' (p. 4). Neo-liberal government, then, stimulates, promotes, and shapes subjects who, self-consciously and responsibly, further their own security and freedom through the market in general and via calculative investment in the risks of the financial markets in particular.

In this regard, the 1980s witnessed a highly successful neo-liberal governmental programme that featured the promotion of direct stock ownership: privatization. Framed by notions of 'shareholder society' and 'popular capitalism', the privatization programmes of the Thatcher and Reagan governments which de-nationalized a wide range of industries, services, and utilities created many first-time shareholders (Burton 1994: 21–3). As Financial Secretary to HM Treasury between 1983 and 1986, John Moore was an important architect of UK privatizations such as that of British Telecom. His particularly revealing account notes that 'Many politicians and financiers doubted whether ordinary people would ever be able to understand equity share ownership or whether ... it is "right" to let them take risks with their money' (Moore 1992: 116). For Moore, however, it is the very promotion of the rationality, risks, and potential returns of equity ownership to the 'ordinary people' that provides the basis for 'successful' privatization programmes (pp. 115–16). Indeed, the share allocation procedures for successive UK privatization programmes explicitly privileged applications made by individuals who, in many cases, were making their first foray into equity investment. Between 1979 and 1991, the number of direct shareholders in the UK increased from 3 million (7% of the adult population) to 11 million (25% of the adult population), subsequently falling to 9 million by 1995 as many investors took returns from the rising share prices of recently privatized companies (Martin 1999: 268, 270). While it may well be the case that many of the shareholders created through privatization did not develop 'any clear sense of what is entailed in shareownership' (Saunders and Harris 1994: 162), showing little interest in the prospects of the companies in which they had invested and not monitoring changes in share prices, privatization nevertheless normalized investment and swept away many of the taboos surrounding equity ownership.

The Building Societies Act of 1986—an important plank of the neoliberal drive to de-regulate 'financial services' in the UK (Knights 1997a)—led to the demutualization of many building societies and their reconstitution as banks, and similarly created many first-time shareholders. Beginning with Abbey National in 1989, a clutch of the UK's largest building societies went public and became banks, especially during the mid-to-late 1990s. In a somewhat ironic twist, demutualization contributed to the partial displacement of thrift by investment by the turning the very thrifty savers who were members of building societies into shareholders in the new bank. Debates over the possible ongoing benefits that members accrued from the mutual status of building societies, dating back to the eighteenth century, largely evaporated as members were offered so-called 'windfalls' in return for their support for demutualization (All-Party Parliamentary Group for Building Societies and Financial Mutuals 2006). Such share windfalls were, typically, equally distributed regardless of the amount held by a member in their account. This, in turn, gave rise to those who became known as 'carpetbaggers'. These were individuals who joined building societies immediately prior to an anticipated demutualization in order to benefit from share windfalls. Carpetbaggers joined building society members in partially sacrificing the guaranteed benefits of membership in return for risks that held the prospect of greater rewards.

There are, of course, many other examples of neo-liberal governmental programmes in Anglo-America that, from the early 1980s onwards, differentiated investment from, and privileged it over and above, thrift and insurance. We will encounter these in the next section of this chapter when we examine mutual fund networks, and especially in Chapter 3 where we turn to consider personal and occupational pensions networks. As we do so, however, we need to be mindful not to collapse our conception of everyday investment as 'financial networks' into the notion of governmentality. To do so would lead us to the simple and crude assertion that the partial displacement of thrift and insurance by investment is a consequence of the programmes and representational practices of neo-liberal government. Investment networks, constituted through a nexus of calculative tools that view risk and the rewards that are assumed to follow in positive terms, are indeed broadly aligned with neo-liberalism and are promoted in a disciplinary manner across governmental programmes. As expressed in Anthony Giddens' *The Third Way* (1998), for example, the embracing of risk has come to stand as a central plank in contemporary governmental programmes. Yet, the emergence and consolidation of networks of everyday investment, in the face of networks of insurance and thrifty saving, is contingent, contested, and has its own genealogy. Technological developments in saving and investment networks cannot be simply 'read off' from an increasingly neo-liberal political and moral context. As we will now explore in relation to mutual fund networks, the apparent and relative rationality of practices of everyday investment began to take hold and become sedimented in important ways not only before the new economy of the 1990s, but before the neo-liberal government of the early 1980s.

Mutual Fund Networks

Mutual fund networks feature strongly in the multiple networks of everyday investment. To borrow explicitly from ANT, they are 'big' actor-worlds that connect the mundane saving routines of Anglo-American society with the networks of the capital markets. Mutual funds are investment trust companies that pool investor's savings, investing those savings in a portfolio of securities according the objectives stated in their prospectuses. Everyday investors own a share or 'unit' (hence the common UK name of 'unit trusts') in the fund, but have no ownership claims on its assets. Investment trusts on both sides of the Atlantic date to the early part of the nineteenth century. The first US mutual fund—the Massachusetts Investors Trust—was created in 1924. 'It was different from the other investment trusts in that it published its portfolio, promised prudent investment policies, and was self-liquidating when investors demanded cash for their investments' (Shiller 2001: 35). The first UK unit trust was launched shortly afterwards by Municipal and General Securities in 1931 (Richards 1987: 27), following a visit to Wall Street by a City of London financier.

Despite the US Investment Company Act of 1940 and the renaming of investment trusts as 'mutual funds'—thereby echoing the more thrifty mutual savings banks and mutual insurance companies—mutual funds remained tainted by the experience of the Wall Street Crash throughout the immediate post-war decades. Although there was a sharp growth in the number of direct shareholders in the US during the latter half of 1950s, with many investors serviced by the countywide brokerage offices of Merrill Lynch, it was not until the so-called 'Go-Go Years' of 1965–8 that investors first came back to the mutual fund, particularly the funds offered by Fidelity (Nocera 1994: 34–52). This, however, proved to be something of a fleeting moment, as the subsequent stock market downturn led savers to retreat from mutual funds to the relatively safety of deposit accounts.

According to Joseph Nocera, business columnist at *The New York Times* and former editorial director at *Fortune* magazine, it was the fashioning of money market funds in the latter half of the 1970s that was crucial in reversing this trend. Money market funds are not strictly mutual funds as we tend to know them today, as they eschewed equities and corporate bonds in favour of short-term instruments, most notably US Treasury Bills (T-bills) and CDs. But, money market funds were a 'seminal invention' because they were 'the first product to cross previously iron-clad boundaries between banks and other financial institutions, not to mention the psychological (but no less iron-clad) boundaries separating "savings" money and "investment" money in the minds of most Americans' (p. 75). The institutional 'boundaries' to investment arose from the regulatory compartmentalization of commercial and investment banking that was put in place in the aftermath of the Wall Street Crash through the Glass–Steagall Act of 1933. While providing savers with a route by which to cross over into the realm of investment and the financial markets, thereby circumventing Glass–Steagall, the appeal of money market funds was also related to another plank of the New Deal financial legislation. Regulation Q—the section of the Banking Act of 1933 that established the power of the Federal Reserve to set interest rate ceilings on deposit accounts—ensured that saving accounts were yielding between 4 per cent and 5 per cent in the mid-1970s. But, with inflation and money market rates considerably higher than these interest rate ceilings for the rest of the decade, and savers, in effect, losing money, money market funds provided 'a way around Q' (Nocera 1994: 78).

Legal action against the Fed by consumer groups, successfully claiming that Regulation Q discriminated against small savers, contributed to the gradual removal of interest rate ceilings from the first months of the 1980s (Krippner 2007). The removal of these ceilings proved, however, to be a slow process and required further legislation in late 1982 (Nocera 1994: 207–25). By the time of what Nocera calls 'the Great Inflation' of 1980 and 1981, and the accompanying monetarist squeeze and hike in interest rates pushed by Paul Volcker as Chairman of the Fed, the 'spread' between the rates available from deposit accounts and money market funds stood at between 11 per cent and 12 per cent. Savings poured into money market funds which, now holding a total of $183 billion in assets, were worth roughly the equivalent of one-third of US commercial bank deposits (pp. 197–220). For Nocera, then, just as the Crash of 1929 and the Great Depression fed the pre-eminence of thrift and widespread suspicion of investment and investment trusts, so 'the Great Inflation' was the key point from which thrift began to be displaced by investment in money market mutual funds. As he puts it:

Previous experience was meaningless. It had been obliterated by inflation . . . the old rules no longer applied. Thrift . . . had long been the great American virtue, something good people practiced as a matter of course. In a time of double-digit inflation, however, thrift was something foolish. . . . Thrift in an inflationary age meant paying for tomorrow's more expensive goods with yesterday's diminished dollars. It was dumb. (p. 191)

For those who contributed to money market funds, 'double-digit infla-tion' had also brought with it double-digit returns. As inflation and interest rates subsided after 1982, the only double-digit returns available were from stock markets which boomed through to the crash of October 1987. From 1982, for investors and would-be investors who had become familiar with and aware of Fidelity, Merrill Lynch, and the other money market fund providers, thrift was still 'dumb'. There were a total of 340 equity mutual funds on offer in the US in 1982, and 6.2 million equity mutual fund accounts (roughly one for every ten family households). By 1998, there were 3,513 equity mutual funds on offer and 119.8 million shareholder accounts (nearly two accounts per family) (Shiller 2001: 35). Between 1991 and 1994 alone, more was invested in US mutual funds than in the period from 1939 to 1991 (Fraser 2005: 515). In the UK, mutual fund networks also consolidated during the 1980s, and especially the 1990s. At the end of 2002, mutual funds accounted for a 22 per cent share of the UK's £1,900 billion of long-term savings, with a further 42 per cent accounted for by occupational and personal pensions. Two decades earlier, mutual funds had not even registered in these figures (House of Commons Treasury Select Committee 2004a).

Mutual fund networks began to take hold after the Great Inflation because, in our terms, calculations of their relative merits became the 'truth' which displaced previously embedded networks of thrift. But, what are the principal calculations of risk through which mutual fund networks materialize, and how have these calculations contributed towards the expansion of mutual fund networks? Just as basic risk/reward calculations lead to the privileging of investment in equities over and above other forms of saving, a range of calculative tools construct and open upon investment choices by facilitating an assessment of the performance of competing investments within the same asset class. Networks of direct investment, for instance, are constituted through tools that enable the calculations of so-called 'fundamental analysis' and 'stock picking'—that is, forecasting the future movement of a stock price, and deciding whether to buy or sell a stock by analysing its current value in the context of other economic data about a company. Such tools include, for example, the price/earnings ratio. In mutual fund networks, meanwhile, 'realized rates of return' expressed as a percentage provide an important calculative starting point that facilitates an assessment of fund performance by the everyday investor. The variance of the realized rates of return from a mutual fund across time is, as with the volatility of an individual stock or bond, measured through standard deviation. This calculates how much a fund's short-term rate of return varies against a longer-term average, such that a higher standard deviation is an indication of a more volatile and risky fund. As David Whitford (1997), writing in *Fortune* magazine, explains to investors and would-be investors:

Even if you are only a casual follower of mutual funds, chances are you've heard of it, since standard deviation, which in this case gauges a fund's volatility, has become an increasingly popular yardstick of risk. . . . If investing is like a roller-coaster ride—and that's as good as any analogy—then standard deviation tells you what to expect in the way of dips and rolls. It tells you how scared you'll be. (p. 149)

Similarly, alongside realized rates of return and standard deviation, a key calculation that is constitutive in mutual fund networks is net asset value (NAV) per share. NAV often features in the listings of mutual funds carried in the 'pink pages' of newspapers The NAV is the current market value of the fund's portfolio of assets divided by the number of shares.

Not only do calculative tools establish the inseparability of risk/reward, then, but they also provide for the calculative measurement of performance and risk across networks of everyday investment. 'Success' in investment thus turns on purchasing, holding, and trading assets that provide returns which are greater than their relative level of risk. Such an understanding of 'success' in investment feeds the prominent place of portfolio diversification in the management of risk. A portfolio of assets is a more or less diversified set of investments that can be weighted across a range of financial instruments. Once held in a portfolio, the risk of an asset is a function not only of its own variance, but also its degree of dependency with the other assets in the portfolio. Risk in a diversified portfolio of assets is less than the average risk of the separate assets—the simple calculative lesson at work in networks of everyday investment that is taken from Harry Markowitz' modern portfolio theory (1959). It is the drive for diversified portfolios that implicitly or explicitly informs much of the appeal of mutual funds. Mutual funds provide everyday investors with an apparent opportunity to diversify their investments in a manner that echoes, and indeed takes advantage of, the portfolio strategies of the professional investors. Such diversification operates both within a single fund, and also across funds, and creates the impression that mutual fund investment is safe, sound, and secure. For everyday investors, portfolio selection across different classes of equities often becomes, in effect, portfolio selection across a range of mutual funds.

Given that mutual funds are typically 'managed funds'—that is, responsibility for establishing and trading a fund's portfolio of assets usually rests with a named individual—the performance record of a 'star' or 'celebrity' asset manager may also feature in the marketing of funds to would-be investors. Indeed, the payment of management fees that significantly eat into the returns of mutual fund investors is grounded in the assumption that asset managers 'add value' and enable investors, through their contributions to a fund, to 'beat the market average' (see Bogle 2005). For those who doubt the capacity of star managers to outperform the market average, there is a low-fee alternative: computer programmed index-tracker mutual funds that are precisely designed and marketed to track and produce the returns from a specific index. According to Nocera (1994), the first celebrity asset manager was Gerald Tsai, who managed Fidelity Capital Fund during the Go-Go Years (p. 47). It was in this period, then, that the performance of mutual funds first became 'an exciting annual race between portfolio managers and the market average' (p. 49). By the time mutual fund networks began to consolidate during the 1980s, it was Peter Lynch, of Fidelity's Magellan Fund, who appeared to stand as 'the greatest mutual fund manger who ever lived' (p. 242). But, what is especially revealing in our terms, is the manner in which celebrity asset managers come to be associated with a particular investment 'style' or 'strategy' that is grounded in particular calculations. Peter Lynch, for example, was famous for diversifying the portfolio of the Magellan Fund by purchasing the stock of mid-size companies that, based on apparently careful and vigilant analysis of their performance and prospects, he believed were likely to grow. Indeed, successful and retiring star asset managers often turn author, and claim to share the secrets of their strategy with the everyday investor (e.g. Bogle 1999). While the presence of celebrity asset managers brings a shiny gloss and degree of personality to the marketing of mutual funds, the appeal of mutual funds continues to lie in their apparent capacity to maximize the returns on offer from the calculative logics of risk/reward.

The extent to which risk/reward calculations and, especially, calculative risk management through portfolio diversification are performative in mutual fund networks is illustrated by the aftermath of both the stock market crash of October 1987, and post-new economy developments in the US. As Nocera (1994) observes of the late 1980s:

Always before, the ugly aftermath of a long bull market had been accompanied by the sound of scurrying feet, as panicked small investors turn tail and ran as far from the market as they could. But after the crash of 1987, small investors did not turn and run, at least not in huge numbers....They *moved* their money, in ways that reflected a new caution, shifting assets from an aggressive fund to a less aggressive one, from an equity fund to a bond fund, from a bond fund to a money market fund. (p. 367–8, *original emphasis*)

Not dissimilarly, in the aftermath of the new economy, there is some evidence that investors are 'less willing to take above-average financial risk than they were in 1999' (ICI and SIA 2005: 17). In this regard, 'balanced' funds with a percentage of assets held in relatively low risk instruments such as government bonds came to the fore. Moreover, in terms of diversification across funds, mutual fund investors turned to index-tracker funds, foreign equity funds, hybrid funds, money market funds, and so on (p. 24). For example, based upon relatively very high returns since 2002, indications are that emerging market funds centred on Latin America or the benchmark stocks of 'BRIC' (Brazil, Russia, India, and China) were particularly popular in 2006 (Thomas 2006).

While mutual fund networks have materialized and expanded through calculative devices of risk/reward in action, then, tax breaks on both sides of the Atlantic since the early 1980s have also supported everyday investment in general, and mutual funds in particular. Tax breaks are effective because they play to the apparent rationality of investment relative to thrift and insurance. As we will see in Chapter 3, the last three decades or so have witnessed several initiatives and developments in pensions—including, for example, the introduction of Individual Retirement Accounts (IRAs) in the US—that have proved essential to accelerating the growth of mutual fund investment. In mutual fund networks themselves, perhaps the most significant tax breaks have been provided by successive neo-liberal governments in the UK. Indeed, it was not until after 1987, following the introduction of Personal Equity Plans (PEPs), that unit trust investment in the UK really took off.

PEPs were the first in a range of tax breaks on saving and investment that have been introduced in the UK in the last twenty years or so. PEPs initially delivered tax-free interest on returns from a plan invested in shares, unit trusts, and corporate bonds, with a minimum of 50 per cent by value of investments held in UK and/or European Union (EU) assets. PEPs were the brainchild of Chancellor Nigel Lawson and were another feature of the Thatcher governments' 'shareholder democracy' programme that included the aforementioned privatization. PEPs were 'not thereby encouraging new saving so much a simple transfers of existing building society and other low-interest savings into the new medium' (Knights 1997b: 222). Although initially privileging direct share ownership (Richards 1987: 89–91), increases over time in the annual ceiling of contributions to a general PEP were accompanied by increases in the proportion that could be invested in unit trusts. While PEPs were joined by Tax-Exempt Savings Schemes (TESSAs) in 1990, thereby providing tax-free interest on a dedicated bank or building society account, TESSAs certainly did not re-balance the taxation regime back in favour of thrifty saving. Replacing PEPs and TESSAs, the Individual Saving Accounts (ISAs) introduced in April 1999 similarly provide a tax wrapper for investments of up to £7,000 per tax year through to 2009/10. Over 16 million people in the UK have an ISA, that is, roughly one-third of the adult population. These everyday savers and investors receive annual tax relief worth a total of £1.6 billion, and their total financial assets within ISAs stand at £160 billion. Although saving in deposit accounts is permitted under ISA guidelines, only a maximum of £3,000 per year can be contributed to a so-called 'cash ISA' (HM Treasury 2005: 111). As such, and continuing the tendency put in place with PEPs, it is equity investment in general and equity-based unit trusts in particular that are privileged through the ISA tax regime.

Concluding Remarks

In this chapter, I have turned 'irrational exuberance'—the prevailing explanation of the transformation of Anglo-American saving and the growth of mass investment—on its head. Drawing on and developing the conceptual themes of financial networks and financial power that were set out in Chapter 1, I have argued that it is because investment is represented, in relative and highly positive terms, as the most rational form of saving that it has come to hold sway in Anglo-American society. Key to the differentiation of investment from thrift and insurance is the contingent nexus of specific calculative tools and technologies of risk that represent future uncertainties as opportunities to be embraced by the investor. Thus, the transformation in saving is characterized by the partial displacement of formerly well-established networks of thrift and insurance by the networks of everyday investment which feature mutual fund and personal and occupational pension funds networks in particular.

I have shown that, in broad terms, the early 1980s was a pivotal moment during which the apparent rationality of practices of everyday investment began to take hold. However, our conceptual theme of financial networks, emerging out of an engagement with ANT, provides, in effect, a reminder that in recognizing the significance of the rise of neo-liberal government in the 1980s we should not bring an unwarranted coherence and strategy to transformations in everyday saving. As our account of the materialization and expansion of mutual fund networks illustrates, the partial displacement of thrift and insurance by everyday investment does not simply map onto or follow from the moral and political shift of liberal to neo-liberal government in the early 1980s.

Contingent and contested technological developments in dynamic networks of saving and investment which, in many instances, preceded the 1980s and addressed quite specific issues, are also significant in constituting the newly ascendant networks of everyday investment. It is to the partial displacement of insurance by investment in Anglo-American pensions, as it turns on neo-liberal governmental programmes and incremental developments in dynamic networks of saving, that we now turn.

3

Pensions and Everyday Investment

Introduction: 'Savings Are Vital to Everyone's Retirement'

Every American deserves to be an owner in the American Dream. That Dream includes a sound pension plan, and adequate private savings...There's nothing better than providing the incentive to say 'this is my asset base, I own it, I will live on it in retirement'.

(President George W. Bush, speech to the SAVER summit, 2002)

The 'Savings Are Vital to Everyone's Retirement' (SAVER) Act was passed by the US Congress in 1997. It mandated the Department of Labor (DoL) to undertake a programme that includes public service broadcasting, public meetings and seminars, educational materials, a dedicated Internet site, and three national summits on pension provision. Summits have been held in 1998 and 2002. The summit planned for 2006 has been delayed. The opening pages of the 2002 summit *Delegate Resources Pack* make a distinction between 'financial education' and 'social marketing'. The former is described as increased public knowledge of financial markets and the latter as comprised of 'action plans...to sell products and services' (DoL 2002: 2). Drawing on the marketing strategies of financial institutions, the organization of the summit featured separate 'breakout sessions' to create action plans for four 'generational cohorts': the so-called 'millennial generation' (under 20s), 'generation X' (20s and 30s), 'baby boomers' (40s and 50s), and 'silent generation' (60s and 70s). Each cohort, conceived of as a distinctive set of financial investors, are deemed to require action plans tailored to their value and lifestyle profiles.

The 2002 SAVER summit and President Bush's speech at the summit provide an illustrative opening insight into the Anglo-American pension networks that are the focus of this chapter. I want to further the argument that contemporary transformations in saving practices are characterized by the partial displacement of thrift and insurance by everyday investment. Assembled through a nexus of specific technologies that 'embrace risk' (Baker and Simon 2002), the calculative performances of everyday investment have come to predominate precisely because they appear, relative to thrift and insurance, as the most rational form of saving. At the SAVER summit, then, it is not so much 'private savings' and thriftiness that are vital in order to provide for an income in future retirement, but the products and services that facilitate financial market investment. 'Ownership' of pension provision now lies with the individual worker who no longer relies upon the collective insurance of occupational welfare and Social Security, but instead creates and carefully manages an 'asset base'—largely through equity-based mutual fund investment—that is to be drawn upon in retirement.

The chapter begins with a brief summary of the pension arrangements or 'pillars' that prevail in Anglo-America. The remainder of the chapter argues that the reworking and re-reckoning of risk in everyday pensions saving, and the partial displacement of insurance by everyday investment that this produces, is embedded through three concurrent processes. Each is addressed in turn. First, neo-liberal governmental programmes to minimize the share of total retirement income that is provided through state-based insurance not only serve to individualize responsibility for retirement saving, but also prompt everyday investment through occupational and personal pension networks. Second, while continuing to provide insurance for their members, defined-benefit (DB) or 'final salary' occupational pension schemes have, over the last four decades or so, increasingly sought to guarantee future retirement benefits through returns from equity investment and trading. I characterize this re-articulation of the calculative technologies of DB schemes, and the new interconnections with the networks of the capital markets that it creates, as a move to insurance through investment. Third, the replacement of DB schemes, as the primary form taken by occupational pensions, by defined-contribution (DC) or 'money purchase' plans involves the substitution of the calculative tools of insurance for those of everyday investment. Participants in DC plans typically invest for their future through equity-based mutual funds, and bear the risk that the returns from those funds will be sufficient to provide for their material well-being, security, and freedom in retirement.

Pensions Pillars

Policy-makers and commentators tend to characterize pension arrangements as comprised of three 'pillars'. The first pillar of state insurance schemes usually comprises two tiers: 'pay-as-you-go' (PAYGO) whereby more or less universal flat-rate transfer payments to those of retirement age are funded through the taxation of employers and those currently in employment; and an earnings-related second tier of payments linked to a greater or lesser extent to individual contributions during working life. Although state insurance began early in the twentieth century, retirement in North American and European societies came to be funded for the most part through PAYGO and second-tier state pensions from mid-century. In the UK, the basic state pension (BSP), dating from 1948, is combined with the State Second Pension which replaced the State Earnings Related Pension Scheme (SERPS) in 2002. In the US and dating from 1935, Social Security currently takes 12.4 per cent in payroll taxes, split equally between employer and employee. Total contributions to Social Security have historically outstripped benefit payments made. The resulting surplus is held in trust (the so-called 'lockbox'). While often 'raided' to cover other government expenditures in recent times, the lockbox retains special Treasury bonds equal to those expenditures. Social Security benefits are not flat-rate, as progressive graduation ensures that the poorest pensioners receive benefits that are disproportionately greater than their contributions.

The second pensions pillar is occupational pensions. Payments to individuals made on or during retirement are paid for through the tax-favoured contributions to a fund made by employers and employees during working life. In the UK in the late 1990s, for example, 46 per cent of employed people were members of occupational schemes. This represents a fall from a peak of 53 per cent in 1967 (Association of British Insurers (ABI) 2000: 17). In broad terms, those who are female, young, employed by small firms, suffer low pay, and endure short-term and/or part-time contracts tend to be excluded from Anglo-American occupational pension schemes. Schemes take two main forms: DB or 'final salary', and DC or 'money purchase'. Although the scale and ratio of contributions by employers and employees vary across both DB and DC, it is the distribution of responsibility and bearing of risk that primary distinguishes final salary from money purchase plans.

Contributions to DB schemes are invested in the financial markets on the behalf of workers by trustees and the asset management industry.

The employer bears the risk that returns on investment may not be sufficient to meet guaranteed benefits, which are calculated according to a prescribed formula based on final salary and/or period of service. In the event of employer bankruptcy, additional insurance of DB schemes is provided in the US by the Pension Benefit Guaranty Corporation (PBGC) and in the UK by the Pensions Protection Fund (PPF). In contrast, under DC plans (which are commonly known as 401(k) plans in the US as around three-quarters of DC plans use the 401(k) tax code), there is no commitment regarding benefits. The individual worker is responsible for deciding the scale of their contributions and between investment options and, ultimately, bears the risk that returns may not be sufficient to provide for their retirement income.

This leaves the final pillar of personal pensions. Here an individual's retirement nest egg is built up through their own dedicated and tax-favoured saving during working life. In the US, personal pensions are savings practices that, while primarily outside of any formal retirement savings schemes or plans, usually take advantage of the tax subsidies available through Individual Retirement Accounts. In 2004, 45.2 million US households (40.4% of the total) owned IRAs which, typically, hold more than one-fifth of a household's financial assets (Holden et al. 2005: 1–2). The total value of all IRA assets at the end of 2003 stood at $3,200 billion. This is around one-quarter of all the financial assets set aside for retirement in the US which also include, for example, the assets of DB schemes and DC plans (p. 2). In the UK, meanwhile, approximately one in every ten workers has an approved and tax-favoured personal pension that utilizes specific DC plans administered by insurers and mutual fund providers. In a close parallel with the US, the total value of UK personal pension plan assets under management is also roughly one-quarter of the total value of all pension assets (Bowman 2001: 423).

State Insurance and Individualization

For the likes of the Organization for Economic Cooperation and Development (OECD) (1998), World Bank (1994), and European Commission (1999), the desired policy objective in the face of a perceived 'ageing society' is clear: to move to a situation where PAYGO and state pension schemes more broadly account for a smaller share of retirement income than at present. The combination of a growing number of retired with increased life expectancy, on the one hand, and a shrinking workforce, on the other hand, leads to an increase in the so-called 'dependency ratio'. This is viewed as leading to a fiscal burden on the state that, without significant tax hikes or benefit cuts, renders current reliance on PAYGO unsustainable over the medium to long term. For the many states in continental Europe in particular, this policy objective necessitates major 'financial market reforms' (OECD 1998: 9) in order that so-called 'prefunded' occupational and personal pension networks, modelled largely on those of the US, can be nurtured (Clark 2003; Engelen 2003; Minns 2001). In the Anglo-American context, where the share of total retirement income provided though occupational and personal pensions networks is high by comparison with Germany, France, and Spain, for example, this neo-liberal programme in pensions takes a slightly different tack. Here a further individualization of responsibility and risk in pension saving networks is underway.

Social theorists including Beck and Beck-Gernsheim (2001) and Zygmunt Bauman (2001) draw our attention to the pervasive processes of individualization at work in contemporary society. The task of performing individual identities has increasingly become not a choice but a compulsion that is shunned by only the most foolhardy. In the terms of Beck and Beck-Gernsheim (2001), we must today *'seek biographical solutions to systemic contradictions'* amidst the disintegration of previously existing collective social forms such as class, family, and welfare state (p. xxii, *original emphasis*). The individualization of responsibility in Anglo-American pensions is, then, symptomatic of a broad but differentiated and uncertain trend. Yet, as Scott Lash (2001) comments, enquiry into individualization by the likes of Bauman and Beck and Beck-Gernsheim tends to neglect the constitutive significance of socio-technical institutions—or what we would call calculative technologies of risk—in the neo-liberal government of change. It is not only that individual responsibility for welfare and security is warranted in economic terms and celebrated in moral terms. Here, as the justifications given by policy-makers for the creation of the Pensions Commission in the UK in 2002 illustrate, state-based insurance is constantly represented as outmoded and 'in crisis'. Individual contributions to state pensions, such as UK National Insurance payments, are cast in negative terms as a tax, and the collective social contract of solidarity across generations and between rich and poor that underpins state pensions is questioned. Alongside these economic and moral arguments, writing the state out of previous welfare commitments also turns on the deployment and promotion of alternative calculative technologies to those of insurance, such that the individual participates in networks of everyday investment and embraces risk in order to adequately provide for their future.

Understood in these terms, and often operating in the name of an 'ageing society' and a 'pensions crisis', disciplinary disincentives that discourage reliance upon state insurance come into view. For example, up until their recent response to the Pensions Commission's final report (2005), successive Labour governments in the UK from 1997 maintained the indexation of BSP benefits to prices as opposed to earnings. Put in place in 1980 by the first Thatcher government and pursued in a wider anti-inflationary policy context, the indexation of BSP benefits to prices significantly eroded pensioners' incomes relative to those in work (Blackburn 2002a: 316–31). Even with the re-indexation of benefits to earnings due to commence from 2012, warnings persist that the BSP alone will continue to provide only the minimum income needed for security and well-being in retirement. Individuals will have to 'extend their working lives', with the state pension age due to rise to 67 between 2034 and 2044 (DWP 2006: 18).

Meanwhile, in the US, the decision to increase the age at which Social Security benefits become payable from 65 to 67 was taken in 1983. This move began to take effect in 2003, and is due to be fully phased in by 2027. Social Security provides the main source of income for two-third of retired Americans and, for one-third of the poorest pensioners, Social Security comprises over 90 per cent of their income (Social Security Administration (SSA) 2004: 3). Social Security also only provides for a relatively low income in retirement by comparison with other first and second pillar arrangements in Europe. Nevertheless, George W. Bush's President's Commission to Strengthen Social Security (2001) offered a range of options that included cuts to be achieved by switching the indexation of benefits to prices as opposed to earnings. However, following his re-election in 2004, Bush's legislative proposals concentrated on the establishment of 'voluntary personal retirement accounts' within Social Security. Under the auspices of creating a so-called 'ownership society'—a notion emphasizing the freedom of individuals to proactively control their own health and retirement prospects through financial market investment (Bush 2005; Dash 2006; Rosenbaum 2005)—the Bush reforms gave individuals the option of diverting up to one-third of their Social Security contributions (with an initial ceiling of $1,000 a year) into a personal retirement account. The proposals would, in effect, have hollowed-out a privatized and marketized space within Social Security for the calculative performance of everyday investment. Proponents of the proposals expected that millions of first-time financial market investors would be created.

Bush's proposals were something of an individualizing-twist on the reform effort made in the closing years of the twentieth century by President Clinton. Clinton's 'Save Social Security First' initiative, which ultimately ran aground amidst the Monica Lewinsky affair, did include a pledge to bolster Social Security by committing more than half of all future budget surpluses to the lockbox. It also suggested, however, that a $700 billion portion of the Social Security trust fund should be invested in the stock market which, assuming returns over and above Treasury bonds, would increase the value of the lockbox and assure the programme's long-term future (Blackburn 2002a: 384–92). There are also some interesting parallels between the Bush proposals and the 1986 Social Security Act in the UK (Waine 2006). The latter offered tax incentives to contract out of SERPS in favour of personal pension arrangements. From 1986 to 1991, two-third of those who were eligible to do so contracted out of SERPS and, in the vast majority of cases, considerably worsened their prospects of a comfortable retirement.

Although President Bush's Social Security reforms stalled and ran out of steam, echoing much of the contestation and debate that accompanied Ronald Reagan's reform efforts two decades earlier (Blackburn 2002a: 354–63), a negative and pessimistic representation of Social Security was reinforced in the process. Social Security benefits constantly appeared throughout the reform effort as barely adequate for a comfortable retirement in the present and certainly inadequate in the future. For example, in his State of the Union Address in 2005, President Bush (2005) described Social Security as 'headed for bankruptcy'. Indeed, the SSA (2004) itself contributed towards this bleak picture, creating considerable disquiet amongst its employees (Pear 2005). At the same time, individuals taking responsibility by investing for their own retirement income were represented throughout the reform effort in positive and optimistic terms. While this included broadly espousing the virtues of an 'ownership society', two features of the prevailing discourse are particularly revealing. First, the administration stressed that reform was not about creating 'private accounts' which would amount to the 'privatization' of Social Security. Instead, it was aimed at establishing 'personal accounts' that would enable 'personal responsibility' (Toner 2005). Second, the administration was quick to defend the place of financial market investment in saving for retirement, extolling its virtues against the criticism that the reforms amounted to 'Social Security roulette'. In the words of Vice-President

Dick Cheney, 'It's been suggested that many people would spend their retirement in poverty, because the investments they choose will be along the lines of lottery tickets, dice games and the racetracks... Over time, the securities markets are the best, safest way to build substantial savings through personal savings' (in Bumiller 2005).

Alongside the disciplinary running down of state insurance and attempts to hollow it out, successive US and UK governments have also created incentives and new regulatory arrangements which, encouraging individual responsibility for investing for retirement, seek to supplement the benefits of state insurance. Most obviously, incentives come in the form of generous tax breaks, currently worth over $120 billion a year in the US and £13 billion annually in the UK (Blackburn 2006a: 111). In line with the headline objective of the first Labour government—to transform the structure of retirement income by reversing the 60:40 ratio of state to occupational and personal pensions (Department of Social Security, DSS 1998)—various recent initiatives in the UK have also sought to stimulate individual investment. For example, the 'stakeholder pension', introduced in 2001, directly targeted 3–5 million low- and middle-income workers who, because they are not members of existing occupational pension schemes, would necessarily rely solely upon the state in their retirement (Ring 2002). Stakeholders are a form of heavily tax-favoured DC occupational pension plan where asset management costs are capped at 1 per cent (now 1.5%) of assets per year. Employers that do not have an existing plan are legally bound to offer (but not to contribute to) a stakeholder pension for their employees. Current government plans for targeting so-called 'retirement undersavers' turn on what has become known as 'BRIT Saver', an update on stakeholder pensions that, due to be introduced in 2012, feature compulsory minimum matching contributions by employers and automatic enrolment (with an opt out) for employees (DWP 2006). The Pensions Act of 2004, meanwhile, reformed and simplified the complex array of taxation regimes that, developing across previous decades, provide relief and breaks on retirement saving. Coming into effect on so-called 'A-day' (6 April 2006), self-invested personal pensions (SIPPs) provide more flexible contribution rules and a wider range of permissible investments.

The recent action of the UK government to simplify the pension taxation regime broadly mirrors much longer-standing programmes in the US. Here a tax code that dates to the Employee Retirement Income Security Act (ERISA) of 1974 is key in the incentives that encourage personal pensions. Although primarily associated with standards for DB occupational schemes, ERISA made provisions for IRAs. These were designed to extend tax-deferred saving for retirement to those who were not already members of occupational schemes, but also gave retiring workers or those changing jobs the option of transferring or 'rolling over' their lump-sum payouts and balances from occupational schemes into an IRA. Contributions to an IRA registered with the Internal Revenue Service (IRS) must take the form of cash, but the IRA owner typically directs the custodian of the IRA to save or invest that cash in a particular way. Over the last thirty years or so, many changes have been made to IRAs. These include increasing the limits that individuals are allowed to contribute to IRAs annually (the maximum in 2006 is $4,000 for those under 50, and $5,000 for those 50 and over), and creating different types of IRA. In terms of the later, three types of IRA are most significant: First, Traditional IRAs, where contributions are tax-deductible or can be made before tax, transactions and earnings within the IRA are tax-free, and withdrawals at retirement are taxed as income. Second, Simplified Employee Pension IRAs, introduced in 1978 and targeted at small businesses and self-employed, where the employer may contribute to a Traditional IRA that is in the employee's name. And, third, Roth IRAs, named after Senator William V. Roth Jr. and introduced in 1997, where contributions are after-tax, but transactions and withdrawals are tax-free. The incentives offered by IRAs have proved to be extremely successful at encouraging individual responsibility for retirement. Changes to the eligibility rules by the tax-cutting Reagan administration in the early 1980s, creating so-called 'universal IRAs', produced a sharp rise in IRA saving, and the introduction of the Roth IRA had a similar if not so pronounced effect (Holden et al. 2005).

What is especially notable for us, however, is the manner in which the composition of IRA assets has changed over time. Saving for retirement through an IRA initially took the predominant form of bank and thrift deposits which accounted for nearly three-quarters of total IRA assets in 1981. As Nocera (1994) notes of the early 1980s and the changes to the eligibility rules put in place by Reagan, 'no one really anticipated much interplay between IRAs and the stock market; it was generally assumed that IRA money would wind up in bank and thrift accounts' (p. 286). But, the share of IRA assets held as bank and thrift deposits fell progressively to 52 per cent in 1986, 36 per cent in 1991, 18 per cent in 1996, and only 9 per cent by 2003. Over the same period, the share of total saving through the annuity products of life insurance companies has remained relatively constant at between 6 per cent and 10 per cent. Back in 1981, mutual funds and securities held in brokerage accounts accounted for only 19 per cent of total IRA assets, but by 2003 the asset share of mutual funds stood at 43 per cent, and brokerage accounts at 37 per cent (Holden et al. 2005: 16).

IRAs have, then, been the significant realm in US personal pensions, the tax-favoured space where the calculative tools and performances of everyday investment have taken hold. Indeed, it was through their pension saving and IRA accounts that many Americans came to perform the new calculative 'truths' about investment for the first time. Reagan's 'universal IRAs' created an opportunity for mutual fund providers, for instance, who targeted their existing money market fund customers. Between 1981 and 1986, 15 million IRA mutual fund accounts were opened (Nocera 1994: 293). In Nocera's terms (1994)

IRAs gave people a way to try on the stock and bond markets for size, to see how they felt, and to become slowly comfortable with the idea of investing. . . . Over time, many people came to believe that it was imperative to maximize the returns they were getting on their IRA account, even at the risk of taking a loss. (pp. 287–8)

IRAs turned out to not only provide incentives for the individual to take responsibility for saving for retirement, but to promote the embracing of risk. The individualization of responsibility in pensions entails not simply a shift from state to individual—or, indeed, some kind of 'privatization' and shift from state to market—but features the partial displacement of insurance and thrift by everyday investment.

DB Pensions and Investment

The expansion of Anglo-American occupational pensions networks during the post-1945 period centred primarily on DB insurance schemes. Given the legal standing of these schemes as trusts, they created mediated investment relationships between their largely skilled and unionized members and sponsoring employers, on the one hand, and the financial markets, on the other. Patterns of inclusion/exclusion in DB schemes were also gendered to a significant degree. For example, in the UK in 1967, only 25 per cent of employed women were members of occupational pension schemes in contrast with 66 per cent of their male counterparts (ABI 2000: 17). The predominantly male members of a DB scheme do not have ownership claims on the scheme's financial market assets, but contribute through routine deductions from payrolls in return for the insurance of a final salary pension in retirement. In Adam Harmes's terms

(2001*a*), workers contributing to DB schemes are 'more akin to passive savers than active investors', their benefits appearing to them as 'more of an entitlement than a return on investment' (p. 106).

The sheer scale of the financial assets of Anglo-American occupational pension schemes, built up over the last half century or so, developed out of the distinct employment relations, family structures, relatively high rates of economic growth, and demographic changes of the post-war Fordist era (Cutler and Waine 2001). Increasing numbers of workers became employed by large firms and public institutions that sponsored DB schemes and, as members of these schemes, workers undertook dedicated savings practices. Blackburn (2002*a*) reckons that by 1999, prior to the bursting of the new economy bubble, the global assets of pension funds were worth $13,000 billion. Around 60 per cent of these assets, or $7,800 billion, belonged to US funds, with those of UK funds worth $1,400 billion. He places these figures in perspective by noting that, according to OECD calculations, the worldwide value of stock markets at the time stood at $23,000 billion (p. 6). In Gordon Clark's (2000) terms, occupational pensions are 'eclipsing all other forms of private savings' in what he calls 'pension fund capitalism' (p. 17). Between one-fifth and one-third of all equities by value in Anglo-America are owned by pension schemes and funds (Hinz 2000: 32; Minns 2001: 27).

A focus on the sheer scale of current pension fund assets would blind us to important changes in DB schemes' portfolios that have taken place over the last four decades or so. By the late 1990s, typically around 60 per cent of US pension fund savings were held in equities, with 30 per cent in fixed-income securities (Clowes 2000: 6). This profile of equity-dominated holdings contrasts sharply with the situation during the 1940s. At this time, it was usual for around one-third of schemes' holdings to take the form of insurance company annuity products, backed by long-term bonds that were held until maturity. Of the remaining two-thirds of holdings, the vast majority were US Treasury (T-bonds) and corporate bonds, with around only 5 per cent held in corporate equities (p. 2). Similarly, in the UK, the average DB scheme held a total of 46 per cent of its assets in domestic equities in 2001, and a further 25 per cent in overseas equities (UBS Global Asset Management 2003: 13). The UK pension schemes' holdings in the 1940s were almost universally fixed-income securities, including UK government bonds (gilts), foreign government bonds, and bonds issued by public utilities (Hannah 1986).

On both sides of the Atlantic, then, the equity holdings of pension schemes gradually increased from the 1950s and 1960s, and accelerated

from the early 1970s into a general trend punctuated only by brief rever-
sals linked to stock market falls, such as that which occurred in 1973–4.
According to Hannah (1986: 74), what initially undermined bond holding
by pension funds was the relatively high rate of inflation that gathered
pace from the late 1950s and eroded fixed-returns. The holding of equities
at the expense of bonds by DB pension schemes continued to accelerate,
however, during the relatively low inflationary climate of the 1980s and
1990s. In these decades, new meanings became attached to the holding
of equities, and assumptions that equities provide a means of avoiding
the corrosive consequences of inflation were augmented by a new calculative embrace of risk/reward. Although holding portfolios of equities was
clearly regarded as a more 'risky' option, the greater rewards that were
assumed to necessarily follow reflected and justified this additional risk.
This circularly reinforcing calculative logic was particularly powerful as
equity markets stormed ahead, first in the early to mid-1980s, and then
for much of the last decade of the twentieth century.

Furthermore, it appeared that greater risks could be managed through
intensified trading and the diversification of portfolios. In the parlance of
those who manage the assets of today's DB schemes, investment strategies must find the right balance between 'core' or 'value', on the one
hand, and 'satellite' or 'growth' assets, on the other.[1] The search for
relatively high returns or 'growth' led pension funds to become prime
movers in a succession of largely discrete fads that focused upon particular
asset classes. For example, pension funds were key investors in corporate
takeovers, merger and acquisitions (M&As), restructuring, and downsizing
during the 1980s (Gourevitch and Shinn 2005: 250; Toporowski 2000),
so-called 'emerging markets' in the mid-1990s (Harmes 2001b: 83–119;
Minns 2001: 137–41), and the new economy during the latter half of
the 1990s. In the midst of the new economy, some of the major US
public pension funds even invested in Enron's off-balance sheet partnerships (known as Raptor I, II, and III, and Jedi I and II) that enabled the
company to hide liabilities and undertake self-dealing (Blackburn 2002b).
As Feng et al. (2001) show more broadly, the combination of core and
satellite holdings in DB schemes' portfolios became reflected during the
new economy period in what they call a 'temporary double standard'.
So-called 'old economy' stocks, held and traded as the core of portfolios
on conservative grounds, continued to be subjected to the disciplines

---

[1] Confidential interview with a representative of a US-owned asset management firm,
London, 4 September 2003.

of shareholder value through tough ROCE (return on capital employed) calculations. But trustees, asset managers, and capital market institutions more broadly were 'prepared to throw capital at new economy companies that had no earnings and uncertain prospects of profiting from digital economies' (p. 481). In addition, US pension funds in particular stoked a boom in new economy related venture capital undertakings. During the 1980s and 1990s, pension fund investments had consistently accounted for 40–55 per cent of US venture capital commitments. The pension funds retained this dominant position as the overall volume of venture capital swelled massively during the new economy bubble.

When the new economy bubble burst, DB schemes on both sides of the Atlantic suffered major losses and, in many cases, were forced to close to new entrants (see below). But this did not lead to a widespread questioning of equity investment, portfolio diversification, and intensified trading, and there is certainly little sign of any retreat into less risky assets. There are, of course, a few notable but relatively rare exceptions. For example, UK chemist Boots Plc announced in October 2001 that, over the preceding eighteen months and under the leadership of its head of corporate finance John Ralfe, its £2.3 billion DB scheme had gradually and secretly sold its equity holdings and purchased bonds. The scheme had thereby 'locked-in' a previous surplus of £250 million generated by rising equity prices that would have otherwise vanished in falling markets (Ascarelli 2002). Cutting sharply against the grain of insurance through equity investment, the Boots' decision produced headlines in the popular media and delivered John Ralfe his fifteen minutes of fame. However, as an article in the *New York Times* by leading pensions journalist Mary Williams Walsh put it in 2003,

If anything, corporate pension managers appear to be moving toward more risk, not less. The composition of pension portfolios is not generally disclosed, so trends are hard to track. But anecdotal evidence suggests that pension managers are turning to hedge funds, real estate investment trusts, emerging markets and other riskier investments, in an effort to recoup the stock losses of the past three years

(Williams Walsh 2003c).

Similarly, in the UK, a widely read industry publication from the same year states that 'Increasingly, pension funds are willing to consider "alternative" investments ... [that] include private equity, hedge funds, gold, commodities, timber, and art and collectables' (UBS Global Asset Management 2003: 52). In search of growth, pension funds have once again been to the forefront of an investment fad in the new millennium, but this time the focus is primarily upon private equity and hedge funds.

Although stock market prices had climbed once again by 2006 to reach the heights of the new economy bubble, the persistence of relatively low yields on long-term government bonds has ensured that large numbers of DB schemes are still confronted by shortfalls in their pension schemes (Coggan and Chung 2006; Lane, Clark and Peacock 2006). The rates of return promised by private equity and hedge funds hold out the prospect of recovering from the losses of the new economy, and thus these funds play a growing role in many pension schemes' portfolios. Private equity funds, such as those run by firms such as Kohlberg Kravis & Roberts, Bain Capital, Blackstone, Texas Pacific, and Carlyle Group in the US, buy up established publicly owned and family controlled firms. A private equity fund therefore holds a 'portfolio' of companies from which, through strategic and operational restructuring to achieve higher profits (so-called 'asset sweating'), it provides investors with returns that are expected to, on average, be considerably greater than those from equities. It is this 'asset sweating' that lies at the heart of the criticisms of private equity made by trade unionists and some politicians and media commentators. Many US pension schemes became partners in private equity funds during the late 1970s and early 1980s (Gross 2000: 36–8), but pension scheme investments in private equity have expanded considerably on both sides of the Atlantic since the turn of the millennium.

Meanwhile, the legal status of hedge funds as private partnerships serves to exempt them from many of the basic legal requirements that apply to investing in the capital markets. This, in effect, licenses their capacity to sell short, use leverage, and take concentrated positions in single assets which, in turn, provides the basis for their promise of superior and spectacular returns (*The Economist* 2006b). Despite ongoing suspicion of hedge funds—stoked by their regulatory position and the collapse of Long-Term Capital Management in 1998 (de Goede 2005b: 132–42), and Amaranth Advisors in 2006 (Anderson 2006)—DB schemes in the US in particular have further embraced the high risk/high return of hedge funds since the collapse of the new economy. Here so-called 'funds of funds' often feature, that is an investment diversified across a range of hedge funds. US pension and other institutional investors now, on average, hold 7 per cent of their portfolio in private equity, and a further 7.7 per cent in hedge funds (Russell Research 2006).

How, then, should we understand the shifting investment strategies of DB schemes, from bonds to equities and, more recently, to the even greater risk/rewards of private equity and hedge funds? In Gordon Clark's account (2000) of 'pension fund capitalism', the changing profile of the portfolios of DB pension schemes since the 1980s owes much to the rise of asset management firms. A few large firms provide asset management services to Anglo-American DB schemes. In the UK, for example, the top five or so firms—Gartmore Investment Management, Schroder Investment Management, Mercury Asset Management, UBS Global Asset Management, Fidelity Investments, BZW, and Prudential Portfolio Management—manage over two-thirds by value of all occupational pension assets.[2] Given that asset managers' earnings are primarily based upon a percentage of the funds that they invest on behalf of others, asset management is a highly profitable business for this select few. As *The Economist* (2003a) magazine has it, 'When things are going right, meaning the stock market is rising steadily each year, there are few industries that can legally make as much money as this one' (p. 4). But, contrary to Clark (2000), and as the terms that collectively name them suggest, what is significant about the rise of asset management firms is precisely the calculative technologies of financial market investment through which they are authorized. Asset managers were, for example, the pioneers in the market application of modern portfolio theory (Clowes 2000: 12–13). In our terms, then, calculative performances in DB networks have—slowly, incrementally, but surely—come to be redefined in action through the calculative technologies of investment.

As a form of insurance, a DB scheme's promise of a 'final salary' pension in retirement, and the security and freedom that it is assumed to provide, rests in the first instance on the statistical and probability calculations of actuarialism. Actuarial practices do not simply measure DB pension schemes' assets and liabilities, but 'contribute powerfully to shaping, simply by measuring it, the reality that they measure' (Callon 1998: 23). On the asset side of the balance sheet, actuarial calculation produces projections on the expected long-term rates of return on investments in equities, hedge funds, corporate and government bonds, and so on. On the liabilities side, it manufactures projections on expected long-term rates of wage increases and the life expectancy of retirees. Risk is thus pooled collectively between all members of the scheme, whether they are retired or still in employment. Accordingly and understood through these actuarial calculations, the task for the trustees charged with managing a

[2] Confidential interview, representative of the Investment Management Association, London, 1 September 2003.

scheme becomes ensuring that assets and liabilities are broadly in balance, and that their scheme can afford to fund the retirement of both current and future retirees.

For much of the twentieth century, managing risk and the balance between assets in liabilities rested on the holding of various bonds that would mature when required to fund the purchase of lifetime annuities for retiring workers. However, the erosion of returns from bonds by inflation, the prospect of higher life expectancy and wages for already maturing schemes, and increasingly complex regulations all encouraged the questioning of the predominant role of insurance companies in organizing and administering schemes (Hannah 1986: 65–80). Demands from trustees for traditional insurance contracts gradually gave way to demands for a combination of specialist actuarial advice, administrative, and asset management services. While employers and trustees struggled to minimize DB scheme liabilities, asset management firms and their calculative techniques held out the scientific promise of future increases on the other side of the balance sheet. This focus on asset growth was given a significant boost in the US by the ERISA legislation which set new regulatory standards for investments by DB schemes (Clowes 2000: 6; Gourevitch and Shinn 2005: 247–8). Today, asset managers—based upon their fee structures, product ranges, claims to expertise, and past performance records—compete to be 'mandated' or contracted by trustees and their consultants to manage all, or typically a specific portion of, a DB scheme's portfolio for a designated period of time (Blake 2003). Some investment management firms specialize in terms of asset class, intra-asset class, and investment styles. So-called 'benchmarks' for asset managers typically contract these firms to outperform average market returns (measured against the major stock market indices and peer performance) by 1–1.5 per cent, and not to under-perform by a similar amount (Myners 2001: 8). As such, the contracts between schemes and asset managers reflect and perform particular positive assumptions about the expertise of asset managers and the optimality of embracing risk/return, and are thereby a microcosm of insurance through investment.

From Defined-Benefit to Defined-Contribution

In this final section of the chapter, I want to argue that a third set of processes in pensions have contributed to the partial displacement of thrift and insurance by everyday investment. This is the drift from

DB schemes to DC plans in occupational pensions, where the latter typically take the form of equity-based mutual funds. What is at stake here is a retreat from the occupational insurance commitments that developed through the post-war era, and an associated individualization of responsibility and risk. This individualization of risk is not, contrary to Stiglitz (2003) for example, simply the transfer of responsibility for the management of investment risks (e.g. volatile stock prices) from trustees and employers to workers. It may well be the case that, as Stiglitz suggests, the risks that an investment turns sour and that well-being in retirement may thus be compromised, are not pooled or spread under DC pensions. But, such a reading would require us to understood 'risks' as objectively identifiable dangers. 'Risk' is also re-invented in DC plans as an opportunity that can be successfully grasped through calculative investment practices in general, and equity-based mutual funds in particular. Individual retirement investors in DC plans are, in short, both calculative risk-bearers and risk-takers.

The drift from DB to DC occupational pension provision took hold in the US during the mid-1980s, and accelerated during the 1990s (Mitchell and Schieber 1998). In 1975, for example, 87 per cent of American workers that were members of an occupational pension scheme were part of a DB plan. By 2001, 58 per cent of those covered by a scheme were members of a DC scheme, a further 23 per cent enjoyed membership of both DC and DB, and 19 per cent were members of a DB plan only (Aizcorbe, Kennickell, and Moore 2003). Put differently, by the turn of the millennium, the total assets of all DC plans were roughly equal to those of DB schemes, despite the latter's maturity (Hinz 2000: 31–2). As Cutler, Waine, and Whiting (2002) argue, the replacement of DB schemes by DC plans is framed by a change in the very parameters through which the organization of Anglo-American corporate activity is understood and judged. In particular, the grip of the mantra of 'shareholder value' as the overriding and disciplinary goal of corporate activity, tightening in the last decade or so, translates into employers' waning commitment to DB pensions. In line with shareholder value and the use of measures such as ROCE, reducing pension costs becomes part of so-called 'value increasing' strategies.

Despite common pressures in Anglo-America to deliver shareholder value, the place of DB schemes as the predominant form taken by occupational pensions in the UK only really began to evaporate relatively suddenly after the turn of the millennium. The bursting of the new economy bubble produced a dramatic decline in the value of DB schemes' portfolios and their returns on investment, pushing many of them deep into deficit (Ciccutti 2003: 20; UBS Global Asset Management 2003: 11). Schemes' deficits on both sides of the Atlantic led to a range of tactics from their sponsors. Some, such as General Motors in the US, initially made significant contributions in order to maintain the solvency of their DB schemes, but have more recently been unable to buck the trend (Hakim and Fuerbringer 2003; Porter and Williams Walsh 2006). Responses by employers have thus included: increasing the retirement age for scheme members; cutting benefits earned through new service; preventing members from taking lump sum pay outs on retirement; requiring that employees either increase contributions or accept lower wage rises as a condition of their continued membership; and, most frequently, closing DB schemes to new entrants who, in most cases, are offered a DC alternative (Watson Wyatt 2003). Indeed, it is arguably only the closure of DB schemes to new entrants in the name of the 'final salary crisis' that has signalled the crisis itself. While the crisis further accelerated a well-developed tendency in the US, it marked a sea-change in occupational pensions in the UK. For instance, an article in *The Financial Times* from March 2003 reported in somewhat shocked tones that three-quarters of DB schemes in the UK are closed to new entrants (Timmins 2003). At present, the trend towards closure to new entrants and provision of a DC alternative continues. It is also being accompanied by employers moving their closed DB schemes off their balance sheets by 'selling them on' to insurance companies to administer (Lane, Clark and Peacock 2006), and also by the closure of DB schemes to existing members.

Governments on both sides of the Atlantic certainly did not seek to reverse the demise of DB schemes in the context of the crisis. Campaigns, such as that undertaken by the UK Trades Union Congress, to defend DB schemes against the threat of closure through the maximization of employer contributions have been of little consequence. That said, it is important to recognize that the move from DB to DC has not been manufactured as the implementation of a clear and coherent neo-liberal governmental programme. It is more akin to a contingent and uncertain drift than a marshalled shift. Three examples are particularly revealing in this regard. First, in the UK, the government has created the PPF which pays compensation to DB scheme members in the event of employer bankruptcy. Modelled on the US PBGC that dates from the ERISA legislation of 1974, the PPF is an additional layer of insurance put in place in the context of the crisis to calm popular protests. The protests of Pension Theft, a group formed to draw media attention to the plight of workers who lost their final salary pensions when their employers went bankrupt, were particularly effective. But, the government's claim that the PPF guarantees the long-term future of remaining DB schemes—made especially in response to charges by a Parliamentary and Health Service Ombudsman report (2006) that members of DB schemes had been misled over the security of the final salary pension promise—nevertheless looks somewhat shaky. Neither the under-funded PPF, nor the deficit-laden PBGC, appear to be in a position to bail out remaining DB schemes in the event of growing employer bankruptcies. And, as Blackburn (2006a: 135–45) suggests, both the PBGC and the PPF are likely to be confronted by a growing number of such bankruptcies. The restructuring of long-established corporations in mature industries, such as steel, air travel, and car production, has come to commonly feature moves in and out bankruptcy, moves which include the passing of often massive pension obligations onto the PBGC and PPF.

Second, both the US and UK governments responded to the final salary crisis by buttressing the operation of remaining DB schemes through changes to the standards used for actuarial calculation. This led, for example, to delays in the implementation timetable for the Financial Reporting Standard (FRS)17 in the UK. Originally due to be mandatory in June 2003, FRS17 serves to minimize the surpluses and amplify the deficits of DB schemes. Assets are to be calculated at current market value rather than through long-term actuarial calculations, and the discount rate is to be based upon corporate bonds rather than an equity-related rate. The discount rate is the rate used in the measurement of the value, in current terms, of a plan's future obligations to members. The discount rate reflects, therefore, expectations about the rate at which a scheme's assets can be expected to increase before its beneficiaries retire (UBS Warburg 2001). In the US, meanwhile, special Congressional measures for DB schemes in the first years of the new millennium, and the Pension Protection Act of 2006, have also focused on changing the standards that apply to discount rate calculations (Williams Walsh 2003a, 2003b, 2003d, 2006b). What is important about these attempts to bolster DB schemes is that their proponents are able to claim that they lead to more precise and transparent measurement, and thereby that they put DB schemes on a sound footing. As such, tinkering with actuarial standards provides a de-politicized and calculative edifice through which an apparent solution to the crisis can be claimed.

Third, and again illustrating the drift from DB to DC, the important place of DC plans and mutual funds in replacing DB schemes was clearly not envisaged when key legislation was initially enacted. In the UK, the decision of Chancellor Gordon Brown, shortly after coming into office in 1997, to remove the tax relief on dividend payments on the shareholdings of DB schemes has subsequently been identified in the popular media as contributing to their demise. But, it seems more likely that Brown was motivated not to crush DB schemes, but to utilize the £5 billion per year saved to spend on new government programmes in health and education. Not dissimilarly, in the US, the introduction of the 401(k) tax code in 1978 and its subsequent clarification by the IRS in 1981 both proceeded without fanfare, and the subsequent importance of the legislation was not recognized by policy-makers at the time (Munnell and Sundén 2004). Contrary to *The Economist* (2002*b*), it was not the case that the introduction of the 401(k) code put 'American private pensions firmly on the defined-contribution track' (p. 13). Rather, in the popular parlance of US pension regulators, 401(k)'s are the 'accidental pension'.[3] That said, once the potential significance of the 401(k) code became apparent, successive US governments have stimulated the take-up of DC plans. For instance, and in the words of US Assistant Secretary of Labor Ann L. Combs (2004), the Bush administration is working to ensure that 'the 401(k) plans of America's workers and their families continue to provide the flexibility, freedom, and security inherent in a vibrant "ownership society" '. This work has included increasing the limits on tax-preferred contributions to 401(k)'s and IRAs, and enabling 401(k) plan administrators to provide workplace investment advice (Andrews 2003; Leonhardt 2003). More recently, as part of the Pension Protection Act, it has also included creating the option for automatic enrolment (with an opt-out) in 401(k)'s (Darlin 2006*b*). Such support for 401(k)'s and DC plans more broadly has, by implication, prompted and sustained the growth of mutual fund networks.

The exact nature of the DC plan available to an individual in the US and UK is determined by the trustees appointed by the plan sponsor (i.e. their employer) who select the plan and the plan administrator. Plan administrators such as Fidelity Investments, UBS Paine Webber, Merrill Lynch, Bankers Trust, and State Street play the role of record keeper, provider of investor education and information (including regular

---

[3] Confidential interview, representative of the Employee Benefit and Security Administration, Department of Labor, Washington, DC, 18 May 2005.

account statements) for members, and intermediary for members' investment decisions. All features of plan administration may be 'bundled' and provided by a single company, or 'unbundled' and contracted between a range of service providers to a greater or lesser degree. DC plans tend to offer individuals a menu of mutual funds covering a range of asset classes and sub-asset classes from which to create their own portfolio. In a so-called 'closed menu plan', all mutual funds are from a single company which is also likely to be the plan administrator. Conversely, several separate mutual fund providers may feature in the increasingly common 'open menu plan'. DC plans often feature a default option whereby assumed gains from equity investment during working life are 'locked-in' during the run up to retirement by a switch into corporate and government bonds. They may also offer individuals a choice between a range of balanced or blended portfolios (so-called 'life-style funds') which are each created to meet various risk/reward targets. Whatever its' exact form, investors in a DC pension plan do largely defer day-to-day financial management to the expert asset managers of mutual funds. Yet, their investment decisions within a scheme—for instance, the choice of buying into, holding or selling a 'blue chip' or 'emerging market' mutual fund—are based on a calculative engagement with risk/reward.

There is, then, currently considerable overlap and intersection between pension and mutual fund networks. This is especially the case in the US, where both the management of IRA assets and the firmly entrenched drift to DC continue to propel everyday investment through mutual funds to new heights. Indeed, according to the ICI (2004), 58 per cent of all mutual fund shareholders in the US made their first investment through a DC plan. That said, the rise to prominence of everyday investment networks in general, and mutual fund networks in particular, continues to entail the partial displacement of thrift as well as insurance in Anglo-American saving. For example, in the US, roughly three-quarters of those households that own equities do hold equities outside of their DC plans, either directly or through additional mutual funds (ICI and SIA 2005). In the UK, meanwhile, developments in mutual fund networks took hold and became consolidated prior to the 'final salary pensions crisis' at the turn of the millennium. The calculative performance of mutual fund investment is increasingly embedded in the prosaic routines of saving, whether or not that saving contributes to the dedicated provision of a pension.

Concluding Remarks

Chapter 2 suggested that the indirect ownership of financial market instruments, made possible through contributions to occupational and personal pensions and mutual funds, is a significant characteristic that marks out the contemporary networks of everyday investment in Anglo-America. Thus, in this chapter, we have concentrated on pensions, pension funds, and saving for retirement, and further explored the argument that transformations in Anglo-American saving hinge on the partial displacement of the calculative risk technologies and performances of insurance and thrift by those of everyday investment. This chapter has shown that, although far from complete, there is a discernable and sustained move from insurance to investment in pensions, a move that is prompted by three broadly concurrent processes of change. First, neoliberal programmes to minimize the share of total retirement income that is provided through state-based insurance not only serve to individualize responsibility for retirement saving, but also to discipline the performance of everyday investment through occupational and personal pension networks. Second, a re-articulation in the calculative technologies of DB occupational pension networks that stretches back across the best part of four decades ensures that the insurance that DB schemes provide for their members increasingly relies upon equity and other relatively high-risk investment strategies. Finally, the drift from DB to DC occupational pensions is significant in eroding employer's commitments to providing insurance for their workers, and in further promoting an individualization of responsibility and risk that rests on mutual fund investment. In Chapters 2 and 3, then, we have situated and embedded transformations in Anglo-American saving, and the rise of everyday investment, in mutual fund and pension networks. We will now turn to consider the embodiment of these transformations, and the making of everyday investor subjects.

4

The Uncertain Subjects of Everyday Investment

Introduction: You Have Been McWhortled!

Appearing for the first time four months after the terrorist attacks of 9/11, the website of McWhortle Enterprises publicized the launch of the Bio-Hazard Alert Detector.[1] The Detector, which 'is small enough to slip into a man's jacket pocket, a woman's purse or child's backpack', was the first product offered by the company to 'the general public'. Based upon McWortle's experience of providing 'defense systems' to the 'far-flung executives' of 'Fortune 500 companies', the Detector works by sensing 'microscopic levels of hazardous bio-organisms and deadly virus organisms'. Owners of a Detector can have considerable 'peace of mind', safe in the knowledge that it 'emits an audible beep and flashes when in the presence of all known bio-hazards'. The huge potential market for the Detector and McWhortle's previous success—as evidenced on its website by customer testimonials and an audio interview with its president Thomas J McWhortle III—led the company to announce an initial public offering (IPO) in a press release of January 25.[2] While McWhortle's stated intention was to file its Registration Statement with the US Securities and Exchange Commission (SEC) five days later in order to enact the IPO, the press release also stressed that 'The SEC has advised us that they have "pre-approved" our IPO because the nation needs a product like this on the market as quickly as possible to protect Americans from terrorism'. Those who responded to the press release by trying to gain a stake in McWhortle through the 'invest now' section of its website were told that the IPO was pre-subscribed, but that Stage 2 bidding was still

[1] http://www.mcwhortle.com   [2] http://www.mcwhortle.com/ipogreenlight.htm

available. However, those who passed through the portal and attempted to participate in Stage 2 bidding were met with the following message: '*If you responded to an investment idea like this... You could get scammed! An investor protection message, bought to you by: the Securities and Exchange Commission.*'

McWhortle Enterprises was one of several hoax investment opportunities created as part of an on-going campaign by the SEC's Office of Investor Education and Assistance. More recent SEC scam sites include a mutual fund called 'Old Glory', a hedge fund called 'Guaranteed Returns Diversified, Inc.', and an investment newsletter called 'Seek to Succeed' that features links to range of spurious investment vehicles.[3] For the savvy investor, there were limited but highly visible clues that indicated that McWhortle was a sting—for example, the SEC does not 'pre-approve' IPOs. Nevertheless, of the 150,000 visitors to McWhortle's website in the three days following the press release, a good number were McWhortled and clicked the 'invest now' option. By January 30, the SEC admitted to the hoax, and SEC Chairman Harvey L. Pitt explained that 'What we're trying to do is warn investors while their guard is down. The next time, when they encounter a real scam, these investors won't let excitement cloud their better judgment'.[4]

It is the attempt to produce 'better judgment' by existing and would-be investors that lies at the heart of not only McWhortle and the other SEC scam sites, but of a wider set of governmental programmes that are currently being undertaken on both sides of the Atlantic in the name of 'financial literacy', 'financial education', and 'financial capability'. For existing investors, the SEC also provides, for example, a range of brochures and pamphlets, a toll-free telephone line, individual assistance by email, and an interactive website (Wyderko 2004). New investors are also targeted, whether in terms of extending pensions provision, or perhaps most disquieting, in terms of initiatives undertaken in schools such as the No Child Left Behind Act of 2001 and Jump\$tart in the US, and the Personal Finance Education Group's (PFEG) work as part of 'citizenship studies' classes in the UK (Odih and Knights 1999). Over-all strategic leadership on financial capability is provided in the UK by the Financial Services Authority (FSA) which, formed in 2000, enacts

---

[3] See, respectively, http://www.growthventure.com/oldglory; http://www.growthventure.com/grdi; and http://www.seek2succeed.com. I thank a representative of the SEC who brought these sites to my attention. Confidential interview, Washington, DC, 16 May 2005.

[4] http://www.sec.gov/news/press/2002–18.txt and http://www.sec.gov/news/headlines/scamsites.htm

statutory duties that commit the regulatory body to promote public understanding of the financial system (FSA 2004*a*). Meanwhile, in the US, December 2004 saw the establishment of the Financial Literacy and Education Commission (FLEC) under the leadership of the Federal Reserve. FLEC aims to coordinate a national strategy across the relevant arms of government. FLEC's mymoney.gov website and toll-free telephone number provide access to relevant financial literacy materials from across government agencies. Common to the wide-ranging drive for financial literacy is a commitment to, at once, empower and discipline the individual to take responsibility for his or her own financial and investment decisions.

The humorous but nevertheless illustrative example of McWhortle, and financial literacy programmes more broadly, serve to orientate our attention to the issue that concerns us in this chapter: the embodiment of transformations in Anglo-American saving, and the making of everyday investor subjects. The previous chapters in Part I have argued that the rise to predominance of everyday investment turns on its representation, relative to thrift and insurance, as the most rational form of saving. Networks of everyday investment—materializing through calculative tools and performances that embrace, measure, and manage risk as opportunity—have partially displaced networks of thrifty saving and collective insurance that construct risk as a possible danger or loss to be minimized. But, the processes of change that feed the predominance of investment as a form of everyday saving also entail the assembly of a neo-liberal subjectivity, the calling up of subjects who make sense of investment in relation to their own security and freedom.

What follows is divided into three main parts. To begin, and through a creative contribution to the literature on neo-liberal governmentality, I mark out my specific route to understanding the making of investor subjects. Concerns with the disciplinary assembly of the 'entrepreneurial self' (Amoore, 2004; Higgins, 2001; O'Malley, 2000) are extended to consider financial and especially investor subjectivity. Investment is conceived of as a contingent and contradictory technology of the self under neo-liberalism, that is, as problematic calculative and self-disciplinary performances that are nevertheless engaged in willingly as part of the ethical production of ourselves as free subjects. The second part of the chapter focuses on the calling up of everyday investor subjects in occupational and personal pension networks. Particular reference is made to the financial literacy programmes of US and UK governmental agencies in the individualization of responsibility and risk in pensions. The final part of the chapter explores the so-called 'investment shortfalls' on both sides of the Atlantic that suggest, in effect, that the subject position of the investor is not simply occupied and performed by individuals in a straightforward manner. Investment as a technology for the calculating and embracing of financial market risk/reward fails to bring order to future uncertainty and instead leads to heightened anxiety; and the performance of investment stands in tension with the practices of work and consumption which also appear as essential to securing, advancing, and expressing individual freedom in neo-liberal society. In short, everyday investors are necessarily uncertain subjects.

Investment as a Neo-Liberal Technology of the Self

A key contribution of the Foucauldian notion of 'governmentalty' is to encourage critical scrutiny of how, through its practices and specific interventions, (neo)liberalism comes to connect 'government, politics and administration to the space of bodies, lives, selves and persons' (Dean 1999: 12). The government of the self by the self is understood as crucial to the operation of power in (neo)liberal society and economy (Miller and Rose 1990). On the one hand, (neo)liberal government respects the formal freedom and autonomy of subjects. On the other hand, it governs within and through those independent actions by promoting the very disciplinary technologies deemed necessary for an autonomous and secure life.

Within the governmentality literature, the financial government of the self by the self is associated primarily with insurance as a technology of risk. For example, David Knights (1997*b*: 224; Knights and Vurdubakis 1993: 734) uses the same phrase to describe the 'financial self discipline' that he sees to be operating in both the nineteenth century and at the end of the twentieth century—'a form of discipline grounded on a social ethic which has economic rationality, planning and foresight, prudence, and social and moral responsibility among its cardinal virtues'. Similarly, while Peters (2001) is broadly typical amongst governmentality writers in drawing attention to the neo-liberal individualization of responsibility for risk, such changes are held to entail developments within insurance as a technology of risk. For Peters (2001), the 'responsibilization of the self' of neo-liberal government calls up 'new forms of prudentialism (a *privatized* actuarialism) where risk management is forced back onto individuals' (p. 91 *original emphasis*). In contrast, a reading of O'Malley's intervention (2004) begins to suggest that the meaning of financial self-discipline is not fixed and static, and is not only performed through the calculative tools of thrifty saving and collective insurance. As O'Malley (2004) asks: 'Surely there is a critical distinction to be made between 19th century exhortations to govern the vicissitudes of life through savings and thrift, and the neo-liberal exhortations for us all to become enterprising investors chancing our wealth on the stock market?' (p. 6).

The calculative performances of prudent insurance and thrifty saving were extremely significant to the liberal government of the self by the self, both during the nineteenth century and for much of the twentieth century. But, the processes whereby everyday investment networks become consolidated, and technologies and performances of investment displace those of insurance and thrift, are embodied transformations. The calculative technologies present in networks of everyday investment call up a subject who embraces financial market risk, deploys various calculative measures of risk/reward in relation to different equities and mutual funds, and manages risk through portfolio diversification. This subject position of the everyday investor is also authorized and legitimated in a broader neo-liberal moral and political discourse. As William Connolly (2002) notes more broadly, 'Built into the dynamic of identity is a polemical temptation to translate differences through which it is specified into moral failings or abnormalities' (p. xiv). In this regard, the concerns of governmentality writers with the assembly of the 'entrepreneurial self', as a signature of neo-liberal government, can be extended to consider aspects of financial subjectivity. New worker subjects are summoned up, for example, who hold the portfolio of skills and experiences that are necessary to embrace the risks and receive the rewards of flexible labour markets (Amoore 2004). As we discussed in the Chapters 2 and 3, neo-liberal governmental programmes demand a similarly entrepreneurial engagement with financial market risks in order to provide for retirement. Although entrepreneurialism apparently shears the financial government of the self from the attributes of prudence and self-denial, it is nevertheless highly disciplinary. Neo-liberal government is not associated with an end of financial self-discipline, but with new forms of financial self-discipline that include investment as a technology of risk.

The contemporary everyday investor subject is, then, somewhat different from the popular investors of the past. As Rob Aitken (2003, 2005, 2007) reminds us, there are, of course, also important continuities. With reference to the advertising campaigns of regional US banks, the Canadian state, and the New York Stock Exchange (NYSE) during the first half of the twentieth century, Aitken explores 'cultures of "popular finance" which both predate and, to some extent, prefigure...recent neo-liberal versions of this story of mass investment' (2003: 296). As he has it, 'the connection of an autonomous self with practices of mass investment' (p. 310) is not exclusive to contemporary neo-liberal government. For us, however, this connection is now amplified, and investment appears to be essential in the course of self-realization. As Aitken (2003) himself observes, the investor subject invoked by the liberal programmes of government which prevailed in North America in the first half of the twentieth century was 'not organized around a monolithic or disconnected identity' (p. 303), but was often enmeshed with images of nation building and citizenship. Such associations with the collective good of the nation are largely absent in the current conjuncture, as investors are encouraged, for example, to diversify their portfolios globally in order to maximize their individual returns. Indeed, 45 per cent of direct and indirect US shareholders hold equities in non-US companies (NYSE 2000). The financial self-discipline of today's investor subjects is seemingly elemental and highly self-serving, performed in the name of individual autonomy and welfare like never before.

How are we to understand the distinctive and unique place of everyday investment in contemporary government? In *The Care of the Self*, the third volume of *History of Sexuality*, Foucault (1984) explores what he terms the 'problematization of *aphrodisia*' in Rome. This was manifest not in 'the form of a demand for intervention on the part of public authority', but as 'an intensification of the relation to oneself by which one constituted oneself as the subject of one's acts' (pp. 39–41). He talks of a series of techniques that permit willing individuals to work on an ethics of the self by regulating their bodies, their thoughts, and conduct. Such 'technologies of the self' not only enable disciplinary self-improvement and contribute to the betterment of society, but also make possible 'the experience of a pleasure that one takes in oneself' (p. 66). Transposed to the contemporary neo-liberal era in which the ethics of self-improvement privilege the material enhancement of individual autonomy and security in the name of a free market society, taking care of the self increasingly involves a portfolio of financial market assets that, carefully selected by the individual through the calculated engagement with risk, holds out the prospect of pleasure through returns. I wish, therefore, to conceive of investment as a contingent and contradictory technology of the self under neo-liberalism, that is, as problematic and precarious calculative performances engaged in willingly as part of the ethical production of ourselves as free subjects.

Let us briefly explore the operation of everyday investment as a neo-liberal technology of the self with reference to the emergence of the so-called 'day trader' in the US amidst the new economy bubble. Day traders were in many ways the epitome of the new economy, a symbolic and 'ordinary' figure who gave up his or her day job to become a full-time investor 'living the bull market at home' (Martin 2002: 48). As was fitting in the context of the new economy, day traders made use of the trading platforms and information services of online brokers. Like all brokers, online brokers such as Charles Schwab and Ameritrade are registered inter-mediaries on an exchange such as the NYSE and/or trading system such as National Association of Securities Dealers Automated Quotation (NAS-DAQ), and earn commission fees for transactions. The provision of online brokerage accounts has been associated with a considerable reduction in fees charged relative to traditional brokers, such that online brokers are also often known as 'discount brokers' which began to offer their services in the mid-1970s (ICI and SIA 2005). Discount brokers such as Schwab differentiated themselves from traditional brokers such as Merrill Lynch by not offering customers costly financial advice, research reports, and so on, and by focusing on the roughly 10 per cent of direct shareholders who are regular and active traders (Nocera 1994: 106–18). More recently, this online discount broker business model has also been taken up by providers of so-called 'mutual fund supermarkets'. On Schwab's Mutual Fund Marketplace, Fidelity's FundsNetwork Xchange, or Vanguard's Fun-sAccess, for example, it is possible for the everyday investor to buy and sell shares in mutual funds at considerably reduced cost. According to NYSE (2000) figures, the average number of daily trades made through US online brokerage accounts increased from 96,200 in March 1997 to 1,371,000 in March 2000.

The proliferation of day trading has been simply attributed by some observers to the promises of massive returns on investment present in the 'new economy' discourse (e.g. Gross 2000). But, the phenomena of the day trader cannot be adequately understood as merely a passing moment in everyday financial subjectivity called up by a fleeting, spec-ulative discourse. Rather, as Baker and Simon (2002) put it, 'the popular interest in day trading seems... to reflect less the promise of easy wealth than the cultural attraction of embracing risk. It represents the possibil-ity of attaining autonomy, leaving behind the frustrations of working for someone else, by risking your own capital' (p. 6). Put differently, simply viewing the emergence of the day trader as a consequence of the 'irrational exuberance' of the new economy bubble obscures the moral, political, and technological context of day trading. The neo-liberal morality of providing for one's material independence as the central component of one's 'freedom' draws on the rationality of investment as a technology. Investors showing enterprise and good economic judgement are not only rewarded through the returns that they achieve, but also enjoy the pleasures of investment. In the aftermath of the new economy, the representation of day traders who 'lost it all' as irrational by media commentators and policy-makers singled them out from the norm and, in effect, rescued investment as a technology of the self from critical scrutiny.

Representations of the Investor in Pensions

While the technologies of calculation present in networks of everyday investment call up a subject who embraces, measures, and manages financial market risk/reward, the subject position of the everyday investor is also authorized in a broader governmental discourse. Fragments of this discourse can be found, for example, in the new financial media explored by Clark, Thrift, and Tickell (2004). The burgeoning of a specialist television and print media during the 1990s transformed investment in the financial markets from 'the preserve of relatively unknown elites' to practices that are 'properly part of middle-class life' (pp. 291–2). As Mark C. Taylor (2004) suggests, a feature of the popular allure of this new media lay in its seeming capacity to entertain as well as inform, to portray financial self-discipline as fun. Similarly, the 'personal finance' sections of bookstores are replete with branded book series, often with accompanying websites, which outline to individuals their responsibilities to care for themselves and guide them through their investment decisions. Indeed, books in 'how to...' series—such as, *Motley Fool, Rich Dad/Poor Dad, Beginner's Guide*, and *...for Dummies*—are a focus for Randy Martin (2002) in his insightful research into the 'financialization of daily life'. In addition to these visual and textual representations of the investor, we could also explore, of course, the advertising campaigns of financial institutions that market all manner of products that make everyday investment possible, or the content of face-to-face financial advice supplied to investors and would-be investors by brokers and advisers. We might also add investor education, whether in schools or as provided at investor seminars, workshops, and conferences. Such seminars feature sessions led by former financiers, TV hosts, newspaper columnists, and authors of personal finance books who, as the slightly colourful and attractive idols or celebrities of everyday investment, stand as apparent founts of knowledge and providers of techniques to be learned and performed.

In this section of the chapter, I want to explore, however, representations of the investor that are present in occupational and personal pensions as specific networks of everyday investment. To this end, we could, again, conceivably engage with a wide range of material. For example, in the US, the websites of an array of consumer and educational bodies—such as the Consumer Information Center, Alliance for Investor Education, American Association of Retired Persons, and National Endowment for Financial Education—all provide information and planning advice on investing for retirement. More specifically, self-help books, websites (e.g. www.401helpcenter.com), and indexes (e.g. Hewitt 401(k) index[5]) are present that support and monitor the practices of 401(k) plan participants. The author has also undertaken non-participant observation studies of the workplace training delivered to defined-contribution (DC) plan members by plan administrators in the UK.[6] Here I want to offer a careful and close analysis of the pension guides produced for popular consumption by US and UK government agencies. These are, in Foucault's terms (1984: 101), 'helpful discourses' in a self-imposed regime for the care of the self. Specifically, we consider guides produced during the first few years of the new millennium by the FSA and Pensions Service (part of Department of Work and Pension (DWP)) in the UK, and the Social Security Administration (SSA) and the Employee Benefits Security Administration section of the Department of Labor (DoL) in the US.

The pension guides produced by Anglo-American government agencies are broadly typical of the outputs of the transformed neo-liberal state. As Crook (1999) notes, as the state sheds welfare, insurance, and regulatory responsibilities, 'state agencies become information and advice bureaux' (p. 179). In terms of pensions, both the US and UK governments are undertaking initiatives to offer advice and information in the name of 'financial literacy' and 'financial capability'. This strategic focus on financial literacy is shared by, amongst others, the World Bank

---

[5] See http://was4.hewitt.com/hewitt/services/401k/

[6] Non-participant observation studies were undertaken in three UK workplaces in late 2004 and early 2005. The plan administrator providing the workplace training was the same organization in each instance, but the employer institution was different.

(see Whitehouse 2000). Policy initiatives in the US have included the SAVER Act discussed by way of introduction to Chapter 3, and the DoL's Retirement Education Campaign of 1995 that immediately preceded the Act. Such schemes are supported more broadly by other branches of government including the Federal Reserve (Braunstein and Welch 2002), and by pensions industry associations that include the Employee Benefit Research Institute and the American Savings and Education Council (Helman and Paladino 2004).

Meanwhile, in the UK, the current government's initial guiding strategic statement on pensions *A New Contract for Welfare* (DSS 1998) includes a chapter entitled 'Education and Trust'. While the content of this chapter has informed some subsequent policies—for example, the creation of the Pension Service, the introduction of combined pension forecasts, and the production by the FSA of the pension guides discussed below—furthering everyday investment for retirement is held as inextricably tied up with wider issues of financial literacy and trust. As *A New Contract for Welfare* has it,

Any improvement in pensions information and public awareness will only have maximum effect if individuals have the basic skills to interpret information and understand the overall financial context in which decisions are made. This will include promoting awareness of the benefits and risks associated with different kinds of investment and providing appropriate information and advice. (p. 87)

In terms of 'trust', individuals' willingness to invest for retirement is believed by government officials to have been destabilized by a series of scandals since the late 1980s.[7] The miss-selling of private pensions to around 650,000 who typically opted-out of their existing DB schemes, the fraudulent use of £420 million worth of assets from the occupational pension schemes of the various companies run by the late Robert Maxwell, and the abandonment by Equitable Life of the 'with-profits' promise made to its personal pension policyholders are all seen to have seriously eroded confidence in the pensions products offered by financial services companies.

Government pension guides typically begin with warnings about the inadequacy of state pensions in providing for retirement income. In the opening words of the principal pamphlet produced by the Pensions Service (2004*a*), for example,

---

[7] Confidential interviews. London, 2 and 3 September 2003. Views expressed by representatives from Government Actuaries Department, Department of Work and Pensions, and HM Treasury.

Everyone needs to plan ahead for retirement. People are living longer and healthier lives, so it is even more important to think about how and when to save for retirement and how long to work. The basic State Pension will give you a start, but to have the lifestyle you want in retirement you need to think about a second pension, and the sooner you can start the better. (p. 1)

For the DoL (2004b) meanwhile, 'Many people mistakenly believe that Social Security will pay for all or most of their retirement needs', but 'A comfortable retirement usually requires Social Security, pensions and investments' (p. 2). It is the prospect of reliance on state pensions leading to the curtailment of freedom and a 'comfortable' lifestyle in old age that looms large in the disciplining of individuals to save for their own retirement. In the words of the DoL (2004b), what is at stake here is 'paying for the retirement you truly desire' (p. 2), 'the dream of a secure retirement' (p. 4).

From the outset, then, government guides juxtapose freedom and financial security against the constraints and exclusions of financial insecurity in order to discipline individual responsibility for pension provision. To return to the DoL (2004b), 'paying for retirement... is ultimately your responsibility. You must take charge. You are the architect of your financial future' (p. 2). The necessary implication, of course, is that not saving for your own retirement is irresponsible. If you experience the uncomfortable lifestyle in retirement that is likely to follow from reliance on state pensions, you only have yourself to blame. A decision not to save for retirement is thus morally questionable. As Stuart Hall (1996) asserts following Derrida, Laclau, and Butler, 'identities are constructed through, not outside, difference... it is only through the relation... to what is not, to precisely what it lacks,... its *constitutive outside* that the "positive" meaning of any term—and thus its "identity"—can be constructed' (pp. 4–5 *original emphasis*). This is certainly the case here, as the stereotype of the insecure, foolish, irresponsible and lazy 'welfare blagger' is a significant but nonetheless absent other in the text of government pension guides. The normative connotations in the words of the DoL (2004b) are clear: retirement may be 'a big purchase' but it requires '*determination, hard* work, a *sound* savings habit, the *right* knowledge, and a *well-designed* financial plan' (p. 3 *my emphasis*).

While represented in government pension guides as responsible for providing for their own future, individuals are nevertheless also encouraged to take advantage of the assistance that may be on offer from their employers through occupational pensions schemes. The FSA (2002b) warns, for example, that 'If you are a member of a salary-based occupational pension scheme, it is unlikely to be in your best interest to change into any type of money purchase scheme' (p. 16). Moreover, employers' contributions to retirement saving are cast as something of a 'free lunch' to be dined upon, and certainly not as 'deferred wages' as is common in the commentaries of trade unionists (e.g. Gerard 2001). The terms and tone of the following from the DoL (2004*b*) are particularly illustrative: 'Does your employer provide a retirement plan? If so, say retirement experts . . . grab it! Employer-based plans are the most effective way to save for your future' (p. 12). They continue, encouraging readers to 'maximize any employer matching funds' when making contributions to a DC plan because 'This is free money!'.

Whether or not they receive support from the employers, readers of government pension guides are left in little doubt that acting responsibly and saving for your own retirement requires calculative performances. Pension guides provide a range of tools that, given various labels, all construct saving for retirement as a de-politicized and technical problem to be solved through rational calculation. The solution to an individual's pension problems is not elusive or contested, but can be found if they adopt the appropriate calculations. Two examples are particularly illustrative. First, the UK guides produced by the FSA often feature so-called 'decision trees'. The FSA (2004*b*) describes decision tress as 'a process of questions and answers designed to help you decide' (p. 2), where questions are posed in a flow chart which require either a yes/no response or a numerical entry. For example, in the FSA's guide (2002*a*) for 'reviewing your plans' and under the heading of 'Are you on track?', the reader is provided with a five-step 'calculator' (pp. 10–17). Step 1 encourages the individual to make a numerical entry in the box provided for their 'target retirement income'. This is supposed to reflect some considerable calculation on the part of the reader about their current income and the likely changes in their financial circumstances (e.g. mortgage) by the time that they reach retirement. Suggestions of a half or two-thirds of current income are made by way of a prompt. At step 2, a number is required for 'expected state pension'. Readers are reminded that individual forecasts can be obtained from the Pensions Service. If the reader is a member of a defined-benefit (DB) scheme, step 3 asks for an entry for 'estimated occupational pensions'. For step 4, a figure is required for 'estimated private pensions', that is, 'how much you might get from money purchase occupational, personal or stakeholder pensions'. In order to enable the reader to arrive at this number, tables are provided for the approximate amount of annual pension income available from a range of annuity products. Finally, at step 5, the individual is told to add together their calculations for steps 2–4, and subtract them from their 'target retirement income' (step 1). A further table is then provided for readers of different ages who need to 'work out' their additional saving requirements. Notably, 'additional saving' in this table is assumed to take the form of investment through a DC pension plan that, somewhat optimistically, will yield 'investment growth of 7 percent per year'.

Second, in the US, the DoL's principal (2004*b*) guide on retirement saving describes itself as a 'booklet that shows you the key tool for making a secure retirement a reality: financial planning' (p. 3). In line with its title (*Saving Fitness*), the guide casts saving for retirement as analogous to an exercise campaign. Sections with titles such as 'A Financial Warm Up', 'Maximizing Your Workout Potential' and 'Staying on Track' all feature, along with images of exercise equipment, scales showing weight-loss, and lean athletic bodies undertaking press-ups and sit-ups! Amidst this portrayal of retirement saving practices as healthy and sexy 'working out' are thus instructions that call up a calculative subject. Readers are told to begin by 'calculating your net worth' (p. 4). This entails adding up the approximate worth of all of your assets (including home and other real estate, vehicles, bank accounts, life insurance, financial investments, and pensions), and subtracting from this figure the sum of your liabilities (including outstanding mortgage payments, credit card and loan debt, and taxes due on income and profits from financial investments). The next task is to 'Estimate How Much You Need to Save for Retirement' (pp. 5–7). Here individuals are directed to use a range of 'financial calculator websites' which all encourage users to move through similar steps to those in the FSA's 'Are you on track?' decision tree (2002*a*).

What, specifically, can be said about everyday investment and the investor subject as they are represented in government pension guides? Reading across the guides, five observations are revealing as to the discourse that specifically summons up everyday investors. First, 'investment' and 'saving' tend to be used interchangeably in government pension guides. Saving practices are investing practices, savers are investors, and saving for retirement is investing for retirement. For example, the FSA (2002*b*) asserts that 'For most people, retirement planning is a long-term goal. So however you decide to save—pensions, Individual Savings Accounts (ISAs), or other investments—you need to put money away regularly over your working years to build up enough assets to give you a worthwhile income when you retire' (p. 8). The interchangeable use of 'saving' and 'investment' in the government pension guides is especially important in privileging and normalizing investment for retirement. A clear and apparently obvious relationship is established between everyday investment and the provision of income for retirement. If one is to be responsible and make calculative saving provision for retirement, one will quite naturally be an investor.

Second, the investor is represented primarily as an equity and/or mutual fund investor. The FSA (2002*b*), for example, states that 'the best way to save towards a long-term goal is to use mainly equities or equity-based investments'. Only when 'you get close to retirement—within, say, five years... it may be sensible to consider locking in the gains you have made [from equity investment] by switching to bonds and deposits' (p. 20). Similarly, for the DoL (2004*b*), those who 'are still young' but saving for retirement are told to 'invest more aggressively. You have years to overcome the inevitable ups and downs of the market' (p. 5). Government guides' discussions of the different investment options available under various schemes and plans also contribute towards this preference for equities. For instance, in a section that offers a general outline of the distinguishing features of equities and corporate and government bonds, the FSA (2002*b*) is quick to point out that 'over medium- to long-term periods (five years or more), the return on equities has tended to be higher than that from deposits or bonds' (p. 44). A subsequent section on 'unit-linked funds' (i.e. mutual funds) available to DC plan members does note that these funds can enable investment in a wide range of instruments including property and fixed-interest bonds. Yet the primary distinction made in the following discussion of unit-linked funds is between two forms of equity fund, that is, actively managed and index-tracker funds.

Third and related to the second, the investor is represented in government pension guides as happy to embrace risks. The standard asset management industry warnings—for example, 'There is a risk that the value of your investment can fall as well as rise' (FSA 2002*b*: 44)—do seem to feature more prominently in UK than US government guides. What is important here is 'how comfortable you feel taking risks with your capital' (FSA 2002*a*: 20). In the US, meanwhile, risk is often portrayed in government guides as an 'opportunity'. For example, the DoL (2004*b*) asks 'Why take any risk at all?' The next sentence quickly answers this question, stating 'Because the greater the risk, the greater the potential reward' (p.10). This is followed by some comparative figures for the average annual returns on a range of various investments since 1926, ultimately showing that the average annual returns from 'large company stocks' (11.2%) have exceeded those from short-term T-bills (3.8%) and long-term US Treasury bonds (T-bonds) (5.3%). It continues, stating that 'None of these returns is guaranteed in the future, but they clearly show the relationship between risk and potential reward' (p. 10). The next section provides details on how to manage risk and maximize potential returns through the diversification of investments across and within categories, while a subsequent section of the guide on 'The Power of Compounding' (pp. 11–12) further reinforces the importance of taking risks to achieve potentially higher rewards.

Fourth, the investor is represented in government pension guides as a financial market player who is active at all times. Taking responsibility for your own pension provision, undertaking the necessary savings calculations, choosing between initial investment options and making regular contributions to a plan is not enough. For the FSA (2002*b*), 'Retirement planning is not a one-off task' (p. 48). 'You should review your investment choices regularly to make sure you are on track to reach your target amount for your retirement' (p. 44). Similarly, for the DoL (2004*b*) 'Financial planning is not a one time process. Life, your goals, tax laws and your financial world have a way of changing, sometimes dramatically' (p. 18). Not dissimilarly, the DoL (2004*a*) tells readers that 'you may want to consult the business section of major daily newspapers, business and financial publications, rating services, the business librarian at the public library or the Internet . . . These sources will provide information and help you compare the performance and expenses of your investment options and other investments outside your 401(k) plan'. The implication is that it is only the active investor who can calculate and manage risk/reward and provide for their own security.

Fifth, the principal government pension guides characterize the investor as both male and female. All individuals, regardless of gender, appear as responsible for producing the financial security necessary for their 'free' and comfortable retirement through active equity investment. Women are indeed much more likely today to be members of an occupational pension plan than they were during the immediate post-war decades. For example, in the UK, 40 per cent of employed women were members of occupational schemes and plans by the late 1990s, up from 25 per cent in 1967. Coverage of male employees fell from 66 per cent to 55 per cent over the same period (ABI 2000: 17). Yet, according to the DoL (2004*b*), there remain 'Facts Women Should Know About Preparing for

Retirement' (p. 11). Readers are advised that 'women need to pay special attention to making the most of their money', and that women tend to 'invest less aggressively'. For both the DoL (2004c) and the Pensions Service (2004b), then, supplementary guides dedicated to women are deemed necessary. The Pensions Service's (2004b) *Pensions for Women* 'tells you about the different issues that affect pensions for women' (p. 1). Here 'women often combine paid work with caring for children, or for disabled or elderly relatives' (p. 5). Readers are told to 'take account of your career and family plans' (p. 25) before considering any pension. Notably, a concern with such 'family plans' does not feature in the calculative financial planning that is recommended in the Pension Service's principal guides. So, while the individual who invests for retirement is both a man and a woman, the representation of the investor in government pension guides is nevertheless highly gendered. The investor subject remains a masculine figure who is deemed best equipped to embrace financial market risk, while the capacity of women investors to provide for their own retirement is constrained by caring and nurturing instincts and an associated lack of aggression.

Making Investors?

The individuals, though not as familiar with the theory of investing as the professionals, have generally received some investment education from their employers. Many have learned about the relationship between risk and return. They have discovered that over the long run stocks have outperformed bonds and other conservative instruments. Many are now able to match their investments with their own financial status, future financial needs, and risk tolerance. They themselves decide how much they will invest in growth stocks or value stocks, large-cap or small-cap stocks, bonds, or guaranteed investment contracts through their decisions about how much to put into which mutual fund options offered by their employers. These employees have become investors...

(Clowes 2000: 3–4)

In this section of the chapter, I want to ask how is it that, contrary to Clowes' confident assertion, the assembly of everyday investor subjects is proceeding in a highly problematic and contradictory manner. For policy-makers and media commentators on both sides of the Atlantic, there is a growing awareness that those targeted by governmental programmes are not, collectively and individually, investing sufficiently or effectively in order to provide for their security. Aside from general fears about declining rates of saving (e.g. *The Economist* 2005c; House of Commons Treasury Select Committee 2004a), so-called 'weak replacement rates' and 'investment shortfalls' are especially and perhaps most starkly apparent in occupational and personal pension networks. For example, the initial report by the Pensions Commission (2004) estimates that 13 million of the UK's 28 million working population are not saving at a level sufficient to provide for a financially secure retirement. The recent final salary pensions crisis is shown to have made matters worse, as investment through occupational pension schemes fell from the equivalent of 1.7 per cent of Gross Domestic Product (GDP) in 2002 to 1.2 per cent of GDP in 2004 (p. 105). Munnell and Sundén's (2004) influential work for the Brookings Institution on 401(k) plans in the US paints a similar picture. Over one-quarter of those who were eligible to join a 401(k) in 2001 choose not to (p. 56), and the poor contribution rates of plan participants (even where these are 'matched' by their employers) raise serious doubts as to the adequacy of plans in terms of their capacity to provide sufficient retirement income (pp. 59–62). 401(k) plan participants are, furthermore, largely failing to undertake the portfolio diversification strategies that basic investment theory deems necessary to the management of investment risk. Indeed, the tendency to hold 'unbalanced' portfolios has been exacerbated as 401(k) sponsors often match their employees' contributions with their own stock (pp. 95–124). This practice was cruelly exposed by the fate of the Enron workers who lost not only their jobs, but also roughly half of their retirement savings which had been invested in the stock of their own employer (Blackburn 2002b). In short, 401(k) participants are far from the calculative financial market players envisioned in government pension guides.

The principal response by Anglo-American policy-makers to current shortfalls in collective and individual investment, and the presence of practices that diverge significantly from the basics of investment theory, has been to step up their financial literacy initiatives. In the UK, this has been accompanied by attempts to: simplify the taxation regimes that apply to investment for retirement through the 'A-day' legislation; stimulate the provision of stakeholder-style 'basic' and low-cost investment vehicles that, as recommended by the reports of Ron Sandler (2002) and the Pensions Commission (2005), target those who are presently excluded from everyday investment; and restore 'trust' in pension and everyday investment networks through a series of re-regulatory moves that have, for example, led to the creation of the new Pensions Regulator

(DWP 2006). While the promotion of financial literacy and the extension of everyday investment to those who are presently excluded may be laudable in its own terms, these policies necessarily miss the point when it comes to the making of investors. Neo-liberal programs represent the investor as a clearly demarcated and unproblematic subject position that can be performed by rational, calculative, and financially literate individuals to further their own security and freedom. Yet, as Miller and Rose (1990) stress, (neo)liberal programs are typically contingent, contested, and contradictory. In their terms, ' "Governmentality" is embodied in innumerable deliberate attempts to invent, promote, install and operate mechanisms of rule . . . But such attempts are rarely implanted unscathed, and are seldom adjudged to have achieved what they set out to do' (p. 11).

I want to argue, then, that two principal contradictions interrupt the processes of identification in everyday investment. Caught amidst these contradictions, individuals do not identify with the subject position of the investor to which they are summoned in an unambiguous manner and, therefore, engage in a mode of 'everyday politics' (Kerkvliet 2005) that negotiates and contests disciplinary power relations in important ways. The first contradiction arises out of the operation of investment as a technology of the self under neo-liberal governmentality. The prospects for individual security and freedom that are held out as possible through investment as care of the self hinge on the returns that are assumed to follow from embracing risk. The financial future is cast as an opportunity that can be taken by the investor who appropriately calculates, measures, and manages risk/reward. By way of illustration, Bewley et al. (2007) claim that the diversification of DC portfolios can provide for the management of stock market volatility in pension saving. In their terms, given the greater rewards that are calculated to be on offer from 'risky' stocks and shares, 'investing in equities for retirement is not scary', but 'investing without equities is scary'. However, the proposed calculative engagement with risk/reward assumes that it is indeed possible to bring some semblance of order to the necessarily uncertain future. It becomes apparent, based on our critical reading of Frank Knight's work on indeterminacy, that this is not a possibility.

Consider, by way of illustration, DC pension plans and annuities. Investment as a technique of risk emphasizes that contributions to a DC scheme should be held in a balanced and diversified portfolio of assets. Everyday investors are encouraged to hold mainly equity-based mutual funds up until their last few years of employment, and then to 'lock in' their presumed returns from these funds by switching into fixed-interest instruments. But, at retirement, DC schemes tend to require that the individual surrenders or 'cashes out' this balanced portfolio in favour of a single financial instrument—i.e. an annuity that will pay an income over the years until death. Given that annuity rates are closely tied to prevailing interest rates and thus fluctuate considerably, retirement investors are thus exposed to uncertainties that arise from not being able to calculate the interest rate at the time of their retirement. The retirement income of those who retired in the late 1990s is, for example, considerably higher than that of those who retired in the first few years of the new millennium when annuity rates (like interest rates) hit historic lows. Pensions consultancy firm Watson Wyatt ran scenarios of what would happen to a hypothetical man who, beginning work at 25, dutifully invested 6 per cent of his pay in a 401(k) plan for the next forty years and then, on retirement, used the account balance to purchase an annuity. If the man had retired in 2000, his balance would have purchased an annuity that paid 134 per cent of his pre-retirement income. But, if he turned 65 in 2003, his 401(k) investments would only be enough to purchase an annuity that replaced 57 per cent of his pre-retirement income (in Williams Walsh 2006a). Fidelity, the leading administrator of 401(k)'s, recommends that workers make sufficient provisions to realize 85 per cent of their pre-retirement income in retirement (Darlin 2006b). What is plain, therefore, is that the fate of even those individuals who have responsibly and skilfully invested for their freedom and security in retirement is determined by luck and good or bad timing.

Unable to bring order to the necessarily uncertain future, the technology of investment, to paraphrase from Crook (1999), actually results in the 'overproduction and undercontrol of risks' (p. 180). The investor subject's attempts to calculate, measure, and manage proliferating risks are increasingly strained by volatilities and uncertainties that cannot be captured and governed by rational expectations. This contraction is compounded by the high fees paid by everyday investors to the asset managers that administer their DC plans and mutual funds, fees that are still payable in the bad times when investments turn sour. As Crook (1999) continues, 'A general information overload' and 'anxiety and insecurity [rather] than a sense of safety and control' follow from 'the arbitrariness and necessary incompleteness of even the most assiduous individual risk calculation' (p. 180). The continual representation of investment as the principal financial means of acquiring material well-being, security, and freedom only serves to heighten this anxiety and, ultimately, to install a sense of perpetual crisis. For some, anxiety and uncertainty manifests itself in a retreat to the relative safety of savings accounts where returns are guaranteed, but more likely is a rejection of saving and financial market investment altogether.

Framed by the explanations of market failure offered by institutional economics (cf. Hodgson 1988; North 1990), recent evaluative reports in the UK in particular tend to represent this rejection of everyday investment as resulting from a 'lack of trust' or 'loss of confidence' in investment. High-profile academics of UK pensions also reach similar conclusions (Clark and Whiteside 2003). The House of Commons Treasury Select Committee (2004*a*), for example, begins from the assumption that there is currently 'a damaging lack of consumer confidence in long-term saving' (p. 3). While the Committee recognizes that the collapse of the new economy bull market undermined popular confidence in investment in broad terms, it holds that 'the fundamental issue was that the industry had a poor record for treating customers fairly' (p. 11). In our terms, the report suggests that everyday investment as a technique of risk for the care of the self is in no way contradictory. Instead, incidences of failure at which the risk/uncertainty contradiction surfaces are cast as the consequence of either miss-selling and miss-information, or unrealistic expectations over the likely performance of particular products. In terms of the latter, for instance, the Committee calls for a 'summary box' of standardized consumer information in the promotional materials for saving and investment products. This is to include an industry-wide 'risk measure' as 'Too often,...savers have bought long-term saving products without any satisfactory explanation of the inherent risks' (p. 17).

At the same time that anxiety and uncertainty come to manifest themselves in the rejection of financial market investment, some individuals have come to perceive their self-interests to be best served by pushing back the frontiers of what it means to be 'an investor'. Put differently, investment as a technology of the self does not take the form envisaged under neo-liberal governmentality as everyday politics intervenes. For example, UK stakeholder pensions not only failed to reach their target market, but have been utilized by the relatively wealthy as providing lucrative tax breaks for additional investment for retirement (Jolliffe 2003). Meanwhile, indications are that large numbers of investors have turned their backs on the financial markets in favour of residential property. A survey undertaken by the ABI (2003) suggests, for example, that 32 per cent of the UK population plan to use income from their property to fund retirement, with 13 per cent expecting their property to provide their main source of income in retirement. Indeed, and as we will explore in detail in Chapter 8, the era of rapidly rising house prices since the latter half of the 1990s has seen the emergence of so-called 'flippers' and 'buy-to-let investors' on both sides of the Atlantic.

Susan Smith's (2006) extensive qualitative research into UK households is revealing as to why individuals have turned to the residential property market to provide for the returns that appear essential to their future security. The explanations that owner-occupiers give for their investments in their homes vary somewhat. For some, investment appears as an 'imperative', while for others it appears as the 'sensible', 'responsible', 'safe', or 'useful' option relative to the risks/returns of the financial markets. As Smith has it, what is especially notable here is 'how, across these discussions, the housing investor is being set up as being even more justified and just than the stockbroker; more respectable still than the most rational of speculators' (p. 18). What seems to be at work here is not a lack of rationality or some kind of 'irrational exuberance', as there is a widespread awareness that residential property is an uncertain and volatile investment. Rather, investment in 'bricks and mortar' is regarded as having both a use-value and obvious materiality. The benefits and rewards of an investment in a home can be used and seen in the routines of everyday life, almost regardless of whether that investment yields returns. While the seemingly intangible and untouchable quality of financial market investment in the 'paper' of equities and bonds creates a tension that always permeates these practices (Maurer 1999), this tension would seem especially germane in the subjectivities of everyday investors.

In addition to the contradiction manifest in investment as a technique of risk, a second contradiction also intervenes in processes of identification such that individuals do not simply perform the subject position of the everyday investor. The subject position of the investor that is summoned up in neo-liberal governmentality is represented as a monolithic and disconnected economic identity. It is the very isolation of the calculative investor that provides the anchor point in representations of close relationships between the risk/return of financial markets, on the one hand, and individual freedom and security, on the other. Such isolation, of course, cannot hold, as investors are also simultaneously workers, consumers, and so on. Just as it is impossible to unambiguously differentiate responsible investors from irresponsible welfare dependents, so investors cannot be clearly demarcated from the subject positions of workers and consumers. This is especially the case when neo-liberal governmental programmes represent savers, workers, and consumers as entrepreneurial subjects. I want to stress, therefore, that the performance of the subject position of the investor stands in tension with the practices of work and consumption which also appear as essential to securing, advancing, and expressing individual freedom.

Alongside the investor subject, neo-liberal government also calls up the 'worker-entrepreneur' in the contemporary restructuring of the productive economy (Amoore 2004). Both the investor and the worker-entrepreneur tend to be represented as responsible and self-reliant figures who embrace risk/reward. Both the securities markets and flexible, downsized, mobile, and contacted-out production appear to present opportunities for individuals who want to progress. Here the successful worker-entrepreneur, who builds their 'career portfolio', will have no problems in also contributing to and managing their own portfolio of equity investments through their DC pension plan and/or mutual funds. However, worker-entrepreneurs necessarily confront new uncertainties over employment contracts, hours, pay, and conditions that, obscured by discourses of risk/reward, are likely to undercut their capacity to perform the subject position of the investor. The responsible investor who builds a portfolio of securities in order to provide for his or her future requires a disposable income to invest. Investment is not a one off event, but a set of ongoing calculative performances of self care that rely, for the vast majority individuals and households at least, on relatively predictable wages. Amongst pension economists, this is sometimes referred to as the 'life cycle hypothesis of saving and wealth accumulation', whereby members of households invest in assets during their working lives which they later rely upon for income. But, far from enabling investor subjects, contemporary restructuring in production and work, embodied through the subject position of the worker-entrepreneur, introduces additional uncertainties into everyday investment practices.

Furthermore, it is particularly ironic that everyday investment, and the associated drive for so-called 'shareholder value' in the name of the investor and financial market efficiency, contributes towards uncertainties over employment. As we will see in Chapter 5, this has been the message for organized labour in the US since the late 1970s, a message that has been taken forward by many of the labour activists who became the 'shareholder activists' of multi-employer and public pension schemes in the 1990s. The key challenge for these activists remains converting workers' investments in corporate securities into greater control over management practices, thereby advancing 'a new paradigm' for pension fund investment that takes into account 'the interests of all stakeholders in the economy in equal measure' (Hebb 2001: 1). But, as will be argued in Chapter 5, shareholder activism in the name of workers has, to date, served primarily to further so-called 'good corporate governance'. This actually further erodes the capacities of corporate managers to undertake strategies that deviate from production patterns that are flexible, lean, and out-sourced. The performance of the subject position of the investor continues to stand in tension with the practices of work.

In addition to the investor subject and the worker-entrepreneur, neoliberal government also calls up consumer subjects who express and communicate their freedom, aspirations, and individuality through commodity ownership and acts of consumer choice (Miller and Rose 1997). As we will explore in depth in Chapter 8, consumer credit has come to play an increasingly instrumental and communicative role in consumer subjectivity, apparently wiping away the need to earn and/or save before a purchase can be made. Indeed, the consumption of credit cards has itself become a means of symbolic expression. What is significant for us, however, is that contrary to the popular discourses that bemoan the growth of consumer credit as a collapse in the values of thrift, the practices of consuming on credit are leading to new forms of financial self-discipline. Calculative performances to manage outstanding future obligations are necessary for borrowers so that credit scores are maintained, for example, and that 'freedom' and 'individuality' can continue to be expressed in the future. There is, then, a contradiction between the consumer and investor as subject positions in neo-liberal government. Even the most disciplined and calculative individual of typical means will, for example, struggle to simultaneously reconcile borrowing for house, car, and consumer goods purchases on the one hand, with contributing to a mutual fund and/or participating in a 401(k) plan on the other. Put differently, while it has long been common for trades unionists to talk of pensions as a collective bargain that defers wages until retirement, in the neo-liberal period investing for retirement is problematic as it requires individual decisions to defer consumption. It is no coincidence, then, that the formation of investor subjects is proving particularly problematic at a time when individuals continue to take part in a frenzied borrowing binge.

Official analytical and strategic reports on investment shortfalls in the US and UK have very little to say about the tensions that are present between the performance of investment, on the one hand, and consumption, on the other. There is, of course, also no mention of the uncertainties and insecurities experienced by worker-entrepreneurs. Interestingly, however, the problems of reconciling investment and credit-fuelled consumption are laid bare in public guides to investment produced by government. Here outstanding obligations arising from consumer credit relations tend to appear as the first enemy of the investor. For example, the DoL's principal pensions guide (2004b) features a section on how to 'Boost Your Financial Performance'. Readers are told that 'There's one simple trick for saving for any goal: spend less than you earn'. The following section instructs readers to 'Avoid Debt and Credit Problems', and tells them that 'High debt and misuse of credit cards make it tough to save for retirement'. Further 'additional tips for handling credit cards wisely' include 'Keep only one or two cards, not the usual eight or nine', 'Pay off the card each month, or at least pay more than the minimum', and 'Leave the cards at home or cut them up!'.

Concluding Remarks

Neo-liberal governmental programmes and representations of everyday investment currently frame debates over how to best to save for the future. Retirement, for example, presently appears as a technical problem to be solved by the individual who calculates, embraces, and bears financial market risk through investment during their working life. Put differently, individuals' confrontations with saving and retirement are immediately de-politicized and no longer elusive or contested once they become anchored in the realm of risk and investment. But, the embodiment of contemporary transformations in Anglo-America saving, and the assembly of everyday investor subjects, is actually producing what we might term 'uncertain subjects'. The so-called 'shortfalls' against the levels of investment that are assumed to be necessary to provide for future security and autonomy suggest, in effect, that the subject position of the investor is not simply occupied by individuals in a unproblematic manner. Investment as a technology of the self is contradictory. It rests on calculating financial market risk/reward, but necessarily cannot bring order to future uncertainty. At the same time, the performance of investment stands in tension with the practices of work and consumption which are apparently also essential to securing, advancing, and expressing individual freedom in neo-liberal society. The making of investor subjects remains precarious, partial, and incomplete, an ambition rather than an achievement, not least because ambitious and aspirational individuals are negotiating and contesting the contradictions and tensions that are present. It is dissent from investment more broadly that is our focus in the next chapter.

5

Socially Responsible Investment

Introduction: Vice Fund

Launched at the end of August 2002, Vice Fund is a mutual fund that is offered in the US by Mutual Advisers, Inc. As detailed in Vice Fund's prospectus and on its website, the Fund provides investors with the opportunity to hold a portfolio of securities in small, medium, and large corporations that operate in the gaming, tobacco, alcohol, and aerospace and defence industries.[1] The Fund has US and foreign assets worth in excess of $50 million, and, in mid-2007, its principal holdings were in the securities of companies such as Altria Group (tobacco and alcohol), Loews Group (tobacco), British American Tobacco, Diageo (alcohol), MGM Mirage (casinos), and Boeing (aerospace and defence). This is, then, a multi-cap equity mutual fund with a difference. The 'philosophy' of GNI Capital, Inc., the Fund's asset manager, is that although these industries are 'often considered politically incorrect', they 'will always be supported and/or consumed and that companies in these industries, if managed correctly, will continue to experience significant capital appreciation in good and bad markets' (Mutual Advisers, Inc. 2006: 2). In line with this philosophy, the Fund's website features pages that make 'The Case For...' stocks in each of the industries that are targeted. For example, 'The Case for Defense Stock Investing' begins as follows:

Afghanistan, Iraq, North Korea. Those would be reason enough to believe in Defense Stocks. Homeland Security and anti-terrorism have become large, profitable industries. So called 'Socially Responsible Investors' would claim that you shouldn't own stocks that have anything to do with defense or weapons. That means that the Aerospace and Defense Industries are to be avoided. Maybe in a

---

[1] http://www.vicefund.com/

perfect world these industries wouldn't need to exist, but until that perfect world does exist, we want to own these stocks.[2]

Between 2002–3 and 2005–6, the annual average realized rates of return for Vice Fund were around 18 per cent, placing it in the top 30 of approximately 650 mid-cap equity funds on offer in the US.

Key to the marketing of Vice Fund as exceptional and idiosyncratic is, of course, its sharp differentiation against the grain of an already present other: the range of 'socially responsible' mutual funds that have come to be offered in the US since the early 1970s and in the UK since the mid-1980s. Indeed, media reports on the returns provided by Vice Fund typically compare it with the returns available from socially responsible investment (SRI) (e.g. Tharp 2007). The example of Vice Fund draws our attention, then, to the well-established financial dissent that seeks to inscribe explicitly moral and ethical concerns into everyday investment. For advocates, activists, and practitioners of SRI, all investments, not simply and only the investments that are included in the portfolio of Vice Fund, are potentially 'politically incorrect', and should be subjected to moral and ethical considerations. The seemingly realistic and rational pursuit of the risk/return of investment by the individual in the name of their material well-being, security, and freedom—that is, the very calculative performances of everyday investment that are the justification for the 'philosophy' of Vice Fund—are challenged by SRI as narrow, short-sighted, and socially and environmentally damaging.

Our focus in this chapter is on the presence, practicalities, possibilities, and problematics of dissent which (re)politicizes everyday investment. Specifically, we will concentrate on two extended and related examples of SRI: first, the so-called 'pension fund socialism' of US multi-employer and public pension schemes; and, second, what we will term 'ethical investment' in mutual fund networks. Pension fund socialism and ethical investment are, of course, not the only mode of dissent present in everyday saving. The rise of everyday investment has been accompanied by various calls, campaigns, and moves that, in effect, seek to defend and return to previously predominant forms of saving that are slipping away. This is particularly the case in pensions where appeals to buttress and strengthen insurance have been manifold. For example, as we discussed in Chapter 3, President George W. Bush's recent attempts to reform Social Security were successfully defeated and, in the UK, a key outcome of the Pension Commission's work has been the reinvigoration of the basic state

---

[2] http://www.vicefund.com/aerospacedefense.html

pension (BSP). Meanwhile, although the defence of insurance has proved much less successful in occupational pensions networks, many unionized public sector employees on both sides of the Atlantic continue to enjoy the benefits of the final salary pension promise despite governmental proposals to undermine them and uncertainties over funding. While the displacement of thrift and insurance by investment is pervasive and pressing, it seems clear that contestation has contributed to ensuring that the triumph of everyday investment is partial and far from complete.

It is perhaps no surprise, therefore, that it is the protection and revival of insurance which tends to occupy social scientists of finance, welfare, and pensions (e.g. Barr 2002; Blackburn 2002a, 2006a; Minns 2001). Within this literature, the defence of welfare rights and entitlements by pension campaigns is often given further bite by trenchant critiques of the place of everyday investment in pension provision. For leading UK writer and activist Robin Blackburn (2006a), for example, the individualization of responsibility and risk in pensions is to be opposed because 'finance is failing us'. Anglo-American personal and defined-contribution (DC) pension arrangements in particular are an expensive, inefficient, and crisis-ridden means of providing for income in retirement. At present, they only serve to create pools of capital that destroy productive economic enterprises in the name of 'shareholder value', provide resources for the inflation of corporate and individual debt, and enrich the 'aristocrats of financialization' (p. 24). What is needed, according to Blackburn, is 'a new way of connecting the individual to the collective, new criteria of social responsibility and new norms of regulation and ownership . . . more collective insurance and larger collective reserves' (pp. 4–5). In terms of 'collective insurance', he proposes not only improvements in pay-as-you-go pensions, but also universal second pensions based on the 'wage-earner funds' model originally proposed by one of the architects of the Swedish welfare state, Rudolf Meidner (see, also Minns 1996). To provide 'collective reserves', Blackburn holds that public claims on future economic revenues should be inscribed against the currently dominant and narrow claims of finance capital. Taxation can buttress BSPs, and a 'share levy' could provide for second pensions whereby companies would issue new shares or bonds in proportion to their profits to a network of funds. The funds, administered by management boards representing workplaces and local communities, would hold these shares and their dividends to generate future incomes for retirees.

While I certainly do not wish to write-off campaigns and proposals to defend and reinvigorate insurance, I am nonetheless wary of simply casting insurance as the only coherent and logical alternative to everyday investment. 'Finance is failing us' may be a tempting mantra to follow, but it emerges through an understanding of financial dissent that works from the binary of power/resistance. Following from our initial remarks on the conceptual theme of financial dissent in Chapter 1, a narrow and exclusive focus on the defence of insurance would reproduce tendencies, found in social scientific research into finance, to privilege collective, public, and organized modes of dissent that turn on the regulatory capacities which state institutions potentially hold over the financial market economy. These tendencies are delimiting in both analytical and political terms, as they lead us to neglect additional dissent that is already present and which holds out possibilities. Put differently, in supporting and waiting for a 'great refusal' against investment, we may pass over and dismiss dissent in the here and now. As Gibson-Graham (1996, 2006) argue more broadly, capitalist market economies are 'proliferative rather than reductive of [economic] forms' (1996: 119; see Leyshon and Lee 2003), and a politics of economic possibility is always present. Rather than a singular and obdurate financial market economy, we are confronted by 'the everpresent opportunity' of building upon existing movements and actions that have already found 'ways to exercise power' and which may point the way to 'new economic futures' (2006: xxiv–xxv).

Eschewing a delimiting focus on insurance, our inquiry into SRI in this chapter also develops a further thread within our conceptual theme of financial dissent: dissent is necessarily ambiguous and compromised. Within the broad church of SRI, both pension fund socialism and ethical investment are significant in politicizing the routines and rhythms of everyday investment, in opening up possibilities for disagreement. Both contribute to alternative discourses of investment, and prompt, cultivate, and embody alternative approaches to investment. Neither, however, installs an indisputable and untainted alternative. In the first part of the chapter, I will focus on the claims that pension fund socialism, arising out of a class-based politics of resistance, can inscribe the collective interests of labour into investment practices. Writing worker's interests into investment practices turns on wresting control over pension funds from the grip of finance capital and the asset management industry. Once control is established, pension fund socialism utilizes what are defined by the Social Investment Forum (2006), the association of SRI institutions in the US, as the three main forms of SRI activism: the targeting of local communities and enterprises for investment; the 'screening' of investments on the basis of ethical criteria; and undertaking shareholder resolutions and campaigns that promote corporate governance reform. Within SRI in the US, public and multi-employer funds account for over 80 per cent by value of all screened institutional investor assets, and public pension schemes are also the leading lights in shareholder activism. As such, public and multi-employer pension funds are a key force in ensuring that one in ten of every dollar invested in the US falls within the category of SRI (Social Investment Forum 2006). But, as I argue, the assertion of a clear and unequivocal working-class subject and interest in financial dissent is problematic. Multiple and contradictory subject positions and interests are at play in shareholder activism in particular.

The second part of the chapter, meanwhile, concentrates on ethical investment in mutual fund networks. The value of assets held in screened mutual funds is relatively small in comparison with screened institutional investor assets. For example, in the US at the outset of 2005, the total assets invested in screened mutual funds were valued at $179 billion compared with $1.49 trillion for screened institutional investments (Social Investment Forum 2006). Nonetheless, socially responsible mutual fund investment is taking hold on both sides of the Atlantic, and is especially significant given the growing prevalence of DC occupational pension plans in which contributors choose from a menu of mutual funds. I argue, however, that the oppositional claims of ethical investment are ambiguous in two crucial respects. The reliance on screening devices provokes a questioning of the prevailing calculative performances of everyday investment and, at the same, constrains the scope for disagreement and dissent by reducing confrontations with everyday investment to a technical and calculative matter. Similarly, the calling up of 'the ethical investor' as a subject of dissent serves to both initiate and contain the politicization of everyday investment. On the one hand, the ethical investor embodies an intimate ethics of cosmopolitanism that challenges prevailing representations of investment as the entrepreneurial care of the self. On the other hand, however, the ethical investor is a subject of dissent who reconciles the personal and the political from within everyday investment networks and through individual value choices alone.

Pension Fund Socialism

In terms of socialist theory, the employees of America are the only true 'owners' of the means of production. Through their pension funds they are the only true 'capitalists' around, owning, controlling, and directing the country's 'capital fund'.

The 'means of production', that is, the American economy ... is being run for the benefit of the country's employees.

(Drucker 1976/1995: 2–3)

As a key early proponent of the benefits of pre-funded occupational pensions in the US, influential management guru Peter F. Drucker gave his argument an interesting spin. As he put it, an 'unseen revolution' has occurred that is producing 'pension fund socialism'. 'Only in the United States are the employees through their pension funds also becoming the legal owners, the suppliers of capital, and the controlling force in the capitalist market' (p. 4). Writing at around the same time as Drucker offered his tongue-in-cheek take on pension funds and 'socialist theory', community activists Rifkin and Barber (1978) questioned the extent to which the economy was 'being run for the benefit of the country's employees'. For them, the US labour movement had to re-orientate their campaigns from the reform of labour law to the control of multi-employer and public pension fund investment if these 'benefits' were to be gleaned. Although the control of pension fund investment had been a subject within 'financial democracy' debates addressed by US liberal think tanks in the late 1950s (Ghilarducci 1992: 111–12), Rifkin and Barber thus kick-started thinking on what has more recently been described as 'a capital strategy for labor' (Hebb 2001: 2). Indeed, they provoked a rebuke from some of the early supporters of pension fund capitalism (e.g. Borjas 1979). Rifkin and Barber's ultimate goal was the rebirth of America's 'Graybelt' manufacturing heartland in the 'North' which, for them, had been starved of investment and subject to 'redlining' by 'the banking community' (p. 6). Given the concentration of 'the largest single pool of private capital in the world' in the multi-employer and public pension funds of the North, 'With control of these moneys, unions and public authorities can begin to take over more and more of the economic-planning and capital-allocation decisions that have, for so long, been the exclusive prerogative of the private capital sector' (pp. 10–11). Ultimately, control over 'pension-fund capital' is, for Rifkin and Barber, 'an opening wedge in the development of basic economic alternatives within the United States' (p. 12).

Drucker and Rifkin and Barber can be seen, then, to have set the terms for subsequent debate and dissent over the investment strategies pursued by US defined-benefit (DB) pension schemes. As we stressed in Chapter 3, DB pension schemes have sought in recent decades to provide insurance through investment, that is, to guarantee future retirement benefits through returns from 'risky' assets. For those following Drucker's lead, the revised investment strategies of pension schemes have contributed significantly to US economic growth and competitiveness by funding, for example, the hi-tech industries of the 'new economy' (e.g. Clowes 2000). In contrast, those following Rifkin and Barber continue to stress that, under the control of asset managers, pension fund investment strategies are speculative, short-term, and discriminatory. Not only does this starve economies of desperately needed long-term productive capital, but also harms the prospects, wages, welfare, and security of workers (e.g. Ghilarducci 1992; Hebb 2001; Toporowski 2000; Useem 1996). Central here is the role that funds and their asset managers play in extracting 'shareholder value' from corporations. Shareholder value shapes, formats, and performs an economy in which financial calculations dominate how the corporation is assessed, prompting destructive practices such as downsizing, sub-contracting, off-shoring, and mergers and acquisitions. It has also become enshrined in the regulatory frameworks of corporate governance that are primarily constituted through agency theory. As Lazonick and O'Sullivan (2000) summarize, agency theorists 'believe that the market is always superior to organizations in the efficient allocation of resources' such that they are 'predisposed against corporate—that is, managerial—control over the allocation of resources and returns in the economy' (p. 16). For 'the market', read investors of all kinds, including pension funds.

The democratic and egalitarian control of fund investment has therefore become a pivotal issue for critics and activists who wish to further workers' interests and establish a genuine pension fund socialism. For Pollin (1995), it is a matter of installing 'democratic-voice' as opposed to 'elite-voice' in pension fund investment decisions. The roots of this struggle for control are to be found in the uncertain property rights that are present in DB schemes. Under property law, it is unclear precisely what members of DB schemes, through their contributions, come to own. For example, one legal interpretation in the late 1990s cast DB scheme assets as 'non-private property' that are entitled to 'protective storage', and therefore as akin to corpses and body parts (in Blackburn 2006a: 157). 'Protective storage' in DB schemes is provided by trustees who, appointed by a scheme's sponsor, have a fiduciary duty to manage assets on behalf of members in the manner of a 'prudent expert'. In short, scheme trustees and scheme sponsors share the desire to maximize investment returns, the former as a consequence of fiduciary duty and the latter as a consequence of their financial bottom line.

Against this backdrop, and following Rifkin and Barber's blueprint, activists' attempts to install workers' control over investment in the last three decades have remained largely confined to the US multi-employer and public pension funds. This activism is supported by networks which extend into the academic community and include, for example, the Pensions and Capital Stewardship Project which is part of the Labor and Worklife Program at the Harvard Law School. US multi-employer funds—also known as 'Taft–Hartley funds' after the 1947 legislation that first regulated their organization—are jointly established by employers and unions. Fund members are unionized, and are typically construction workers and teamsters who are likely to be employed by different firms during their working lives. Built up through the post-war era, multi-employer pension funds currently hold assets worth in excess of $430 billion (Marens 2004: 110). While fiduciary duty applies to the trustees that administer multi-employer funds, their boards are divided equally between union officials and representatives of the corresponding employers' association. Meanwhile, although there is no guarantee that union officials will serve as trustees of public pension funds, the extensive unionization of the state and local government employees that are the members of these funds does make representation on their boards a strong possibility (Rifkin and Barber 1978: 224–8). The strategic importance of the public funds for pension activists stems from the sheer size of the assets that they command. Their size also ensures that they are much more likely than private single-employer funds to manage their own assets, rather than contracting out to the consultants and asset management firms. Currently only five of America's twenty largest pension funds by assets are private single-employer schemes (General Motors, IBM, General Electric, Boeing, and Ford), with the remaining fifteen all public pension funds. The top five largest funds are all public funds, in a list that is topped by the California Public Employee Retirement System (CalPERS). CalPERS covers 1.4 million public employees and retirees and, at September 2005, had assets worth a massive $196 billion.[3]

Once some form of control over investment is established, pension fund socialists concentrate on three main forms of activism. First, labour's capital is channelled into so-called 'economically targeted investments' (ETIs). For many public pension funds, this targeting concentrates on so-called 'community investment' in a wide range of infrastructural projects within their 'home' state, projects as diverse as public golf courses and social

---

[3] http://pionline.com/page.cms?pageId=624

housing (Gross 2000: 27–54). For multi-employer schemes, meanwhile, ETIs tend to explicitly support unionized employment. For example, the Union Labor Life Insurance Company and the American Federation of Labor-Congress of Industrial Organizations' (AFL-CIO) Housing Investment Trust (HIT) currently holds in excess of $5 billion in real estate loans made to developers who employ unionized labour. HIT was joined by the Building Investment Trust (BIT) in 1988, a $1.5 billion conduit through which investors channel workers' capital into real estate (hotels, office buildings, etc.) that is managed by those who do not oppose the unionization of labour (Marens 2004: 116). Despite tripling in value between 1994 and 2000 (Calabrese 2001: 93), the cumulative value of multi-employer ETIs remains, however, extremely small in the context of the overall holdings of US pension funds. Suspicions abound amongst trustees about union involvement in investment practices that arise largely out of the kickbacks which came to bind the Teamsters' Central States fund and a string of Las Vegas casinos during the 1960s and 1970s. Despite a 1994 endorsement by the DoL suggesting that ETIs do not necessarily stand in tension with the fiduciary duty of trustees, and recent campaigns such as the Heartland Labor Capital Project co-sponsored by AFL-CIO and United Steelworkers of America to raise awareness of the benefits of ETIs (Calabrese 2001), these suspicions persist.

Second, pension fund activists have promoted the use of 'screening' devices that bring 'ethical' considerations to bear in fund's investment strategies. Screening draws on the legacy of many civic associations, most notably churches and universities, that have sought for centuries to avoid investment in the so-called 'sin stocks' of alcohol, tobacco, and gambling industries (Sparkes 2006). Amongst the US public pension funds, by way of example, CalPERS incorporated SRI criteria into its domestic and overseas investments following a trade union campaign in 2002. The consequences of this were most immediately felt in the 'Permissible Country Index' (PCI) which CalPERS deploys in relation to its investment in emerging markets (Hebb and Wójcik 2005; Soederberg 2006a). The PCI provides a set of weighted quantitative measures against which the appropriateness of investments are screened and judged. Adherence to international labour standards does feature in the PCI, and poor scores in this regard provided the justification for CalPERS decision to divest from Thailand, Malaysia, Indonesia, and the Philippines in 2002. That said, the weighting given to labour standards remains low relative to financial market factors such as liquidity, volatility, settlement systems, and transaction costs, and

CalPERS continues to regard emerging markets as a short-term investment option.

The third form taken by pension fund activism is, then, 'shareholder activism'. The focus here is corporate governance reforms that not only oppose the restructuring plans of recalcitrant managements, but also tend to create new legal rights for shareholders in the process. Such is the importance of shareholder activism that O'Connor (2001) argues that corporate governance has displaced labour law to become the key site for contestation between capital and labour in the US. A significant initial milestone in the development of shareholder activism was the coming together of three craft unions and seventeen public pension funds to found the Council of Institutional Investors in 1985. As Marens (2004: 113) notes, the formation of the Council drew activists' attention to the use of shareholder resolutions in order to cajole corporate governance reforms. The Council now represents more than 130 pension funds who, collectively, hold in excess of $3 trillion in assets. While Securities and Exchange Commission (SEC) rules prevent labour disputes from being raised through shareholders resolutions, all other decisions by corporate managers can be targeted by shareholder activists. The shareholder activism of pension fund socialism has thus become increasingly bound up with the technicalities of proxy voting and shareholder resolutions (Marens 2004). Resolutions are typically advisory in nature, such that even when they receive majority support they are not binding on management. Once a company is targeted by a resolution, it is commonplace for funds and other institutional investors to voice their concerns in private meetings with executives. These meetings take place in the shadow of the likely shareholder vote on the resolution and, if shareholders concerns are addressed, lead to the withdrawal of the resolution. Resolutions often address the independence of executive boards from shareholders, the removal of financial disincentives that discourage takeovers (so-called 'poison pills'), and the structure of compensation boards that award excessive 'fat cat' executive salary packages including stock options, 'golden hellos', and 'golden parachutes'.

Leadership in the shareholder activism of pension funds has come from the trustees of major public funds such as CalPERS, CalSTRS (California State Teachers Retirement System), and the New York City Employees Retirement System. Trustees on the boards of these funds have links to, or are widely regarded as sympathetic to, organized labour. CalPERS have been the standard bearers for US shareholder activism since the mid-1980s. They were the first of the massive public pension funds to heighten their proxy voting activity, and late California State Treasurer Jesse Unruh was a key figure in the formation of the Council of Institutional Investors (Ghilarducci 1992: 126). More recently, the $300 billion of losses incurred by public pension funds as a result of the collapse of Enron further galvanized CalPERS and CalSTRS, often in conjunction with trustees from New York, Connecticut, North Carolina, Iowa, and elsewhere, to more aggressively pursue those who they see as damaging the interests of their workers and retirees (Greider 2005). For example, taking advantage of the Private Securities Litigation Reform Act of 1995 which clamped down on profiteering by the legal profession and gave institutional investors the lead role in investor class-action suits, the New York State Common Retirement Fund wrested a $6 billion payout from investment bankers in the wake of the collapse of WorldCom (Donovan 2005). Current campaigns to advance 'shareholder democracy' and make majority voting binding in shareholder resolutions are, meanwhile, being spearheaded by the American Federation of State, County, and Municipal Employees (*The Economist* 2006a).

Research by Gourevitch and Shinn (2005) suggests that shareholder activism led by the multi-employer and public pension funds has an efficacy which can be seen to have had a significant impact upon US corporate governance. In our terms, this mode of financial dissent is itself constitutive in the transformations in everyday saving that forge close relationships with the capital markets. To be sure, Gourevitch and Shinn attempt to steer clear of the normative arguments of pension fund socialism. But, starting from the premise that the politics of competing interests and the institutional aggregation of preferences shapes the contours of corporate governance, Gourevitch and Shinn identify 'owners', 'managers', and 'workers' as the three key sets of competing interests. The contending interests of owners and managers have long been asserted in economic and legal analyses of corporate governance, the former as wanting control and protection, the latter as wanting autonomy and discretion (e.g. Berle and Means 1932). For Gourevitch and Shinn, however, recognizing the operation of a workers interest in corporate governance is crucial to understanding why US arrangements have changed in recent decades. According to Gourevitch and Shinn, US corporate governance has come to stand as something of an outlier globally, and as the best fit with 'an external, diffuse *shareholder* model' which they contrast with the 'internal concentrated *blockholder* model' (p. 4 *original emphasis*). Under the shareholder model, it is 'investor owners', which include workers via their pension schemes, who have been successful in establishing arrangements for the supervision, assessment, disciplining, and punishment of managers. Indeed, by the mid-1990s, DoL regulations required that all pension funds' trustees vote on shareholder resolutions and even encouraged them to negotiate with managers and submit their own resolutions.

The significance of workers interests and pension fund activism in the constitution of US corporate governance comes through most strongly in Gourevitch and Shinn's (2005) comparative study where they contrast the US and UK cases. The distinctive nature of many public pension funds in the UK, whereby member's contributions are not invested but instead flow into the state's coffers, effectively rules them out of shareholder activism. There are, of course, a few notable examples. These include the Universities Superannuation Scheme, the Environment Agency pension fund, the Trades Union Congress (TUC) pension fund, a handful of local authority plans, and the activism of Hermes which has its roots in the massive British Telecom pension scheme and also manages assets for funds that are mostly public, union, or employee-based (Clark and Hebb 2005; Gourevitch and Shinn 2005: 240). But, these are exceptions and, as advocates of UK shareholder activism Mackenzie and Sullivan (2006) recently put it, 'The mainstreaming of responsible investment still has a long way to go' (p. 348). In order to explain the UK's 'fit' with the shareholder model, Gourevitch and Shinn thus turn to political institutions, and distinguish between 'majoritarian' and 'consensus' ideal-types. The former are likely to 'generate policies that encourage patterns of diffuse governance' and are exemplified by the UK, while the latter tend to 'generate blockholding' and are exemplified by Sweden (p. 10). As such and in contrast with the US, the UK's 'fit' with the shareholder model is related not only to the distinctive trajectory of the British economy, the primacy of financial interests, weak managers and workers, but also to the centralized majoritarian state apparatus which, especially after Margaret Thatcher came to power in 1979, promoted minority shareholder protections (pp. 259–62).

Gourevitch and Shinn's research (2005) also begins to hint, however, at the ambiguities and ambivalences present within US pension fund socialism as a mode of dissent in everyday investment. Gourevitch and Shinn suggest that the move towards the shareholder model of corporate governance in the US is a consequence of a new 'coalitional alignment' between 'workers and owners [who] combine to contain managerial agency costs and preserve the security of their investments and pensions' (p. 8). This 'transparency coalition' focuses on furthering the authority of the SEC to ensure that adequate and reliable information is available on management practices and corporate performance (p. 255). The coalition proved particularly influential, for example, in framing the Sarbanes-Oxley legislation, which included the creation of the Public Accounting Oversight Board to develop and enforce standards, and a code of ethics for Chief Financial Officers (pp. 257–9). Gourevitch and Shinn's 'transparency coalition' casts doubt, then, on the construction by pension fund socialists of a singular and unified working-class subject and interest in dissent. Pension fund socialism ontologically juxtaposes workers against finance capital as an already dominant and controlling other. A sense of unity, interest, and purpose amongst workers is created through the securing of a singular foe—you are either with us, or you are with them.

For Gourevitch and Shinn (2005), workers newly found support for transparency and minority shareholder protections is explained by the ways in which the position of some as pension fund members creates change in their rational preferences. Rather than assuming the collective interests of workers and focusing on their apparently rational preferences, I would suggest an alternative route to understanding the ambiguities of pension fund socialism as a mode of dissent. In Gibson-Graham's terms (1996), pension fund socialism can be seen as an example of a 'capitalocentric' reading of contemporary finance—it assumes the all-pervasive and totalizing power of capital, and thus demands resistance by workers which steps outside of those power relations. Indeed, echoing pension fund socialism, for Gourevitch and Shinn (2005), power is wielded by competing collective interests that seek to secure their preferences. But, as the re-reading of Laclau and Mouffe (1985) provided by Butler, Laclau, and Žižek (2000) reminds us, while 'new social movements often rely on identity-claims, . . . "identity" itself is never fully constituted; in fact, . . . identification is not reducible to identity' (p. 1). There is an antagonism or incommensurability between identification and identity. We should not fear the 'failure' of a single and coherent working-class interest in dissent from investment, but should 'value this "failure" as a condition of democratic contestation itself' (p. 2). For us, workers who are members of pension funds are, at once, consumers, investors, and shareholders, and are also likely to be men, baby-boomers, credit card holders, fathers, and so on. So, while pension fund activism may succeed in enlivening a radicalized working-class subjectivity, that subjectivity will be a partial and fragmented solidarity.

Shareholder activist campaigns for corporate governance reform are particularly illustrative of the how the multiple subjectivities of pension fund members play themselves out in ambiguous dissent. In Ghilarducci's terms (1992: 131–2), shareholder activists have embraced discourses of property rights in corporate governance campaigns and, therefore, have become defenders of one of the central pillars of financial power at the same time as seeking to further the interests of workers. As described by CalPERS (1995: 1, *original emphasis*), for instance, shareholder activism is 'the prudent exercise of *ownership* rights, toward the goal of increased share value'. For those involved in shareholder activism, it is often prefaced not on an explicit challenge to the drive for shareholder value, but on the assumption that 'good corporate governance' and financial performance simultaneously benefit pension fund members, workers, and wider shareholders. It becomes common, for instance, for pension fund socialists such as Tessa Hebb (2001) to talk of workers, pension fund members, communities, corporations, shareholders, and so on as 'stakeholders'. Consider, by way of further illustration, the phrase 'CalPERS effect' which is widely used by US asset managers and institutional investors. What is particularly striking is that the 'CalPERS effect' does not refer to the consequences of the fund's activism in the name of workers, far from it. Rather, the 'CalPERS effect' refers to the consequences for the stock prices of those corporations who are included on CalPERS annual hit list for poor financial performance and corporate governance practices. As the financial results and governance of these firms typically improves in response to pressure from CalPERS, so their stock price tends to outperform the relevant benchmark indices (CalPERS 1995).

In sum, carried forward through targeted investment, screening, and especially shareholder activism, there is certainly little doubt that pension fund socialism contributes to the (re)politicization of DB schemes investment strategies. In William Greider's terms (2005), 'remote skirmishes over esoteric financial rules' have become 'a very visible political fight'. As the standard bearer for pension fund activism, CalPERs has, in particular, been in the eye of the political storm. Yet, the subjects and interests present in this mode of dissent are far more indistinct than tends to be assumed by pension fund socialists. These ambiguities casts serious doubts on Greider's claims (2005), for instance, that CalPERS and pension fund activism more broadly is 'pursuing far-ranging possibilities for reforming the economic system' and is nothing short of 'the vanguard of a new kind of reform politics'. As our next extended example of ethical investment illustrates though, recognizing the absence of a singular and unified working-class subject and interest is not politically paralyzing and certainly does not render SRI impossible as a mode of financial dissent.

Ethical Investment

Both pension fund socialism and ethical investment (re)politicize the routines and rhythms of everyday investment. They provide unconventional discourses on investment and seek to script, induce, and embody alternative approaches to investment. Within SRI as a mode of financial dissent, ethical investment nonetheless differs from pension fund socialism in crucial respects. Ethical investment does not appear to posit a singular subject and interest of dissent against finance capital as an already dominant other, but instead summons up an explicitly moral and ethical investor who pursues their own individual values within a broad-based cosmopolitanism. Where pension fund socialism seeks collective control of investment, ethical investment seeks a deeper individualization that enables ethical choices. These differences between pension fund socialism and ethical investment are, in part, a consequence of the specific contexts that they each confront: pension fund activism is focused on DB pension networks and their unclear property ownership structures; and ethical investment is concerned with mutual fund and DC pension networks which, as we argued in Chapter 4, call up an entrepreneurial investor subject who embraces the risk/reward of the financial markets to further their own well-being, freedom, and security. Aside from these contextual differences, however, whereas pension fund socialism attempts to write the interests of workers into investment through the binaries of individual/collective and personal/political, ethical investment, in effect, assumes no such disjunctions.

The differences between pension fund socialism and ethical investment in this regard are revealed, for example, in the commentaries offered by supporters of SRI on the drift from DB to DC occupational pensions. Pension fund socialists tend to oppose the individualization of responsibility and risk that the move from DB to DC carries forward on the grounds that it undercuts the possibilities for collective political action. For Greider (2005), for example, if California Governor Arnold Schwarzenegger's proposals to break up CalPERS by offering public employees DC accounts had been successful, they would have dispersed 'its financial power' and diluted 'its ability to exercise reform leverage'. For advocates and activists of ethical investment, meanwhile, DC pension plans, and the mutual fund networks with which they connect and overlap, hold no such fears or dangers. For example, in their recent survey of ethical investment in US DC pension plans, the Social Investment Forum (2007) suggests that 'the outlook for SRI fund options appears strong'

(p. 2). The survey found that 19 per cent of DC plan sponsors currently offer one or more SRI options to plan members, with an additional 41 per cent of plan sponsors expect to add an SRI option within the next three years. Not dissimilarly, the UK Social Investment Forum (2006) has trumpeted its success in lobbying the DWP to commit itself to including an SRI option within the 'BRIT Saver' initiative that is due to come into effect in 2012.

Mutual fund networks provide the primary terrain through which individualized ethical investment tactics are pursued. War and international campaigns were important catalysts that stimulated the contemporary development of ethical mutual funds. The initial proliferation of ethical mutual funds in the US in the early 1970s was a reaction to the Vietnam War, as the Pax World Fund and the Dreyfus Third Century Fund broadened the 'sin stocks' that investors could avoid by adding the stocks of the nuclear industry and military and defence contractors. Meanwhile, campaigns of divestment from South Africa's apartheid regime in the 1970s and 1980s also generated support for ethical mutual funds on both sides of the Atlantic. The first ethical unit trust offered in the UK— the Friends Provident Stewardship—appeared in 1984 (Dreblow 2005). Increasingly, however, ethical investment has borrowed from and built on the technologies and marketing strategies of mainstream mutual fund networks. It is in the last decade or so, then, that ethical mutual fund investment has really taken off.

In the US, the cumulative value of investments across 201 ethical mutual funds at the beginning of 2005 stood at $179 billion, up from only $12 billion across 55 funds as recently as 1995 (Social Investment Forum 2006: 7). Ethical investment in the UK is a somewhat fledgling venture in comparison, with around 450,000 ethical investors holding £6.1 billion in assets across 63 funds at the end of 2005.[4] The UK, however, has also witnessed a sharp increase in ethical investment in recent years. In 1995, the total value of UK ethical investments stood at £792 million. The principal specialist providers of ethical mutual funds in the US are Calvert Group, Citizens Advisors, Domini Social Investment, Dreyfus Corp., MMA Praxis, New Covenant, Parnassus, and Pax World Funds. Mainstream providers may also offer ethical options within their 'family of funds', such as Citigroup's Smith Barney Social Awareness Fund. In the UK, the main providers include AEGON, Barchester, Co-operative Financial

---

[4] http://www.eiris.org

Services, Friends Provident, Impax Group, Quadris, and Rathbone Green-bank. The websites and publications of industry associations (e.g. Social Investment Forum, UK Social Investment Forum) and specialist infor-mation services (e.g. Ethical Investment Research Services, SRI World Group) also guide and support ethical investors and would-be ethical investors.

The ethical investor will typically chose from a menu of mutual funds that have been 'screened' and branded according to various 'negative' or 'positive' criteria. The former as 'value-based avoidance screening' (Social Investment Forum 2006: 4) leads to the omission from portfolios of companies linked, for example, to the arms trade, while the latter enables investment in companies that, for example, are involved in recycling and conservation. Negative screening clearly has it roots in the long-standing avoidance of 'sin stocks' by certain investors. For example, the first US investment fund to develop and adopt what might be called 'sin stock screening' in 1950 was Pioneer Fund, a fund that was originally opened in 1928 to meet the needs of Christian investors (Social Invest-ment Forum 2006: 3). Today, the negative screening out of traditional sin stocks remains the most common feature of US ethical mutual funds, with tobacco and alcohol far and away the main concerns of ethical investors (Wander and Malone 2007). That said, the majority of US ethical mutual funds incorporate five or more social and environmental screens (Social Investment Forum 2006: 8–9).

Positive screening, on the other hand, has recently become closely associated with investments in companies in all sectors of economies that show evidence of 'corporate social responsibility' (CSR)—that is, com-panies that have reported and audited procedures, standards and codes for dealing with issues of environmental sustainability, health and safety, employer-employee relations, human rights, and so on (Hill et al. 2007; Scholtens 2006). In the terms of the Social Investment Forum (2006), positive screening is 'based on the principle that investors actively seek to support companies whose social and environmental records are con-sistent with good corporate citizenship' (p. 4). The association between ethical investment and CSR is reflected in, and constituted through, the emergence of indexes of the shares of firms that are deemed to be taking CSR standards seriously. In the US, the Domini 400 Social Index, launched back in 1990, combines negative and positive screening techniques to exclude the stocks of 250 firms listed on the mainstream Standard & Poors Ratings Group (S&P) 500 index, and adds a further

150 positively screened firms. The Dow Jones Sustainability Indexes include the stock of what are considered to be the top 10 per cent of CSR performers across a range of economic sectors. In the UK, meanwhile, the FTSE4Good indexes which were launched in July 2001 only include companies that are found by FTSE to reach CSR standards. Overall, such indexes provide a two-dimensional graphical visualization of the returns available over time from what are calculated to be 'ethical stocks' (Aitken 2007). Returns from these stocks can thus be easily compared or 'benchmarked' against the returns available from mainstream or 'non-ethical' stocks, and the returns from ethical mutual funds can be tracked and judged against a market average by the ethical investor. Indexes also make possible index tracker mutual funds, whereby the so-called 'passive investment' of computerized trading programmes reduce the management costs associated with ethical investment. For instance, Co-operative Financial Services currently provide the CIS FTSE4Good Tracker Fund.

In addition to their assembly through the devices of negative and positive screening and associated indexes, ethical mutual funds are also likely to be offered by asset management firms that are engaged in shareholder activism related to corporate governance and CSR issues. This activism may include direct dialogue with managers, the filing of shareholder resolutions, and proxy voting in support of shareholder resolutions. A report by the Social Investment Forum (2005) suggests, for example, that providers of ethical mutual funds in the US are twice as likely as providers of mainstream funds to support shareholder resolutions on corporate governance issues through their proxy voting. Indeed, following the introduction of new rules by the SEC in 2003, mutual fund providers must now publicly disclose their proxy voting guidelines and past records. For the ethical investor, the interrogation of the shareholder activism of mutual fund providers in relation to both corporate governance and CSR is thus made possible. To this end, the Social Investment Forum website includes a guide for ethical investors that not only compares funds according to their financial performance and screening devices, but also includes links and telephone numbers for those investors who wish to follow up on each fund's advocacy and proxy voting records.

Amidst the promises and possibilities of ethical investment as a form of financial dissent are, however, certain ambiguities that ensure that SRI does not provide a coherent, indisputable, and untainted alternative to mainstream everyday investment. To be fair, ethical investment does not seek to be an unequivocally oppositional mode of dissent. But, I want to suggest that the oppositional claims of ethical investment are more problematic than tends to be acknowledged by advocates and activists. First, let us consider the manner in which ethical investment materializes in large part through the inclusion of screening devices into the portfolio selection models of mutual fund providers and asset managers. It is, after all, the use or otherwise of such screens that marks out an ethical from a 'non-ethical' mutual fund. As we suggested in Chapter 1 by drawing on actor-network theory (ANT) and the 'new accounting history', the taken-for-granted and established calculative instruments and devices of financial market networks are nonetheless dynamic and subject to contestation. Key to the transformation of Anglo-American everyday saving and the forging of close relationships with the capital markets, as the subsequent chapters in Part I have made plain, is the displacement of saving networks that materialize through thrift and insurance as calculative techniques of risk by networks of everyday investment. Although representations of investment as the most rational form of saving thus hinge on the apparent objectivity, efficiency, and functionality of the calculative techniques of investment relative to those of thrift and insurance, this should not obscure the dynamism of networks of everyday investment. The advance of screening techniques is, in effect, the contestation and (at present) limited reconfiguration of the calculative tools of risk/reward through which mutual fund networks are constituted.

Once screening is understood in these terms, ambiguities can be seen to be present in ethical investment as a mode of dissent, ambiguities that are rooted in the elusive power and politics of calculation. On the one hand, as Andrew Barry (2002) observes, the legacy of Max Weber's work on rationality has been the awareness amongst sociologists that calculation and measurement in all its forms is 'an essentially anti-political instrument' (p. 272). Calculation re-casts political questions as technical issues to be solved, and is therefore 'thought to reduce the space of the political and to limit the possibility for disagreement' (p. 272). The political, social, and moral questions about whether we should save and how we might go about saving are, for instance, cut down to size by calculative devices. They are re-situated in the domain of the market economy and, in the context of neo-liberal programmes of government in particular, such questions become a matter of which mutual fund investments will best provide for individual freedom and security. On the other hand, however, as Barry has it:

Measurement and calculation do not only have anti-political effects. They do not just have the effect of restricting political controversy in the economic field. They also, at the same time, provide the basis for an opening up of new objects and sites of disagreement. (p. 274)

Calculation can be (re)politicizing precisely because, as we have already noted, financial market networks are constituted through fallible, contradictory, and dynamic calculative tools of risk. In Barry's terms, measurement and calculation are 'fragile' and 'inventive' (pp. 274–9). The inventive development of screening devices may highlight weaknesses in fragile calculations of risk/reward that, for example, disregard the uncertainties created by poor CSR standards. Poor CSR standards may come to have a negative impact on the corporate brand which, in turn, results in declining consumer sales and threatens shareholder value. Debate ensues that potentially focuses not only on appropriate investment techniques and the relationships between sustainability and shareholder value, but on the social and environmental consequences of corporate economies more broadly. The use of screening devices ensures, then, that ethical investment simultaneously closes down and opens up the routines and rhythms of everyday investment to disagreement and dissent.

Second, the ambiguities of ethical investment are also related to the subject of dissent—'the ethical investor—that is summoned up. As with the ambiguities that arise from the calculative screening techniques of ethical investment, the calling up of the ethical investor serves to both initiate and contain the (re)politicization of everyday investment. On the one hand, the explicit moralizing representations of the ethical investor challenge the implicit moral assembly of the subject position of the mainstream investor. As we argued in Chapter 4, the embodiment of networks of everyday investment turns on the forging of a subject who pursues an ethics of the self through disciplinary and calculative self-improvement. Ethical investment interferes with this rationalization. It does not deny that investment is closely bound up with the care of the self, but operates through an intimate ethics of cosmopolitanism. The intensified subjectivization of power carried through processes of individualization creates opportunities for immanent dissent that become connected in unpredictable but potentially progressive ways. It is the individual's responsibility to codify their own values and norms through their own investment practices, and the betterment of the self becomes inseparable from universal improvement and progress towards, for instance, public health, temperance, peace, a cleaner environment, and so on. For example, under a heading of 'Pluralism and Diversity', the Social Investment Forum's principal (2006) publication states that 'The broad range of social screens used by SRI mutual funds provides socially responsible investors with a wide array of investment options to meet their specific concerns, from both financial and social standpoints' (p. 9). The investor, and by extension financial market investment, need not be selfish and can be virtuous in the name of 'the social'.

On the other hand, however, the summoning up of the ethical investor as the subject of dissent tightly constrains political engagement with the rise of everyday investment. As Aitken (2007) notes by drawing on Foucault's reading of 'ethics' as 'the conscious practice of freedom', a politics of ethics prompts only an individualized activism that has delimiting consequences for dissent in everyday investment. The personal and the political are to be reconciled from within mutual fund networks and through individual value choices alone. Scope for the political questioning of the need for investment in the name of the care and freedom of the self is significantly reduced. This can be seen, for example, in the constant tendency, present throughout the prospectuses, websites, indexes, information services, and academic writing concerned with ethical mutual funds, to compare the returns from ethical investment with those of mainstream investment (e.g. Banner, Derwall, and Otten 2007; Becker and McVeigh 2001). If the ethical investor can have their cake and eat it—profits do not have to be sacrificed for personal principles, but can happily co-exist—then there is clearly little space for disagreement and for the (re)politicization of investment as a technology of the self.

The universalizing claims of ethical investment obscure a quite specific prescription of what improvement and progress in 'the good society' might actually look like. Diversity is to be celebrated, but only within clear and settled boundaries. Ethical investment envisages a society of active citizens who provide for themselves and their others by fully exercising their rights and responsibilities as property owners in a shareholding democracy (e.g. Hancock 2005). But, drawing on the work of William Connolly (2002), the relational securing of the identity of the 'ethical investor' can be seen to actually reinforce the making of the neo-liberal subject position of 'the investor' which, as Chapter 4 stressed, also turns on its differentiation from thrifty savers and those irresponsible individuals who continue to rely on state insurance. If 'to act ethically is often to call some comforts of identity into question' (p. xiv), as Connolly contends, then ethical investment as a mode of financial dissent would actually seem to be quite 'unethical'. There is little scope within a shareholder democracy, where only ethical investors can express their values, for what Connolly terms 'agonistic respect' between investors, savers, and those who rely on the BSP, for example. Ethical investment does not recognize the contestability of identity of the investor from the perspectives of savers or welfare recipients. It closes down the space that might otherwise 'cultivate reciprocal respect across difference' and 'negotiate larger assemblages to set general policies' (p. xxvi). As Connolly suggests, no 'fixed code, austere set of procedures, or settled interpretation of moral universals' should structure these negotiations which will necessarily be difficult and always ongoing (p. xxx).

Concluding Remarks

In Part I of this book, we have situated the unprecedented relationships that prevail between contemporary Anglo-American society and the capital markets of 'global finance' in the transformations of everyday saving. We have characterized these transformations as the partial displacement of thrift and insurance by investment as the newly predominant form of routine saving. It has been shown that the positive and emphatic representation of investment as the most rational form of saving, the operation of calculative devices for the embracing of risk/reward in discrete networks, and the moral, technological, and political programmes of neo-liberal government that include the mass assembly of the uncertain subject of 'the investor' have all, taken together, made the materialization of everyday investment possible. As such, our analysis across the previous chapters has contributed towards the (re)politicization of the apparently rational and scientific performances of everyday investment, opening them up to critical scrutiny and stressing the power relations, contingencies, and contradictions present in their development.

In this chapter, we have, furthermore, considered the presence, practicalities, possibilities, and problematics of dissent in everyday investment. Aware of the delimiting political and analytical consequences of concentrating solely on attempts to defend and reinvigorate social insurance, we have explored SRI as a mode of dissent present within occupational pensions and mutual funds as the principal networks of everyday investment. Focusing on pension fund socialism and ethical investment, I have argued that discourses of SRI succeed in politicizing the routines and rhythms of everyday investment by stimulating, supporting, and embodying alternative approaches to investment. I have also argued, however, that SRI is an ambiguous and compromised mode of financial dissent. The assertion of a clear and unequivocal working-class subject and interest in financial dissent by pension fund socialists is problematic, and the screening techniques and cosmopolitan subject of ethical investment serve to simultaneously initiate and contain the politicization of everyday investment.

Part II

Borrowing

6

The Boom in Everyday Borrowing

Introduction: £1.3 Trillion and Rising

In the closing months of 2004, fears about the scale of borrowing by individuals and households in the UK reached fever pitch in the mainstream media. For the first time, the outstanding financial obligations of households grew to over £1 trillion. While the lion's share of the £1.05 trillion owed by UK households at the end of November was related to mortgage borrowing (£867 billion), it was the £58 billion owed to credit card companies and the further £125 billion of obligations arising from other unsecured consumer lending that especially attracted the media's attention (figures from FSA 2005: 57). It was highlighted, for example, that households in the UK account for roughly two-thirds of the outstanding credit card obligations of the entire European Union (Halligan 2005). The overall scale of UK household borrowing had not only reached new heights, but the gradual and relatively steady increases of the previous few decades had given way to rapid growth. The ratio of household's outstanding obligations to post-tax income increased from roughly 100 per cent to 150 per cent between the late 1990s and 2005 (Bank of England 2006a: 39). In 2004 alone, the annual growth rates for lending to UK households by the major UK banks were a staggering 25 per cent on credit cards, and 15 per cent for both unsecured consumer loans and mortgages. While these annual growth rates subsequently slowed to stand at between 6 per cent and 8 per cent for all categories of lending by the first half of 2006, the total outstanding financial obligations of UK households nevertheless reached in excess of £1.3 trillion (p. 25).

Individuals and households in the UK have, of course, been far from alone in their borrowing binge. As part of what he terms the 'global debt bomb', economic historian James Clayton (2000) traces, in quantitative terms, the growth in household borrowing in the Group of 7 (G-7) societies during the last three decades of the twentieth century. Across the G-7 states—Canada, France, Germany, Italy, Japan, UK, US—household liabilities as a percentage of household income rose from 53 per cent in 1985 to 74 per cent in 1996 (p. x). Nevertheless, these trends have been most prominent and unrelenting in the US and the UK. Like their counterparts in the UK, individuals and households in the US have significantly extended their borrowing over the last thirty years or so. US households' outstanding obligations as a percentage of GDP showed only a marginal increase from 11 per cent to 12 per cent between 1960 and 1970, exploding subsequently to reach 51 per cent by 1980, 65 per cent by 1990, and 69 per cent by 1997 (p. 7). By way of comparison, outstanding sovereign and corporate obligations stood at 60 and 41 per cent of GDP, respectively, in 1997 (p. 7). Again, similar to their counterparts in the UK, Americans have taken on significantly more debt in recent years. By the end of 2004, US households' outstanding mortgage obligations were the equivalent of 60 per cent of GDP, and outstanding consumer credit obligations equal to a further 18 per cent of GDP (Joint Economic Committee 2004: 2).

How is it that these high and unprecedented levels of personal and household borrowing have become routine and mundane for so many in Anglo-America? In this chapter, I will situate the boom in the two principal sets of market networks of Anglo-American everyday borrowing—consumer credit and mortgage networks—and argue that it is only through qualitative transformations in these networks, which include the forging of close relationships with the capital markets of 'global finance', that the boom has been made possible. The argument moves through two main sections. I start by addressing consumer credit networks in general, and especially credit card networks. For sociologists of consumer credit (Calder 1999; Frank 1999; Klein 1999; Medoff and Harless 1996; Olney 1991; Ritzer 1995, 2001; Schor 1998), consumerism prompts expanded borrowing but, contrary to the common sense which prevails in the context of the current boom, the spread of credit money relations does not signal an illogical and dangerous demise of thrift and prudence. Rather, consumer credit furthers the inherent instrumental rationality of monetary relations, and thereby serves to bring a semblance of order to the irrational self-gratification of consumerism. While the stress placed by this literature on the apparent scientific rationality of consumer credit relations is thus highly insightful, instrumental rationality is nevertheless far from innate in money and finance. It has to be established and assembled, and constantly re-assembled, in more-or-less discrete networks. I illustrate this with reference to the emergence and consolidation of the new consumer credit networks that we typically associate with the credit card. Credit card networks have not displaced previously established consumer credit networks that typically make use of loans and instalment plans, but provide highly significant additional capacities for everyday borrowing. Echoing our analysis of saving and investment networks in Chapters 2 and 3, I stress the contingent constitution of booming credit card networks as rational and scientific through specific calculative tools and performances—revolving credit, payment and authorization systems, and credit reporting and scoring.

The second section of the chapter turns our attention to the close interconnections that have become consolidated between mortgage and consumer credit networks, on the one hand, and the networks of the capital markets, on the other. It is common for academics, journalists, and policy makers to emphasize that the everyday borrowing boom, in the US especially, is reliant upon disintermediated global capital flows which finance a ballooning current account deficit. Such capital flows are, however, understood largely in isolation from the lengthening and dynamic reconfigurations of mortgage and consumer credit networks. I argue that the overlapping and intersecting of previously disconnected and detached networks has materialized through new calculative devices and performances which rationally figure and manage the uncertainties of future repayments by everyday borrowers as 'default risks'. Particular attention is paid to the default risk management techniques of lenders—especially asset-backed securitization, but also so-called 'structured finance' and the use of credit derivatives—that turn on the issue and trading of default risk-related instruments in the capital markets. Buoyed by the confidence and legitimacy of an apparent newly found calculative capacity to break down and communicate uncertainties as risks, and intersecting with seemingly deep and liquid markets for the trading of those risks, mortgage and consumer lending has exploded.

Consumption and Consumer Credit Networks

What is perhaps most striking about the sociological literature on consumer credit is that, for the most part, it is not motivated by a desire to understand consumer credit as such. Rather, starting from a concern with consumption, the boom in everyday borrowing is explained largely as the outcome of the advance of the logics of consumerism. For Medoff and Harless (1996), for example, it is only the struggle to 'maintain a standard of living' based on 'consumer habits' that can explain why US individuals and households have continued to spend despite falling real wage rates (pp. 15–16). Others such as Frank (1999), Klein (1999), and Schor (1998) see booming consumer credit as less a consequence of material survival in the context of falling wages, and more as licensing the relentless pursuit of status and social prestige in a consumerist society. Either way, consumer credit appears to play a somewhat functional role as the structural forces of consumerism march on.

Consumer credit is also understood in the sociology literature as necessarily giving rise to disciplinary obligations of repayment. Drawing in large part on conceptual insights from Weber (1978), Simmel (1990), and Bell (1976), the focus is upon how the assumed rationalities of credit money relations prevent the irrationalities of consumerism from spiralling out of control. For George Ritzer (1995, 2001), for instance, the rationalization of consumer society is carried forward by the credit card industry. Rationalization in this sense is a de-humanizing process whereby systems are put in place that focus narrowly on the optimum means to ends. Meanwhile, for Lendol Calder (1999), the moral legitimation of a credit boom lies in the creation of a widespread awareness that consumption on credit is not simply a self-indulgent option associated with the demise of thrift, but actually requires 'discipline, hard work, and channelling of one's productivity toward durable consumer goods' (pp. 30–1). Disagreeing with Daniel Bell's (1976) classic work on the apparent disjunction between cultures of consumerism and economies of work, Calder stresses that 'if there is a hedonism in consumer culture, it is a disciplined hedonism' (p. 31). This is because, as he puts it, ' "easy payments" turned out to be not so easy', such that 'consumer credit made . . . the culture of consumption less a playground for hedonists than an extension of Max Weber's "iron cage" of disciplined rationality' (pp. 28–9). Klein (1999) broadly concurs, casting consumer credit as 'creating social control through implicit and explicit controls on the consumption of material and experiential social products' (p. 2).

Georg Simmel's (1990) social theory of money, originally published over a century ago, most strongly and skilfully advanced the argument that the spread of monetary relations carries with it the quantitative logic of instrumental rationality which leads us to ask only 'how much?' and not 'what and how?'. As Zelizer (1994) summarizes, it was this inherent feature of modern monetary relations, and the associated 'homogenization and flattening of social ties' (p. 2), that, for Simmel, was the key to the power of money. The sociology of consumer credit would seem to share Simmel's conviction. Although more recent contributions to the social theory of money and finance similarly recognize that rationality is indeed a strong tendency in modern money, there is, nonetheless, a growing awareness that money, as a social relation, can and does take many forms (e.g. Dodd 1994; Ingham 2004; Zelizer 1994). By implication and in our terms, instrumental rationality cannot be assumed to be an inherent feature of all modern monetary relations and all manner of financial networks. Rather, what we see are multiple monetary and financial networks in which the appearance of scientific rationality has to be secured and remade in specific forms, and remains contingent, contested, and open to (re)politicization.

The assembly and reproduction of apparently rational consumer credit networks can be explored in the contemporary period with reference to increasingly consolidated credit card networks which have contributed significantly to the boom in Anglo-American everyday borrowing. The total value of US household's outstanding credit card obligations rose fivefold between 1980 and 1997, outstripping the rate of growth in outstanding mortgage obligations and coming to account for an increasing share of the total (Clayton 2000: 29). To be sure, credit card networks have not displaced previously established consumer credit networks. Based around innovations in consumer loans and especially instalment plans, these networks first emerged during what Calder (1999) calls 'the credit revolution' of the 1920s and 1930s. After considerable interruption by the Great Depression and world war, everyday borrowing networks flowered in the 1940s and 1950s to finance the mass consumption of consumer durables (Calder 1999; Olney 1991). Credit card networks have come to provide, therefore, highly significant additional capacities for everyday borrowing in the contemporary period. They enable multiple purchases of 'small ticket' items, objects, and leisure experiences, on the one hand, and have produced innovations in lending techniques that are now embedded across multiple borrowing networks, on the other. As Calder (1999) puts it when he compares the credit revolution and the contemporary period, the current era is characterized by 'more lenders' and 'more methods' (pp. 291–2). I will stress here that the 'methods' and 'lenders' of credit card networks are contingently constituted as rational and scientific through three sets of specific calculative tools and performances: revolving credit, payment and authorization systems, and credit reporting and scoring.

Revolving Credit

Store cards provided by retailers, and later by oil companies and the airline industry, date from the early twentieth century. These early forms of credit card were essentially ring-fenced instalment plans settled on a monthly basis. The universal third-party credit cards which have become so familiar in the last few decades first emerged, meanwhile, in the post-1945 period. What marks out credit card networks, then, is the extension of a portable line of credit by the card issuer and not by a producer or retailer as merchant. The first universal third-party credit cards—the Diners Club Card of 1949 and the American Express card of 1951 in the US, and the British Hotel and Restaurant Association card in the UK— were conceived of as a useful facility for the subsistence requirements of the travelling salesman. The 'universality' of these cards was heavily circumscribed, and issuers or providers were non-banks who earned fees from both cardholders and merchants in return for bringing them together. As with store cards, the outstanding balances of the holders of the first third-party credit cards had to be settled at the end of each month (Mandell 1990: 1–10). The place of the universal credit card in making possible the contemporary consumer credit boom turns, therefore, on its reconfiguration through the calculations that provide for revolving credit. As Montgomerie (2006) stresses, revolving credit creates a distinct and ongoing network of relationships between individuals, card issuers, and the financial markets.

The first universal credit cards with revolving credit facilities were provided by Chase Manhattan and Bank of America in 1958, utilizing a tool that had been used in the late 1940s by the likes of Gimbel's and Bloomingdale's on the accounts of low-to-middle income store cardholders who struggled to settle their accounts at the end of each month. The legitimacy of revolving credit calculations, and thus the production of credit card networks, has nevertheless been subject to considerable contingency across several decades. For example, Chase Manhattan's credit card plan which featured 350,000 cardholders and 5,300 retailers by the end of its first financial year in 1958/9 collapsed in 1962 due to high operating costs and bad debts (Klein 1999: 28; Mandell 1990: 29). More broadly, issuers' opportunities to profit from universal credit cards with revolving credit facilities during the 1970s were undercut by several factors. For example,

US states imposed ceilings on the interest rates chargeable on unsecured credit. These usury laws came to an end, in effect, with the Marquette decision taken by the Supreme Court in 1978. The decision held that usury laws only applied to credit card issuers in the state in which they were located, and not the state in which the cardholder was located. Issuers therefore booked or relocated their credit card operations to offices in those states with the most lenient usury laws such as South Dakota and Delaware. This undermined the effectiveness of laws elsewhere, and initiated a 'race to the bottom' as states competed to attract banking business (Warren and Warren Tyagi 2004: 128–9; Watkins 2000). Additional barriers to profit included limits on lending by income category, relatively high rates of inflation, and the attitudes of the main merchants who shunned universal cards in favour of their own store cards (Manning 2000; Mandell 1990: 48–9). It was not until the 1980s, then, that the performance of revolving credit calculations by issuers and cardholders slowly became normalized.

For the issuers of universal cards, revolving credit calculations have become increasingly central to the profitability of their business. As Guseva and Rona-Tas (2001: 635) put it, 'the goal of the credit card business is to extend for as long as possible the period during which interest is charged on a purchase, as interest is the richest source of profit'. Issuers of cards can make profits in three main ways: by charging annual fees to cardholders; through receipt from merchants of a small percentage (usually 1–2%) of the value of each transaction made using their cards; and from the interest paid by cardholders each month on their revolving balances (Ritzer 1995: 35–6). In the US, where the major card issuers such as Citigroup, Chase Manhattan, Bank of America, MBNA, and First Chicago have come to face stiff competition from so-called non-banks such as General Electric (GE Capital) since the mid-1980s, the charging of annual fees is now rare on standard cards. Similar competitive pressures are also at work in the UK, where Barclays, HSBC, Lloyds TSB, Natwest, and Halifax face challenges from issuers as diverse as Virgin, Marks & Spencer, and Tesco. That said, penalty fees for late payment or exceeding credit limits have, for example, become more common (House of Commons Treasury Committee 2003: 30; McGeehan 2004). The growing volume of purchases made on credit cards more broadly has also put pressure on transaction fees.

The experience of the 1980s proved significant to credit card issuers in emphasizing the profitability of revolving credit. The relatively high interest rates that prevailed early in the decade appeared to have little effect on cardholders who continued to increase their unpaid monthly balances. The issuers took advantage, and as the '1980s wore on, the interest they charged on revolving credit came to bear little or no relation to the prevailing rate of interest. For example, between 1980 and 1992, the Federal funds rate fell from 13.4 per cent to 3.5 per cent while the average credit card interest rate actually rose from 17.3 per cent to 17.8 per cent (Medoff and Harless 1996: 12). Credit card issuers shifted the focus of their marketing campaigns from so-called 'convenience users' or 'deadbeats', who pay off their account in full at the end of each month, to 'revolvers'. The latter were typically offered increased credit limits, reward schemes, loyalty programmes, and, more recently, interest free periods on balance transfers from one card to another (see Chapter 8). By the mid-1990s, then, 80–90 per cent of the profits made by credit card issuers came from interest paid by cardholders on their unpaid balances (Medoff and Harless 1996: 12; Guseva and Rona-Tas 2001: 636). In the terms of those working for credit card lenders, those borrowers who meet their repayments in full at the end of each month are 'freeloaders' and 'deadbeats'.

Authorization and Payment Systems

As Jeacle and Walsh (2002) make clear, the first store cards issued by US department stores in the 1920s corresponded with highly significant transformations in authorization and payment arrangements. The numbered cards provided a means for identifying the cardholder, creating a 'de-personalized' alternative to simple familiarity between the merchant and their customer. Cardholder's accounts were also reorganized, as individualized index card systems replaced the store-wide ledger. This made it possible to simultaneously check the credit lines of customers, and to record payments at the point of sale. The gradual consolidation of contemporary credit card networks and their revolving credit facilities has similarly required the development of authorization and payment technologies, namely and primarily the systems operated by Visa and MasterCard.

Bank of America's BankAmericard operation was the first to begin to establish a national network in the US from 1966. In one respect and in the context of regional banking restrictions, this national expansion rested on the BankAmericard symbol and brand being licensed to other issuing banks. Indeed, by 1971, National BankAmericard Inc. (renamed Visa in 1976) was established as a separate legal entity from Bank of

America, a joint venture involving member banks in a structure that limited the obligations and liabilities of the partners. Today, Visa has 21,000 member financial institutions across 300 countries and territories.[1] The re-branding of BankAmericard as Visa was explicitly motivated by a strategy to shed its obvious American heritage for the purpose of global expansion. In a parallel set of developments, other card issuers formed a competing US national network called the Interbank Card Association, which became known as MasterCharge in 1969, and MasterCard in 1980 (Mandell 1990: 31). BarclayCard, which was the largest single national network in the UK at the time, linked up with Visa in the 1970s, while the UK's Access universal card system shortly afterwards became part of the Interbank and then MasterCard network.

While the national and global expansion of Visa and MasterCard rests in part, then, on their standing as credit card brands that are franchised to issuing banks, it has also required the installation of vast authorization and payment systems which link the terminals, tills, and 'cash registers' of retail merchants and 'read' the individual information on each card's magnetic strip. It is now widely accepted among retailers that the introduction of terminals in order to enable credit and debit card transactions will increase sales volume—the amount of cash in a wallet or purse places a ceiling on the value of a possible purchase. Such assumptions are, for example, currently driving the introduction of wireless terminals by mobile merchants (e.g. plumbers and pizza delivery companies) (Kingson 2005). Moreover, the whole edifice of so-called 'e-commerce' as a 'cashless economy' has entailed massive investment in the development of specific and 'secure' on-line authorization and payment systems. Yet, the widespread introduction of terminals and systems and, therefore, the embedding of credit card networks, was initially highly contingent. For example, credit card use in America's principal department stores only took hold once J.C. Penney signed an agreement with Visa in 1979 and began to introduce terminals and accept cards (Mandell 1990: 48–9). Store cards and credit cards issued by the main US retailers (e.g. Sears) continued to outnumber those carrying the Visa and MasterCard logos through to the mid-1980s. Meanwhile, in the UK, the major high-street retailer Marks & Spencer refused to accept third-party credit cards into the late 1990s.

It is easy to forget that the act of swiping or inserting a credit card at a merchant's terminal—perhaps the signature performance of the everyday

---

[1] http://www.usa.visa.com/about_visa/about_visa_usa/index.html

borrowing boom—is only made possible by the intermediary technologies of Visa and MasterCard which, in effect, bring the merchant, their bank, and the card issuer together in a calculative moment that typically lasts between 8 sec and 20 sec. From initial swipe to authorization and completion of the sale, a range of checks take place: is the card known to have been stolen; does the sale breach the credit limit of the cardholder; and does the transaction deviate from their usual purchase patterns? Confirmation of identity is provided by the cardholder through either signature or, more recently, the entry of a 'personal identification number' (PIN). The obligations between the card issuer and the merchant's bank that arise from a sale are, furthermore, cleared through payment systems which offset the sum of the multiple obligations that are likely to exist between the two institutions (Mandell 1990: 61–2). Should a purchase be made using a debit card, these payment systems provide for the instantaneous transfer of funds. VisaNet, the world's largest authorization and payments system, currently processes more than 3,700 transactions every second at its peak, and comprises enough fibre optic and communications cable to encircle the globe nearly four hundred times.[2]

Credit Reporting and Scoring

Alongside revolving credit and authorization and payment systems, the calculative tools and performances of credit reporting and scoring have made possible the emergence and consolidation of credit card networks. The significance of these tools arises from the ways in which they enable issuers to construct, measure, and manage the uncertainties over the future meeting of outstanding obligations by cardholders. Credit reporting and scoring figure and manage so-called 'credit' or 'default risk', and thus provide card issuers with a calculative and apparently scientific means of feigning control over a necessarily uncertain future. As Guseva and Rona-Tas (2001: 623) have it, 'Unless uncertainty is transformed into risk so that rational calculation becomes possible, general-purpose, revolving consumer credit cannot develop on a mass scale'.

Through to the last few decades of the twentieth century in the US, uncertainties surrounding future repayments by consumer borrowers tended to be managed by merchants themselves who kept open-book accounts for long-term and well-known customers. The significance of 'trust' and 'reputation' in lending decisions was supplemented by early

[2] http://www.usa.visa.com/about_visa/about_visa_usa/index.html

forms of credit reporting, that is, (at this time) the practice of collecting information about borrowers' character and habits from key members of their communities (e.g. attorneys, bank clerks, postmasters, etc.) (Guseva and Rona-Tas 2001: 629). Uncertainties arising from lending through store cards and the first universal third party credit cards were managed in a similar manner. In the UK, meanwhile, retail bank networks and their managers provided local sites for the gathering of embodied tacit knowledge on prospective borrowers through to the 1980s (Leyshon and Thrift 1999: 441). It was not until 1965 that Credit Data Corporation, based upon information provided by the large California banks, produced the first nationwide computerized US credit bureau. This provided an accessible database of standardized information on the financial situations of existing and potential credit cardholders. Today, there are three national providers of credit histories in the US: Experian, TransUnion, and Equifax (Guseva and Rona-Tas 2001: 629–30). Each maintains around 190 million credit files, and taken together, they issue about 1 billion credit reports annually.

The first credit scoring techniques were also developed in the mid-1960s, although their roots extended back to screening techniques used by mail order firms in the 1930s. The aim of credit scoring is to calculate the probability that a credit cardholder will default, given their employment, financial, and residential/family histories (Ritzer 2001: 84–6). Specifically, probabilities are calculated for ability to pay, intent to pay, and so-called 'stability' and 'accountability'. All (weighted) scores are summed, and then compared against an upper- and lower-threshold by the card issuer. In Ritzer's (2001) terms, credit scoring therefore reduces 'the individual quality of credit worthiness to a simple, single number that "decides" whether or not an applicant is, in fact, worthy of credit' (p. 85). In the US, a credit score is also known as a 'FICO score', short for the Fair Isaac Corporation of Minneapolis that undertakes much of the scoring. A maximum FICO score is 850 and the minimum 300. The average is 720, and a score below 620 places an individual in the 'risky' category (McGeehan 2004). Making an application for a credit card has thus become highly standardized and largely impersonal, requiring that details on occupation, length of time in current residence, and so on are provided on an application form. Information from this form is combined with credit reports and, if necessary, verification of income, in order to arrive at a credit score.

The gradual shift over the last three decades or so from the more directly relational and 'face-to-face' management of uncertainty to the calculations of credit reporting and scoring as technologies of risk is characterized by Leyshon and Thrift (1999), drawing on Latour (1987), as the rise of 'at-a-distance' means of distinguishing between 'good' and 'bad' customers. Yet, credit reporting and scoring tools took time to become embedded. For example, in the US, it was only in the wake of the rampant fraud and defaults that followed from card issuers' unscreened and unsolicited mass mail-shots that credit reporting and scoring began to take hold. In the UK, meanwhile, it was not until 'a period of experimentation that began in the 1980s' and through 'a process of trial and error' that credit scoring became a tool employed by the financial services industry (Leyshon and Thrift 1999: 436). Again, this was a period in which defaults and bad debts were on the increase following a phase of intense market competition but, in the UK, established credit scoring tools could be imported ready-made from the US (pp. 443–4).

The reach of these 'at-a-distance' techniques is currently such that more than 80 per cent of all the credit cards in the US are, for example, issued by institutions to cardholders with whom they have no other financial relationship (Guseva and Rona-Tas 2001: 627–8). As credit reporting and scoring replace the discretion of loan officers with the rationality of statistical and algorithmic analysis, they figure in new ways what is deemed to be knowable about the likelihood of defaults. Written in to the procedures of card issuers, credit scoring has thus ultimately made possible a massive expansion in both the numbers of cardholders and the revolving credit facilities at their disposal. Common in this regard is so-called 'risk-based pricing', whereby interest rates paid by different holders of the same card vary according to their credit scores as the primary means for measuring their credit/default risk (see Chapter 7). Such variations in interest rates are in addition to the different rates that apply across the ranges of cards offered by issuers where, for example, Platinum cardholders will typically pay lower rates of interest than those who do not hold such 'premium cards'. The on-going surveillance of the financial activities of cardholders by credit bureaus also provides information which may be used to alter the interest rate pertaining to that card (McGeehan 2004). Overall, given the apparent success of credit reporting and scoring as calculative tools for the management of default risk in credit card networks, the performance of a so-called 'credit check' has become a ubiquitous feature of all contemporary market networks of borrowing, 'the obligatory point of entry to the retail financial system' for Leyshon and Thrift (1999: 448). At the same time, as Edward Chancellor (2005) has it, 'By expanding the universe of creditworthy borrowers and increasing the confidence with which banks lend, credit scoring has facilitated the rapid growth of consumer debt in recent years...' (p. 61). In our terms, the seeming control over the uncertain future that credit reporting and scoring gives to lenders provides the basis for more lending to a greater number of borrowers.

Capital Flows and Everyday Borrowing Networks

Alongside an emphasis on consumerism and the associated collapse of thrift, it is also common for accounts of the boom in US everyday borrowing in particular to draw attention to capital movements within disintermediated global markets. *The Economist* (2002*a*, 2003*b*, 2005*c*) magazine's recent surveys and special reports on the world economy stress, for example, the extent to which world economic growth has come to rest on the spending and borrowing habits of US governments and consumers. The US borrowing boom—and, by implication, given Britain's growing current account deficit, the Anglo-American boom— has and continues to made possible by capital inflows from Germany, oil-exporting states, and especially Japan, China, and the rest of Asia. Asian central banks in particular have purchased massive holdings of US bonds, thereby working to support their own export industries and against the appreciation of their currencies against the dollar (Duncan 2003). In Paul Krugman's terms, 'Americans are making money selling each other houses with money borrowed from the Chinese' (in Scurlock 2007: 26).

Following from this analysis, it is the sustainability of the US borrowing boom that becomes the greatest concern for policy makers. The IMF (2004) warns, for instance, that a rupture in the pattern of liquid capital flows into the US poses the single greatest threat to what they call 'global financial stability'. Meanwhile, prior to his recent appointment, the current Chairman of the Federal Reserve Ben S. Bernanke propounded what is known as the 'global savings glut' thesis. This suggests that the US has been able to continue to attract capital inflows during a period in which interest rates have hit historic lows (i.e. since 2000) precisely because saving rates elsewhere exceed rates of investment. Thus, debate has come to turn on whether the liquid savings glut is 'a temporary and largely cyclical phenomenon', or 'the result of long-term structural shifts and is likely to last for years, perhaps decades' (*The Economist* 2005*c*: 5). For those who take the former position, the US and world economies are heading for a so-called 'hard landing' (e.g. Bonner and Wiggin 2006; Pettifor 2006), with opponents of this view such as Bernanke predicting a 'soft landing'.

Explanations of the borrowing boom that concentrate on quantitative global movements of capital remain, however, partial and limited. As scholars of IPE point out, there is no smooth and seamless global financial market where power and politics do not impinge on movements of capital. It is not an irony that the position of the US as 'consumer of last resort' in the world economy has become financed by those outside the US since the early 1980s, but a direct consequence of US financial power and seignorage (Germain 1997; Helleiner 1994; Seabrooke 2001; Strange 1986). Furthermore, as we stressed in Chapter 1, there is no singular global financial market or system, but multiple, dynamic, and more-or-less discrete networks of finance that may intersect to a greater or lesser degree. Popular accounts of the place of the capital markets in the boom in everyday borrowing have very little to say about the constitution of the boom in transformed networks that have close linkages with the capital markets. Global capital flows only fund the Anglo-American borrowing boom because of the constitution of longer everyday networks of borrowing that now overlap and intertwine with the networks of the capital markets.

Key to the materialization of transformed and lengthened borrowing networks has been a reconfiguration in the means through which lenders manage the uncertainties surrounding the future repayments of borrowers. Leyshon and Thrift's (1999) characterization of the management of the possibilities of default in everyday networks of borrowing during the post-war years as 'relational' and 'face-to-face' is certainly not far from the mark. However, calculative performances of so-called 'default risk' were common. For instance, under the relatively short and unconnected mortgage networks of this period, the saving and loans (S&Ls), thrifts, and building societies that dominated lending calculated and managed the category of default risk. UK building societies, for example, typically constructed conservative lending conditions with respect to the type of borrower and type of property—calculated through loan-to-income and loan-to-value ratios respectively—and by requiring that mortgagors were covered by the insurance industry. In the US, meanwhile, default risk for low- and middle-income earners was addressed through federal insurance or guarantees provided by the Federal Housing Association (FHA) and the Department of Veterans Affairs (DVA). The contemporary reconfiguration of mortgage and consumer credit networks is not, then, a simple shift in how the possibilities of default are conceived, that is, a move from uncertainties that lay beyond prediction to the statistical and predictive calculation of risks (Stuart 2003). Rather, the contemporary period has witnessed an on-going intensification and reformation of default risk calculation, measurement, and management. While the techniques of credit reporting and scoring have become increasingly significant in this regard, they are only part of the reconfiguration of default risk. Further calculative devices of default risk are also pivotal in the constitution of lengthened and booming networks of mortgage and consumer borrowing.

During the post-war period, banks tended to manage the default risks arising from mortgages and consumer loans through one of the principal calculative tools of accountancy, the balance sheet. It is the balance sheet that names and determines mortgages and loans are 'assets' that have to be matched by savings and other forms of capital as 'liabilities'. A mortgage lender would, for example, issue a mortgage, collect and monitor payments, and hold the 'asset' on their balance sheet until the interest and principal was paid. Non-bank lenders, meanwhile, undertook practices of factoring transactions which, while enabling them to sell on their receivables, did not create a liquid secondary market (Partnoy 2004: 76). Contemporary calculative tools of default risk target the management of the asset side of the balance sheet. Assets are broken down into 'elementary risk factors' and 'become an object of stochastic evaluation' (Aglietta and Rebérioux 2005: 142). As Aglietta and Rebérioux continue, 'The essential consequence of this logic of risk decomposition is the possibility of risk transfer. Risk transfer makes it possible to spread risks over the broadest population of financial investors' (p. 143). In our terms, mortgage and consumer credit networks become bigger and closely interconnected with the networks of the capital markets. The operation of tools of default risk calculation and management, especially asset-backed securitization but also so-called 'structured finance' and the use of credit derivatives, turns, then, on the issue and trading of default risk-related instruments in the capital markets.

Asset-Backed Securitization

Asset-backed securitization is the practice of 'bundling' or 'pooling' together a stream of future repayments arising from everyday borrowing to provide the basis for the issue of, and payment of interest and principal on, securities (typically fixed-rate bonds known as asset-backed securities or ABS). In short, assets are commodified and liquidified in a particular way. Thus, the process of asset-backed securitization involves the transfer of a pool of relatively homogeneous assets from the lender ('originator' or 'issuer') to a special purchase vehicle (SPV). The SPV, which typically has trust status under law, finances the transfer of these assets through the issue of tradable securities. The trust status of the SPV makes the securities attractive to investors, as 'even if the bank filed for bankruptcy protection, the trust's assets would be secure' (Partnoy 2004: 77). The payment of interest and principal on the securities is directly dependent on the aggregated cash flows (which themselves are repayments by everyday borrowers) arising from the underlying pooled assets. The major investment banks tend to play a critical role in the organization of the securitization process and the marketing of securities to investors of all kinds.

The first significant growth in ABS practices took place in the US in the late 1970s and 1980s, with the residential mortgages of S&Ls and thrifts providing the underlying assets bundled together—so-called 'mortgage-backed securities' (MBS). Today, while it receives relatively little attention from academics, policy makers or the financial media, the US MBS market is one of the largest bond markets in the world. At the end of 2004, the total value of outstanding T-bonds stood at $3.944 trillion, compared to $5.473 trillion for MBS. Even during the period of federal government profligacy between 2000 and 2004, the increase in the value of outstanding T-bonds by around $1 trillion paled by comparison with the near $2 trillion increase for MBS in a period of booming mortgage lending and house price rises (Bond Market Association 2004a). While highly lucrative for those involved, the secondary market for trading in MBS/ABS remains limited by comparison with corporate and sovereign bond markets. The value of daily trading in the secondary market for US MBS, which is by far the most liquid of all ABS markets, is roughly half that of trading in the benchmark T-bond market.

An especially notable feature of MBS in the US is the role played by so-called 'government-sponsored enterprises' (GSEs). These include the Government National Mortgage Association (Ginnie Mae), the Federal National Mortgage Association (Fannie Mae), and the Federal Home Loan Mortgage Corporation (Freddie Mac). The historical roots of these institutions date to the Great Depression and New Deal legislation of the 1930s, and the desire to support house ownership amidst economic hardship and ongoing income inequalities. At present, Ginnie Mae does not buy or sell mortgage loans or issue MBS, but guarantees the timely payment of principal and interest on MBS that are issued on federally insured or guaranteed loans. Formed in 1968, Ginnie took over these operations from Fannie Mae which, dating from 1938, became a 'private' corporation after its first thirty years. Fannie and Freddie Mac (formed in 1970) both purchase and hold mortgages in their portfolios through the issue of MBS, effectively performing the role of SPVs for the significant portion of the US MBS market. As Carruthers and Stinchcombe (1999) summarize: 'The demand for funds by householders to invest in illiquid houses could be met by investors demanding liquid investments only if the government made home mortgages more liquid' (p. 361). The mortgages purchased by Fannie and Freddie have to comply with guidelines designed to ensure that they support the mortgages of ethnic minorities and low-, moderate-, and middle-income earners. The value of outstanding so-called 'agency MBS' (i.e. those issued by Fannie or Freddie or guaranteed by Ginnie) stood at $3.547 trillion by 2004, with the so-called 'private-label' MBS originated by market institutions worth $1.926 trillion (Bond Market Association 2004b).

From the mid-to-late 1980s, ABS on both sides of the Atlantic moved beyond mortgages to increasingly embrace a wide range of everyday borrowing obligations for which it is possible to aggregate and forecast a stream of future repayments—for example, car loans (certificates for automobile receivables, the 'CARs market'), credit card receivables (certificates for amortizing revolving debts, the 'CARDs market'), and student loans. More recently, the 'assets' securitized have broadened still further to include all manner of aggregated and predicted income streams that arise from, for example, household rents, phone bills, and infrastructural developments in transportation, education, telecommunications, power generation, and so on (Leyshon and Thrift 2007). According to Securities Industry and Financial Markets Association (2006) figures, the value of outstanding bonds in the US CARs market increased from $59.5 billion to $234.5 billion between 1995 and 2003, with the value of the CARDs market increasing from $153.1 billion to $401.9 billion over the same period. So-called 'centralized lenders' and non-banks who depend on the wholesale markets to raise capital are among the largest originators of non-mortgage ABS programmes in the US, including GMAC for CARs, and MBNA, GE Capital, and Capital One for CARDs. In both the US and UK, however, mortgages remain by far the largest single asset group that is subject to securitization. While rapidly growing in continental Europe, securitization and ABS markets remain largely Anglo-American. The UK, for example, accounts for roughly 60 per cent of the European market (Davies 2006*b*).

Securitization is written into the performances of lending through the accounting calculations of the balance sheet. ABS is a particular form of 'off-balance sheet' accounting, whereby assets are isolated, repackaged and sold on the capital markets, and liabilities are thus reduced. The movement of assets off-balance sheet is pivotal for the operations of non-banks and centralized lenders in mortgage and consumer credit networks (Pryke and Whitehead 1994). The common practice by banks of separating out their credit card businesses from the rest of their operations (and thus from their liabilities in the form of personal savings) is also only possible due to off-balance sheet accounting. More broadly, the movement of assets off-balance sheet enables credit card issuers, mortgage, and consumer lenders to generate new assets while holding only a relatively small capital base (whether in the form of personal savings, capital market borrowing, or share capital). In the parlance of ABS practitioners, there is 'no need for match funding for asset growth'.[3] Consider, for example, the expanded mortgage lending in the UK during the 1990s by HBOS and Northern Rock who, in contrast with the major commercial banks, do not hold massive volumes of saving deposits on their liabilities side. More recently, the so-called 'customer funding gap' of the major UK banks—that is, 'the amount of customer lending not financed through customer deposits'—grew from 0 per cent to 11 per cent between 2001 and 2005 as lending expanded significantly (Bank of England 2006*a*: 28).

Pressures to manage balance sheets were felt particularly strongly by US S&Ls during the early 1980s, stimulating their initial involvement in MBS (Wharf 1994: 318–20). Off-balance sheet accounting by some Anglo-American mortgage lenders also figured prominently in relation to their attempts, during the late 1980s and early 1990s, to meet the minimum capital adequacy requirements established under the Basel Committee on Banking Supervision's Basel Capital Accord (Basel I). This practice of moving assets off-balance sheet to provide 'regulatory capital relief on the liabilities side' has, however, become much less significant since the introduction of the Basel II Accord in 2001.[4] A key difference between Basel I and Basel II is that the 'regulatory capital' required under the

---

[3] Confidential interview, representative of a specialist securitization servicer company, London, 24 January 2005.

[4] Confidential interview, representative of the Risk Mitigation Department, Financial Services Authority, London, 26 January 2005.

conditions of the former is largely circumscribed within the 'economic capital'—that is, both capital at risk and as a buffer for shocks—which is the focus of the self-regulatory in-house risk assessment models that are legitimated by the latter (de Goede 2004; Power 2005). Both off-balance sheet accounting and risk assessment models target efficiency gains in relation to capital.

In a similar vein, off-balance sheet accounting also simultaneously makes it possible to 'avoid tax leakage' (Ashman and Black 2002: 63), and may well be closely related to the accounting devices of tax avoidance. The movement of assets off-balance sheet to an SPV, the associated issue of ABS, and the resulting pattern of cash flows, are all potentially subject to taxation (Harrower 2002). Taxes on the transfer of assets can be subject to capital gains tax, for example, while the issue of securities may require stamp duty to be paid and payments may necessitate withholding tax. The SPVs to which assets are transferred from an originator's balance sheet are, therefore, in many instances registered in jurisdictions such as the Cayman Islands for US-based originators, and Jersey, Luxembourg, and Dublin for UK-based originators. Each jurisdiction provides the lengthened networks of Anglo-American mortgage lending and consumer credit with regulatory spaces that shelter ABS programmes from taxation.

The calculative judgements of the principal bond rating agencies—most notably S&P, Moody's Investor Services, and Fitch Investors' Service—are also significant in figuring ABS. The authority of the rating agencies is derived from their apparently expert deployment of the seemingly objective tools of credit rating (Sinclair 2005). Their ostensible vigilance and continuous monitoring appears necessary to the generation of their principal product in relation to each bond issued: 'a letter symbol reflecting a relative ranking on a scale from most to least creditworthy' (Sinclair 1994: 138–9). Such is the authority of the agencies that their top 'AAA' (triple-A) rating of the first issues of MBS in the UK proved, for instance, to be crucial in establishing confidence among investors.[5] Similarly, as Asian central banks diversified their holdings in US bond markets from 2003, the AAA rating of agency MBS proved crucial to their attractiveness. In the twelve months to October 2004, the total value of central bank holdings of agency MBS increased from $52 billion to $2,444 billion (Chancellor 2005: 55). And, again, for non-mortgage ABS more broadly, investors initially 'rushed to buy' because they 'typically received very

---

[5] Confidential interview, former director of Barclays Capital, London, 24 January 2005.

high credit ratings' (Partnoy 2004: 77). Once rated, a set of bonds issued in the CARDs market, for example, become relatively transparent financial instruments for investors. They are comparable, at a glance and in terms of risk, both with MBS, corporate and sovereign bonds, on the one hand, and with other bonds in the CARDs market, on the other. To follow the example through, the credit scores of the cardholders whose repayments are bundled together to provide the basis for the bond issue form an important point of reference for the rating given to the bonds. As Guseva and Rona-Tas (2001: 632) put it, 'The calculation of the risk of a security on the secondary market rests on the primary calculation of the risk of the card debt portfolio.'

Structured Finance

The calculations of the bond rating process also underpin the practices of so-called 'structured finance' which have come increasingly to the fore in ABS programmes. Indeed, the terms 'securitization' and 'structured finance' are coming to be used somewhat interchangeably, and the organization of the securitization process by the principal investment banks tends to take place through their structured finance divisions. Here the instruments issued through the process of ABS take the form of collateralized bond obligations (CBOs), or collateralized debt obligations (CDOs) more broadly. CDOs are 'structured', whereby the 'senior tranche' of bonds is differentiated from the 'first loss' or 'equity' tranche, and from the various 'mezzanine layers' in between. The senior tranche is highly rated as a relatively low-risk and low-yielding set of CDOs, while the potential for default is born disproportionately by holders of the first loss tranche of CDOs which, accordingly, receive a low credit rating as relatively high-risk and (potentially) high-yielding bonds.

According to Bank of England (2006a) figures, the global value of CDOs now stands at $1 trillion, roughly the equivalent of the funds currently under management by hedge funds which have received far greater attention in the financial and popular media. In this regard, it is important to note that the growth of markets in CDOs has not been solely related to ABS and consumer credit networks. Indeed, for Partnoy (2004), 'CBOs are one of the threads that run through the past fifteen years of financial markets, ranging from Michael Milken to First Boston to Enron and WorldCom' (pp. 77–8). That said, figures from the Securities Industry and Financial Markets Association (2006) on the value of ABS outstanding in the US, subdivided by instrument, give a strong indication, for example, of the growing use of CDOs in consumer credit networks. The value of outstanding CDOs in the US increased from a mere $1.2 billion in 1995 to $296.9 billion by the third quarter of 2006. CDOs only accounted for 0.4 per cent of all outstanding ABS in 1995, but are now equivalent to 14.7 per cent of the total. The slight falls since 2003 in the value of outstanding CARs and CARDs ABS that are registered in these figures would also seem to reflect the growing prominence of CDOs.

The development of structured finance is, then, regarded by practitioners as the tailoring of ABS programmes to the different 'appetites for risk' held by potential investors.[6] While the interest paid to all investors who hold ABS is, in effect, their reward for taking on and bearing default risk, the limited but more-or-less certain returns from AAA rated MBS, for example, may not be attractive to certain investors. Investors in ABS calculate, strategize, and justify the purchase, holding, and trading of default risk-related instruments through the assumptions and models of asset management. As we discussed in relation to DB pension schemes in Chapter 3, asset management is highly significant to the constitution of the networks of the contemporary capital markets. For pension funds and other institutional investors seeking to further diversify their portfolio into lower-risk instruments, then, AAA rated MBS may well be regarded as providing an alternative to equally highly rated sovereign and corporate bonds. Similarly, within a CDO issue, the lower-risk senior tranche typically appeals to pension funds and insurers, while the higher-risk tranches are attractive to mutual funds, structured investment vehicles, and hedge funds. In a further and particularly illustrative example, US banks, S&Ls, and thrifts, as originators of MBS programmes, have also sought to diversify their own portfolios through the purchase of MBS issued by other institutions (Coles and Hardt 2000). The assumption here is that default risk can be effectively managed through the diversification of assets, an assumption that strikes a particular chord with MBS originators whose business remains regionally concentrated despite the removal of federal banking restrictions (*The Economist* 2004).

While for the most part, then, it is ABS that has been constituted through the isolation and breaking down of the assets of mortgage and

---

[6] Confidential interview, representative of a London subsidiary of US-owned investment bank, Newcastle-upon-Tyne, 9 February 2005.

consumer credit providers through the calculative prism of 'default risk', structured finance and the active management of assets understood as a portfolio of risks has more recently also stimulated derivatives practices. Rather than repackaging assets and moving them off-balance sheet by selling them on to investors, credit derivatives contracts are used by lenders to manage the default risks that are associated with their assets. In short, it is not assets that are commodified and liquidified, but the default risks calculated for those assets that are commodified and liquidified. The principal contracts take the form of credit default swaps (CDS), and also so-called 'synthetic CDOs' which create tranches of CDS.

The most common credit derivative, CDS, has been around for a decade or so and continues to be central to the rapidly accelerating growth of credit derivatives. The total value of outstanding credit derivatives in 1996 was $180 billion, growing to $893 billion by 2000, $5,021 billion by 2004, and $20,207 billion by 2006 (Barrett and Ewan 2006). Much of the growth in issuance of CDS has been related to banks' lending to their corporate customers and, according to Partnoy (2004: 374–6), is the principal reason why the major US corporate bankruptcies of the first years of the new millennium (Enron, Global Crossing, Kmart, WorldCom) did not also bring down their bankers. But, a CDS contract operates much the same for corporate and everyday borrowers. In mortgage and consumer credit networks, buyers of CDS contracts, derived from a specific set of 'reference assets' (e.g. personal loans) on their balance sheet, 'sell on' only the default risks that have been calculated for those assets and not the assets themselves. In return for receiving a regular premium for the ownership of default risk, sellers of CDS are liable to provide contingent funds to the lender should 'specified credit events' (defaults) occur in relation to the reference assets. The standardization of probably calculations for defaults on different groups of reference assets, such as for personal loans to prime borrowers, ensures that CDS can be traded between sellers in secondary markets (Aglietta and Rebérioux 2005: 163). Banks and insurance companies tend to be the principal buyers and sellers of CDS. Banks not only protect themselves against the default risks associated with their own assets but, at the same time, effectively diversify their asset base by selling protection to others. Roughly one-third of banks' volume of credit derivative activity is related to their loan book which includes lending to everyday borrowers, and two-thirds is related to trading (Barrett and Ewan 2006).

Concluding Remarks

This chapter has begun our inquiry into everyday borrowing in contemporary Anglo-America. I have focused on the boom in everyday borrowing, and the qualitative transformations in consumer credit and mortgage networks that have made it possible. By situating the boom in the principal market networks of everyday borrowing, the account offered differs from existing explanations. These view the boom as either a function of the spread of consumerism and the collapse of prudence that results, or as primarily reliant on disintermediated global capital flows that fund current account deficits. Specifically, I have stressed the contingent constitution of booming credit card networks through specific calculative tools and performances—revolving credit, payment and authorization systems, and credit reporting and scoring. And, furthermore, I have explored the reconfiguration of mortgage and consumer credit networks. Materializing through calculative devices which measure and manage the uncertainties of future repayments as 'default risks', transformations in mortgage and consumer credit have realized longer networks that now closely overlap and interconnect with the networks of the capital markets in terms of the issue and trading of default risk-related instruments. Lenders have thus supported a greater scale of mortgage and consumer borrowing than would have otherwise been the case. By the middle 2004, the issuance of ABS by value exceeded corporate bond issues for the first time (Chancellor 2005: 57). But, as the vast sums residing in the capital markets have come to sustain this extended lending, important questions remain. First, has the qualitative transformation of everyday borrowing created more inclusive networks where the capital markets, in effect, become democratized and made to work for all? Second, how has the transformation and boom in everyday borrowing manifested itself in the re-assembly of everyday financial subjectivities and the re-making of financial self-disciplines, and what tensions and contradictions are present in the processes of identification? Third, what forms of dissent have emerged in the course of the boom in everyday borrowing, and what are the prospects and problematics of dissent in everyday borrowing? The following chapters in this part of the book will address each of these questions in turn.

7

The Inequalities of Everyday Borrowing

Introduction: 'Market Completion'

> Without a sub-prime market, some borrowers by virtue of poor credit
> history, unstable income, and other characteristics are unable to qual-
> ify for a mortgage. With a subprime market, there is a more complete
> credit supply schedule with the market pricing for poorer credit qual-
> ity in the mortgage rate. By completing the capital market, subprime
> lenders reduce borrowing constraints. The result is a social welfare
> gain. (Chinloy and MacDonald 2005: 153)

Contemporary Anglo-American mortgage and consumer credit networks are characterized by qualitative transformations that have made
possible not only an unprecedented boom in everyday borrowing, as
Chapter 6 has shown, but also what economists Peter Chinloy and Nancy
MacDonald call 'market completion'. During the 1980s, and since the
early to mid-1990s in particular, greater numbers of individuals and
households have taken out mortgages, instalment loans, and revolving
credit as a matter of routine. An 'incomplete' market has been replaced
by 'a more complete credit supply schedule' as previous 'borrowing constraints' have been reduced, developments that Nocera (1994) similarly
casts as contributing to 'the democratization of finance'. A highly significant feature of these transformations, especially from the 1990s, has been
the rise of sub-prime finance. The specialist lenders or 'non-banks' that
are typically present in sub-prime networks make available car loans, debt
consolidation loans, credit cards, and, in particular, mortgages. So-called
'non-conforming' or sub-prime borrowers usually have low, irregular, or
unverifiable incomes, and/or poor credit histories and scores. But, for
sub-prime borrowers, the 'social welfare gain' of qualifying for mainstream credit comes at a price. 'Market pricing' for 'poorer credit quality'

borrowers ensures that sub-prime borrowers pay considerably higher rates of interest than borrowers who are categorized as 'conforming' or 'prime'.

In this chapter, then, we are interested in inequalities of everyday borrowing that, over the last decade or so, have become increasingly marked by hierarchical variations in the interest rates paid by borrowers. To draw on a distinction made by Newman and Wyly (2004), what primarily concerns us is not the 'exclusionary redlining' of borrowers, but their 'exploitative greenlining' (p. 53). Redlining undoubtedly continues—even when borrowers have similarly incomes, an African-American applicant in the Unites States of America (US) is twice as likely as a white applicant to be denied a mortgage, for example (Squires 2003: 5). Nonetheless, our focus here is on the ways in which 'market completion' in everyday borrowing, carried forward by such developments as the consolidation of sub-prime networks, is far from egalitarian. The crisis that has ruptured US sub-prime mortgage networks since late 2006 looms large at the time of writing, and we will explore this in detail as part of the concluding chapter of this book. For now, the rise of sub-prime finance is explored as part of the wider developments whereby credit relations have expanded in terms of both scale and scope. How are the inequalities of everyday borrowing produced through and across market networks of everyday borrowing, networks that include sub-prime and also 'alternative' or 'informal' finance where home credit lenders, payday loan providers, cheque-cashing services, pawnbrokers, sale and buyback shops, mail order companies, and rent-to-own retailers prevail?

Policy makers, activists, and social scientists tend to draw a clear dichotomy between 'inclusion' and 'exclusion' in addressing issues of contemporary financial inequality. However, as the first section of this chapter will make plain, this binary reduces a concern with inequalities to a largely singular question: are borrowers excluded from 'mainstream' or 'formal' market finance? Those experiencing inequality are thus necessarily assumed to occupy a marginalized space somewhere beyond the limits of mainstream market networks. In contrast, I will argue that the dichotomous representation of an abnormal and informal space of financial exclusion, and the associated designation of the borrowers that occupy that space as 'alternative', 'high risk', 'sub-prime', and so on, actually contributes to justifying the charging of relatively high rates of interest by lenders present in these realms. And yet, at the same time, the operations of alternative and informal lenders are made possible precisely by close interconnections with mainstream financial and capital market networks.

The second section of the chapter explores this argument in detail by concentrating on the differentiation of 'sub-prime' from 'prime' finance, and on the assembly of high-interest sub-prime networks. Sub-prime networks are shown to be constituted through calculative devices and performances that, as I argued in Chapter 6, are also pivotal to the materialization of the transformation and boom in mainstream market networks of everyday borrowing. It is through the incremental adoption, development, and application of techniques of 'prime' finance—most notably, credit reporting and scoring that first took hold in credit card networks, and default-risk management that leads to the issue and trading of securities backed by the outstanding obligations of mortgagors, credit card holders, and so on—that sub-prime has been produced. Credit reporting and scoring techniques are not primarily used by sub-prime lenders to 'include' or 'exclude' potential borrowers. Rather, when combined with marketing strategies, these technologies provide the basis for the sorting, profiling, targeting, and pricing of customers through the prism of risk. This is known as 'risk-based pricing', that is, the categorization of borrowers according to calculations as to their likelihood of default, and the charging of graduated rates of interest based on these categorizations. Closely related, sub-prime lender's assets are moved off-balance sheet, and the 'pooled' future repayments of their 'risky' borrowers provide the basis for extensive programmes of securitization and structured finance. These techniques are especially significant in sub-prime networks because specialist lenders lack the capital base of liabilities held by banks and, as such, are largely reliant for asset growth on the rating, structuring, and issue of bonds backed by borrowers' future repayments.

Inclusion/Exclusion and New Inequalities

The Anglo-American everyday borrowing boom that accelerated in the 1980s was an expansion in both the scale and scope of credit relations. As the level of total collective borrowing soared, so credit and the obligations of repayment became mundane for greater numbers of individuals and households (Burton 1994; Grant 1992). Confronted by the 'debt crisis' of the first years of the decade that curtailed much of their international lending, the major Anglo-American banks came to welcome the custom of many of those 'at home' who they had previously marginalized. James Grant (1992) captures this in typically colourful terms: 'The descendants of the clientele of loan sharks became the valued credit-card "members" of leading banks' (p. 3). In the early 1990s, however, this expansion of everyday borrowing was briefly curtailed. Recession, falling residential property prices, rising personal bankruptcies, and bank and S&L failures were all contributing factors. Moves to further transparency, weed-out disreputable lenders, and reassure recently created 'financial consumers' also played a part, as regulators subjected the 1980s wave of deregulation that had unleashed the 'bonanza of selling' to critical scrutiny (Morgan and Sturdy 2000: 231–9). During the first years of the last decade of the twentieth century, then, in Leyshon and Thrift's (1995) terms, 'finance capital' was 'retreating to a middle-class heartland'. This 'credit crunch' appeared to represent a moment when the financial system's 'inherent tendency to discriminate against poor and disadvantaged groups' surfaced once again (p. 314; cf. Dymski and Veitch 1996). The period witnessed a 'flight to quality', a process involving 'a strategy of risk avoidance' and 'financial infrastructure withdrawal' (p. 313). Only the relatively wealthy and those deemed credit-worthy and 'less risky' appealed to banks operating in consumer credit and mortgage networks who, at the same time, began to selectively dismantle their costly branch networks in rural and inner city areas (Tickell 2000).

It was against this backdrop that social scientists first turned to the notion of 'financial exclusion' to explain the dynamics of financial inequality. In the words of Leyshon and Thrift (1995), for example, 'financial exclusion' was the outcome of 'processes that serve to prevent certain social groups and individuals from gaining access to the financial system' (p. 314). The experiences of the excluded stood in stark contrast and as the corollary to those of their other: the affluent suburban 'superincluded' who were 'cherry picked' by banks for the cross-selling of loans, mortgages, credit cards, and all manner of insurance and investment products (Leyshon and Thrift 1996; Leyshon, Thrift, and Pratt 1998; Leyshon et al. 2004). American scholars in particular had long noted the marginalization, discrimination, and 'redlining' of borrowers by so-called 'mainstream' lenders and insurers on the grounds of income, gender, inner-city location, and especially race (for review, see Dymski 2005a; Squires 2003). But, the rubric of 'financial exclusion' nevertheless appeared to bring into sharp relief the dynamics of contemporary financial inequality. For instance, for perhaps the most influential academic commentator on US financial inequalities, Gary Dymski (2005b), the widespread articulation of 'financial exclusion' involves 'a generalisation of the idea of race-based discrimination in banking markets, to encompass customer-class distinctions other than race and ethnicity per se' (p. 441).

It provides a 'new terminology' that has 'opened the way to bolder and more extensive ... analyses' (p. 441).

Since the early to mid-1990s, a further step-wise acceleration of the boom in everyday borrowing has once again been characterized by not only a massive increase in the scale of consumer and mortgage borrowing, but also by the involvement of greater numbers of individuals and households. More borrowing is now, in short, being undertaken by many more people. In the UK, for example, the proportion of households with access to mainstream consumer credit increased from 61 per cent in 1989 to 73 per cent in 2002 (Brooker and Whyley 2005: 1). Furthermore, there are indications that, in consumer borrowing networks at least, it is precisely those outside of the 'middle-class heartland' of finance who are borrowing most relative to their income. For example, in the UK, figures from the Bank of England's British Household Panel Survey show that while unsecured borrowing as a percentage of income increased for all income categories between 1995 and 2000, far and away the greatest increase took place in those households with income less that £11,500 (in House of Commons Treasury Select Committee 2003: 35). Meanwhile, growing numbers of owner-occupiers on both sides of the Atlantic have, for the first time, become incorporated into mortgage networks.

How are we to understand these recent developments, and where do they leave the rubric of inclusion/exclusion as we seek to apprehend contemporary financial inequalities? In contrast with the early 1990s, what is perhaps most notable about 'financial exclusion' is the manner in which it is now a conceptual touchstone for government agencies, policy makers, and community activists. Although policy discourses of financial exclusion do not subject the processes of inclusion/exclusion to critical scrutiny in the manner of social scientific analyses, questions of inequality are nonetheless similarly reduced to a largely singular issue: whether or not individuals and households can access ideal-typical 'mainstream' and 'formal' market networks. For a recent contributor to the *World Bank Research Observer*, then, those who experience 'involuntary exclusion ... lack access because, for example, barriers to access the formal financial system are too high or costs are unreasonably high or because they do not have a credit record' (Claessens 2006: 210). Financial inequality becomes, in short, a matter of 'deficient access' (p. 212). In the UK, the ministerial Foreword of the document guiding current government policy on this issue describes financial exclusion as 'those living on low incomes [who] cannot access mainstream financial products such as bank accounts and low cost loans' (HM Treasury 2004). This informs a three-pronged strategy where 'promoting financial inclusion' is seen to hinge upon creating greater 'access': 'access to banking services', 'access to affordable credit', and 'access to free face-to-face money advice'. Implementation is supported by the Financial Inclusion Fund, amounting to a £120 million commitment over three years, and the Financial Inclusion Taskforce, which is charged with managing and monitoring the process.

In the US, the exclusion created by financial infrastructure withdrawal from inner city areas from the early 1990s has been taken up by community reinvestment activists and advocacy groups. Described by Squires (2003) as 'an emerging social movement' (p. 3), community reinvestment advocates have 'used a variety of tools to pursue their objectives of increasing access to credit in underserved markets. These include public education, litigation, demonstrations, partnerships, and direct delivery of services, among others' (p. 7). The community reinvestment movement has its roots in the struggles of the late 1960s and 1970s to establish state and federal legislation outlawing redlining on the grounds of race—for instance, the Fair Housing Act of 1968, the Home Mortgage Disclosure Act of 1975, and the Community Reinvestment Act (CRA) of 1977—and the umbrella organization for the movement, set up in 1990, is the National Community Reinvestment Coalition.[1] The CRA has been a key focal point for subsequent activism. Extended to apply to S&Ls as well as banks in 1989, and revised again in 1995 and in recent years, the CRA includes provisions for the rating of financial institutions by Federal regulators on such measures as the distribution of loans by neighbourhood and borrower income characteristics, and the distribution of branches. Regulators are required to take ratings into account when institutions apply for permission to, for example, open a new branch or merge with another institution. Significantly for the community reinvestment movement, the CRA also makes provision for third parties to challenge such applications. Although very few challenges result in the denial of an application, they nonetheless tend to lead to delays and adverse publicity that are costly to financial institutions. As such, the 'challenge process provides leverage that several groups have used to negotiate reinvestment or CRA agreements' (Squires 2003: 11). CRA agreements worth in excess of $1 trillion have been established in all regions of the US which cover, for instance, increases in mortgage, home-improvement, and small-business lending to racial minorities and low income families; changes in mortgage underwriting standards for particular categories of borrower; new

---

[1] See http://www.ncrc.org/

branches in urban areas; and the establishment of joint implementation and monitoring committees (pp. 11–12).

By reducing financial inequalities to the issue of access, policy and activist discourses of financial exclusion give the impression that everyday borrowing has a clear and unambiguous inclusive inside, on the one hand, and an excluded outside, on the other. The manner in which networks of consumer credit and mortgage finance have come to embrace a growing number of individuals and households as 'insiders' in the last decade or so is to be celebrated. As HM Treasury (2004) observes in glowing terms, for example, 'the majority of households have seen a dramatic rise in the availability, flexibility and affordability of credit' (p. 28). At the same time, financial exclusion, like the broader discourse of 'social exclusion', demarcates a static, uncompetitive, and residual economic space occupied by those on low incomes which lays beyond ' "normal" society—normality being defined in terms of proximity to ideals of "global" economic participation and consumption' (Cameron and Palan 2004: 19). In an era of neo-liberal government, the socially excluded who 'cannot or will not overcome the inertia of the past, those who cannot come up to speed with either the global economy or the privatized state', are consigned 'to another realm: a place where the emergent norms . . . do not, or do not yet, apply' (p. 131). As such, the rubric of financial exclusion licences only a de-politicized and managerial politics of financial inequality, that is, programmes and initiatives in inner-city 'hot spots' that either promote inclusion in mainstream financial services, or which address the problems of those who remain consigned to so-called 'alternative' or 'informal' finance.

Everyday borrowing is indeed discriminatory, hierarchical, and marginalizing, but these inequalities increasingly cannot be addressed through the binary of inclusion/exclusion. For one thing, inequality and discrimination is now less a matter of access credit and abandonment, and more a matter of the differential interest rates that borrowers pay to lenders across both mainstream and alternative networks of borrowing. For example, while the community reinvestment movement under the provisions of the CRA contributed to partially holding back the tide of financial exclusion in US cities (Leyshon and Thrift 1995: 323; Tickell 2000: 240–1), even advocates such as Squires (2003) note that increased financial inclusion in US since the early 1990s is also a story of new lenders making high-interest markets in areas that were previously regarded as too risky and off-limits (pp. 5–6). Retaining the rubric of inclusion/exclusion makes it difficult to recognize these inequalities.

Consider, for example, the following somewhat confusing statement from Gary Dymski (2005b): 'Financial exclusion does not mean the absence of credit for a portion of the population: far from it. Those who are excluded need credit, are provided it and pay much more for it, than the financially included' (pp. 451–2). But, to go further, the dichotomous representation of the inequalities of everyday borrowing in terms of inclusion/exclusion actually contributes to the constitution of those inequalities. The new inequalities of price arise out of both the disjunctions between, and complex intersections and overlaps that bind, 'mainstream' and 'alternative' networks of everyday borrowing. The demarcation and diagramming of an abnormal and alternative space of financial exclusion actually makes possible the charging of relatively high rates of interest by lenders present in that realm, while the operations of the alternative and specialist lenders that occupy that space entail close connections with mainstream financial and capital market networks.

Taken together, 'door step' or home credit lenders, payday loan providers, cheque-cashing services, pawnbrokers, sale and buyback shops, mail order companies, and rent-to-own retailers are commonly described as comprising the 'alternative' or 'informal' sector. Such a representation gives the impression that this is some kind of local economic backwater that, so to speak, stands at the margins and caters for the marginalized. It would seem that it is, by definition, different from the mainstream, a distinct and quite specific realm. Two related implications follow. First, those 'risky' borrowers on a low income who are only able to access credit available from lenders in this sector will necessarily pay much higher rates of interest for a specialized service. Second, as the space of the excluded, the 'alternative' sector cannot thus be described through less respectable categories such as predatory, exorbitant, or usurious. It is something of a sad irony that the very representation of door step lenders, payday loan providers, and so on as the 'alternative' antithesis of the 'mainstream', as the realm of the financial excluded, actually contributes to the legitimation of high interest lending.

By way of example, door step lenders in the UK, such as Provident Financial, Cattles, and London Scottish Bank, provide small short-term cash loans of typically several hundred pounds to one in twenty (roughly 3 million) regular low-income borrowers (Collard and Kempson 2005). These borrowers meet their obligations through weekly cash payments made to agents visiting their homes, hence the terms 'door step' or 'home credit'. The high rates of interest paid by door step borrowers— usually well in excess of 100 per cent annual percentage rate (APR)—also marks them out from the mainstream. Current government initiatives to improve 'access to affordable credit' include the promotion of re-regulated credit unions and not-for-profit community finance institutions that lend at rates of interest well below those of door step lenders (HM Treasury 2004; see Chapter 9). As such, the relatively high rates of interest charged in these networks are recognized as a policy problem. Yet, door step lenders have successfully defended the interest rates that they charge in the face of government scrutiny and legal challenge by consumer groups. For instance, in June 2004, the National Consumer Council lodged a super-complaint with the Office of Fair Trading (OFT) on the home credit industry, claiming that there were limited incentives for lenders to compete on the interest rates that they charged to borrowers. The OFT forwarded the issue to the Competition Commission which has subsequently sought to improve transparency, but has rejected calls for interest ceilings.[2] The rates were justified on the grounds that the door step business is distinctive from the mainstream: customers are 'high risk'; their loans are short-term and reflect the demands of borrowers for this form of credit; and the door-to-door administration favoured by borrowers is also highly costly (Brooker and Whyley 2005).

While playing to its seeming disjunction and disconnection from main-stream lending, the materialization of high-interest alternative finance rests, at the same time, on interpenetration with mainstream and capital market networks. As Rob Aitken's (2006) notion of 'fringe finance' suggests, the discriminatory spaces and practices of alternative finance are interstitial, that is, neither completely inside nor outside of mainstream finance. Despite the small volumes of credit provided by door step lenders, payday loan shops, and so on, this remains 'big business' (Caskey 1994; Palmer with Conaty 2002). The major firms that operate in these rapidly expanding networks, such as Dollar Financial Group, First Cash Financial Services, and Provident Financial, are profitable multinational enterprises. Internet payday loan offerings in the US are offshore for regulatory and taxation purposes. In the UK, leading pawnbroker Cash Converters is an international franchise operation that began in Australia, and premier rent-to-own retailer BrightHouse is part of the Thorn Group Plc which is owned by Japanese investment bank Nomura Holdings. Furthermore, the door step lenders, payday loan providers, and cheque-cashing services of fringe finance also have close operating relationships with the major

[2] For details, see http://www.competition-commission.org.uk/inquiries/current/homecredit/index.htm

banks and their technical infrastructures (Aitken 2006). These include, for example, partnerships to evade state loan and interest rate restrictions in the US; the use of mainstream authorization, clearing, and payment systems by internet payday loan companies; and lines of credit and capital loans provided by the banks to the alternative lenders. In the UK, meanwhile, Fidelity International is the largest holder of share capital in Provident and Cattles. Indeed, it should be stressed that payday lending, the largest and fastest growing form of fringe finance, almost always requires that the borrower deposits a post-dated personal cheque as security for a loan. A personal cheque can, of course, only be written once the signatory is the holder of a mainstream account. As Aitken (2006) summarizes, 'Capital, as it is constituted through and at its fringes, operates not in a space wholly separate from its "others", but precisely across and under the lines that are said to separate it from those "other" worlds in the first place' (p. 493).

Sub-Prime Time

It would seem to be the case, then, that the dichotomous representation of a separate and abnormal space of financial exclusion is constitutive in the charging of the high rates of interest that prevail in that realm, and that the operations of alternative lenders are made possible precisely by close interconnections with mainstream financial market institutions and networks. In the remainder of the chapter, I want to explore this line of argument in detail with reference to the rise of sub-prime finance in general, and sub-prime mortgage networks in particular. As a category, 'sub-prime' applies to relations and obligations present across all manner of everyday borrowing networks. Although specialist sub-prime lenders are almost always niche non-banks, they are often subsidiaries of mainstream financial firms or, as with Fairlane Credit of Ford Motor Credit Co., for example, dedicated operations within the finance arms of major conglomerates. Sub-prime may also relate to the use to which a borrower intends to put the credit that they obtain. For example, a loan on a car over five years old, or a mortgage on a home constructed from irregular materials, may be deemed 'sub-prime'. That said, it is the assessment of the characteristics of a borrower's economic and financial life that will most likely determine whether or not their borrowings are deemed to fall within the category of sub-prime. Sub-prime borrowers include those with a low, irregular, and/or unverifiable income—such as workers on temporary employment contracts or the self-employed—and those with poor credit histories and scores that result, for instance, from no previous borrowing record, past failures to meet borrowing obligations, or bankruptcy.

While including automobile loans (Schiffin 1996), credit cards (Carey 1996; *The Economist* 2005*a*), and, increasingly, debt consolidation loans that are typically secured against the home (Moss 2004), sub-prime borrowing has become highly significant in Anglo-American mortgage networks in general, and US mortgage networks in particular. Mortgage networks have a distinctive feature that makes them particularly amenable to the 'risky business' of sub-prime lending: all loans are secured against the home as an asset or collateral. Added to this, there is also the possibility that those assets may increase sharply in value, a possibility that is certainly not present when a sub-prime car loan is secured against an aging vehicle that is depreciating in value, for example. Between 1994 and 2003, the rate of growth in the total value of US sub-prime mortgage originations—an average of 25 per cent per annum—far outpaced the rate of growth in prime mortgage lending. In 2003, originations of sub-prime mortgages reached $330 billion, up from only $35 billion a decade earlier. This increase in sub-prime mortgage lending ensured that it came to account for just less than 10 per cent of total US mortgage lending in 2003 (Kirchhoff and Block 2004). The rate of increase in sub-prime mortgages accelerated again from 2003 through 2006, with new originations in 2006 standing at somewhere between $605 billion and $625 billion (*The Economist* 2006*c*, 2007*b*). Such was the scale of these new originations that sub-prime came to account for between one-fifth and one-quarter of all new mortgage originations in the US in 2006. Add to this so-called 'Alt-A' mortgages—that is, 'near-prime' mortgages based on little or no documentation as proof of income, or mortgages with high loan-to-value ratios—and this figure climbs to 40 per cent (*The Economist* 2007*c*). At the same time, previous state-insured support for low-income and minority borrowers waned. The FHA insured 19 per cent of all mortgages originated by banks in 2000, but only 5 per cent in 2005 (Bajaj and Nixon 2006*b*). Homeownership in the US reached 64 per cent of the adult population in 1970, and did not rise any higher until after the explosion of sub-prime mortgage finance from 1994. By 2004, the homeownership rate in the US reached 69 per cent (Samuels 2007).

While roughly half of mainstream mortgages in the US are new originations for purchases, this share falls to around a quarter in sub-prime networks where the majority of originations refinance existing obligations.

In the parlance of practitioners, the 'churn rate'—that is, the regularity with which borrowers remortgage—is considerably higher in sub-prime networks. A sub-prime mortgage is much more likely to be what is known in popular parlance as a 'refi'. Key sub-prime mortgage lenders such as Ameriquest, New Century Mortgage, and National City grew from the mid-1990s to become important financial market institutions in their own right. Indeed, such was their growth (and profits) that major banks sought to gain a foothold in sub-prime mortgage networks. High profile acquisitions included, for example, Citigroup's purchase of Associated First Capital in 2000, and HSBC's 2003 takeover of Household International which, at the time, was the leading sub-prime mortgage provider in the US. Lenders in US sub-prime mortgage networks have close working relationships with the realtors, appraisers, and brokers who are based in the inner-city areas where the majority of sub-prime borrowers, often African Americans and Hispanics, make their homes. The arrangement fees and commission payments made to brokers in particular ensure that they are, in effect, sub-contracted arms of the principal lenders.

Although sub-prime mortgage networks in the UK remain somewhat limited by comparison with the US, they are a similarly growing and increasingly important feature of mortgage finance (Munro et al. 2005). Roughly one-quarter of UK borrowers are unable to access mainstream mortgage finance. Specialist lenders—such as Paragon, Kensington Mortgage Company, and Southern Pacific Mortgages—and subsidiaries of banks, building societies, and major US conglomerates—such as Abbey National's HMC, Britannia's Verso, HBOS's Birmingham Midshires, Bradford and Bingley's Mortgage Express, Citigroup's Future Mortgages, GE Capital's iGroup, and GMAC RFC—target these borrowers. As with the US, what Munro et al. (2005) term 'the public face of the industry' tends to be the independent or tied brokers who receive commission fees from lenders (p. 26). The overall value of sub-prime mortgages in the UK is difficult to determine, as the Council of Mortgage Lenders do not separate-out sub-prime in their figures for the industry. Nevertheless, according to Burton et al. (2004), the value of new sub-prime mortgage lending grew by 20 per cent in 1999 alone, and is currently the equivalent of between 5 and 10 per cent of the total UK mortgage market.

So, how are high-interest sub-prime networks constituted? It would be easy to overlook the manner in which the category of 'sub-prime' is itself significant: it demarcates a realm of financial practice that will witness the charging and payment of 'non-standard' rates of interest and relatively high arrangement fees because borrowers' are deemed to be 'risky' and their credit histories and circumstances will often require special attention. Once demarcated, the seeming logic of sub-prime becomes hard to question. For example, while Munro et al. (2005) are concerned by the ways in which sub-prime mortgage lenders may exploit 'vulnerable consumers', for them 'it is clearly fair to charge a higher interest rate to reflect the higher risks of default among such borrowers' (p. 2). At the same time, as Wyly et al. (2006) show, the apparent 'inclusion' experienced by sub-prime mortgagors, especially by comparison with the marginalization of individuals and households in inner-city areas during the 1950s and 1960s, limits the scope for critical questioning of the rates of interest that they pay. As they summarize: 'if unfair denial and exclusion was so bad, many people ask, what is wrong with lenders eager to make loans to all, including those with bad credit?' (p. 108). This is especially the case in sub-prime mortgage networks, where deeply engrained assumptions about the individual and collective benefits of home-ownership for all (see Chapter 8), reinforced through policy initiatives to promote these benefits to those on low incomes (Munro et al. 2005: 6; Shlay 2006), tend to further undermine questions of affordability. In sub-prime mortgage networks, the interest rates paid by borrowers are usually at least 3 per cent over those that prevail in prime mortgage networks and are often much higher.

Also significant to the constitution of sub-prime is the manner in which the category rests on an apparent disjunction and disconnection from the 'excluded' space and practices of 'alternative' finance. Burton et al. (2004) draw our attention to many of the differences between sub-prime and alternative finance. For instance, sub-prime finance can include very sizeable loans to fund, for example, a house purchase, whereas door step lenders, payday loan providers, and cheque-cashing services provide short-term forms of credit in small amounts. Sub-prime finance is directly marketed through telesales and internet, tabloid newspaper, and targeted television advertisements. It tends to be delivered in an electronic and highly automated manner through on-line applications and call centre networks. In contrast, the marketing of alternative finance is limited, and assessments of creditworthiness and mechanisms of delivery are labour intensive and face-to-face. But, I would argue that in terms of the inequalities produced in and across these realms, their differentiation is also itself significant. The choice of the prefix 'sub' implies a secondary category within the mainstream. Immediately, then, sub-prime lending and its borrowers are demarcated from what might be called 'non-prime'. And, as such, it becomes logical and reasonable to expect that the rates of interest that are paid by sub-prime borrowers will be both higher than those paid by prime borrowers, and lower than those paid by those who are consigned to the world of alternative finance. In short, the hierarchical naming of realms of finance and their borrowers itself contributes to the materialization of distinct networks and the manufacture of inequalities in the price of credit.

While emerging out of their discursive differentiation, sub-prime networks and the rates of interest payable by sub-prime borrowers are nonetheless primarily and scientifically constituted through calculative technologies and performances that have also made possible the current boom in mainstream everyday borrowing. Consider, for example, the following quote from the cover story of *The Banker* magazine in August 2001:

Mortgage banks everywhere hear the news: ex-bankrupt businesspeople, struggling divorcees, freelancers and the self-employed are your best customers not your worst. Stop trying to lend at low margin to accountants, lawyers and civil servants who are reliable but earn the bank peanuts. Instead, find the customers who used to be turned away; by using modern techniques, in credit scoring and securitization, they can be transformed into profitable business. (Kochan 2001: 3)

The differentiation of the category of sub-prime borrowers is one thing, but lenders capacity to 'find' and 'transform' those customers requires the adaptation, development, and innovation of 'modern techniques'— or what we call calculative technologies of risk—in sub-prime networks.

Risk-Based Pricing

After the apparent initial success of credit reporting and scoring in credit card networks, the widespread performance of these techniques across a wide range of everyday borrowing networks during the late 1980s and early 1990s supported the profiling of low-risk borrowers who were 'cherry picked' by lenders. But, in concentrating their attention on these borrowers, mainstream lenders, in effect, sorted but neglected a particular category of borrower or 'market space' that became the focus for others (Burton et al. 2004: 13). This is a significant 'market space'. For example, in US mortgage networks, borrowers with a FICO score above a threshold of 620 (up to a maximum of 850) are deemed prime, leaving around 20 per cent of the individuals in the US that are being monitored and measured by the credit report and scoring companies as 'sub-prime' (Chinloy and MacDonald 2004: 153). In US credit card networks, meanwhile, the threshold is slightly higher at 670 (Carey 1996), creating an even larger sub-prime market space.

The targeting of borrowers who are deemed 'risky' under the techniques of credit reporting and scoring by sub-prime lenders has also materialized through a strategic marketing discourse. While banks and financial services organizations were relatively slow to adopt marketing strategies in comparison with other sectors of the economy, they were nonetheless transformed into 'customer-orientated' organizations during the 1980s (Burton 1994; Morgan and Sturdy 2000). As a purported academic profession, marketing proceeds from the claim that the 'needs' of consumers can be established and known. It follows that this knowledge is pivotal to an organization's 'marketing strategy', that is, the tailoring of products to the needs of consumers. Consumers' disparate needs are statistically analysed and categorized, leading to the manufacture of 'market segments' for particular products (Morgan and Sturdy 2000: 163–4). For mainstream lenders, as Gary Dymski (2005*b*) summarizes, 'The search for financial customers then is quite different than in even the recent past', as 'thick sets of somewhat heterogeneous borrowers and depositors in well-defined geographic markets' are replaced by 'thin sets of well-defined and homogeneous borrowers and depositors, in shifting sets of geographic markets' (p. 449). In sub-prime networks, meanwhile, the combination of credit scoring techniques and marketing strategy leads not only to the targeting of a 'thin' sub-prime market segment, but also to the sorting, stratification, and mining of that market segment into a series of more closely defined 'thin sets'. As Burton et al. (2004) suggest, although credit scoring calculations are, to a large extent, separated from marketing and sales strategies, credit bureaux information is nevertheless central to the so-called 'prospect databases' and 'forensic marketing' that are used in sub-prime finance (p. 12). Credit reports and scores are, in effect, 'being used not just to minimize the chance of customers defaulting on a loan but in terms of assessing how the firm can maximize the profit it can make from that customer' (p. 14).

Making and maximizing profits in sub-prime lending has, therefore, come to turn on so-called 'risk-based pricing'. Risk-based pricing was first established among home and car insurance providers during the mid-1980s, whereby potential policy-holders deemed to be 'high risk', either as a consequence of living in certain postcode areas or a 'bad' record of previous claims, were required to pay substantially greater premiums than those deemed 'low risk'. In sub-prime borrowing networks, the techniques of credit reporting and scoring, market segmentation databases, and default risk management come together to make possible the categorization of borrowers according to the likelihood of their default, and the charging of graduated rates of interest based on these categorizations (Leyshon and Thrift 1999). Both prime and sub-prime lenders are confronted by differential uncertainties as to whether borrowers will meet their future repayment obligations. But, sub-prime lenders in networks of everyday borrowing have led the way in the attempt to pre-emptively fold those future uncertainties into the present. Honed in sub-prime networks, risk-based pricing has subsequently taken hold in mainstream or 'prime' consumer credit and mortgage finance. For example, in the UK, the major banks attracted considerable attention from consumer organizations and the popular media in 2006 after they stopped quoting typical APRs in their advertising of branch-based loans (Gilmore 2006). Under the Consumer Credit Act of 2004, a typical APR that features in an advertisement for a particular loan, credit card, and so on must be charged to a minimum of 66 per cent of borrowers. The move away from advertising typical APRs was framed by the banks as necessary given the development of what they termed 'personal pricing'.

In risk-based pricing, both the future and the past meet in the stratified risk calculations and pricing decisions that are made in the present, as probabilities for default for different categories of borrower are determined on the basis of inference from statistics on past credit records. This includes the use of the 'artificial intelligence' and 'modelling' through rules of association in order to identify, for instance, patterns of 'good payment behaviour' by particular borrowers that inhabit seemingly high-risk categories (Carey 1996: 14). Risk-based pricing is, furthermore, not simply a one-off calculation (Burton et al. 2004: 6–7). Should an existing borrower fail to regularly keep up with their repayments, they are deemed more risky by the lender and are sanctioned through the ratcheting-up of the interest rate that they pay. Some sub-prime lenders may also progressively lower rates as borrowers successfully meet their obligations. Ultimately, and in theory at least, 'The higher interest rates (and higher fees) charged . . . insure that loans . . . will remain profitable even if a fairly high default rate is realized' (Dymski 2005b: 450).

A simple illustration of risk-based pricing in sub-prime networks is provided by the range of Visa credit cards offered in the UK by Vanquis Bank, an arm of Provident Financial.[3] These include the 'Abacus Card' for those who are 'new to credit' or have had 'credit problems in the past', and

[3] http://www.vanquis.co.uk/home/home.aspx?ref=GO_AT&affid=vanquisbank

the 'Blue Card' targeted at those who 'need to rebuild their credit rating'. Each card has a different 'typical APR'—39.9 per cent for the Abacus Card, and 29.9 per cent for the Blue Card—revealing that individual cardholders within each of these two categories will be paying graduated rates of interest according to, for example, the extent of their 'credit problems in the past'. In sub-prime mortgage networks, meanwhile, risk-based pricing becomes part of the origination process. US mortgage networks, for instance, witnessed the adoption of automated underwriting software systems during the 1990s. These are systems that are based on standards produced by Freddie Mac and Fannie Mae, have resulted in much faster loan decisions, and have enshrined the importance of credit scores, segmentation, and risk-based pricing into the origination process (Gotham 2006: 251; Stuart 2003: 124–8). Confronted by a potential sub-prime mortgagor, automated underwriting systems thus provide two routes by which a loan could be originated. First, in both the US and UK, mortgage underwriters are afforded 'discretion' to take account of 'extenuating circumstances' that may have led to a past 'credit event' (Stuart 2003: 97–8). This could include, for instance, a failure to meet obligations arising from borrowing on a credit card, and the underwriter may assemble supporting paperwork that demonstrates an 'individual's current ability and willingness to repay' (Munro et al. 2005: 17). Should an underwriter 'manually override the score' (Stuart 2003: 130), a key consideration may be whether or not a potential sub-prime mortgagor's credit position is 'improving' or 'deteriorating' at the point of application. Second, eschewing manual underwriting and the assembly of additional paperwork, originators can utilize the multiple risk/interest rate categories for borrowers present in underwriting systems (Stuart 2003: 130). In short, risk-based pricing creates a range of graduated categories of borrower which can be deployed in the name of 'personal pricing'.

It is important to note that in the materialization of sub-prime networks, the calculative edifice of risk-based pricing has also served to de-politicize the inequalities between prime and sub-prime borrowers in terms of interest rates charged (e.g. Crews Cutts and Van Order 2003). The technical and scientific justification of the relatively high rates of interest paid by sub-prime borrowers is significant in several respects. It is common for proponents to suggest, for example, that, without such techniques, credit would not be available to many of those that demand it. As a representative of Barclaycard told the UK House of Commons Treasury Select Committee (2003) inquiry into credit card interest charges, risk-based pricing means that they can 'offer cards to people who would not be offered them under a system where there was only one rate' (on p. 27). The apparent objectivity of risk-based pricing is also an important defence against the accusation that the rates of interest paid by sub-prime borrowers arise from discriminatory lending on the grounds of race, class, and (inner city) location (Warren and Warren Tyagi 2004: 135–7; Wyly et al. 2006). Such accusations could provide the basis for a legal challenge in the US, for instance, where the Equal Credit Opportunities Act of 1976 outlaws such discrimination. While it is clear that the typical US sub-prime mortgagor, for example, is indeed an African American living in a deprived urban neighbourhood, the relatively high rates of interest paid by these borrowers become, from the perspective of risk-based pricing, the outcome of impartial and detached economic calculation as opposed to prejudice.

Sub-Prime and the Capital Markets

The rise of sub-prime mortgage networks, especially in the US, is widely recognized to have produced changes in urban housing landscapes as owner-occupation has advanced. For example, for Wyly et al. (2006), areas of 'dilapidated inner-city housing' are witnessing processes whereby the payment of rents to local landlords is being replaced by mortgage repayments to 'a national sub-prime lender who gets investment capital from Wall Street and the global financial markets' (p. 109). For these writers, such processes are viewed as a consequence of the power and reach of finance capital becoming extended, for the first time, into areas of inner-city housing. This interpretation pays very little attention, however, to the place of the technologies of securitization and structured finance in the constitution of sub-prime mortgage networks, networks that are big, long, and closely interconnected with the networks of the capital markets. As I suggested more broadly in the previous chapter, the re-articulation of default risk calculations and management—principally through the technologies of asset-backed securitization and structured finance that hinge on the issue and trading of default risk-related instruments—has been highly significant in the materialization of a boom in everyday borrowing that is funded through the capital markets. In this part of this chapter, then, I want to focus on the constitutive importance of these technologies in the rise of sub-prime finance and the inequalities produced through and across its networks. Specifically, I want to suggest that the significance of ABS and structured finance is magnified in sub-prime networks in four main ways.

First, specialist sub-prime lenders are almost exclusively non-banks or 'centralized lenders' who, in contrast with the banks, S&Ls, and building societies, do not hold a stock of savings capital on their balance sheets as liabilities. Sub-prime lenders typically enjoy large short-term lines of credit provided by their bankers who may also be their parent company. This provides operating capital for the initial making of loans, mortgages, and so on. Sub-prime lenders are also usually 'small cap' public corporations, or owned in partnership by banks and all manner of institutional investors (Bajaj and Haughney 2007). Although diverse in terms of ownership and sources of investment capital, then, sub-prime institutions are nonetheless reliant upon the techniques of securitization for the continuous expansion of their loans book, that is, for 'asset growth'.

Unlike banks who may be able to match increasing assets against increasing liabilities on their balance sheets, sub-prime lenders must move assets 'off-balance sheet'. Key in this regard are lenders' securitization programmes that 'bundle' the future obligations of borrowers as the basis for payments of interest and principal on the bonds that are issued. In the parlance of sub-prime practitioners, under this 'originate and distribute model' the balance sheet is not 'weakened' by the growth of risky assets. Investors in sub-prime ABS receive, of course, a premium over and above the interest that is payable on 'conforming' or 'prime' ABS, with the extent of this premium measured in terms of 'spreads' against prevailing prices for 'risk free' government bonds. While the extent to which borrowers' future obligations are securitized has increased across all networks of everyday borrowing in the last couple of decades, sub-prime has been an important factor in these developments. In US mortgage networks in 2006, for example, around three-quarters of all mortgages were securitized, up from approximately half at the end of the twentieth century (Stuart 2003: 22; *The Economist* 2007c). This growth can in large part be traced to the greater prominence of sub-prime lenders and borrowers within mortgage networks.

Second, the calculative tools of credit rating that are evidently utilized in an expert and objective manner by the principal agencies— Moodys, S&P, and Fitch—are particularly significant in securitized sub-prime lending. Given the 'risky assets' that are securitized, the calculative judgements of the credit rating agencies are especially germane to the authorization of the resulting bonds. Put differently, while the allocation of a simple letter rating to all ABS reduces investment research costs and creates apparent transparency and comparability for investors, it also brings a degree of standardization and certainty that would otherwise be lacking in the risk/reward characteristics of sub-prime ABS. Indeed, sub-prime lending is sometimes known in the US as 'B-and-C lending'. This refers to the ratings that are usually given to sub-prime ABS, and immediately differentiates these bonds from the AAA-rated bonds that are backed by prime mortgages, for example. The ratings given to sub-prime ABS provide an 'at a glance' indication of the 'quality' of the borrowers who are pooled as the basis for a bond. For example, although the majority of sub-prime MBS are rated B and C, ratings given to these bonds range from AAA-minus for a near-prime pool of borrowers who have a FICO score of between 580 and 620, to E for a pool of borrowers who have been bankrupt in the last twelve months. Investors confidence in the uniformity of the calculations that link the pools of borrowers underlying sub-prime MBS and the rating it receives is also furthered by the underwriting standards, provided by Freddie Mac and Fannie Mae, which lenders tend to follow (Stuart 2003: 22). The categorization of borrowers during the origination process, in terms of credit score, verification of income and so on, is explicitly linked to their aggregation into the pools that back rated securities.

Third, while structured finance techniques have become increasingly prominent across all networks of everyday borrowing over the last decade, the capacity to slice and dice a sub-prime ABS issue into a wide-range of CDOs with differing risk/reward characteristics is especially important. Robin Blackburn (2006b) provides a simple hypothetical example of a sub-prime ABS issue structured into ten tranches. The bottom and most risky tranche represents the first tenth of borrowers who default on their obligations, and holders of these CDOs are the last to be paid when the underlying interest payments are made; the next tranche represents the second tenth of defaulters; and so on up to the top tranche (p. 44). Structured finance makes it possible, then, to disperse particular risks across different CDOs into 'digestible chunks' and, at the same time, to concentrate risk in others (*The Economist* 2007d). As such, a sub-prime ABS issue can be made attractive to investors with contrasting 'risk appetites' and 'risk tolerances'. It is even possible to derive what are known as 'investment grade' CDOs, rated BBB and above, from a sub-prime asset portfolio. It also becomes possible to derive and demarcate what is known as the 'residual' or 'first-loss-' or 'equity-tranche'. This may be held by sub-prime lenders themselves, their parent banks, or by investors who may have an option to force the issuer to buy it back should so-called 'early payment default' problems develop with the underlying repayments. The investment bank that underwrites a sub-prime ABS programme may hold the residual, although, as Blackburn (2006*b*) emphasizes, the focus of the investment banks tends to be the top or middle tranches which 'will be far more secure yet will pay a good return' (p. 45). As the institutions that organize and market securitization and structured finance programmes, investment banks have first option when it comes to buying the bonds and CDOs that are produced.

Fourth, and again related to the risky nature of the assets that are securitized and structured, the importance of the derivative techniques of credit default swaps is amplified in sub-prime networks. There is, in short, little need for CDS contracts related to triple-A rated MBS. In simple terms, a CDS is an agreement whereby one party makes a series of payments to another in return for compensation in the event of a specified default or 'credit event'. Investors in sub-prime bonds may use CDS to insure themselves against defaults but, given the potential volatility of sub-prime bonds, CDS are also the focus for trading by hedge funds and others who bet on defaults without owning the bonds themselves. It is possible, for instance, for a hedge fund to 'short' sub-prime bonds through CDS, that is, to bet that the prices of a particular group of bonds will fall and to reap rewards from that fall (Anderson 2007). ABX Home Equity indexes make reference to baskets of CDS on tranches of bonds backed by sub-prime mortgages, and are differentiated in terms of both the bonds' ratings and their date of origination. So, for example, the ABX.HE 07-1 BBB minus index comprises credit default swaps referencing 20 US sub-prime MBS rated BBB minus issued in January 2007. The indexes thus provide the basis for calculations that cost the insuring of bonds against losses.

Concluding Remarks

In posing a series of critical questions about 'the democratization of finance' at the outset of this book, one of our concerns lay with the inequalities that have prevailed as unprecedented relationships have been forged between Anglo-American everyday financial routines and the capital markets. In terms of everyday borrowing, we are confronted with an apparent paradox. On the one hand, the boom in everyday borrowing is an expansion in both the scale and scope of credit relations. Some kind of 'democratizing' process of 'inclusion' would appear to be at work, whereby lengthened and highly connected networks have come to embrace borrowers who are far from middle-class in terms of income, residency, and so on. On the other hand, however, this 'democratization' is hollow and hierarchical as recently included borrowers, as well as those who are marginalized by prime and sub-prime lenders, pay significantly higher rates of interest on mortgages, loans, and revolving credit. As this chapter has shown, once we reject the dichotomy of inclusion/exclusion as a category of understanding, and instead ask how inequalities are produced within and across more-or-less discrete networks, it becomes clear that inequalities are an inherent feature of contemporary everyday borrowing.

Throughout the chapter, I have stressed two principal features that mark the production of what Newman and Wyly (2004) so aptly describe as 'exploitative greenlining'. First, the demarcation and differentiation of anomalous, specialist, and excluded spaces of finance populated by low-income, high-risk, and sub-prime borrowers actually contribute to the charging of relatively high rates of interest by lenders present in those realms. The recent decision in the UK not to impose interest rate ceilings on door stop lending is broadly mirrored, for example, by debates in the US on sub-prime mortgage lending which suggest that risk-based pricing is not discriminatory. Second, high-interest networks of everyday borrowing are not separate from mainstream financial and capital market networks, but are interstitial in nature. Sub-prime networks have been shown, for example, to have materialized through the development and application of the calculative techniques credit scoring, asset-backed securitization, and structured finance that, initially at least, were the preserve of mainstream or 'prime' market networks. In terms of the techniques and performances of lenders, then, there is clearly a sense in which there is little that is distinctive about booming networks of everyday borrowing, whether they be 'mainstream' and 'alternative', 'formal' and 'informal', or 'prime' and 'sub-prime'. It is also the case that the constitution of booming networks of everyday borrowing where sharp inequalities prevail is not limited to the techniques and performances of lenders. The transformation and boom in everyday borrowing are also embodied processes, and it is to these processes that we now turn.

8

The Uncertain Subjects
of Everyday Borrowing

Introduction: 'Cavalier Debtors'

When announcing the financial results of UK bank Lloyds TSB for the
first six months of 2006, Chief Executive Eric Daniels launched an attack
on what he called 'cavalier debtors' (Ringshaw 2006). Bad debts had
increased by 20 per cent at Lloyds during this short period, and now
totalled £800 million. £632 million of the £800 million arose from
retail borrowers reneging on their obligations to the bank. The results
for retail lending by other leading UK banks during this period told a
similar story. HSBC's bad debts surged by 36 per cent to £365 million,
and HBOS reported a 26 per cent increase to £592 million. At Barclays,
meanwhile, the retail banking division's bad debt was up 42 per cent to
£198 million, and Barclaycard's 11 million customers produced a similarly
sharp rise in bad debts, up by 37 per cent to £696 million (Davey 2006).
It was, however, Daniels' decision to speak out and reprimand Lloyd's
customers which provoked considerable attention from the financial and
popular media. Company chief executives don't tend to openly blame
their customers for poor financial results. But, coming in the same week
as the Bank of England's Monetary Policy Committee (MPC) decided to
raise interest rates by 0.25 per cent to 4.75 per cent, the first rise in
over two years, Daniel's words also seemed to capture a broader current of fear that everyday borrowers had indeed over-extended themselves. For example, writing in *The Times*, Miles Costello (2006) warned
that 2006 would see a record number of 100,000 personal insolvencies,
'meaning someone is entering formal insolvency every minute of the
working day'.

Daniel's comments about 'cavalier debtors' remind us that the contemporary transformation and boom in Anglo-American everyday borrowing are embodied processes. As I will argue in this chapter, the ever-greater outstanding financial obligations of a majority of individuals and households, created primarily through mortgage and consumer credit networks, entail the disciplinary summoning up of the subject of the responsible and entrepreneurial borrower. A failure to meet outstanding obligations is to be 'cavalier', casual, careless, irrational, and irresponsible. Even when critical attention comes to focus on the practices of lenders, for example, neo-liberal policy recommendations tend to concentrate upon the rationality of responsible borrowers as 'consumers'. For the House of Commons Treasury Select Committee (2003), then, 'certain sections' of the UK credit card industry 'are currently engaged in practices which can give rise to some consumers "sleep walking into a situation of over commitment" where a small change in circumstances can turn manageable debt problems into disasters' (p. 37). The 'practices' to which they refer include the automatic and unsolicited increase of credit limits, offering teaser rates, and reducing minimum monthly payments, and the "sleep walking..." quote is taken from a submission to the Committee by a representative of Citizens Advice. Yet, the Committee focus their recommendations, and those of a follow-up report (House of Commons Treasury Select Committee 2005), on the transparency of pricing structures and marketing methods. They demand action from the OFT and the Department of Trade and Industry (DTI) to protect the consumers of credit. Calls for standardized and transparent information from lenders on interest rates are made, for instance, because it will ensure that borrowers can make rational and informed consumption decisions.

I have already suggested in Chapters 1 and 4 that a feature of the everyday life of global finance is the assembly of neo-liberal financial subjectivities, of entrepreneurial subjects who routinely perform changed forms of financial self-discipline. Focusing on the embodiment of transformations in everyday saving and the making of investor subjects in pension and mutual fund networks, Chapter 4 argued that prudence, insurance, and thrift are being displaced by the embracing of the risks/rewards of the financial markets through investment as a calculative technology of the self. I also stressed the contingency, contradictions, and ambiguities present in these processes of identification. Now, there are, of course, important differences between the subjects of everyday saving and borrowing. For example, in contrast with the situation that prevails for investor subjects, very few mortgagors or credit card holders are aware of the networked relationships that have come to bind their borrowing performances with the capital markets. Nevertheless, in what follows, I want to further explore the summoning up of neo-liberal entrepreneurial financial subjectivities. I will round-out and develop the argument that thrifty and prudent forms of financial self-discipline are being supplanted. As Eric Daniels' comments about 'cavalier debtors' illustrate, it is not the case that the boom in everyday borrowing is made possible by the assembly of subjects who abandon financial self-discipline in favour of consumptive freedoms. This is not a move from thrift to spendthrift. Rather, prudence and thrift are displaced by new moral and calculative self-disciplines of responsibly and entrepreneurially meeting, managing, and manipulating the outstanding obligations that arise from extended borrowing.

The summoning up of a self-disciplined borrower as a consumer who is at once both responsible and entrepreneurial can be seen, for example, in the embedding of credit reporting and scoring techniques across networks of everyday borrowing. As part of the apparently increased control over the uncertainties of default risk that these devices produce for lenders, 'irresponsible' borrowers who fail to meet their outstanding obligations are punished not only by legal enforcement mechanisms but also through worsened credit scores and higher rates of interest. A responsible borrower who holds a good credit report will, in contrast, be offered relatively lower rates of interest. In the US, the Federal Trade Commission (2006) has recently amended the Fair Credit Reporting Act in order to create greater transparency with regard to an individual's credit report and score. But, a credit score is not simply something to be discovered by individuals. It is also the focus for self-disciplinary entrepreneurialism. For example, on both sides of the Atlantic, as the main credit agencies such as Equifax, Experian, and Fair Isaac Corporation offer individuals the opportunity to purchase access to their credit histories/scores, they also provide tips and guidelines on how to improve a credit score. For example, Equifax encourages individuals to 'level the playing field' with potential lenders by purchasing what they call 'Score Power', an individualized package of report and tools for management that feature the 'Interactive Score Simulator' to show how certain actions may change a credit score.[1] Such simulators are also being used by credit counselling agencies as an educational tool (Bayot 2003). Similarly, for those borrowers who find that their

---

[1] https://www.econsumer.equifax.com/consumer/sitepage.ehtml?forward=cps_detail&pageMod=prodMod

credit report/score is an obstacle to securing access to credit at reasonable rates of interest, the burgeoning array of 'personal finance' literature now available in book stores also includes publications such as Rose's (1997) *The DIY Credit Repair Manual*. Websites have even emerged for companies that offer to improve individual's credit scores by 'piggybacking' them on the credit cards of those who have good scores—that is, their names are added to the credit card account for a fee.

Although the embodiment of the transformation and boom in everyday borrowing extends across networks of borrowing, then, the precise form taken by the responsible and entrepreneurial borrower also varies somewhat within different networks of borrowing which are constituted through more-or-less discrete calculative technologies and performances. As such, the first part of the chapter focuses on the responsible borrowers of contemporary credit card networks, a subject position that we will call the 'revolver'. Revolvers not only regularly make use of the revolving credit facilities, but also manipulate their outstanding balances in order to further their consumptive freedom and security into the future. Revolvers may also express and communicate their freedom, aspirations, and individuality through the consumption of credit cards themselves. The second part of the chapter concentrates on the responsible and entrepreneurial borrower of contemporary Anglo-American mortgage networks. Here I will suggest that mortgagors are no longer what Grey (1997) calls 'suburban subjects', that is, owner-occupiers who view their home as essential in meeting their aspirations. Rather, the borrowing boom in mortgage networks rests on the assembly of mortgagors as what we will call 'leveraged investors'. Leveraged investors are owner-occupiers who view residential property as an asset that will grow to realize returns. Not only do these returns appear as essential for freedom and security in the future, but they require the disciplines of responsible and extended borrowing in the present. In the third and final part of the chapter, we move to consider the tensions and contradictions that are present in the assembly of responsible and entrepreneurial borrowers, and thereby reveal the incomplete and precarious performance of these subjectivities. Rising stock markets and house prices in the last decade or so have ensured that, for the most part, the contradictions that would otherwise interrupt these processes of identification are yet to surface widely. It is precisely those on low wages, who are also likely to be tenants and not leveraged investors, who are at present struggling to perform new forms of financial self-discipline. In short, the subjects of the transformation and boom in everyday borrowing are necessarily uncertain subjects.

Revolvers: Calculative and Communicative

Reading the Foucauldian literature on (neo)liberal governmentality, responsible borrowers can be viewed as not simply dominated or manipulated, but as aspirational and intentional consumer subjects called up and mobilized in a specific moral, political, and technological context (Miller and Rose 1997). The making of responsible borrowers plays on central features of liberal subjectivity, namely freedom and security. As de Goede (2005b) argues, while nineteenth-century legislation abolished previous legal statutes that punished debtors through imprisonment, it nonetheless firmly assigned responsibility for credit relations to borrowers and rearticulated the logic that determines that the borrower who does not meet their outstanding obligations will suffer a curtailment of their freedom. As such, in de Geode's terms, 'a strict regime of guilt and punishment still underlies modern debtor–creditor power relations' (p. 157). The individual who, for example, declares themselves bankrupt and is legally excused their credit obligations suffers not only moral condemnation, but also finds that their access to credit and thus their material well-being, freedom, and security, is taken away. Furthermore, as the performance of multiple and multifaceted financial subject positions becomes a moral code across a range of networks of everyday saving and borrowing in the neo-liberal era, so prudent responsibility in meeting outstanding obligations is joined by the entrepreneurial management and manipulation of those obligations. To borrow a phrase from James Scurlock (2007), individuals have become 'debt surfers' who perform new self-disciplines to 'ride larger and larger waves of debt without wiping out' (p. 2). In credit card networks, the self-disciplined subject of the responsible and entrepreneurial borrower is assembled, specifically, as what we will call the 'revolver'.

The calculative technologies of revolving credit call up revolvers who both extend their credit card borrowing, and tend not to meet their outstanding obligations in full at the end of each month. Roughly two-thirds of Americans regularly make use of revolving credit facilities and, in effect, begin to perform the subject position of the revolver (cf. Ritzer 1995: 34). The outstanding obligations of US revolvers average out at around $13,000 each (Moss 2004). Given that it is these revolving balances that are the key to profitability for card issuers, recent innovations such as cash-back reward cards are an explicit attempt to concentrate those balances on a single card. The 'average' American in 1999 had eleven credit cards, up from seven in 1989 (Clayton 2000: 90). Representations of the revolver clearly play on the relationship between money and freedom noted by Simmel (1990) and others, such that consumer credit appears as 'a source of freedom from the bondage of the need to earn and save before purchase becomes possible' (Shaoul 1997: 81). It follows that the holder of a large number of credit cards with sizeable revolving credit limits on each feels particularly liberated. The revolver has, then, an important other, a subject for whom the inability to access credit results in a serious curtailment of freedom.

The technologies of credit reporting and scoring and authorization and payment ensure that a successful revolver is a responsible borrower. Revolvers must necessarily make at least minimum repayments on their outstanding obligations at the end of each month. Such regular payment of obligations, in the context of fluctuating patterns of income and expenditure, comes to be normalized. Making these payments is likely to result in the further extension of a line of credit, and a good repayment history may well mean that a borrower is targeted by additional credit card issuers. At the same time, card-holders are made aware that deviation and the failure to meet at least minimum repayments will be punished. Should they forget, a letter, phone call, and eventually home visit from a lender or a sub-contracted firm of collection agents will follow non-payment. Deviation is represented as irrational, as the credit ratings of so-called 'delinquents' are downgraded and their access to credit dries up. Delinquents can no longer experience the consumptive freedom and security that comes through revolving credit.

The financial self-discipline of the revolver has, furthermore, come to turn not only on making and planning repayments, but on the entrepreneurial and calculative management and manipulation of outstanding obligations. Three examples are especially illustrative. First, and perhaps most simply, revolving credit assembles a responsible borrower who is able to extend the time horizons across which they will meet their outstanding obligations. In the UK, for example, the average duration that cardholders take to clear their outstanding balances increased from three months in 1997, to five months in 2002 (House of Commons Treasury Select Committee 2003: 45). For many revolvers who increase their outstanding obligations, the overall ratio of monthly payments to income will remain largely unchanged.

Second, perhaps the signature performance of the revolver during the last decade or so has been the transfer of an outstanding balance from one credit card to another. The motivation here is to take advantage of reduced introductory-offer interest rates ('teaser rates') in order to, in effect, reduce outstanding obligations. The personal finance sections of major newspapers, as well as the countless money advice websites, provide tables listing the best available current offers that, for example, provide zero per cent interest payable on balance transfers for a twelve-month period. Nearly 4.5 million cardholders in the UK have taken advantage of teaser rates and transferred their revolving balances to another card (Meyer 2005). The frustrations of the credit card industry with those who regularly and routinely transfer their outstanding balances from one card to another and so on, leading them to label such entrepreneurial individuals 'rate tarts', has furthermore only served to reinforce such practices. The 'rate tart' who searches on-line for the best deal on a balance transfer is, as in the traditional colloquial sense of the term 'tart', a promiscuous woman of unsound virtue who is to be condemned. However, given the ambiguous meaning of 'tart' in contemporary parlance and its general association by the young with a hedonistic life-style, the implication is also that those represented as a 'rate tart' may be gaining pleasure and enjoyment at the expense of a less promiscuous other. Some leading credit card issuers in the UK, such as Barclays, Egg, and MBNA, moved in mid-2005 to profit from these pleasures by imposing charges of around 2 per cent on balance transfers. In a period of historically low interest rates, however, large numbers of issuers continue to make it possible for savvy and canny revolvers to regularly move their balance from one card to another at no cost.

Third, and related to the second, simultaneous performances of everyday borrowing across overlapping credit card, loan, and mortgage networks call up revolvers who substitute credit card obligations for alternative repayments at lower rates of interest. This so-called 'debt consolidation' has come to concentrate on mortgage refinancing, equity withdrawal, and so-called 'home-owner loans', especially in the period of low interest rates and rising house prices from the latter half of the 1990s in the UK, and between 2000 and 2004 in the US. Relatively high-interest unsecured credit card borrowing is substituted for relatively low-interest secured borrowing. By way of illustration, mortgage equity withdrawal in the UK increased from −£1.4 billion in the fourth quarter of 1995 to £13.5 billion by the first quarter of 2003 (Anderson 2004: 49). Meanwhile, in the US, as the rate of increase for total unsecured consumer borrowing slowed from 2001, this coincided with a sharp increase in outstanding mortgage obligations. While partly related to roaring house prices and the changing subjectivities of residential property ownership that we discuss in the next section, there are also strong indications that, in the words of the Joint

Economic Committee (2004) of the US Senate, 'many households have re-financed their homes in part to pay off higher interest debt' (p. 2). According to a Freddie Mac (2005) brochure, a staggering $500 billion worth of home equity was released through re-mortgaging in the US from 2002 to 2005. And it appears that roughly one-quarter of those who have refinanced their mortgages in recent times in the US have increased their obligations in order to pay off consumer debts (Aizcorbe, Kennickell, and Moore 2003: 25–6; Moss 2004). For Alan Greenspan (2004), then, there is little doubt that this debt consolidation is a rational move: 'the surge in mortgage refinancings likely improved rather than worsened the financial condition of the average homeowner'.

Although representations of the revolver assemble a calculative and self-disciplined subject by playing on a highly materialist conception of freedom and security, these processes of identification also simultaneously feature revolvers who express and communicate their 'success' and individuality through the credit card(s) that they hold. Neo-liberal subjects are summoned up who define themselves not just by the freedom to purchase and by what they buy, but by the plastic that they use to make a purchase. Here the long-standing role of the credit card in authorizing the identity of the cardholder takes on a significant twist. As the physical form taken by cards has moved from paper cards and dog-tag-like plates to plastic cards with magnetically encoded strips, so card issuers have marketed the opportunities for cardholders to communicate particular identities. Aside from authorizing identity, the use value of a credit card is limited to, for example, removing ice from a frosted car windscreen or chopping out a line of cocaine. But the 'value' of a particular card to its holder goes far beyond these uses, standing as an important symbolic good; that is, as an object owned by individuals as a means of constituting their subjectivity and signalling and communicating this with others. Holding a particular credit card signals the attainment, and enables the projection of, a particular entrepreneurial sense of self.

The manner in which the credit card has come to stand as a significant object in the mediation of consumption is recognized to some degree by Klein (1999) who offers an analysis of the representations of financial consumers present within credit card advertising campaigns. According to Klein (1999), by the late 1970s and especially the 1980s, 'Each credit card became an individual commodity subsequently marketed as painstakingly as the facilitated purchases of consumer products or experiences' (p. 29). There is, then, 'a science within the process of selling credit cards... Advertising agencies sample consumer demand through focus groups... testing completed commercials through storyboard research analysis, and commissioned studies through consumer research organizations' (p. 84). Nevertheless, Klein continues to suggest that understanding the consumer credit boom requires that we focus on the making of subjects of (non-financial) consumption in the first instance. Klein's detailed analysis, for example, concentrates on Visa's television advertising commercials of the early 1980s. These included 'Back To School', featuring a woman cardholder in her forties overcoming barriers to college access, and 'Houseboat', which was based around a family of four purchasing a run down boat, making the necessary alterations and sailing off into the sunset!

For nearly three decades now, credit cards of different colours have been marketed as providing a means for communicating the size of the line of credit at the cardholder's disposal. Not surprisingly, so-called 'prestige cards' have seen the most sustained initiatives in this regard. With the launch of their first 'gold cards' in the early 1980s, Visa and MasterCard created a means of distinguishing those with the greatest access to credit from the 'normal' cardholder (Mandell 1990: 81–3). Subsequent initiatives have focused on the production of platinum cards as an advance on gold and, most recently, on the introduction of apparently highly prestigious black cards. For example, the American Express Centurion Black Credit Card is targeted at those who travel extensively with their work, offers a range of benefits such as hotel upgrades and concierge services in return for an annual fee, and is available by invitation only to those who have held an American Express Platinum Card for some time. The representation of revolvers who communicate their success, freedom, and security through the colour of their credit card has not, however, been limited to prestige cards. A television advertising campaign in the UK during the first years of the new millennium is an illustrative case in point. The soundtrack for American Express' Blue Card campaign was provided by New Order's 'Blue Monday', the highest selling 12 inch vinyl single of all-time and widely regarded as one of dance music's classic records. The 'cool blue' images from the campaign represented the card as the choice of the upwardly mobile, fashion-conscious night-clubber.

Aside from the colour of credit cards, so-called 'affinity cards' are also marketed as providing revolvers with an object through which to attain and project a particular sense of self. Affinity cards date from the mid-1980s, as issuers sought to market cards to a greater number of Americans, and to reach out to those who might, for the first time, consider holding more than one card or switch from a previous card. Three types of affinity card have subsequently emerged (Klein 1999: 33; Mandell 1990: 80–1). So-called 'product benefit cards' offer bonuses or what are known in the industry as 'rebates' (e.g. air miles, savings on branded products) for usage. While these cards may be held by those who wish, for example, to construct and communicate themselves as regular, upwardly mobile air travellers, it is perhaps 'lifestyle cards' and 'personality cards' that are more explicitly symbolic goods by design. 'Lifestyle cards' seek to respond to and enable the manufacture of certain interests by the cardholder, especially in charitable causes which receive donations when the card is used. 'Personality cards' meanwhile are typically embossed with photos of celebrities, or the colours of a favourite sports league or team.

Mortgagors: Leveraged Investors

While almost all mortgagors in Anglo-America are unaware that their ability to borrow on a greater scale in the contemporary period rests on the reconfiguration of mortgage networks to create close intersections with the networks of the capital markets, the production of extended, responsible, and entrepreneurial borrowing is nevertheless impossible without the calling up of subjectivities of residential property ownership. As John Flint (2003) shows, the liberal governmental drive for home-ownership throughout much of the twentieth century consistently summoned up apparently enterprising, autonomous, and secure owner-occupier families through their juxtaposition against an other: dependent, trapped, and insecure renters who place welfare demands upon the state. Grey (1997) similarly emphasizes that the making of what he term's 'suburban subjects', playing on conceptions of freedom and security in the course of liberal government, is, at once, individualizing, normalizing, and disciplinary. As he summarizes, 'Individualising: this is mine, I bought it, it is for my personal use. Normalising: I am a home owner, a responsible citizen, a person of property. Disciplinary: I must work and pay for my house, or lose my status as a normal individual if I cannot' (p. 49).

Owner-occupation has thus been held out as an aspiration for all in an explicitly moral economy that demarcates what is respectable and acceptable, on the one hand, from that which is unrespectable and unacceptable on the other. Consider the following description from Warren and Warren Tyagi (2004) which nicely captures the deep-seated representations of home that owner-occupation plays to and articulates:

To the overwhelming majority of Americans, home ownership stands out as the single most important component of 'the good life'...Homes mark the lives of their children, setting out the parameters of their universe. The luck of location will determine whether there are computers in their classrooms, whether there are sidewalks for them to ride bikes on, and whether the front yard is a safe place to play. (p. 20)

Indeed, a failure to meet the aspiration of home-ownership is represented as very much a consequence of irresponsibility and a lack of discipline on the part of the individual, a failure of the family. Nothing else and no-one else is to blame. In popular parlance, renters spend 'dead money' and fail to get 'a foot on the property ladder'. Once on that ladder, individuals seek to further the security and freedom of themselves and their children, whether in the name of local crime figures or proximity to good schools.

In the US, the programmatic form taken by the governmental discourse of suburban subjects has been such that tax subsidies and institutional arms of the state are dedicated to the promotion of owner-occupation. Interest on mortgage repayments is, for example, tax deductible. The current remit of the so-called 'government-sponsored enterprizes'—Ginnie Mae, Freddie Mac, and Fannie Mae—includes the further extension of owner-occupation to minorities and low-income individuals and families. For example, Freddie Mac (2005) describes a 'mission' to 'stabilize the nation's mortgage markets and expand opportunities for homeownership' (p. 4). Similarly, Fannie Mae (2005) portrays itself as having 'a public-spirited mission to expand homeownership opportunities for low- and moderate-income families and to make the cost of mortgage credit as affordable as possible' (p. 7). While both Freddie and Fannie are significant, then, in the secondary mortgage markets and techniques of mortgage-backed securitization that we discussed in Chapters 6 and 7, Freddie Mac (2005) also promotes, for example, 'aggressive outreach programs, homebuyer education and innovative mortgage products' which 'help ensure that more minority families can achieve the dream of owning their own homes' (p. 5).

In the UK, although the making of suburban subjects has not been the preserve of dedicated state institutions, encouraging owner-occupation has nonetheless been a largely continuous feature of governmental programmes. In Susan Smith's (2006) terms, 'expectations that pick out, prioritise and reaffirm certain moral sentiments and values' about home-ownership have been pursued 'through technologies of regulation, contractual agreements, and other styles of formalisation imposed on interpersonal relations' (p. 13). A stark example in this regard was the 'right to buy' policy of the Thatcher government in the early 1980s that relied heavily on the notion of a 'property-owning democracy'. The policy offered tenants in state-owned council housing the option to purchase their homes at considerably discounted prices, and stressed the independence and material well-being associated with home-ownership. The offer was taken up by around two million households, contributing towards a major expansion in home-ownership in the UK that has continued into the new millennium. Owner-occupied housing increased from 9.8 million in 1981 through to 13.1 million in 1991, and 14.6 million by 2001 (69% of the total housing stock). Indeed, such has been the success of the assembly of suburban subjects in the UK that 85 per cent of those in mid-life currently live in owner-occupied housing.[2]

While the concerted making of suburban subjects has been a largely continuous feature of Anglo-American liberal government for the best part of a century, the neo-liberal period is currently witnessing not only an apparent tightening of the perceived relationships between owner-occupation, freedom, and security, but also a subtle change in the subjectivities of owner-occupiers. Given that roughly two-thirds of owner-occupiers are mortgagors, this change is highly significant in the embodiment of the borrowing boom and the associated transformation of mortgage networks. As Susan Smith (2006) suggests with reference to the UK, Anglo-American owner-occupiers are 'entangled in the materiality of housing, the meaning of home and the mobilisation of money' (p. 1). The way in which these entanglements come together and are articulated is undergoing change that is framed by governmental programmes, representations of home, and changes in mortgage networks. For Smith, a shift is occurring in 'household's dispositions', 'away from a tendency to opt for ownership ... towards an inclination to bank on housing by design' (pp. 5–6). There can be little doubt that this shift is embodied in the emergence of what she calls the 'investor figure' of 'housing's new financial order' (p. 5). As owner-occupation has become normalized to the extent that it is indeed the norm, so 'What matters is what kind of owner you are; and this is tied to what kind of asset you own' (p. 14).

Owner-occupation has become, then, an entrepreneurial, financial, and housing strategy as the home becomes an object of leveraged investment.

---

[2] Figures from confidential personal correspondence, representative of the Office of the Deputy Prime Minister, 26 May 2005.

Autonomy and welfare for owner-occupiers, would-be owner-occupiers, and their children increasingly appears to turn less on the home as an individual space of shelter and refuge, and more on the financial returns achieved from house price rises. What is especially notable is the changing form taken by mortgages in order that the home becomes an object of leveraged investment. In the UK during the 1980s, for example, with-profits endowment mortgages became increasingly popular, accounting for more than eight out of ten mortgages issued by 1988. Instead of a straight repayment mortgage, where the borrower meets outstanding obligations of capital and interest over the length of the agreement, with-profits endowment policies were designed so that borrowers paid back just the interest on the loan and, at the same time, contributed to a life insurance policy or unit trust fund. Tax relief was available on both these payments. At the end of the mortgage term, it was expected that the funds which the insurance policy or unit trust had built up would be sufficient to pay back the principal of the loan as well as provide a capital sum. As Morgan and Sturdy (2000) have it, for mortgagors, 'the way in which they owned their home and were paying back the loan on it was now integrally and more explicitly tied with wider processes of investment in the capital markets' (p. 108). As it became clear by the late 1990s that these investments would not be sufficient to realize mort-gagors' repayments, let alone realize an additional capital sum—a crisis that the government casts as the widespread 'miss-selling' of an unsuitable product to mortgagors who were often not made aware of the 'risks' that they were taking (House of Commons Treasury Committee 2004b)—the experiment with endowment mortgages largely came to an end. But, just as endowment mortgages facilitated investment in the financial markets (investments that over 6 million people in the UK are still relying on to meet the outstanding principal on their mortgages), so have straight repayment mortgages subsequently come to be represented as enabling home-ownership as investment. Furthermore, as Smith (2006) argues, the advent of mortgage-equity withdrawal and innovative mortgage products (e.g. over-mortgaging, flexible, offset, and current account mortgages) ensures that investment in a home is becoming increasingly related to consumptive freedom, security, and opportunity in the present, as well as in the future in general, and in retirement in particular.

Once construed as an entrepreneurial act of investment, owner-occupation requires the responsible meeting of mortgage repayments in the present and until the interest and principal has been paid. Maintaining, increasing, and ultimately releasing housing wealth is impossible without the self-discipline of responsible borrowing, but with that responsibility would now seem to come investment returns from the home. The mortgage becomes 'good debt' when compared with the 'bad debt' of credit card borrowing in particular (Scurlock 2007: 33). Not only do previously common representations of the mortgage in popular parlance as 'a millstone round your neck' all but disappear (McCulloch 1990), but individuals and couples become seemingly quite content to commit an ever greater proportion of their income to mortgage repayments. In the UK, for example, according to Council of Mortgage Lenders figures, the average mortgage balance increased from £52,572 in 2001 to £90,177 in 2006. Assuming a capital repayment mortgage at an interest rate of 5 per cent (the base rate prevailing in both 2001 and 2006), this translates into an increase in monthly payments from £307.37 to £527.17 (Halligan 2006). Related, traditional loan to income ratios governing the amount that a mortgagor can borrow have been relaxed. Some UK lenders, including Abbey, Bristol & West, and Northern Rock, will now lend up to five times salary for both single and joint mortgage applicants. Although there are restrictions—for example, applicants to Abbey must have a relatively high annual income and a good credit score—this represents a considerable increase on the traditional ratios of three and a half times individual income, and two and three-quarters of joint income (Francis 2006a). In the US, meanwhile, so-called 'stated income loans' or 'liar loans' permit the mortgagor to declare an income which is not verified by the lender with reference to tax returns or pay checks (Scurlock 2007: 35–6).

Furthermore, once the owner-occupier is summoned up as a leveraged investor subject, individuals and couples appear to be more likely to take up mortgage products that enable them to entrepreneurially reduce and manage their obligations, at least in the short-term. Borrowers on both sides of the Atlantic may lengthen the term of their mortgage. The traditional 30-year fixed-rate mortgage in the US has been joined, for instance by a 40-year equivalent. This serves to reduce the month-on-month repayment obligations but, of course, borrowers repay a much greater amount over the full-term of the mortgage. Meanwhile, writing in the *New York Times*, Damon Darlin (2006a) suggests that 10.2 per cent of all new mortgages in the US in 2003 were interest-only, meaning that borrowers pay only the interest for an initial period. This figure rises to 26.7 per cent for 2005, with a further 15.3 per cent of mortgages in 2005 taking the form of flexible, payment-option, and negative amortization loans. Under flexible and payment-option arrangements, borrowers choose how much to pay each month. For negative amortization mortgages, monthly repayments gradually increase as they are set at levels which are insufficient to cover the interest and principal of the loan. Underpinning many of these new mortgage products is the assumption that house prices will rise, creating equity for the leveraged investor who can 'cash out' this equity in order to meet future and rising repayments.

It is clear that the re-articulation of the home as an object of leveraged investment has been especially marked in the context of the recent boom in residential property prices. For example, in the five years to the end of 2003, total outstanding mortgage borrowing in the US climbed by $2.25 trillion, an increase of over 50 per cent (Chancellor 2005: 71). Interestingly, the re-articulation of the home during this period has also become part of popular culture. Property television programmes—such as *Location, Location, Location* in the UK, and *Flip This House* in US—expressly seek to encourage viewers to 'trade up the housing ladder' and maximize the returns from their investments. Here owner-occupier investors are summoned up as 'flippers' who, by moving house or 'flipping' at regular intervals in a rising market, treat their home-life as an entrepreneurial exercise in investment. The burgeoning popular financial print media and newspaper supplements also regularly feature advice on how to become a flipper, and on the possible returns available from residential property when compared to financial market investment (e.g. Birger 2005; Francis 2006*b*). By featuring advice on how best to sell your home, programmes such as *Location, Location, Location* also dovetail with the 'home improve-ment' and 'do-it-yourself' consumerism that, developing from the 1980s, is manifest in dedicated superstores, television programmes, and maga-zines. While representing the home as a space of individual expression, media advice on home improvement nevertheless tends to focus on how to follow current trends in order to meet the expectations of potential buyers. As such, owner-occupiers are always represented here as potential sellers, and their aspirations for improved security and freedom become related to the material gains of rising house prices. For some leveraged investors, then, re-mortgaging releases equity that, for example, funds a small extension or a new bathroom in the latest style.

The calling up of owner-occupiers as leveraged investors is now quite explicit in UK government policy. The discourse of so-called 'asset-based welfare' is beginning to travel into government policy from think-tanks such as the Institute for Public Policy Research. A 2005 government initia-tive to further extend owner-occupation called 'Homebuy', for instance, describes homes as 'not just places to live . . . they are also assets'. It also casts itself as 'enabling more people to share in increasing asset wealth' (in

Smith 2006: 15). Indeed, current policy debates are coming to question, by way of illustration, whether the concentration of around half of UK and US households' assets as housing wealth is a risky investment, and how best to enable retirees to draw down their housing wealth. For example, Robert Shiller (2003) claims that 'the financial tools that will allow ordinary folk to cope with increased uncertainty, and to insure against adverse economic events, are already being developed' (p. 90). Such 'tools' include risk-management hedging techniques for housing wealth that Shiller himself has been involved in developing. Several attempts in both the UK and US to establish derivatives contracts for residential property have been undermined by the apparently unrepresentative nature of the indexes that provide the basis for contracts. Indexes that track price movements are likely to lag behind current trends, for example. What is distinctive about the Case-Shiller Indexes launched by the Chicago Mercantile Exchange, then, is that they claim to be more authoritative as they are based on repeat sales figures for the same property.[3]

While the assembly of owner-occupiers as leveraged investors has been especially pronounced in the recent house price boom, shifts in popular culture, government policy, and financial techniques would seem to suggest that the leveraged investor is here to stay. What is less clear at present is the place of the residential property investor more broadly in neo-liberal society. Both the UK and US witnessed a sharp increase in what are commonly known as 'buy-to-let investors' during the house price boom, that is, owner-occupiers who have sought specialist mortgage finance to purchase additional houses, with mortgage repayments covered by the rental income generated by the property purchased (Scanion and Whitehead 2005). In the UK, for example, the value of outstanding buy-to-let mortgages rose from £2 billion at the end of 1998 to £47 billion by June 2004 (Pensions Commission 2004: 194). Similarly, according to the National Association of Realtors, 23 per cent of all house purchases in the US in 2004 were made for investment purposes and not for owner-occupation. A further 13 per cent was accounted for by vacation home purchases (*The Economist* 2005*b*).

As we suggested in Chapter 4, buy-to-let investment sits somewhat uneasily within governmental programmes in occupational and personal pensions in particular which inculcate the financial market investor as a unitary subject. An especially revealing example in this regard are the regulations governing what assets can be purchased and held, for

---

[3] http://investor.cme.com/ReleaseDetail.cfm?ReleaseID=174818

tax purposes, in the new UK self-invested personal pensions (SIPPs) (see Chapter 3). Prior to their introduction in April 2006, it was widely expected that funds held in a SIPP could be used to purchase buy-to-let properties and second homes, as well as all manner of financial instruments. Higher-rate taxpayers would thus have received a 40 per cent discount on their buy-to-let investments, because contributions to a SIPP are, in effect, tax free. Personal pension providers began to establish property funds for those SIPP holders who, although they did not want to become buy-to-let investors, nevertheless wanted to hold some property in their portfolios (Budworth 2005). There was even some discussion as to whether it would be worth owner-occupiers 'purchasing' their own home through their SIPP, and then leasing it back to themselves. But, when the guidelines on SIPPs were finally announced in December 2005, buy-to-let properties and second homes (but not real-estate investment funds) were excluded from the list of permissible investments under SIPPs.

Busted Borrowers?

Policy makers on both sides of the Atlantic readily acknowledge that the boom in everyday borrowing has produced, in quantitative and aggregate terms, a rapid increase in households' outstanding obligations that out-strips relatively stagnant household incomes (e.g. Aizcorbe, Kennickell, and Moore 2003; Bank of England 2006a; Greenspan 2004; Joint Economic Committee 2004). But, when total collective household assets (income and other sources of wealth) are weighted-up against total collective household borrowing as liabilities, such measuring of the everyday borrowing boom tends to support somewhat optimistic analyses. This is especially the case for the first few years or so of the new millennium, whereby sharp increases in mortgage and consumer borrowing on the liabilities side for households in both the US and UK are, in effect, justified by house price rises and the re-bounding stock market on the assets side. In the terms of a recent *Financial Stability Report* by the Bank of England (2006a), for example, 'Aggregate household balance sheets in the United Kingdom are strong. Although personal indebtedness has increased rapidly, so too has the stock of housing and financial assets' (p. 16). Similarly, for Alan Greenspan (2004), speaking prior to his retirement from the Federal Reserve, 'Overall, the household sector seems to be in good shape, and much of the apparent increase in the household sector's debt ratios . . . reflect factors that do not suggest increasing household financial stress'.

As quantitative analyses of a collective and singular household balance sheet give the impression that the boom in everyday borrowing is relatively unproblematic, they also, in effect, represent the subject position of the responsible and entrepreneurial borrower as being occupied in a fairly straightforward manner. New forms of financial self-discipline are routinely performed by the vast majority of borrowers without distress. This rather rosy representation is certainly dented somewhat by rising insolvency rates on both sides of the Atlantic. In the UK, for example, insolvency rates stood at around 0.02 per cent of adult population in the mid-1980s. This increased sharply to around 0.10 per cent in the early 1990s, fell back to roughly 0.07 per cent for the next decade, and, since 2003, has spiked to stand at approximately 0.22 per cent in 2006 (Bank of England 2006a: 17). The significance of increased insolvency rates is, however, somewhat brushed-off by policy makers who commonly represent insolvency as either an unfortunate individualized experience, or a regulatory creation. In terms of the former, instances of insolvency are commonly represented not as the outcome of irresponsible borrowing or lending, but as the result of 'external shocks' suffered by borrowers such as loss of employment, divorce, and ill-health. The House of Commons Treasury Select Committee's (2003: 36–7) findings on 'over-indebtedness' in the UK suggest, for example, that changes in individuals' employment, health, and family circumstances are the most likely sources of problems for those who find themselves unable to meet their outstanding obligations (on the US, see Sullivan, Warren, and Westbrook 2000; Warren and Warren Tyagi 2004).

The extent to which regulations are significant has, meanwhile, also begun to feature strongly in recent times in policy makers' accounts of insolvency. In the UK, the Enterprise Act of 2002 led to the introduction of a new insolvency regime in April 2004. Alongside a reduction in the period of automatic discharge for bankrupts from three years to one year, the Act made provisions for Individual Voluntary Arrangements (IVAs). IVAs are formal agreements whereby a debtor agrees to repay a proportion of their outstanding obligations to creditors, but does not lose ownership of their assets as under bankruptcy. For the Bank of England (2006b), then, although 'the increase in insolvency may be related to there being more borrowers, as well as rising individual debt burdens... Legislative changes may also be behind the most recent spate of insolvencies. One possibility is that the new regime is perceived as more debtor friendly' (p. 8). Not dissimilarly, in the US, the reaction of borrowers in the period immediately prior to the recent tightening of the bankruptcy regime has led the Bush administration to argue that tightening was indeed appropriate. Under the new regime, individuals who earn more than the median income in their state, and who are capable of making repayments of at least $6,000 on outstanding obligations over a five-year period, are no longer able to have their debts wiped out for a fresh start as under the Chapter 7 provisions of the bankruptcy code. Instead, they will have to seek protection under Chapter 13 of the code which requires a repayment schedule, and undergo a newly introduced financial counselling programme (Egan 2005). Between the enactment of the legislation in April 2005 and its introduction a few months later in mid-October, a rush and then scramble to bankruptcy ensured that filings were up by around 20 per cent on the previous year (Dash 2005).

Once insolvency is represented by policy-makers as an unfortunate individualized experience, or as a response to the prevailing regulatory regime, this legitimates and licenses the continuation of policies that concentrate on the making of responsible and entrepreneurial borrowers. A particularly illustrative example in this regard is the initiative currently being pursued in the UK in the name of 'tackling over-indebtedness' (DTI and DWP 2004, 2005). The tackling over-indebtedness agenda, which cross-cuts various institutional arms of government, centres on 'improving the efficiency of the consumer credit market', and advancing 'social equity' by reducing the debt problems experienced by low-income families (2005: 8–9). In short, it seeks 'prevention and cure' (p. 11). But, revealingly, prevention is said to require 'an increase in levels of financial capability and awareness . . . so that individuals can take control of their finances and participate actively and effectively in the credit market' (p. 8), while the key to 'cure' becomes 'free debt advice' (e.g. National Debtline, Consumer Credit Counselling Service) and 'face-to-face debt advice' (p. 12). 'Prevention' is thus linked with the National Strategy for Financial Capability led by the FSA (2006), while cure is wrapped up with the Promoting Financial Inclusion initiative led by HM Treasury (2004). The content of both 'capability' and 'advice' is, of course, dominated by guidance on the meeting, management, and manipulation of outstanding obligations.

While advancing the financial literacy of everyday borrowers is quite laudable in its own terms, it certainly misses the point when it comes to the assembly of responsible and entrepreneurial borrowers. The self-disciplined financial subjects that are summoned up through the moral discourse and political programmes of neo-liberal government, and through the calculative technologies of mortgage and consumer credit networks, are clearly demarcated as monolithic subject positions. As

Burton et al. (2004) note of credit reporting and scoring, for example, these technologies are 'constructed on the basis of a linear conception of the subject who is expected to have a stable or continuously improving employment and credit career' (p. 5). Responsible borrowing can thus be performed by self-disciplined, rational, and calculating individuals to further their own security and autonomy both in the present and into the future. But, to return to Burton et al., subjects 'may not necessarily have continuous life-chance careers, and/or the stable life experiences that are the life-blood of credit scoring techniques' (p. 5). For us, more broadly, tensions and contradictions interrupt the processes of identification in the everyday borrowing boom, ruptures that certainly cannot be overcome by greater financial literacy. Caught amidst these contradictions, individuals cannot identify with the subject position of the responsible borrower in a certain and unambiguous manner. For some, these contradictions are already manifest in over-indebtedness and insolvency. For the vast majority of the 'asset rich' who are also in regular and well-paid employment, the contradictions are yet to surface in a widespread struggle to meet outstanding obligations.

Three contradictions are at work. The first and second contradictions relate to the manner in which, for many everyday borrowers, the extension of outstanding obligations has not been met by comparable increases in income. Not surprisingly, it is the poorest in society, those with a limited and shrinking income in relative and real terms, who find it hardest to make ends meet. According to the DTI (2005), over half of those who they define as 'over-indebted' in the UK—that is, as having difficulty meeting credit commitments or paying household bills—earn less than £7,500 per annum. Yet, many low-income households are very highly skilled in the management of the obligations that arise from their borrowing. It is not then simply the case, then, as Medoff and Harless (1996) suggest, that the relative stagnation of real wages alongside extended everyday borrowing will ensure that the boom will inevitably come to a very sticky end. There are, nonetheless, two contradictions specific to the embodiment of contemporary boom in everyday borrowing that are currently surfacing in low-income households, interrupting and rendering precarious the performance of the subject position of the responsible and entrepreneurial borrower.

First, the borrower that is summoned up in the boom appears as a disconnected and unitary subject, a figure that is disembedded from all but his/her financial relations. But, as we noted in Chapter 4, alongside financial subjects who routinely perform new forms of self-discipline, neo-liberal government also calls into being the 'worker-entrepreneur' in the contemporary restructuring of the productive economy (Amoore 2004). Both the responsible borrower and the worker-entrepreneur are represented as self-reliant figures. The flexible, downsized, mobile, and contacted-out worker who necessarily encounters uncertainties over employment contracts, hours, pay, and conditions is, however, very poorly placed to perform the new forms of financial self-discipline. Just as investment is not a one-off event but a set of on-going calculative practices that are undercut by uncertainties over employment, so the meeting, management, and manipulation of on-going borrowing obligations are reliant upon relatively predictable wages. This contradiction is experienced first, foremost, and most strongly by precisely those low-income individuals and households who are the most 'flexible' in their work. The situation is further compounded because low-income flexible workers are also more likely to have outstanding obligations arising from loans, mail order purchases, and door-step lenders, as opposed to obligations from credit card spending (Tudela and Young 2003: 2). It is a sad irony that those who most need the room for manoeuvre of revolving credit because of the nature of their working lives are the least likely to be permitted by issuers to hold a credit card.

As Warren and Warren Tyagi's (2004) account of the rise of bankruptcy in the US illustrates, low-income household's precarious performances of the self-disciplines of responsible and entrepreneurial borrowing are likely to be all the more problematic where borrowers are also fathers and mothers. Based upon the largest single study of bankrupt families in the US, Warren and Warren Tyagi suggest that the typical case of bankruptcy is thus: a two-parent, two-income family with one or more children that is struck by unemployment, long-term illness, or divorce. Confronted by real wages that are stagnant at best, moral pressures to maximize freedom, security, and opportunities for their children, and rising housing costs, insurance payments, day-care bills, and so on, US family incomes are already stretched and fully committed. Add to this the summoning up of revolvers and leveraged investors, and the meeting, management, and manipulation of outstanding obligations necessarily becomes problematic as soon as the family experiences strife. As Warren and Warren Tyagi put it, 'Married parents are in trouble because they have spent every last penny and then some just to buy a middle-class life for their children' (p. 10). Single-income and single-parent families do not, of course, escape these disciplines and pressures, and are even more likely to become bankrupt should the vagaries of flexible labour markets strike.

Second, the performance of the subject positions of responsible and entrepreneurial borrowing has increasingly come to turn on new forms of financial self-discipline more broadly, especially financial market investment and leveraged investment in residential property. But, low-income individuals and households are, of course, the least likely to have savings of any kind, and are the most likely to be renting their home. As the Bank of England (2006a) is forced to admit with regard to indebtedness in the UK, 'The benign overall picture masks areas of vulnerability... House price rises have not benefited renters, who typically have lower and more volatile income' (p. 16). Already confronted by rising living costs and knife-edge labour market flexibility, exclusion from the growth of asset-based wealth leaves many low-income households with little choice but to extend their borrowing yet further.

The third contradiction that interrupts processes of identification in the everyday borrowing boom holds the potential to be experienced not only by those on low incomes, but also much more widely. The performance of multiple neo-liberal financial subject positions—primarily 'the investor' on the savings side, and 'revolver' and 'leveraged investor' on the borrowing side—has been largely complementary for the last fifteen years or so. Massive increases in financial asset prices have been followed by similarly substantial residential property price rises, the latter in conjunction with historically low rates of interest for mortgagors. But, the tight relationships between investment and responsible and entrepreneurial borrowing come to stand in sharp tension when financial and property prices decline to any significant degree, and when interest rates begin to rise. That this gaping contradiction did not seriously rupture the recurrent and routine performances of the subject position of the responsible borrower during the 1990s and into the first five years or so of the new millennium is, ultimately, a consequence of a highly uncertain conjunctural confluence of factors. For example, the collapse of the new economy stock market bubble from the turn of the millennium coincided with a period of rapid house price growth. As the widespread practices of debt consolidation during this period illustrate, responsible borrowers were able to draw directly on those house price rises through mortgage re-financing and equity withdrawal. To a lesser extent, the stagnation and, in some regions, downturn in US residential property prices since 2004 has coincided with a re-bound on the financial markets that has seen, for instance, the Dow

Jones average surpass the heights it reached during the new economy bubble.

At the time of writing, however, there are strong indications that this contradiction is beginning to surface and is being lived in the increasingly precarious performances of responsible and entrepreneurial borrowers. Interest rates on both sides of the Atlantic are on the rise, and there appears little scope at present for borrowers to engage in another round of debt consolidation. Most starkly, US sub-prime mortgage networks are currently experiencing a deep and pervasive crisis that, as we will see in our concluding chapter, has provoked widespread fears that the bankruptcies of sub-prime mortgagors and lenders may prove to be just be the tip of the iceberg. Elsewhere and more broadly, regulators and lenders are, at once, talking up the prospects of a 'soft landing' while preparing for the worst. For example, the implications of a major downturn in the UK housing market have already prompted action from policy-makers. In November 2006, the FSA suggested that, as a matter of good practice, UK mortgage lenders should 'stress test' their risk management systems through a scenario that assumed a 40 per cent fall in residential property prices and a 35 per cent repossession rate (Hosking 2006). Recent historical precedents clearly form the basis for this scenario: UK average house prices fell by 15 per cent between 1989 and 1992, but some regions experienced declines approaching 40 per cent. Banks are obliged by the FSA to stress-test hypothetical adverse movements in asset prices, interest rates, and exchange rates to ensure that they have a sufficient capital cushion, but how robust stress-testing procedures actually are turns on the assumptions that are made. The FSA described a 40 per cent fall in UK house prices as a 'severe but plausible scenario'.

Concluding Remarks

Dominant representations of everyday borrowing currently serve to silence political debate over the ever-expanding outstanding obligations of a majority of individuals and households in Anglo-America. Extended borrowing presently appears as a technical problem to be solved by the responsible and entrepreneurial individual who meets, manages, and manipulates his own obligations. A failure to borrow responsibly is to seriously compromise one's freedom and security. As I have shown in this chapter, the new self-disciplines of the responsible and entrepreneurial borrower tend to take more-or-less specific forms in relatively discrete networks of everyday borrowing: 'the revolver' who furthers his line of credit, manipulates balances, and communicates their associated freedom through the design of their credit card; and 'the leveraged investor' as a mortgagor who extends and manages their borrowing because their home as an asset will provide not only shelter and refuge but for financial returns.

While the transformation and boom in everyday borrowing are indeed embodied processes, I have also argued in this chapter that the processes of identification are far from unproblematic. The assembly of responsible and entrepreneurial borrowers is shot through with tensions and contradictions which interrupt the processes of identification. Caught amidst these contradictions, individuals cannot identify with the subject position of the responsible borrower with any degree of certainty. While the contradictions are most strongly experienced at present by those on low incomes and/or those who are categorized as sub-prime, the performance of new self-disciplines remains precarious for many. The making of responsible and entrepreneurial borrowers remains necessarily partial and incomplete, an ambition rather than an achievement.

9

Dissent in Everyday Borrowing

Introduction: 'My Saviour Doesn't Live in Washington, DC'

James D. Scurlock's 2007 film and accompanying book *Maxed Out* begin with his meeting with Dave Ramsey. Ramsey, an ex-bankrupt and evangelist, is the host of a number one Tennessee radio talk show which broadcasts from a building in downtown Nashville. The building also houses Ramsey's 'Financial Peace University', an organization that offers a twelve-step programme to borrowers who are experiencing problems meeting their outstanding obligations. As a documentary film maker, Scurlock's approach in *Maxed Out* is to offer a series of vignettes that draw out what he regards to be the unrealistic levels of individual and household indebtedness that prevail in the US. Thus, Scurlock shows how Ramsey's success and fame is based on the down-to-earth and practical advice that he gives to the callers to his radio show, like 'the stern parent they never knew but they wish they had' (Scurlock 2007: 3). This advice to callers features such suggestions as selling their gas-guzzling cars, getting a second job, and holding garage sales. For Ramsey, 'Debt is evil. Debt is so evil, in fact, that Dave advocates paying cash for everything, with the exception of a mortgage, which should be no longer than fifteen years' (p. 4). Indeed, 'Dave thinks that obesity and indebtedness are flip sides of the same moral failing' (p. 6). In Ramsey's own words, 'Is it any surprise...that people who go into debt elect people who go into debt? I don't think it's the other way around...My saviour doesn't live in Washington, DC. That's not where he lives' (on p. 6).

Scurlock's meeting with Dave Ramsey illustrates what I regard as the three most significant tendencies present within dissent in everyday borrowing. First, dissent in everyday borrowing is often grounded in long-standing religious 'truths' about credit relations that inform a search for 'salvation'. Ramsey holds a Puritanical distaste for borrowing and, for him, a return to thrift is the order of the day. The writings of academics and journalists who are critical of the boom in everyday borrowing and fearful of its consequences are also, for example, sometimes implicitly or explicitly coloured with the Puritanical condemnation of the decline of thrift (e.g. Grant 1992). As Calder (1999) has it more broadly, 'the heights of thrift continue to offer a powerful interpretive narrative for understanding the economic and cultural history of debt' (pp. 25–6). But, the religious truths about credit relations that are often a prominent feature of dissent in everyday borrowing are not limited to the Puritanical virtues of thrift. Arguably more prominent is the sin of usury, especially as it is held to manifest itself in the excessive rates of interest charged by so-called 'predatory lenders'. The charge of 'predatory lending' is usually made against the sub-prime, door step, pay day, and other 'alternative' lenders that we encountered in Chapter 7. For instance, on the final page of *Maxed Out*, Scurlock (2007) directs his readers to 'learn how to protect yourself against predatory lending' by visiting the website of Americans For Fairness In Lending (AFFIL) (p. 248). Formed in 2006, AFFIL is an umbrella organization for social movements of legal activists, consumer advocates, civil rights campaigners, financial literacy champions, religious groups, and so on. The AFFIL website includes references to usury from relevant books in the Bible, and a brief timeline on the regulation of interest rates that stretches back nearly 4,000 years.[1]

Second, dissent in everyday borrowing is inclined to work from the assumption that a clear and coherent alternative can be established, that 'salvation' can be achieved. For Dave Ramsey and the evangelists that Scurlock meets in the US 'Bible belt', the boom in everyday borrowing is a consequence of the moral failings of individuals who distastefully gorge themselves on credit. As such, the return of those individuals to the righteous path of thrift and self-denial is held out as providing a patent and arrant pathway out of the moral malaise. *Maxed Out* satirizes and dismisses this view, as, for Scurlock, the transformation and boom in everyday borrowing has been driven by the power of Wall Street, the complicity of politicians, and the profiteering of mortgage and consumer credit lenders. Nonetheless, *Maxed Out* continues to retain and proffer the view that dissent in everyday borrowing can achieve an apparent and reasoned alternative. The decline of thrift is not condemned on moral grounds by Scurlock, and instead predatory lending at usurious

---

[1] http://www.affil.org/

rates of interest provides the focus for his denunciation. It follows that restrictions on predatory lending and usury—for example, reforms which force lenders to use credit scoring techniques in a way that gives sufficient weighting to a borrower's income and their ability to meet their repayments—lie at the heart of what Scurlock calls the 'solutions' that are available (pp. 239–46).

The encounter between James Scurlock and Dave Ramsey also highlights a third important tendency within dissent in everyday borrowing. More often that not, dissent in everyday borrowing begins from the portrayal of over-indebted individuals as victims who have been hoodwinked and swindled by predatory lenders. Not only is it the case that they must learn the real truths about credit relations, and that clear and coherent alternatives must be established in their name, but it also tends to follow that uninitiated individuals are not generally in a position to participate in dissent. When Scurlock mocks Ramsey's evangelism for thrift—he notes, for example, that Ramsey's radio show is sponsored by a Nashville pawnshop—he is, in effect, exemplifying this third tendency within dissent in everyday borrowing. In *Maxed Out*, over-extended borrowers are very much the victims in the story. Consider, for instance, Scurlock's (2007) description of those who phone-in to Dave Ramsey's show:

The callers, as ever, are lost. They are trapped. They cannot help themselves. They do not understand their lives. They do not understand the terms of their credit card agreements and car loans. They are afraid. They are good people, however. They are just confused. Their hearts are willing but their minds are weak. (p. 3)

Once individual borrowers are portrayed as victims, the only realistic and worthwhile mode of dissent appears to be collective resistance that undertakes educational campaigns and lobbies policy makers to regulate predatory lending. For leading US financial activists Warren and Warren Tyagi (2004), for instance, the real victims of predatory lenders are 'families in financial trouble' and, as such, they call for a widespread mobilization of lobby groups (p. 159). For them, 'Liberal or conservative, faith-based or secular, any group that sees its mission as *families* should have interest rate regulation and bankruptcy protection at the very top of its agenda' (p. 162, *original emphasis*; see also Pettifor 2006). Similarly, for Scurlock, the 'saviour' does indeed 'live in Washington, DC', and organizations and movements that come together under the banner of AFFIL are key to activating the potential control of state authority over everyday borrowing.

In this chapter, I want to suggest that the three tendencies within dissent in everyday borrowing that come into view in Scurlock's encounter with Dave Ramsey are analytically delimiting and politically troubling. As I stressed in Chapter 1, my concern to develop the conceptual theme of financial dissent draws on an awareness of the shortcomings of the dominant approaches to resistance which assume and seek out a 'single locus of great Refusal' (Foucault 1976: 96). This locus comes together through calls for 'truthful' accounts of the realities of untamed financial power, and for organized and collective action to install publically re-regulated financial markets as a coherent alternative. The current tendencies within dissent in everyday borrowing broadly reflect, then, the dominant approaches to financial resistance. As I began to detail in Chapter 5, however, multiple modes of dissent are present in the everyday life of global finance that are likely to be passed over and dismissed as insignificant in the search for a great refusal. In further elaborating this argument in this chapter, I want to concentrate on two modes of dissent in everyday borrowing that, perhaps not surprisingly, do not feature in *Maxed Out*: the interventions of artistic projects that (re)politicize everyday borrowing without propounding either a religious or ethical truth about credit relations, or a clear and reasoned alternative to the prevailing situation; and credit unions that seek the local provision of 'not for profit' cooperative credit in the face of predatory lending and failures of market and state.

Although drawing attention to credit art and credit unions highlights further political possibilities that are neglected by the search for a great refusal in everyday borrowing, this chapter will nonetheless also underline the ambiguities of these modes of dissent. The artistic projects that I examine in the first part of the chapter (re)politicize everyday borrowing precisely by playing on the difficulties of personal and political confrontations with credit relations. Credit art projects do not follow the disempowering assumption that the individual borrower who engages with them is an unfortunate and unknowing victim of financial power, but also suggest that perceived personal and political commitments in everyday borrowing cannot be simply reconciled. Credit art also shows that disturbing the settled moralities and meanings of everyday borrowing is possible without recourse to an alternative truth of one kind or another. Indeed, such artistic 'making strange' may well be less alienating and exclusionary than modes of dissent that hinge on appeals to religious truths in particular. However, the desire of credit art projects to emphasize the complications and difficulties of dissent in everyday borrowing, alongside their unwillingness to mark out an unequivocal alternative, can also prompt feelings of helplessness and confusion.

The second section of the chapter turns to examine credit unions as a mode of dissent which (re)politicizes everyday borrowing, which open up to disagreement the meeting, management, and manipulation of extended borrowing in market networks. Like credit art, credit union dissent also does not understand borrowers as victims, but calls up a subject of dissent who reconciles perceived personal and political commitments though performances that are, at once, intimate and collective. Rooted in the co-operative movement, credit unions are strongly grounded in a philosophy of mutual self-help that, at once, manifests itself in a mode of dissent that is 'not-for-profit' and which rejects the efficacy of state regulation and intervention. I suggest, however, that credit union dissent does not provide an unequivocal oppositional alternative to market networks of everyday borrowing. Ambiguities are present in this mode of financial dissent, arising out of the place of technologies of calculation and state regulation in the constitution of credit unions. While calculative performances make possible credit unions as financial institutions that are sustainable without the profit motive, they are nonetheless de-politicizing to the extent that it becomes difficult to discern between credit unions and market institutions. At the same time, although public legal provisions are essential to the materialization of credit unions, those provisions are also de-politicizing as credit unions increasingly become constituted as 'near-market' and, as in UK, are incorporated as 'social enterprises' into wider governmental initiatives to advance 'financial inclusion'.

Credit Art

The capacity of artists work to (re)politicize the ways in which the instrumental rationality of monetary relations draws a 'veil' over social relations is reasonably well documented (e.g. Shell 1995; Velthuis 2005). As a mode of dissent, this 'money art' (de Goede 2005*b*: 168) tends to be concerned with the 'drawing', distribution, or destruction of money in its note form. Money artists have often 'drawn' money to question the meaning and values that are attributed to paper money. As Marc Shell (1995) notes, 'A piece of paper money is almost always a representation, a symbol that claims to stand for something else or to be something else' (p. 80). It is this 'something else', typically communicated and visualized through the political, religious, and economic inscriptions and iconography that adorns state minted money, which tends to be parodied by money art (de Goede 2005*a*: 382–4). For example, artists such as J.S.G. Boggs and Lorenz Spring have subtly replaced the words and symbols on dollar bills with alternatives, while Andy Warhol drew dollar bills and reproduced the dollar sign in an array of colours and styles in order to play on the manner in which the ownership of art becomes a symbol of wealth. The extent to which those artists who draw money have often fallen foul of counterfeiting laws further illustrates the political significance of their work.

Various performance artists have distributed money as a gift for 'free' or, as in Jonier Marin's 'Money Art Service' from the early 1970s, sold it at below face value (Shell 1995: 115; Velthuis 2005: 62–4). This is a politicization of the value of money whereby the act of 'giving' creates non-monetary obligations that disturb the deeply entrenched meanings that are attached, for example, to a dollar bill or a five pound note. Not dissimilar, the destruction of money starkly agitates established under-standings of the value that is typically ascribed to it. For example, the trustees of the K Foundation, Bill Drummond and Jimmy Cauty, burnt £1 million in cash on the Scottish island of Jura in August 1994. The money had been accumulated through the sales of their dance music act KLF, and the ashes that resulted were compressed to manufacture a single house brick. The incineration was filmed, and a year later the pair toured the UK with their movie *Watch the K Foundation Burn a Million Quid*. As part of the tour, Drummond and Cauty engaged audiences in debate as to the meaning of their act of dissent.

If, as de Goede (2005*b*) claims, 'money art' can 'disturb, and help undermine naturalized financial practices by raising the questions that need to be silenced in order for money and financial practices to operate on a daily basis' (p. 171), what of what we might call 'credit art'? What of artistic modes of financial dissent that explicitly agitate and disturb settled and deeply engrained calculative assumptions about borrowing, and what it means to be a borrower? Is credit art, like money art, 'up to the task of enlightening us about—hence loosening—the various knots of aesthetic, political, and economic belief' (Shell 1995: 137) embedded and embodied in everyday borrowing? There are certainly a number of credit art projects through which we might pursue these questions. For example, money is a central leitmotif in Barbara Kruger's photographic provocations of the representations and dynamics of power (Kruger 2005). Kruger's most famous work, from 1987, features a hand clutching a bright red rectangle, and the words on the rectangle read 'I shop therefore I am'. I want to focus in detail here, however, on Kate Bingaman-Burt's 'Obsessive Consumption' project because it provides a particularly illustrative example of the possibilities and problematics of credit art.[2]

Bingaman-Burt, an Assistant Professor of Graphic Design at Mississippi State University, began Obsessive Consumption in 2002 by taking photos of all of the objects and experiences that she purchased, producing a 28-month visual archive of her everyday routines as a consumer that was made publically available on her website. In September 2004, 'Credit Card Drawings' became the second iteration of the project, a series of nine by twelve inch pen and ink line drawings that reproduce her credit card statements in a sketch style. Credit Card Drawings thus feature the logos of the credit card issuers to which she has outstanding obligations, and all the details that are typically listed on such statements including monthly expenditure, APR's and other charges, credit limits, previous payments, special offers, warnings, offers of assistance, and so on. Each drawing is named according to the credit card provider that has issued the statement, and the month and year of the statement—for example, Illustration 1 below is called *First National July 2005*. At the outset of Credit Card Drawings, Bingaman-Burt committed herself to drawing all of her statements until her obligations had been met. This was no small undertaking, then, as Bingaman-Burt had built up considerable revolving balances on six credit cards during her time at art school. And, as you might expect from a project that probes the obsessive nature of consumption, Bingaman-Burt likes to shop. As she puts it in a statement on her agent's website, 'Personal consumer spending and monthly credit card statements ferociously fuel my work'.[3] By July 2007, however, she had paid off three of her cards. Credit Card Drawings can be purchased from the Obsessive Consumption website, with the purchase price determined by minimum payment due on the statement concerned. So, for example, *Chase October 2005* is currently for sale at $135, plus postage and packing.

The Obsessive Consumption project also includes a series of twenty-four by twenty-four digital prints based on the logos of the six credit card issuers with whom Bingaman-Burt has had revolving credit—Chase, First National, MBNA, USAA, Target, and Juniper. Multiple logos are printed in rows by way of background, and a large number (the APR on the card concerned) is printed over the logos through the middle of the picture. The Juniper digital print, for instance, has 19.99 running through its

[2] http:/www.obsessiveconsumption.com
[3] http://www.jenbekman.com/artists/kate_bingaman-burt/statement.php

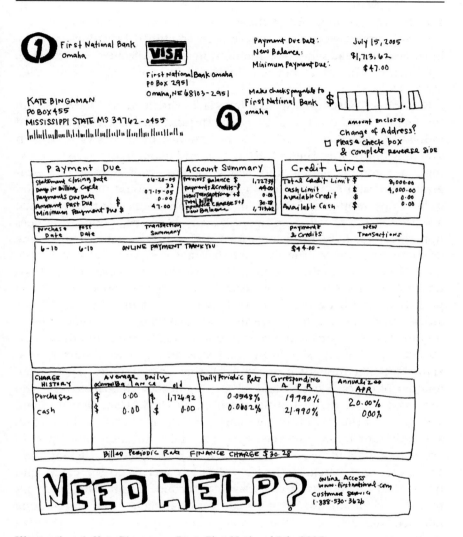

Illustration 1 Kate Bingaman-Burt, *First National July 2005*

centre. As part of a line called 'Sewn and Stuffed', Obsessive Consumption also includes handstitched dollar sign dolls made out of vintage fabrics in various colours and patterns, and pillows featuring either the logos of credit card issuers or the APRs that they charge. More recently, Bingaman-Burt has added a daily pen and ink line drawing of objects purchased to the Obsessive Consumption project, and an accompanying 'What Did

You Buy Today?' blog. All of these works are also available to purchase from the project website, and have been combined in various ways by Bingaman-Burt at a series of exhibitions in several US cities. For example, one such exhibition, at Indiana University in January 2006, was called 'APR:CPR'.

Obsessive Consumption, and especially Credit Card Drawings and the related soft furnishings, deny the disjunctions—private/public and individual/collective—that tend to be assumed by modes of dissent in everyday borrowing. The transformation and boom in everyday borrowing is not simply a matter of individual victims being suckered into ever-greater outstanding obligations by the forces of capital that lay beyond them. Consumption and borrowing are performances that the individual is quite capable of reflecting upon. Dissent in everyday borrowing does not, therefore, have to be organized and collective and in the name of those who know little of what they are involved, but can be the kind of personal confrontation with consumption and credit relations which Obsessive Consumption seeks to provoke. As Rob Walker (2006) puts it, summarizing the words of Bingaman-Burt in a *New York Times* article, 'Her hope . . . is to engage an audience on a more conceptual level, inviting them to think about consumption and obsession and their after-effects . . . The objects she creates and sells are, in a way, simply "souvenirs" of that thought process'. The same article quotes Jim Coudal, founder of Chicago design and advertising agency Coudal Parters, who requested to buy the first of Bingaman-Burt's Credit Card Drawings and thus gave her the idea of selling them. For Coudal, Credit Card Drawings are significant in two respects. First, they take 'an anonymous part of everyone's life and make you look at it in a completely different way'. The credit card statement is, after all, both specific to the credit card holder and ubiquitous in everyday life. Second, Credit Card Drawings play on the 'production' of the credit card statement in an empowering manner. The statement is 'completely produced by machine . . . No human touches it, except for the human at the other end, who has the card— and who affects the content of that statement by the purchases they make'.

For Obsessive Consumption and Credit Card Drawings, however, per-ceived personal and political commitments in everyday borrowing can-not be simply reconciled. Rather, they are necessarily ambiguous and problematic. Obsessive Consumption itself is, at once, an artistic project, a brand, a shop, and a blog. It was created, in Bingaman-Burt's own words, 'to showcase my love/hate relationship with money, shopping, branding, credit cards, celebrity, advertising and marketing'.[4] There are, undoubtedly, aspects of Credit Card Drawings that draw explicit attention to and question the self-disciplinary routines and obligations of everyday borrowing. For example, the text 'Need Help?' is much larger in *First National July 2005* than in the original statement. Furthermore, the Drawings already near two-hundred in total, and Bingaman-Burt's hard work will not be completed until the revolving balances on all of her credit cards are cleared. There is, however, a considerable degree of humour and playfulness when she states in a personal statement that 'I do this as a penance for my sins.'[5] As she puts it elsewhere, 'I don't want to preach, I just want to make aware.'[6]

In contrast to the tendencies that prevail in modes of dissent in everyday borrowing, Bingaman-Burt does not offer a clear assault on the evils of everyday borrowing grounded in religious truths. Consider, for example, Ann Pettifor (2006) who relies upon the spectre of usury to draw attention to the inequalities of everyday borrowing which, as we suggested in Chapter 7, are increasingly marked by hierarchical variations in interest rates. Pettifor's call 'to revive moral standards and set clear *ethical* benchmarks by which to regulate credit and debt, and rein in the finance sector' is made on the grounds not only of the teachings of Christianity, but also on 'Islam's success in discrediting usury' (pp. 13–14, *original emphasis*). Pettifor is seeking to apply broadly the same ethics that she championed while president of the Jubilee 2000 campaign, and which contributed to initiatives to reduce and cancel the outstanding obligations of the 'highly indebted poor countries' (de Goede 2005b: 153–61; Pettifor 1998). What matters for Pettifor (2006) are 'principles that place limits on levels of indebtedness... that recognize that creditor and lenders are co-responsible, share responsibility with the debtor, for debts; that bad loans make bad debts; that losses as well as gains, must be shared' (p. 171). But, Bingaman-Burt's Credit Card Drawings show that it is possible to disturb the settled calculations, moralities, and meanings of everyday borrowing without recourse to an alternative truth of one kind or another, and that dissent in everyday borrowing is not rendered ineffectual as a consequence. As William Connolly (2002) suggests more broadly, while religious faith should have a place in financial dissent, the making of universal claims on religious grounds also undermines the possibilities for the negotiation of difference and disagreement in the course of dissent.

---

[4] http://www.jenbekman.com/artists/kate_bingaman-burt/statement.php
[5] http://www.jenbekman.com/artists/kate_bingaman-burt/statement.php
[6] http://relatetothis.blogspot.com/2007/05/interview-with-kate-bingaman-burt.html

Bingaman-Burt's 'making strange' of everyday borrowing may well be less alienating and exclusionary, then, than modes of dissent that hinge on appeals to religious truths.

Credit art as a mode of dissent is, however, far from unproblematic. As Velthuis (2005) notes of artistic interventions in the market economy more broadly, they do not 'circulate easily, despite the many attempts of artists to reach a broader audience'. The visual communication of art also ensures that it is unable to 'convey detailed concepts or arrive at unambiguous statements about economic processes' (p. 13). Moreover, the manner in which artists of the market economy typically collapse the dichotomy between criticism and affirmation, an established convention within art criticism, can lead to the charge that art, as a form of knowledge about economy, loses its political potential as it 'deems all interpretations to be temporary, contingent and unstable' (p. 18). The emphasis placed by Credit Card Drawings on the complications and difficulties of dissent in everyday borrowing, for example, alongside an unwillingness to mark out an alternative, could prompt feelings of confusion and helplessness. A visitor to Bingaman-Burt's website could, for example, purchase a 'souvenir' of their visit, and extend the revolving balance of one of their credit cards, without giving the process much thought. Indeed, one of the upshots of the Obsessive Consumption project for Bingaman-Burt has been a feature article in a magazine for artists called 'The Artists Guide to Making Money'. So, to borrow terms from Leyshon and Lee (2003), while credit art may contribute greatly to 'thinking the economy otherwise', it does not lend itself to 'performing the economy otherwise'.

Credit Unions

As a mode of dissent in everyday borrowing, credit unions are of significance precisely because they provide an evident and effective means of 'performing the economy otherwise'. The transformations of contemporary finance—and, in particular, the withdrawal of the infrastructures of mainstream market networks from urban and rural communities in the early 1990s—have coincided with the proliferation of various locally grounded networks of money and credit. For example, Local Exchange Trading Schemes (LETS) and so-called 'alternative currencies' have attracted considerable attention from social scientists of finance who are interested in their economic and political possibilities (e.g. Lee 1999; Maurer 2003; North 2007; Thrift and Leyshon 1999; Williams, Aldridge, and Tooke 2003). LETS and alternative currencies seek to formalize and expand already present social relations of mutuality and reciprocity by denominating exchange in monetary units. In a LETS, members list the activities that they are willing to trade in a directory. The association keeps records for the transactions that are made and assemble individual accounts, and the money in circulation is thus strictly notional book money. By way of illustration, in the UK, Manchester LETS which operated from 1992 through to 2005 denominated trade in 'bobbins' as book money, with one bobbin the equivalent of one pound sterling. Members were free to negotiate in their trading and their creation of bobbins, but work and activities were typically either charged at a flat rate of one bobbin, or at a rate of six bobbins per hour. The name 'bobbin' invoked both Manchester's textile industry of the past, and to the popular local expression of 'it's bobbins' which implies that something is of little value (North 2007). Alternative currencies, meanwhile, actually take a physical form such as paper or coin. Perhaps the most established and celebrated example of an alternative currency in Anglo-America is the Ithaca HOUR from upstate New York. One Ithaca HOUR is supposed to index one hour of labour time, but in circulation it has come to be equivalent with $10. HOURs are the established medium of exchange in local farmers' markets and stores in Ithaca, and some relatively large businesses offer to denominate their employees' wages in HOURs (Maurer 2003).

In the context of our inquiry into dissent in everyday borrowing, however, it is credit unions that are of particular interest. There are undoubtedly similarities between LETS, alternative currencies, and credit unions. All are economic performances that are forged through small and explicitly disconnected 'local' and 'moral' networks that are differentiated from and, in some instances, expressly opposed to, mainstream market networks (Thrift and Leyshon 1999). Dating from Germany in the 1850s, and first appearing in the UK in the 1964 and the US in 1908, credit unions, like LETS and alternative currencies, witnessed a surge in political interest in the 1990s. But, in contrast with LETS and alternative currencies, saving and borrowing transactions within a credit union are denominated in the prevailing national currency. Furthermore, while LETS make borrowing possible because members do not need to earn monetary units in order to buy the services of another member, a credit union, as the name suggests, is a formally constituted organization that facilitates saving and borrowing.

The legal status of a credit union is as a financial cooperative. Credit unions are owned and democratically controlled by their members, and, according to the Association of British Credit Unions Ltd. (ABCUL), 'offer savings and great value loans plus they are local, ethical and know what their members want'.[7] Any profits made are either reinvested in the credit union, or distributed to members as a dividend. In order to be a member of a particular credit union, an individual must fall within the 'common bond' that defines that union. A common bond may be community based, determined by place of work, or by belonging to an association or church, for example. In the US, significant initial growth in credit unions came in the 1920s and 1930s, as both state and federal policy makers made legal provisions for their establishment. This period also witnessed the creation of a national newsletter for members, and the formation of the Credit Union National Association (CUNA) (CUNA 2005). Growth in the number of credit unions, members, and total assets continued steadily through to the 1970s. Subsequently, although the number of credit unions has fallen as a consequence of amalgamations, membership and total assets have continued to increase. By the end of 2006, 8,662 credit unions in the US had 88.2 million members—around one-quarter of the adult population—and assets worth $732.5 billion. The tradition of dual chartering continues, with federally chartered credit unions contributing slightly more to each of these figures than their state chartered counterparts.[8] Credit unions in Britain, meanwhile, numbered 540 in September 2005, with 363 registered with ABCUL. British credit unions have roughly 600,000 members, and hold £400 million in savings.[9] In contrast with the US, credit unions in Britain do not feature strongly in everyday saving and borrowing routines, and the initial surge in growth of British credit unions did not begin to take hold until the 1990s.

Viewed against the backdrop of the tendencies that prevail in dissent in everyday borrowing, what is distinct about the ways in which credit unions (re)politicize the meeting, management, and manipulation of extended borrowing and open this up to possible disagreement? Credit union dissent is relatively distinct in the ways in which the binaries of personal/political and individual/collective are denied. Credit union dissent is, at once, intimate and voluntary, on the one hand, and mutual and collective, on the other. The scope and meaning of this mutuality is determined in large part by the common bond, but the political significance of that mutuality would seem to vary, in broad terms, between US and

---

[7] http://www.abcul.coop/page/about/intro.cfm
[8] http://advice.cuna.org/download/US_totals.pdf
[9] Figures from Association of British Credit Unions Ltd, private correspondence, 17 July 2007.

UK credit unions. Reflecting the initial development of US credit unions in the context of the deep and wide dislocations of the Great Depression, members were and continue to be economically diverse (Hannan, West, and Baron 1994). In contrast, as Paul Jones (2005) suggests, the step-wise growth in British credit unions in the 1990s was marked by 'phil-anthropic intent to serve the poor and over-indebted' and was often linked with governmental 'social exclusion' initiatives in deprived areas (p. 13; also Donnelly and Haggett 1997; Fuller and Jonas 2003). UK credit unions are much more likely than their US counterparts, therefore, to call up an explicitly economic-political subject by playing on mutuality in attracting and retaining members. Personal financial performances are combined with a political purpose. For example, British credit unions at present typically pay a saver an annual dividend of between 2 per cent and 3 per cent, such that they are certainly not competing with market institutions for 'consumers'. As the ABCUL have it, 'when you invest in your local credit union, you know that the only people you are benefiting are your neighbours or colleagues'. As they continue, 'Credit unions keep money within a community, because there are no outside shareholders to pay'.[10]

The distinctiveness of credit unions as a mode of dissent in everyday borrowing also hinges on the manner in which public institutions are not regarded as the focal point for dissent, or as the basis for the creation of economic and financial alternatives. The traditions of mutual self-help that have infused the cooperative movement since the formation of the Rochdale Society of Equitable Pioneers in 1844 continue to be present in credit union dissent. Credit unions and credit union activists stress a philosophy that combines autonomy and independence, on the one hand, with community participation and democracy, on the other. Indeed, it is perhaps appropriate that social scientific analyses of credit unions tend to ask whether, as resistance to established power relations, credit unions can be said to be explicitly oppositional and to provide an unequivocal alternative to market networks of everyday borrowing. Leyshon and Thrift (1995), for example, cast credit unions as 'alternative institutions of accumulation', as '*institutions of resistance* rather than com-pliance' (p. 324, *original emphasis*). Whether credit union dissent can be understood in such certain terms is, however, open to debate.

Fuller and Jonas' (2003) intervention is revealing in this regard. They identify a need to introduce some dynamism into understandings of the

---

[10] http://www.abcul.coop/page/about/saving.cfm

political possibilities of British community credit unions, and try to transcend the categorical binary of 'alternative'/'mainstream'. Fuller and Jonas thus construct a threefold typology and sliding-scale between *'alternative-oppositional'*, *'alternative-additional'*, and *'alternative-substitutive'* (p. 57, *original emphasis*). Alternative-oppositional institutions are characterized as engaging in 'the process of actively and consciously *being* alternative— as embodying something "different" in value or operational terms, whilst simultaneously representing a rejection of more non-alternative, or mainstream forms and their identities' (p. 57). Alternative-additional institutions 'represent an additional choice to other extant institutions, whilst not necessarily being distinguishable in the sense of *being* alternative' (p. 57, *original emphasis*). Finally, alternative-substitute institutions 'act as a form of substitute (or even as institutions of last resort) for institutions that are no longer present, and which may or may not be engaged in *being* alternative' (p. 57, *original emphasis*). Drawing on these categories, Fuller and Jonas conclude that 'community credit unions have traditionally played a role in carving out alternative-oppositional economic spaces for individuals and communities seeking access to convenient, low-cost ways of saving and borrowing' (p. 70). However, debates and cleavages within the national credit union movement, and the incorporation of credit unions into government programmes to address 'financial exclusion', are framing activism which is orientated towards 'alternative-additional/substitutive forms'. As Fuller and Jonas somewhat wistfully remark, 'the space for community credit unions to retain their financial autonomy and alternative-oppositional identity may be contracting' (p. 70).

Fuller and Jonas's research into the dynamic developments in British community credit unions is rich and insightful. Indeed, we will return to consider recent developments in community credit unions and their incorporation in governmental programmes below. However, Fuller and Jonas's typology and analysis reinforces the binary of power/resistance that often informs social scientific inquiry into financial dissent. The result is the representation of community credit union dissent as an untainted form of localized cooperative resistance that is being compromised by powerful forces from without which pull it towards the mainstream. In contrast, I would stress that certain ambiguities are necessarily present in credit unions as a mode of dissent in everyday borrowing. Although credit union dissent undoubtedly (re)politicizes everyday borrowing performances in a number of important ways, these ambiguities ensure that it cannot stand as an unequivocal oppositional alternative to the transformed and booming market networks of everyday borrowing.

The ambiguities present in credit unions as mode of dissent in everyday borrowing arise out of the place of both technologies of calculation and state regulation in the constitution of credit unions. Let us consider and illustrate each of these ambiguities in turn. On the one hand, calculative technologies make possible the performance of credit unions as 'local' and not-for-profit financial institutions. Just as a balance sheet, for example, does not simply describe a bank's financial position but actually helps to constitute what we understand as a bank, so basic calculations for savings, loans, capital, reserves, insurance, and so on are key in the assembly of a credit union. There is also a sense in which the calculations that are common to banks—for example, calculations of profitability and shareholder value—provide the other against which credit unions come to differentiate themselves. Credit unions are different because they are not bound by these calculations. At the same time, comparisons between market institutions and credit unions are often reduced to a pair of numbers, that is, the interest rates payable on a loan taken out from each set of institutions. Potential credit union members are encouraged on the websites of both the ABCUL and CUNA, for example, to make use of loan calculators that will make plain to them the lower rates of interest that are offered by credit unions.

The place of calculative technologies in the materialization of credit unions is, on the other hand, also de-politicizing to the extent that it may become difficult to discern between credit unions and market institutions. This would seem to be especially the case as credit unions seek to expand their membership and lending, informed by the assumptions of economies of scale (Jerving 2007). For example, in the US, CUNA puts it in the following terms: 'you need to understand your market to grow your membership.'[11] In order to assist credit unions in maintaining their 'competitive edge', CUNA thus provide a range of 'best practice' and 'peer learning' tools, analyses, surveys, profiles, and so on. The extent to which the drive to increase membership is regarded as a marketing exercise by the leadership of US credit unions was, furthermore, starkly illustrated by CUNA's 1998 decision to appoint a 'Project Differentiation Committee'.[12] The Committee produced an example of a 'Statement of Commitment to Members', and encouraged all credit unions to produce their own similar

---

[11] http://advice.cuna.org/reports/memb_research.html
[12] http://www.cuna.org/pol_affairs/grassroots/project_d/project_dif.html

statements. While the statements are supposed to emphasize the cooperative roots of credit unions and encapsulate the differences between them and market institutions, the initiative was also a reflection of the ambiguities in credit unions as a mode of dissent. Those administering credit unions and writing a statement are told to 'Think of the Statement as a "Philosophy Policy"—similar in nature to your asset/liability management policy, but focusing instead on the philosophical aspects of your operations.' It is telling, then, that an 'asset/liability management policy' is already in place and is likely to be familiar to credit union administrators.

Recent debates between community credit union activists in Britain over the so-called 'instrumentalist' and 'idealist' models are, in effect, a manifestation of the ambiguities of credit union dissent that arise from the place of calculative techniques within it. The distinction between the instrumentalist and idealist models was initially made by Berthoud and Hinton (1989) in an attempt to demarcate what they saw as two contrasting ideologies within British credit unions. While instrumentalists emphasize the role of credit unions in efficiently providing for the savings and loans of as many people as possible, idealists stress the making of loans to those most in need and the empowering participation of those individuals and communities in the administration of small-scale credit unions. Since the late 1990s, following from concerns that many community credit unions were too small to be effective and that membership was not growing as fast as had been expected, instrumentalists have sought to press forward their agenda. By the end of the 1990s, 85 per cent of British credit unions were organized through community common bonds, but employer bond credit unions contributed half of the total credit union membership and 70 per cent of the total assets (Jones 2005: 14). For Paul Jones (2005), an academic advocate of the instrumentalist model, 'British credit unions are more successful when they develop as market-orientated social enterprises able to build effective partnerships with banks, government and the private sector to serve low-income communities' (p. 13). Members become customers in the first instance, individuals who are more likely to be eligible to join a credit union if common bond areas are extended and smaller credit unions are amalgamated. The traditional practice of requiring members to save over a certain period before they are permitted to borrow is to be phased out, replaced by calculative assessments of ability to repay. The efficiencies of rigorous calculation and accounting methods are held to be key to attracting new savers because, 'as market-orientated social enterprises', credit unions will be in a position to offer them more attractive dividends.

The ABCUL has clearly been persuaded of, and is now seeking to take forward, the instrumentalist model. For example, between 2002 and 2004, the ABCUL, with support from Barclays Bank and the Office of the Deputy Prime Minister, piloted a new system of calculations in nine community credit unions. This system is called PEARLS. Developed by the World Council of Credit Unions (WOCCU), PEARLS is 'a financial monitoring and business tool' that 'is invaluable to helping credit unions grow and develop, enabling them to better serve their target market' (ABCUL 2005: 5). It provides a series of standardized ratios to monitor the stability and financial performance of a credit union across the six areas that make up the PEARLS acronym. For instance, under 'Protection', the ratio for 'bad debt provision' sets a standard of 35 per cent of capital set aside. The manner in which PEARLS, in effect, re-constitutes a credit union through calculative technologies is perhaps best captured by the following from the ABCUL (2005) report that trumpets the pilot: 'financial discipline and rigor are essential qualities if you are going to run a financial intermediary, on low margins, serving an inherently risky membership profile' (p. 3). Note how the credit union is described as 'a financial intermediary'; the not-for-profit and cooperative status of the credit union becomes running 'on low margins'; and the members of the credit union are regarded not as individuals engaged in mutual self-help but as 'inherently risky'. In terms of the latter, those credit unions participating in the PEARLS pilot also became part of 'an affinity arrangement between ABCUL and Equifax', making use of 'a bespoke credit scoring tool' (p. 21).

What of the ambiguities in credit unions as a mode of dissent in everyday borrowing that arise out of place of the state in the constitution of credit unions? On the one hand, public legal provisions are essential to the materialization of credit unions as an alternative to market networks of everyday borrowing. State policy makers are in a position, then, to enable and promote credit unions as an alternative to market institutions. In the UK, for example, the key legislation, the Credit Unions Act, dates from 1979, and the regulation of credit unions by the FSA since 2002 has ensured that members are now protected in compensatory schemes that also apply to savers in banks and building societies. On the other hand, however, the public legal provisions through which credit unions are constituted also have potentially de-politicizing consequences for this mode of financial dissent. Indeed, on both sides of the Atlantic, recent regulatory initiatives and policy programmes have rendered credit unions increasingly problematic as a mode of dissent.

In the US, the reduction of credit union political activism to technical and regulatory concerns is particularly acute. The Credit Union Legislative Action Council, for example, is the tenth largest political action committee in the US in terms of contributions made to the campaign funds of those who stand for election. In terms of recent and current regulatory changes, the 1998 Credit Union Membership Act was the culmination of a debate over whether the nature of the common bond should be changed such that 'social business members' could be eligible to join credit unions. By 2006, one in four credit unions were admitting business members and providing business loans (Schenk 2006). The Credit Union Regulatory Improvement Act, meanwhile, was referred to the House Financial Services Committee in March 2007. If it were to be passed into law, the Act would move credit unions towards a risk-based approach to the calculation of capital, for instance, and would increase the limits that currently apply to the making of small business loans. As with the 1998 legislation, what is particularly notable about the market-orientated Regulatory Improvement Act is that CUNA is lobbying hard for its introduction. As the Association put it by way of endorsement for the Act: 'Regulatory relief for credit unions will help improve productivity and efficiency in a competitive and dynamic marketplace, and will translate into better and lower-cost service to credit union members'.[13]

In the UK, meanwhile, the relationship between credit unions and governmental programmes has undergone a significant change since the late 1990s. In Fuller and Jonas' (2003) terms, 'credit unions are being appropriated by the state under a selective instrumentalist guise' (p. 64). As the initial local governmental support of credit unions in the name of 'social inclusion' has given way to their incorporation into national governmental programmes in the name of 'financial inclusion' (see Chapter 7), so credit unions have become more akin to market institutions. During the late 1990s, local government intervention and support for community credit unions included small grants for set up costs, free office accommodation, and advice and training. By the end of the decade, local authorities were spending near to £10 million per annum on supporting credit union development (Jones 2005: 14). From the turn of the millennium, and since 2004 in particular (HM Treasury 1999, 2004), credit unions have come to form a key plank in policy initiatives that seek to address 'access'

---

[13] http://www.cuna.org/gov_affairs/legislative/issues/2007/curia.html

to affordable sources of credit at rates of interest below those that prevail in the 'alternative' sector.

While the shifting place of credit unions in UK neo-liberal governmental programmes is partly related to their repositioning as part of a national financial inclusion strategy, it would also seem to reflect a set of subtle change of emphasis within the main elements of the so-called 'social economy' agenda. As Amin, Cameron, and Hudson (2003) summarize it, UK governmental initiatives to utilize the 'social economy' or 'third sector' (not market, not state) seek to restore the economic vitality of local communities while promoting self-reliance and needs-based service provision. But, as they also note, despite representations of the social economy as self-reliant and self-financing, very few social economy enterprises are able to sustain themselves and tend to reply on public sector grants and/or service contracts. This was precisely the situation that prevailed with community credit unions by the late 1990s, whereby an emphasis on the 'needs' of deprived areas had resulted in increased local government expenditures and credit unions that were far from self-reliant. For example, in August 2001, one of the largest community-based credit unions, in Camberwell in south London, was saved from collapse. According to local MP Harriett Harman, 'If Camberwell had gone under it would not only have been a devastating blow to the policyholders and the area, but potentially disastrous for the credit union movement. We faced the prospect of members up and down the country taking their money out' (in Inman 2001). Although a 'cash call' among its members by the British Bankers' Association led to an agreement to provide a set of loans to the Camberwell credit union, this did not prove necessary. Instead, Camberwell credit union was taken over by neighbouring Southwark credit union. Southwark council also provided a £25,000 loan, topped up by loans from credit unions across the country, and £30,000 in donations were received from philanthropists.

So, in preparing credit unions for an effective role in combating financial exclusion, HM Treasury has driven forward an agenda that requires market-orientated changes in the ways in which credit unions are organized and operate in the name of self-financed expansion. These changes have, in part, been legislated through the introduction of the new regulatory regime within which credit unions now find themselves. FSA regulation of credit unions entails, for example, liquidity and capital adequacy requirements. But, regulatory changes are also spurred on by those within credit unions who favour the instrumental model. For Paul Jones (2005), for example, regulatory changes to date have not been sufficient. He even goes as far as to argue in favour of the removal of interest ceilings on credit union lending which currently stand at 26.8 per cent APR. In his terms, 'for any lender, small labour-intensive, high-risk loans are not economically viable in any numbers at this annual percentage rate' (p. 17). In sum, although, as Fuller and Jonas (2003) stress, the intensifying pressures for the constitution of market-orientated instrumentalist credit unions will continue to be contested by some activists, credit unions will nonetheless remain an ambiguous mode of dissent in everyday borrowing.

Concluding Remarks

Across Part II of this book, we have situated the boom in Anglo-American everyday borrowing in transformations in the principal market networks of mortgage and consumer borrowing. Emphasis has been placed on the contingent constitution of booming networks through specific calculative tools and performances of risk, especially as this realizes longer networks that now closely overlap and interconnect with the networks of the capital markets and feature the issue and trading of default risk-related instruments. Lenders' confidence in their apparent calculative capacity to break down and communicate uncertainties as risks, and intersections with seemingly deep and liquid markets for the trading of those risks, has created an explosion of credit. While many more borrowers are now incorporated into networks of everyday borrowing than was the case just a few decades ago, it has been shown that inequalities continue to be discursively and calculatively produced such that both the recently included and the marginalized pay considerably higher interest rates. The transformation and boom in everyday borrowing is embodied through the summoning up of a responsible and entrepreneurial subject who meets, manages, and manipulates his growing outstanding obligations. Tensions and contradictions are present, however, in the assembly of responsible and entrepreneurial borrowers such that performances of this subject position are incomplete and precarious. Our analysis in the previous chapters in Part II has, then, contributed towards opening up the apparently rational and scientific performances of everyday borrowing to disagreement by stressing the power relations, contingencies, and contradictions integral to their development.

Furthermore, in this chapter, we have addressed the presence, practicalities, possibilities, and problematics of dissent in everyday borrowing. We began by outlining the principal tendencies within dissent in everyday borrowing—the grounding of dissent in religious truths, and organized and collective action, in the name of the victims of predatory lending, to install publically re-regulated financial markets as a coherent alternative— and suggested that these tendencies are delimiting in analytical and political terms. The chapter has explored, therefore, two modes of dissent in everyday borrowing that would tend to be neglected in most accounts and regarded as politically insignificant. A focus on credit art and credit unions has continued our attempt to stress the multiple modes of dissent present in the everyday life of global finance, and to consider their possibilities. Credit art projects do not follow the disempowering assumption that the individual borrower who engages with them is a victim of financial power, but also suggest that perceived personal and political commitments in everyday borrowing cannot be simply reconciled. Credit art also shows that disturbing the settled moralities and meanings of everyday borrowing is possible without recourse to an alternative truth. Credit union dissent similarly does not understand borrowers as victims, but summons up a subject of dissent who reconciles perceived personal and political commitments though cooperative performances that are both intimate and collective. The efficacy of state regulation and intervention is also rejected by credit unions as a mode of dissent. At the same time, however, it has been shown that credit art and credit unions are ambiguous and compromised as modes of dissent. Both serve in their different ways to, at once, open up and close down the scope for disagreement over everyday borrowing and for thinking and performing everyday borrowing otherwise.

Conclusion: The Sub-Prime Mortgage Crisis

Introduction: 'A Niggle in an Arcane Corner of the US Mortgage Market'

The completion of the final manuscript of this book during August 2007 has coincided with deep ruptures in US sub-prime mortgage networks feeding into a serious breakdown in the world's capital markets. Since the end of February and throughout the summer months, fears about the perilous state of US sub-prime mortgages had contributed to bouts of considerable stock and bond market volatilities. But, on Thursday, 9 and Friday, 10 August, and amidst widespread uncertainties and sharp price changes across all markets, the European Central Bank (ECB), the Federal Reserve, and central banks in Japan, Canada, and Australia made available emergency loans totalling over $320 billion in the money markets at rates of interest below prevailing rates (Bajaj and Landler 2007). The ECB boosted money markets further on the following Monday, and by Friday, 17 the Federal Reserve had lowered the discount rate, that is, the rate at which it lends to banks. The slow evaporation of liquidity from bond markets over the preceding months had reached a crescendo and, without this pre-emptive intervention, a so-called 'credit crunch' seemed likely to lead the money markets to seize up. The commercial banks who dominate the money markets were at this moment only willing to provide short-term credit to each other at inflated interest rates, unsure precisely which of their number were struggling to deal with the fall-out from the crisis (Creswell 2007). The hedge fund arms of several major banks had recently been wound-up due to their investments in sub-prime MBS, and serious questions were being asked of the webs of lending and borrowing that bound all manner of financial institutions to investments in CDOs

230

arising from sub-prime securitization programmes and also private equity deals.

The problems in US sub-prime mortgage networks first began to come to light during the latter half of 2006, as 'delinquency rates'—that is, the percentage of borrowers falling behind by two months or more on their repayments—spiked quite sharply. By March 2007, this rate was running at 13 per cent, more than double the already rising 6.2 per cent rate of June 2006 (Bajaj and Nixon 2006b; *The Economist* 2007c). Sub-prime mortgages originated in 2005 and, especially 2006, were, then, proving particularly problematic. In the parlance of the industry, mortgages of this 'vintage' proved to be 'sour'. As the number of foreclosures in sub-prime networks also began to grow in March 2007, foreclosure rates on all mortgages also reached their highest levels since records were first kept in 1970 (Bajaj 2007a). Swamped by returns due to the early payment default clauses in their securitization programmes, a large number of small- and medium-sized sub-prime mortgage lenders either went out of business—36 by mid-March 2007 according to *The Economist* (2007 f)—or were purchased by Morgan Stanley, Merrill Lynch, Citigroup, Barclays, Deutsche Bank, and others at apparently bargain prices. HSBC's announcement of an overall record profit for 2006/7 in late February was overshadowed by the setting aside of a massive $11 billion of capital to cover bad debts going forward, and the chief executive and vice chairman of its US sub-prime mortgage arm HSBC Finance Corporation (created when HSBC acquired Household International in 2003) were forced to step down (*The Economist* 2007a). Credit derivative indexes for sub-prime MBS fell sharply during this period, and sub-prime lending was largely curtailed.

From May 2007, the difficulties experienced by sub-prime borrowers and lenders began to reverberate through to those who had invested in sub-prime MBS and CDOs, and then rippled into the capital markets more broadly. A total of roughly $100 billion worth of sub-prime mortgages were estimated to be 'bad debts' and the situation appeared likely to worsen, with defaults expected to reach $300 billion by the end of 2008 (White et al. 2007). Hedge funds that had invested in the most risky tranches of sub-prime mortgage CDOs were, perhaps not surprisingly, the first to experience major problems. Needing to liquidate their positions, the funds were unable to find any investors willing to take these instruments off their hands. UBS closed a fund that had lost over $120 million from investments in sub-prime bonds in May, for example, and two funds owned by major US investment bank and dominant mortgage market player Bear Stearns also suffered a high-profile closure in late June (*The Economist* 2007*a*). During July and August, hedge funds and structured investment vehicles (SIVs) as far and wide as the UK, Germany, The Netherlands, and Australia all reported problems arising out of investments in sub-prime MBS and CDOs. SIVs seek to take advantage of interest rate arbitrage, borrowing short-term with the backing of the banks that typically own and run them, and investing in ABS and CDOs (Tett, Davies, and Cohen 2007).

The close support provided to hedge funds by the major investment banks—for instance, a prime broker not only contributes to financing the leveraged or 'geared' investments of a fund, but also lends them stocks so that they can sell short—also ensured that they were far from immune to the sub-prime losses. Accordingly, their share prices oscillated wildly during the summer months. Given that many of the same hedge funds and banks that held sub-prime bonds had invested in the CDOs issued by private equity firms in the recent boom of high-profile buy-outs, liquidity also began to drain from these market networks (Davies and Scholtes 2007). Credit spreads—that is, the graduated premiums that riskier borrowers must pay over and above the benchmark interest rates for government borrowing—widened sharply. Private equity buy-outs had also inflated stock market prices in recent times, and so, in turn, stock markets also fell sharply on 9 and 10 August. French bank BNP Paribas suspended withdrawals from three funds that had significant investments in sub-prime MBS, citing the complete evaporation of liquidity in certain market segments. Countrywide Financial, the largest independent mortgage lender in the US, warned that, despite its limited involvement in sub-prime lending, it was struggling to find buyers for private label MBS and that it could not continue to hold large volumes of assets on its balance sheet without additional lending from banks. And, finally, the central banks began making liquidity available in the money markets.

It is unclear at the time of writing what the consequences of the 'credit crunch' will be over the coming months and years. However, on the basis of the analysis put forward in this book, what is clear is that, contrary, to *Financial Times* journalist Richard Beales (2007), the crisis is not simply an isolated case of 'a niggle in an arcane corner of the US mortgage market' that 'has escalated into what looks ever more like a global liquidity and credit crunch'. Rather, the current ructions in the world's financial markets are rooted in precisely that which has been the focus of this book: the unprecedented relationships, built up across the last three decades or so, between Anglo-American everyday financial life and the capital markets. I have sought throughout this book not merely to reveal, elucidate, and critically question these relationships, but also to argue that they should be (re)valued in our understanding of contemporary finance. The US sub-prime mortgage crisis is, of course, a desperate situation for the former mortgagors who have now lost their homes. But, it also provides a stark and timely illustration of the wider arguments made here. The extra-ordinary gyrations that are presently gripping the capital markets have arisen out of ruptures in the ordinary payment routines of mortgagors. The common sense representation of everyday saving and borrowing as of secondary importance to the apparently 'bigger' developments of global finance is found seriously wanting when that which appears at the margins actually comes to occupy centre stage.

The category of 'everyday life' has, in ontological terms, underpinned my argument throughout this book. Everyday life is not, and cannot be, merely 'residual'. As I suggested in the Introduction, there is a need to turn the established representations of contemporary finance as 'global finance' inside out and on their head. The development of the four prin-cipal conceptual themes that I initially set out in Chapter 1—networks, power, identity, and dissent—has created purchase for my critical analysis of the everyday life of global finance in the subsequent chapters. Devel-oping these themes has enabled an analysis that follows through on the initial ontological move to take everyday life seriously. In this concluding chapter, then, I want to return to each of these conceptual themes in the context of the US sub-prime mortgage crisis. As the discussion below will show, if we ground an analysis of the crisis in concepts that have been developed to reveal and revalue the significance of everyday routines in contemporary finance, the result is an interpretation of the crisis that is quite different to that which prevails among policy makers and media commentators. Contrary to dominant interpretations, the crisis is not simply an anomalous outcome of problems largely specific to US sub-prime mortgage lending. Rather, it is also profoundly related to the wider transformations that have created unprecedented relationships between Anglo-American everyday borrowing, on the one hand, and the capital markets of global finance, on the other.

Financial Networks

As it has been developed here by drawing primarily on actor-network the-ory, the conceptual theme of financial networks has been pursued across two main dimensions. First, contemporary finance has been decentred in a manner that eschews hierarchical representations of space and scale such as 'global' and 'local', and which views contemporary qualitative transformations in multiple and more-or-less discrete saving and borrowing networks as entailing their lengthening, overlap, and intersection with the various networks of the capital markets. The conceptual theme of financial networks has thus enabled an analysis that recognizes the unprecedented relationships between everyday finance and the capital markets but, at the same time, does not collapse into the belief that the former is just a new playground that has become occupied by the latter.

Second, we have emphasized the significance of dynamic calculative tools and performances of risk to the constitution of networks of everyday saving and borrowing. Chapters 2 and 3 stressed, for example, that the materialization of qualitatively transformed everyday saving networks has been made possible by the partial displacement of techniques of thrift and insurance by those of investment. Similarly, Chapter 6 emphasized the contribution of the techniques of credit scoring and default risk management to the constitution of the transformation and boom in everyday borrowing networks. The confidence and legitimacy arising from a newly found calculative capacity to break down and communicate uncertainties as risks, alongside intersections with seemingly deep and liquid markets for the trading of those risks, were shown to be key to the explosion of consumer and mortgage lending.

US sub-prime mortgage networks are, in our terms, especially long and interconnected when compared with prime mortgage networks. Although the new techniques and performances of default risk produce close intersections between prime mortgage networks and the networks of the capital markets, in sub-prime lending these overlaps are particularly extensive. As was detailed in Chapter 7, sub-prime mortgage lenders are typically non-banks that, while appearing to stand at the margins and to cater for the marginalized, are highly reliant upon capital provided by mainstream institutions and the markets. In the course of the current crisis, it is the extensive points of intersection across sub-prime mortgage networks that have ensured that the repayment problems of mortgagors have fed so clearly and rapidly into the wider capital markets. For example, popular media coverage of the crisis currently tends to emphasize the ways in which the hedge funds that held many of the riskiest tranches of 2005 and 2006 vintage sub-prime CDOs have been forced to wind-up their operations. The hedge funds were highly leveraged and thus, in turn, those banks that have provided the hedge funds with much of their capital have also been drawn into the crisis. Yet, the overlaps between

US sub-prime networks and the capital markets are certainly not limited to intersections between lenders' securitization programmes, on the one hand, and a few isolated hedge funds and their bankers, on the other.

The accounts of those sub-prime mortgage lenders recently forced out of business provide further insights into who, precisely, had been buying the sub-prime MBS and CDOs that were issued. Although primarily the preserve of investment banks, commercial banks, insurance companies, and hedge funds, some US everyday investors had also purchased these risky instruments via their mutual fund contributions (Morgenson 2007b). Add to this the holdings of 'prime' mortgage-backed securities by mature pension schemes and, for that matter, schemes' stakes in hedge funds, and something quite startling begins to emerge out of the sub-prime mortgage crisis. The contemporary relationships between everyday saving and borrowing and the capital markets have become so omnipresent that savers are not just reliant upon returns from the corporations and governments in which they have invested—and, by extension, upon their own productivity, choices, and deductions as workers, consumers, and taxpayers. Savers have also become, in some instances at least, directly reliant for investment returns on their own repayments as borrowers.

What of the significance of calculative tools and performances of risk to the constitution and crisis of US sub-prime mortgage networks? The principal argument put forward in Chapter 7 was that the extension of lending to greater numbers of borrowers in recent decades has not produced a genuine or democratic 'financial inclusion', far from it. Rather, stark inequalities in the interest rates paid by borrowers are produced through the differentiation of 'prime' from 'sub-prime', for example, and, in sub-prime networks, through techniques of risk-based pricing, securitization, and structured finance. These tools provide the means through which the uncertainties of lending to those designated 'sub-prime' are calculated, priced, and rationalized as 'risks'. When combined with the positive recasting of risk as opportunity by the technologies of investment that we covered in Part I, sub-prime MBS and CDOs as packages of risk/reward thus become very attractive to a range of investors. But, as we have noted at various points in this book, calculative techniques and performances of risk can necessarily only provide for the feigning of control over an uncertain future. For example, in Chapter 4, it was suggested that the performance of the subject position of 'the investor' is rendered precarious and incomplete by the inherent failure of risk calculations to bring order to uncertainty. For us, the risk/uncertainty contradiction would also seem to be crucial to understanding the US sub-prime mortgage crisis.

Unable to capture, measure, and mange future uncertainties, risk technologies have been at the heart of the crisis. Given that risk-based pricing
failed, in its own terms, to effectively price risk in US sub-prime mortgage
networks, it is not surprising that this calculative edifice has already come
under some critical scrutiny from policy makers and media commentators. Attention has concentrated on the extent to which the relative
infancy of sub-prime networks meant that there was a lack of 'historical
data' on which inferences from past statistics could be used to calculate
future probabilities of default for different categories of borrower. Furthermore, the historical data that was available for sub-prime mortgagors only
encompassed the period of relatively low and stable interest rates and
rising house prices since the early 1990s. So, for example, when seeking
to defend the failure of staff at HSBC Finance Corporation to predict the
scale of defaults by their borrowers, Chief Executive of HSBC Michael
Geoghagan noted that 'You've got to have history for analytics...the
fact of the matter is there [isn't history] for the adjustable rate mortgage
business when you've had 17 jumps in US interest rates' (in *The Economist*
2007*b*). Yet, for us, what is notable is that existing scrutiny of the place
of risk-based pricing in the crisis assumes that future uncertainties could
indeed be priced through vigorous calculation if sufficient information
was, or could be, stored in databases and so on. What is missing, at
present, is recognition of the contradictions of risk-based pricing.

Confronted by potential sub-prime mortgagors, risk-based pricing produced faith among lenders and their investors that it was possible to
price for the future uncertainty of whether an individual borrower would
meet their obligations. Indeed, automated underwriting systems actually
reinforced the apparent control of the future offered by risk-based pricing.
Automated underwriting made it possible in instances where a mortgage
applicant was categorized as 'refer/eligible' or 'refer/ineligible' by underwriting systems—meaning that, for one reason of another, they could not
be considered an 'investment quality loan' on the secondary markets—
for a loan to be approved '*without further manual underwriting* by simply
offering that applicant a higher interest rate' (Eggert 2007; Stuart 2003:
128 *original emphasis*). Speeding-up the mortgage process and realizing
commissions appeared to hold no danger or downside for lenders on a
case-by-case basis. And, yet, the collective future uncertainties of mortgagors necessarily escaped calculation.

It is widely recognized that the credit scoring techniques from which
risk-based pricing is derived focus only on an individual's past credit
history (see Leyshon and Thrift 1999). They do not take into account the

possibility that a future change in economic conditions (e.g. recession, fall in property prices, rising interest rates) will effect not only prospects for an individual borrower, but also the large numbers of borrowers on a lender's books. Risk-based pricing in sub-prime networks similarly only calculates default rates for individuals within a particular category. In the terms of those seeking to develop and perfect techniques of risk-based pricing, they do not currently address so-called 'default correlation'. Writing prior to the crisis and based upon their analysis of the portfolio of a major US sub-prime mortgage lender, Cowan and Cowan (2004) warn, for instance, that 'as credit quality declines, the importance of default correlation increases... ignoring default correlation in the development of credit risk models for subprime portfolios would lead to considerable model risk' (p. 755). For us, however, the failure of risk-based pricing to take into account 'default correlation' led to considerably more that 'model risk'. It ensured that, when widespread defaults arose linked to interest rate rises and house price falls, sub-prime lenders incurred losses that were not only uncalculated but on a much greater scale than could have been predicted.

Given the close relationship between risk-based pricing, on the one hand, and the rating of the instruments that are created through securitization and structured finance, on the other, the contradictions of the former have also permeated through to the latter. While the credit rating calculations of S&P, Moodys, and Fitch are in themselves necessarily undercut by an incapacity to fully capture an uncertain future through the prism of risk, this contradiction is heightened when credit rating rests on the risks calculated for particular categories of everyday borrower. The failure of credit rating calculations and agencies in the course of the sub-prime crisis has certainly attracted considerable political and media attention. Although rising delinquencies and foreclosure rates among sub-prime borrowers were apparent in late 2006, the credit rating agencies did not begin to downgrade the associated securities until the spring of 2007. Moreover, the original rating of CDOs in particular as 'triple-A'—which in sovereign and corporate bond markets represents an instrument as low risk and highly liquid—is being seriously questioned (Beales and Scholtes 2007). The House Financial Services Committee of the US Congress and the European Commission are, at the time of writing, planning investigations into the role of the credit rating agencies in the crisis (Buck 2007). However, it appears highly unlikely that an acknowledgement of the contradictions of scoring, pricing, and rating risk will figure in their deliberations. Instead, it is the specific ratings assigned to CDOs, and relationships between the rating agencies and their clients—those issuing MBS and CDOs pay the agencies for their services—that will likely be the focus for investigations.

The risk/uncertainty contradiction, as it is manifest in the calculative technologies of securitization, also began to surface in the course of the crisis. The techniques of securitization can be seen to be 'pro-cyclical': that is, they encourage a proliferation in the scale and scope of lending in the 'good times', over and above that which would take place if loans remained on lenders books; and they result in a sharper tightening of lending in the 'bad times', and thereby increase the possibility of a 'credit crunch' (Chancellor 2005). As noted by the lone critical contributor to the Senate Banking, Housing and Urban Affairs Committee's session on the place of securitization in the crisis, the movement of default risks off-balance sheet means that fee-hungry lenders may pay insufficient attention to the default risks of their borrowers (Eggert 2007). More broadly, the Bank of England (2007) worry that the sub-prime crisis suggests that 'the "originate and distribute" model' of lending dilutes 'incentives for the effective screening and monitoring of loans' (p. 22). Operating in a not dissimilar vein to the contradictory dynamics of risk-based pricing, then, securitization contributes to, and provides the incentives for, the making of more and more loans on a case-by-case basis. But, at the same time, there remain significant doubts as to the place of the capital markets in addressing collective future uncertainties.

The 'spreading' of default sub-prime mortgage risks through the tools and performances of securitization and structured finance is viewed in highly favourable terms by two recent contributors to the IMF's working paper series (Kiff and Mills 2007). Writing prior to the central bank interventions of August 2007, Kiff and Mills argue that

The dispersion of credit risk to a broader and more diverse group of investors has . . . helped to make the U.S. financial system more resilient. The magnitude and scale of losses being currently experienced in subprime mortgage markets would have materially impacted some systematically-important U.S. financial institutions in the traditional originate-and-retain business model. (p. 12)

Kiff and Mill's position is consistent with other orthodox financial economists and policy makers who emphasize the efficiencies of disintermediated finance. For the Bank of England (2006a), for instance,

Financial engineering of this type does not alter the financial sector's aggregate credit exposure to the non-financial sector. It does, however, alter the distribution of risk within the financial sector by concentrating it in some securities and reducing it in others. This can improve systemic stability if risk is held by those with the greatest capacity to absorb losses. (p. 21)

But, as the Bank notes on the same page, 'investors in these securities are vulnerable to macroeconomic risks that affect many of the underlying ABS at the same time'. The sub-prime mortgage crisis has provided the first significant moment when such 'macroeconomic risks' have been felt in ABS and CDO markets, and provides 'an important test of the structure of this market and its performance in response to stress' (Bank of England 2007: 22; also *The Economist* 2006c, 2007d). That the sub-prime mortgage crisis appears at the time of writing to have fuelled a wider credit crunch would seem to indicate, however, that the risk/uncertainty contradiction ensures that this 'test' has been failed (*The Economist* 2007e, 2007g). 'Risk spreading' may not actually 'improve systemic stability'. Rather, once flaws in risk calculations, in effect, become apparent, and uncertainties come to prevail, 'risk spreading' may actually contribute to what we might call 'systemic uncertainty'.

Given that the default risk management techniques of securitization and structured finance are (as Chapter 6 has shown) also pivotal to the materialization of the transformation and boom in everyday borrowing, the presence of such systemic uncertainties is particularly troubling. The risk/uncertainty contradiction is apparent not just in the securitization programmes of US sub-prime mortgage lenders, but in the trading of claims on the default risks of everyday borrowers more broadly. To put this differently, the possibilities of what Keynes (1961) famously termed the 'liquidity illusion' are now much more likely in mortgage and consumer lending than was the case in the relatively short and disconnected networks of the past. The 'liquidity' of the capital markets that has supported Anglo-American mortgage and consumer borrowing over the last few decades is, after all, a matter of investors' expectations and faith in risk calculations (Carruthers and Stinchcombe 1999). Should the rationality and scientific accuracy of the calculative techniques and performances of credit scoring, credit rating, and securitization come to be questioned beyond sub-prime networks, then a credit crunch would be much more widely felt by everyday borrowers.

Financial Power

The conceptual theme of financial power has in part been developed in this book to stress the power relations and politics at play as market networks are constituted through calculative tools and performances of risk. Drawing on Foucault's (1980) work on power/knowledge, and the extension of this work with reference to modern finance by Marieke de Goede (2005*b*), the representation of everyday saving and borrowing routines as rational, scientific, and legitimate has been viewed throughout as crucial to their materialization. In Chapter 2, for example, it was argued that the consolidation of everyday investment is not the outcome of some mass 'irrational exuberance' (Shiller 2001), but has been made possible precisely because, relative to thrift and insurance, investment appears as the most rational form of saving. In stressing the power relations and politics of representation, the conceptual theme of financial power has also been explored by examining the ways in which the calculative technologies of saving and borrowing networks are also imbricated and deployed in liberal government. Following from and contributing to the Foucauldian-inspired literature on 'governmentality', Chapters 2 and 3 emphasized, for example, that transformations in everyday saving arise from reconfigurations in calculation that are underway, at once, in both dynamic financial networks and shifting governmental programmes. While the embracing of risk through the tools of investment is an essential part of the apparatus of neo-liberal government and is promoted in a disciplinary manner across governmental programmes, the transformation of everyday saving is nonetheless contingent, contested, and not simply reducible to the rise of neo-liberalism. Similarly, in Chapter 8, the embodiment of responsible and entrepreneurial borrowers was seen to combine neo-liberal regulatory, welfare, and bankruptcy regimes which summon up an asset-holding consumer of credit, on the one hand, and the calculative techniques and performances of credit card and mortgage networks, on the other.

In marking out and developing the conceptual theme of financial power in this way, one of my chief concerns has been to counter two alternative and more established perspectives. First, social theorists of money tend to associate financial power with the processes of modernity and, in particular, with the instrumental rationality and homogenization of social relations that is assumed to be carried forward by the spread of modern money and finance. This perspective is especially evident in the research into consumer credit by sociologists, but, as the chapters that comprise Part II have shown, the apparent scientific rationality produced by the spread of credit relations is assembled, negotiated, re-assembled, and contested across more-or-less discrete networks. Second, social scientists of finance typically cast financial power as the material resources and rent-seeking ownership claims of finance capital as a specific economic group and class interest. Given the long-standing and diverse intellectual lineage of this second perspective on financial power—it draws on Marx, Keynes, and an array of social democrats and social liberals—it is perhaps not surprising that it has come to feature in current coverage of the US sub-prime mortgage crisis.

The crisis provoked, for instance, a stinging response from Larry Elliott (2007) of *The Guardian* newspaper in the UK. For Elliott, sub-prime finance and the ensuing crisis is a direct consequence of the power of Wall Street's 'moneychangers' who 'are back, bigger and badder than ever'. Here sub-prime lenders and brokers are 'a bunch of snake-oil salesmen, hucksters and crooks' that 'fleeced millions of vulnerable Americans'. The calculative technologies that we have identified as significant to the constitution and crisis of sub-prime networks—especially risk-based pricing, securitization, and structured finance—are held to be 'pure hokum' that gave 'the scam a veneer of bogus credibility'. Although less strident and explicit than Elliott in their opposition to the power of Wall Street, some US policy makers and media commentators also point the finger of blame at the lending practices which stoked the 'bubble' in sub-prime mortgages. Contingent conditions are typically acknowledged to have contributed to both the inflation and bursting of bubble—most notably, rising and then falling house prices, and low and then increasing interest rates. But, particularly as the crisis has deepened, sub-prime has become associated with lax-lending and get-rich-quick predatory profiteering. In Edward Chancellor's (2005) terms, the sub-prime mortgage debacle is thus being cast as typical of 'the anatomy of credit bubbles', whereby 'unsound banking' and 'Bending of the rules, evading regulations or ignoring traditions that have restricted lending in the past' all took hold (pp. 12–14). For example, underwriting assessments of new borrowers by sub-prime lenders are identified as having been, at best, cursory and, at worst, largely non-existent. For Christopher J. Dodd (2007), Chairman of the Senate Banking Committee, lenders originated mortgages 'on the basis of the value of the property, not the ability of borrowers to repay. This is the fundamental definition of predatory lending'. There are indeed clear indications that many sub-prime lenders in the US in 2005 and 2006, most notably HSBC, provided simultaneous second mortgages which, in effect, pushed loan-to-value ratios up to 100 per cent and even higher (The *Economist* 2007c).

In contrast with readings of the crisis that either explicitly assert or implicitly assume that it can be traced to the power, interests, and greed of finance capital, the conception of financial power developed in this book leads to an interpretation that emphasizes the materialization of the crisis through contradictions in key calculative technologies of risk. These technologies do not serve as 'a veneer' in the seemingly separable realm of sub-prime finance that is populated by 'crooks', but are also pivotal to the assembly of all manner of prime networks and their interconnections with the capital networks. To be sure, the transformations in everyday saving and borrowing that we have covered in this book have massively enriched those, in Wall Street and the City, that we tend to know as 'finance capital'. The emergence of US sub-prime mortgage networks is no exception in this regard. There is also a sense in which the representation of financial economies through the calculative prism of 'risk' makes possible the accumulation of profits in the present, and the colonizing of profit opportunities in the future (Blackburn 2006*b*). Yet, contemporary transformations in Anglo-American saving and borrowing have not been imposed and ideologically legitimated from 'the outside' by finance capital, but are contingently embedded and embodied 'inside' the power relations of everyday networks and neo-liberal government. In (re)politicizing sub-prime and making the power relations at work intelligible, we need to open-up sub-prime—and by implication, everyday borrowing networks more broadly—to contestation by stressing the fragilities, tensions, and contradictions of the apparently scientific risk technologies that feature in the de-politicized constitution of present and future.

Financial Identity

The conceptual theme of financial identity has been developed here to enable scrutiny of the embodiment of transformations in everyday saving and borrowing. Questions of financial identity, and especially the assembly of everyday financial subjects and subjectivities, are rarely considered by social scientists. Drawing on insights from Foucault's later work, Chapters 4 and 8 have thus explored the making of multiple everyday financial subjects—'investors', 'revolvers', and 'leveraged investors'—as crucial to the embodiment of mutual fund, occupational pension, credit card, and mortgage networks. Throughout, stress has been placed on the ways in which the calling up of financial subjects plays on central features of liberal subjectivity, namely freedom and security. As such, I have argued that transformations in everyday saving and borrowing are embodied through the summoning up of neo-liberal financial subjectivities, of individual subjects who recurrently and routinely perform new and changed forms of financial self-discipline. While Chapter 4 suggested that investment and the embracing of risk/reward now stands as a significant technology of the self, Chapter 8 suggested that this supplanting of prudence and thrift is accompanied by new self-disciplines of responsibly and entrepreneurially meeting, managing, and manipulating the outstanding obligations that arise from extended borrowing.

Chapters 4 and 8 also stressed the contingency, contradictions, and ambiguities present in processes of identification. Neo-liberal everyday financial subjects are what we have termed 'uncertain subjects', that is, the performance of subject positions and new self-disciplines is problematic, precarious, and always incomplete. For example, investment as a technology of the self is contradictory as it rests on calculations of financial risk/reward that cannot bring order to future uncertainty. The representation of financial subjects as disconnected and unitary subjects, figures who are somehow isolated from all but their financial relations, cannot be maintained. For instance, the performances of investment and responsibly meeting outstanding borrowing obligations both stand in tension with the flexibilized practices of the 'worker entrepreneur' (Amoore 2004) which are apparently also essential to securing, advancing, and expressing individual freedom in neo-liberal society. Both investment and the meeting of obligations require a relatively stable income, but this is undercut by uncertainties of over employment, pay, and so on.

In the context of the crisis of US sub-prime mortgage networks, the account provided in Chapter 8 of the calling up of what we called 'leveraged investors' would seem to be of particular relevance. The embodiment of extended sub-prime borrowing can thus be related to the assembly of individuals as owner-occupiers who regard their home not merely as a space of shelter and refuge, but as an asset that will grow to realize returns. While these returns appear as essential for freedom and security in the future, they also require the disciplines of responsible and entrepreneurial extended borrowing in the present. Indeed, as was shown in Chapter 8, governmental programmes in the US explicitly seek to further owner-occupation and asset-based wealth accumulation by targeting those individuals within society that are also most likely to fall within the category of 'sub-prime'. It is against this moral, political, and technological backdrop, then, that the vast majority of US sub-prime mortgagors came to turn to so-called 'affordability products' from 2004 onwards.

As was emphasized more broadly in Chapter 8, once the owner-occupier is summoned up as a leveraged investor, individuals and couples are more likely to take up mortgage products that enable them to entrepreneurially reduce and manage their obligations in the short term. In sub-prime networks, 'affordability products' included negative amortization loans and various forms of 'adjustable rate mortgages' (ARMs). From 2003, 'hybrid' or 'interest-only' ARMs became the norm in sub-prime networks. Under an interest-only ARM, the length of time over which interest and repayments are to be made is compressed, and the first two or three years are taken as a 'teaser' period at the outset of the mortgage. For example, under a so-called '2/28 hybrid', the first two years provide a 'teaser' period, and the remaining payments are made over the subsequent 28 years. At the end of the teaser period, the mortgage 'resets' to a substantially higher interest rate and monthly repayment. The entrepreneurial manipulation of outstanding obligations by the leveraged investor is an important self-discipline within an interest-only ARM. Underpinning this form of mortgage is the assumption that the mortgagor will take up a 'refi' before the option period comes to an end and monthly payments rise. House price rises during the option period will create equity that can be 'cashed out' to meet the future and higher repayments of the refinanced mortgage. However, a nasty surprise lay in store for those sub-prime borrowers who took out their interest-only ARMs during 2004 and 2005: interest rates rose and house prices fell during their initial option periods (Bajaj and Nixon 2006a; *The Economist* 2007c, 2007f).

Overall, a quarter of all mortgages in the US in 2006 were ARMs, a figure that rises to over three-quarters in sub-prime networks and higher still in California, the cities of the South, and along the Texan border with Mexico where sub-prime borrowers are concentrated (Bajaj and Nixon 2006a, 2006b; *The Economist* 2007b, 2007f). The prospect that these mortgages will reset to higher rates, and that few will be able to refinance to improved rates, ensures that a cloud will continue to hang over US sub-prime mortgagors for some time to come. The re-setting of interest rates on ARMs has been projected to result in around one-quarter of these mortgagors finding themselves in negative equity by 2008, and further one-third in default (*The Economist* 2007c). Shortly after the sub-prime mortgage crisis broke, then, the Federal Deposit Insurance Corporation moved to establish new and more restrictive underwriting standards that apply to banks who offer ARMs to prime mortgagors (*The Economist* 2007b).

Drawing on our analysis of the assembly of the uncertain subjects of the everyday life of global finance, however, the problems that ARMs generated for sub-prime mortgagors can be seen as far from an isolated incidence. Like the problems experienced since 2000 by recent retirees who have been confronted by very poor annuity rates (see Chapter 4), so the interest rate and house price changes that undercut adjustable-rate mortgagors are not just a case of misfortune and bad timing. Rather, the performance of neo-liberal everyday financial subject positions is necessarily precarious, undermined by contradictions and tensions that emerge in self-disciplines that turn on the calculation of the future. As William C. Apgar, assistant housing secretary in the Clinton administration, aptly puts it in relation to debt consolidation, for example, house equity 'can't be used as an everlasting reserve fund for folks who have more expenses than income on a perpetual basis' (in Moss 2004). The contradictions of risk/uncertainty and of manipulating outstanding mortgage obligations do not surface in abstract terms, but are lived in the repetitious performances of everyday savers and borrowers.

Financial Dissent

The conceptual theme of financial dissent, as it was set out in Chapter 1, drew attention to the 'curious and politically problematic search for a great refusal' (Foucault 1976: 96) by social scientists of finance. This search was held to manifest itself in research that: seeks to expose the 'true' material horrors of finance in the name of those who suffer; assumes the binary of power/resistance, often looking to the regulatory authority of public institutions as the means through which an unequivocal alternative can be established; and supposes that resistance must take particular collective and organized forms. In contrast, through the development of the conceptual theme of financial dissent, I have sought to: open up the highly technical and thoroughly de-politicized performances of finance to critical scrutiny because it is precisely this which is central to the exercise of power; recognize the inseparability of power and resistance, such that dissent is always ambiguous and, at least in part, compromised in one way or another; and emphasize the presence of multiple forms of dissent in the everyday life of global finance.

This book, then, should be seen as broadly consistent with the spirit of critique that, as highlighted in the Introduction, has motivated many academics of everyday life. It is indeed clear that contemporary transformations in saving and borrowing routines introduce vulnerabilities, volatilities, and inequalities into Anglo-American everyday life that were previously absent. As it has been developed here though, the theme of financial dissent will no doubt frustrate those who would prefer an irrefutable rejection of the unprecedented relationships that now bind everyday finance with the capital markets. As Chapters 5 and 9 have shown, there are at present modes of dissent that do incontrovertibly reject the shift to everyday investment, for example, and which seek to install seemingly untainted alternatives through collective and organized politics. Chapter 5 began by noting the presence, for instance, of collective calls and campaigns to defend and reinvigorate previously predominant forms of saving, most notably insurance. Analytically and politically, my concern has not been to play down such modes of dissent, but to recognize the delimiting consequences that follow from the search for a great refusal that these modes of dissent tend to reflect and promote. Chapters 5 and 9 have concentrated, therefore, on the analysis of modes of dissent that would seem likely to be dismissed and neglected by those searching for a great refusal. At the same time, both chapters have explored the political possibilities and problematics of modes of dissent, rather than judging them in terms of their capacity to forge unequivocal alternatives. For instance, Chapter 5 concentrated on SRI even though it does not, by any means, represent a clear alternative to everyday investment. But, whether as pension fund socialism or ethical investment, SRI nonetheless provides competing representations of the purpose of investment that prompt and embody activist approaches to investment.

My analysis in Chapter 9 of dissent in everyday borrowing would appear to be particularly relevant to understanding the dissent that has emerged in the context of the US sub-prime mortgage crisis. The crisis has witnessed the principal tendencies that, as was suggested at the outset of Chapter 9, are often present within dissent in everyday borrowing more broadly. First, religious 'truths' that lead to the condemnation of usury have found expression in the course of crisis, often underpinning the denunciation of sub-prime lenders as predatory. Second, dissent in the sub-prime crisis has also been marked by the tendency to assume that a solution can be found in order to realize an apparent and reasoned alternative. Third, calls for regulatory control over sub-prime lending are made on the grounds that sub-prime borrowers, as victims of predatory lenders, are largely unable to help themselves. All three tendencies have come together in the critical contributions made to various hearings of the House Committee on Financial Services, the Senate Committee on Banking, Housing, and Urban Affairs, and the Congressional Joint Economic Committee.

Congressional concerns to date have centred on the role of public authority in preventing a similar crisis in the future. There has been much handwringing over the relationship between the lax and predatory lending that built up in the boom, and the lack of federal regulatory and supervisory authority in relation to sub-prime lenders as non-banks. Senator Charles E. Schumer, Democrat of New York, told a hearing of the Congressional Joint Economic Committee, for example, that the sub-prime mortgage debacle was 'a terrible instance where a lack of oversight has led to a Wild West mentality among unscrupulous lenders and, frankly, the exploitation of large numbers of financially unsophisticated borrowers' (in Peters and Andrews 2007). At the same hearing, Federal Reserve Chairman Ben Bernanke conceded that it would be worth considering whether Congress should give the Fed and others the authority to enforce regulations on mortgage lenders who are non-banks. Banks are subject to the oversight of the likes of the Federal Reserve, Federal Deposit Insurance Corporation, and the Office of the Comptroller of the Currency. In contrast, non-bank sub-prime mortgage providers are only covered by the consumer protection regulations enforced by the Federal Trade Commission, and by secondary mortgage market regulations policed by Department of Housing and Urban Development (Rushton 2007). Patchy state-level regulations apply to the licensing of non-banks, brokers, and servicers, with only half of the states having laws against predatory lending.

In terms of bailing out sub-prime borrowers as the 'victims' of the crisis, meanwhile, the attention of activists and policy makers has come to focus on Freddie Mac, Fannie Mae, and the Federal Housing Association. These are the principal government-sponsored enterprises involved in supporting mortgage lending to minorities and those on low incomes. According to Stuart (2003), the pressure on Freddie and Fannie to make mortgages available to these groups led them to begin to relax underwriting standards in the 1990s. In addition, as sub-prime mortgage networks developed, Freddie and Fannie purchased sub-prime MBS, holding around 15 per cent of all sub-prime MBS in 2006 (Bajaj 2007b). In the wake of the crisis, Freddie and Fannie have withdrawn from the purchase of all MBS backed by ARMs that do not conform to the new guidelines created by the Federal Deposit Insurance Corporation. Therefore, in effect, Freddie and Fannie have withdrawn from the purchase of sub-prime MBS. Amidst the liquidity crisis of August 2007, however, Fannie Mae proposed to invest a further $72 billion (equivalent of 10% of its existing portfolio) in the struggling sub-prime and Alt-A sectors of the MBS market (Dash 2007). The move was blocked, however, by the regulator, the Office of Federal Housing Enterprise. In line with the arguments put forward by the Bush administration, the regulator suggested that these sectors lay outside of Fannie Mae's remit, and that further progress was needed to clean up the institutions books after the accounting scandal of 2006. Meanwhile, the Federal Housing Association has been identified as key in plans to bail-out borrowers who experience problems with defaults on their obligations (Bajaj and Nixon 2006b; *The Economist* 2007c). Calls have been made for the rules governing the activities of the FHA to be re-written in order that it can re-finance those sub-prime mortgages that are in default.

Although dissent that seeks federal regulation of predatory sub-prime lenders and to bail out defaulting sub-prime borrowers is laudable in its own terms, it misses the point somewhat in the light of the analysis and arguments put forward in this book. As Chapters 5 and 9 have stressed, financial dissent is necessarily ambiguous and compromised, and the search for a great refusal and a coherent and logical alternative will always end in disappointment. Drawing on this argument, I would like to close with two points that I see as most relevant to financial dissent in the context of the sub-prime crisis. First, given the place of contradictory risk technologies at the heart of the crisis, the politics of calculation is highly significant to on-going dissent. Yet, as our analysis of SRI and credit unions has illustrated, the ambiguities of financial dissent are often found in the politics of calculation. Contesting predominant calculative tools and performances, at once, opens up and closes down possibilities for (re)politicization and disagreement. This can be seen, for example, in the current attempts of legal activists and organizations, such as AFFIL and National Association of Consumer Advocates, to draw attention to the problems that securitization techniques have created for borrowers facing foreclosure.

On the one hand, it is certainly the case that securitization enshrines in new ways the long-standing legal principle that the borrower is responsible for meeting outstanding obligations. When a mortgagor experienced repayment problems in the short and relatively disconnected networks of the post-war era, lender and borrower could renegotiate the terms of those obligations in order to avoid foreclosure. In contrast, in long and densely interconnected sub-prime networks, there is little scope for co-responsibility at moments of distress. Strict investor protections included within securitization programmes often thwart any attempts by the servicers, charged with mortgage repayment collection, to renegotiate mortgagors' loan agreements (Kiff and Mills 2007; Morgenson 2007*a*; Scholtes 2007). Recent guidance issued by federal regulators urging banks to work with sub-prime borrowers who are in default is, then, of little consequence (Beales et al. 2007). On the other hand, however, focusing dissent on the legal definitions of particular responsibilities of parties within securitization programmes is de-politicizing. The wider question as to whether borrower and lender should actually be co-responsible for future obligations is reduced and narrowed down to a specific technical and procedural matter.

Second, and finally, financial dissent that identifies a particular group and/or set of institutions and practices as clearly to blame for the sub-prime crisis—whether predatory lenders, ARMs, or the credit rating agencies, for example—may well be politically disabling. As we noted in our analysis of SRI as a mode of financial dissent in Chapter 5, apportioning blame in this way contributes not only to securing a singular foe as scapegoat, but also to securing the identity of those who are assumed to oppose that foe. For pension fund socialists, for example, the representation of finance capital as the powerful enemy to be overcome at the same time secured a working-class subject of dissent in pensions. In the sub-prime crisis, meanwhile, pointing the finger at predatory lenders, or their cosy relationships with the credit rating agencies, rather conveniently secures the identity of responsible 'prime' lenders and borrowers. Given that the calculative techniques and performances of risk that have proved so contradictory in sub-prime networks also make possible embodied prime networks of everyday borrowing, this relational representation of a realm occupied by responsible lenders and borrowers is especially problematic. Financial dissent in the sub-prime crisis needs to call into question not only those who would seem to be implicated in the excesses of sub-prime networks. If there is to be a genuine and ethical 'democratization of finance', we must also be prepared to question the broader and seemingly secure networks, calculative performances, and identities of the everyday life of global finance.

Bibliography

ABCUL (2005). *An Introduction to PEARLS in Britain*, London: Association of British Credit Unions Ltd. Available at: http://www.abcul.org/lib/liDownload/344/PEARLS%20in%20the%20UK.pdf

ABI (2000). 'The Pensions System in the United Kingdom', in OECD (eds.), *Private Pensions Systems and Policy Issues*. Paris: OECD, pp. 9–22.

—— (2003). *Adequacy, Affordability and Incentives: A Better Future for State Pensions*, London: Association of British Insurers. Available at: http://www.abi.org.uk/BookShop/ResearchReports/37%20Adequacy,_affordability_and_incentives.pdf

Abolafia, M. Y. (1996). *Making Markets: Opportunism and Restraint on Wall Street*. Cambridge, MA: Harvard University Press.

Aglietta, M. and Rebérioux, A. (2005). *Corporate Governance Adrift: A Critique of Shareholder Value*. Cheltenham, UK: Edward Elgar.

Aitken, R. (2003). 'The Democratic Method of Obtaining Capital—Culture, Governmentality and Ethics of Mass Investment', *Consumption Markets and Culture*, 6(2): 293–317.

—— (2005). 'A Direct Personal Stake: Cultural Economy, Mass Investment and the New York Stock Exchange', *Review of International Political Economy*, 12(2): 334–63.

—— (2006). 'Capital at Its Fringes', *New Political Economy*, 11(4): 479–98.

—— (2007). *Performing Capital: Toward a Cultural Economy of Popular and Global Finance*. Basingstoke, UK: Palgrave MacMillan.

Aizcorbe, A. M., Kennickell, A. B., and Moore, K. B. (2003). 'Recent Changes in U.S. Family Finances: Evidence from the 1998 and 2001 Survey of Consumer Finances', *Federal Reserve Bulletin*, 89: 1–32.

Aldridge, A. (1998). 'Habitus and Cultural Capital in the Field of Personal Finance', *The Sociological Review*, 46(1): 1–23.

All-Party Parliamentary Group for Building Societies and Financial Mutuals (2006). *Windfalls or Shortfalls? The True Cost of Demutualisation*, London: All-Party Parliamentary Group for Building Societies and Financial Mutuals. Available at: http://www.mutuo.co.uk/pdf/windfallsorshortfallsfinal.pdf

Amin, A., Cameron, A., and Hudson, R. (2003). 'The Alterity of the Social Economy', in A. Leyshon, R. Lee, and C. Williams (eds.), *Alternative Economic Spaces*. London: Sage, pp. 27–54.

Amoore, L. (2004). 'Risk, Reward and Discipline at Work', *Economy and Society*, 33(2): 174–96.

—— (2006). ' "There is no great Refusal": The Ambivalent Politics of Resistance', in M. de Goede (ed.), *International Political Economy and Poststructural Politics*. Basingstoke, UK: Palgrave MacMillan, pp. 255–74.

—— and Langley, P. (2004). 'Ambiguities of Global Civil Society', *Review of International Studies*, 30(1): 89–110.

Anderson, J. (2006). 'Betting the House and Losing Big', *New York Times*, 23 September, online edition.

—— (2007). 'Winners Amid Doom and Gloom', *New York Times*, 9 March, online edition.

Anderson, S. (2004). *The CML Mortgage Market Manifesto: Taking the Past into the Future*. London: Council of Mortgage Lenders.

Andrews, E. L. (2003). 'Bush's Plan for Pensions is Now Given Low Priority', *New York Times*, 26 February, online edition.

Appadurai, A. (1996). *Modernity at Large: Cultural Dimensions of Globalization*, Minneapolis, MN: University of Minnesota Press.

Arrighi, G. (1994). *The Long Twentieth Century: Money, Power and the Origins of Our Times*. London: Verso.

Ascarelli, S. (2002). 'Equities Get the Boot', *Wall Street Journal*, 16 January. Available at: http://www.johnralfe.com/displayArticle.php

Ashman, I. and Black, J. (2002). 'CDOs and Structured Finance Transactions: The Cayman Islands Perspective', in J. Borrows (ed.), *Current Issues in Securitisation*. London: Sweet & Maxwell, pp. 59–65.

Augar, P. (2000). *The Death of Gentlemanly Capitalism: The Rise and Fall of London's Investment Banks*. London: Penguin.

Bajaj, V. (2007a). 'Bad Loans Put Wall St. in a Swoon', *New York Times*, 14 March, online edition.

—— (2007b). 'Freddie Mac Tightens Standards', *New York Times*, 28 February, online edition.

—— and Haughney, C. (2007). 'Tremors at the Door', *New York Times*, 26 January, online edition.

—— and Landler, M. (2007). 'Mortgage Losses Echo in Europe and on Wall Street', *New York Times*, 10 August, online edition.

—— and Nixon, R. (2006a). 'Re-financing, and Putting off Mortgage Pain', *New York Times*, 23 July, online edition.

—— —— (2006b). 'Subprime Loans Going from Boon to Housing Bane', *New York Times*, 6 December, online edition.

Baker, T. and Simon, J. (2002). 'Embracing Risk', in T. Baker and J. Simon (eds.), *Embracing Risk: The Changing Culture of Insurance and Responsibility*. Chicago, IL: University of Chicago Press, pp. 1–26.

Bank of England (2006a). *Financial Stability Report*, London: Bank of England. Available at: http://www.bankofengland.co.uk/publications/fsr/2006/fsrfull0606.pdf

Bank of England (2006b). *Inflation Report*, London: Bank of England. Available at: http://www.bankofengland.co.uk/publications/inflationreport/ir06may.pdf

——(2007). *Financial Stability Report*, London: Bank of England. Available at: http://www.bankofengland.co.uk/publications/fsr/2007/fsrfull0407.pdf

Banner, R., Derwall, J., and Otten, R. (2007). 'The Ethical Mutual Fund Performance Debate', *Journal of Business Ethics*, 70(2): 111–24.

Barr, N. (2002). *The Welfare State as Piggy Bank: Information, Risk, Uncertainty, and the Role of the State*. Oxford: Oxford University Press.

Barrett, R. and Ewan, J. (2006). *British Banker's Association Credit Derivatives Report 2006*. London: British Banker's Association.

Barry, A. (2002). 'The Anti-Political Economy', *Economy and Society*, 31(2): 268–84.

——Osborne, T., and Rose, N. (1996). *Foucault and Political Reason: Liberalism, Neoliberalism and Rationalities of Government*. London: UCL Press.

Bauman, Z. (2001). *The Individualized Society*. Cambridge: Polity Press.

Bayot, J. (2003). 'You Might Want to Put Your Credit to the Test', *New York Times*, 29 June, online edition.

Beales, R. (2007). 'US Niggle Became Global Problem', *FT Weekend*, 11–12 August, 2.

——and Scholtes, S. (2007). 'Critical Focus Turns on Rating Agencies', *Financial Times*, 16 August, 35.

——Chung, J., Scholtes, S., and Wighton, D. (2007). 'Sub-prime Leniency Demanded', *FT Weekend*, 30 June to 1 July, 17.

Beck, U. (1992). *Risk Society: Towards a New Modernity*. London: Sage.

——and Beck-Gernsheim, E. (2001). *Individualization*. London: Sage.

Becker, E. and McVeigh, P. (2001). 'Social Funds in the United States: Their History, Financial Performance, and Social Impacts', in A. Fung, T. Hebb, and J. Rogers (eds.), *Working Capital: The Power of Labor's Pensions*. Ithaca, NY: Cornell University, pp. 44–66.

Bell, D. (1976). *The Cultural Contradictions of Capitalism*. New York: Basic Books.

Bello, W., Bullard, N., and Malhotra, K. (2000). 'Introduction', in W. Bello, N. Bullard, and K. Malhotra (eds.), *Global Finance: New Thinking on Regulating Speculative Capital Markets*. London: Zed Books, pp. ix–xii.

Berle, A. A. and Means, G. C. (1932). *The Modern Corporation and Private Property*. New York: Commerce Clearing House.

Bernstein, P. L. (1996). *Against the Gods: The Remarkable Story of Risk*. New York: John Wiley & Sons.

Berthoud, R. and Hinton, T. (1989). *Credit Unions in the United Kingdom*. London: Policy Studies Institute.

Best, J. (2005). *The Limits of Transparency: Ambiguity and the History of International Finance*. Ithaca, NY: Cornell University Press.

Bewley, R., Ingram, N., Livera, V., and Thompson, S. (2007). 'Who's Afraid of the Big Bad Bear? Or, Why Investing in Equities for Retirement is Not Scary and Why

Investing Without Equities is Scary', in H. Bateman (ed.), *Retirement Provision in Scary Markets*. Cheltenham, UK: Edward Elgar, pp. 14–44.

Bingham, N. and Thrift, N. (2000). 'Some New Instructions for Travellers: The Geography of Bruno Latour and Michel Serres', in M. Crang and N. Thrift (eds.), *Thinking Space*. London: Routledge, pp. 281–301.

Birger, J. (2005). 'Meet the Flippers', *Money*, 34(4): 83–6.

Blackburn, R. (2002*a*). *Banking on Death or, Investing in Life: The History and Future of Pensions*. London: Verso.

—— (2002*b*). 'The Enron Debacle and the Pension Crisis', *New Left Review*, 14: 26–51.

—— (2006*a*). *Age Shock: How Finance is Failing Us*. London: Verso.

—— (2006*b*). 'Finance and the Fourth Dimension', *New Left Review*, 39: 39–70.

Blake, R. (2003). 'The 2003 Pension Olympics', *Institutional Investor*, May, 41–6.

Bleiker, R. (2000). *Popular Dissent, Human Agency and Global Politics*. Cambridge: Cambridge University Press.

Blyth, M. M. (2002). *Great Transformations: Economic Ideas and Political Change in the Twentieth Century*. Cambridge: Cambridge University Press.

Bogle, J. C. (1999). *Common Sense on Mutual Funds: New Imperatives for the Intelligent Investor*. New York: John Wiley & Sons.

—— (2005). *The Battle for the Soul of Capitalism*. New Haven, CT: Yale University Press.

Boltanski, L. and Chiapello, E. (2006). *The New Spirit of Capitalism*. London: Verso.

Bond Market Association (2004*a*). 'Outstanding Levels of Public and Private Debt'. Available at: http://www.bondmarkets.com/story.asp?id = 323

—— (2004*b*). 'Outstanding Volume of Agency and Non-agency Mortgage-backed securities'. Available at: http://bondmarkets.com/story.asp?id = 1256

Bonner, B. and Wiggin, A. (2006). *Empire of Debt: The Rise of an Epic Financial Crisis*. Hoboken, NJ: John Wiley & Sons.

Borjas, G. J. (1979). *Union Control of Pension Funds: Will the North Rise Again?* San Francisco, CA: Institute for Contemporary Studies.

Bowman, J. (2001). 'Coverage of Private Pensions in the United Kingdom', in OECD (ed.), *Private Pensions Conference 2000: Insurance and Pensions, Private Pensions Series No. 3*. Paris: OECD, pp. 417–24.

Boyer, R. (2000). 'Is a Finance-led Growth Regime a Viable Alternative to Fordism? A Preliminary Analysis', *Economy and Society*, 29(1): 111–45.

Braunstein, S. and Welch, C. (2002). 'Financial Literacy: An Overview of Practice, Research, and Policy', *Federal Reserve Bulletin*, November: 445–57.

Brenner, R. (2002). *The Boom and the Bubble: The US in the World Economy*. London: Verso.

Briys, E. and de Varenne, F. (2000). *The Fisherman and the Rhinoceros: How International Finance Shapes Everyday Life*, Chichester, UK: John Wiley & Sons.

Brooker, S. and Whyley, C. (2005). *Locked In, Kept Out: The Extent of Competition Within the UK Home Credit Industry*. York, UK: Joseph Rowntree Foundation. Available at: http://www.jrf.org.uk/bookshop/eBooks/1859353002.pdf

Buck, T. (2007). 'Rating Agencies Targeted in EU Probe into Subprime Crisis', *Financial Times*, 16 August, 1.

Budworth, L. (2005). 'Property Funds Lure Pension Investors', *The Sunday Times*, Money section, 1. 25 September.

Bumiller, E. (2005). 'Overhauling Retirement is Worth Risk, Cheney Says', *New York Times*, 14 January, online edition.

Burchell, G., Gordon, C., and Miller, P. (1991). *The Foucault Effect: Studies in Governmentality*. Hemel Hempstead, UK: Harvester Press.

Burton, D. (1994). *Financial Services and the Consumer*. London: Routledge.

——Knights, D., Leyshon, A., Alferoff, C., and Signoretta, P. (2004). 'Making a Market: The UK Retail Financial Services Industry and the Rise of the Complex Sub-prime Credit Market', *Competition and Change*, 8(1): 3–25.

Bush, G. W. (2005). 'State of the Union Address'. Available at: http://www.whitehouse.gov/news/releases/2005/02/20050202-11.html

Butler, J. (1997). *Excitable Speech: A Politics of the Performative*. New York: Routledge.

——(1998). 'Merely Cultural', *New Left Review*, 227: 33–44.

——Laclau, E., and Žižek, S. (2000). *Contingency, Hegemony, Universality: Contemporary Dialogues on the Left*. London: Verso.

Bygrave, M. (1998). 'From Wall Street to High Street', *The Guardian*, Weekend Supplement, 25 July, 24–9.

Cain, P. J. and Hopkins, A. G. (1986). 'Gentlemanly Capitalism and British Expansion Overseas', *Economic History Review*, 39(4): 501–25.

Calabrese, M. (2001). 'Building on Success: Labor-Friendly Investment Vehicles and the Power of Private Equity', in A. Fung, T. Hebb, and J. Rogers (eds.), *Working Capital: The Power of Labor's Pensions*. Ithaca, NY: Cornell University Press, pp. 93–127.

Calder, L. (1999). *Financing the American Dream: A Cultural History of Consumer Credit*. Princeton, NJ: Princeton University Press.

Callon, M. (1986). 'Some Elements of a Sociology of Translation: Domestication of the Scallops and the Fishermen of St. Brieuc Bay', in J. Law (ed.), *Power, Action and Belief: A New Sociology of Knowledge*. London: Routledge & Kegan Paul, pp. 196–233.

——(1998). 'Introduction: The Embeddedness of Economic Markets in Economics', in M. Callon (ed.), *The Laws of Markets*. Oxford, UK: Basil Blackwell, pp. 1–57.

——(1999). 'Actor-network Theory—The Market Test', in J. Law and J. Hassard (eds.), *Actor Network Theory and After*. Oxford, UK: Blackwell, pp. 181–95.

——(2005). 'Why Virtualism Paves the Way to Political Impotence: A Reply to Daniel Miller's Critique of The Laws of Markets', *Economic Sociology: European Electronic Newsletter*, 6(2): 3–20.

CalPERS (1995). 'Why Corporate Governance Today? A Policy Statement, 14 August, California Public Employee Retirement System'. Available at: http://www.calpers-governance.org/viewpoint/default.asp

Cameron, A. and Palan, R. (2004). *The Imagined Economies of Globalization*. London: Sage.

Campbell, J. Y. (2006). 'Household Finance', *The Journal of Finance*, 61(4): 1553–604.

Carey, J. J. (1996). 'The Sub-prime Credit Market: Identifying Good Risks for Unsecured Cards', *Credit World*, 85(1): 13–16.

Carruthers, B. G. (1996). *City of Capital: Politics and Markets in the English Financial Revolution*. Princeton, NJ: Princeton University Press.

—— and Stinchcombe, A. L. (1999). 'The Social Structure of Liquidity: Flexibility, Markets, and States', *Theory and Society*, 28(3): 353–82.

Caskey, J. P. (1994). *Fringe Banking: Check-Cashing Outlets, Pawnshops, and the Poor*. New York: Russell Sage Foundation.

Castells, M. (1996). *The Information Age: Economy, Society and Culture, Volume 1— The Rise of the Network Society*. Oxford, UK: Blackwell.

Chancellor, E. (1999). *Devil Take the Hindmost: A History of Financial Speculation*. Basingstoke, UK: MacMillan.

—— (2005). *Crunch Time for Credit? An Inquiry into the State of the Credit System in the United States and Great Britain*. Hampshire, UK: Harriman House Ltd.

Chinloy, P. and MacDonald, N. (2005). 'Subprime Lenders and Mortgage Market Completion', *The Journal of Real Estate Finance and Economics*, 30(2): 153–65.

Ciccutti, N. (2003). 'Everything You Ever Wanted to Know about Pensions but Were Afraid to Ask', *Bloomberg Money*, 66: 16–24.

Claessens, S. (2006). 'Access to Financial Services: A Review of Issues and Public Policy Objectives', *World Bank Research Observer*, 21(2): 207–40.

Clark, G. L. (2000). *Pension Fund Capitalism*. Oxford, UK: Oxford University Press.

—— (2003). 'Pension Security in the Global Economy: Markets and National Institutions in the 21st century', *Environment and Planning A*, 35(8): 1339–56.

—— (2005). 'Money Flows Like Mercury: The Geography of Global Finance', *Geografiska Annaler*, 87(2): 99–112.

—— and Hebb, T. (2005). 'Why Should They Care? The Role of Institutional Investors in the Market for Corporate Social Responsibility', *Environment and Planning A*, 37(11): 2015–31.

—— and Whiteside, N. (2003). 'Introduction', in G. L. Clark and N. Whiteside (eds.), *Pension Security in the 21st Century: Redrawing the Public-Private Debate*, Oxford, UK: Oxford University Press, pp. 1–20.

—— Thrift, N., and Tickell, A. (2004). 'Performing Finance: The Industry, the Media and its Image', *Review of International Political Economy*, 11(2): 289–310.

Clarke, D. B., Doel, M. A., and Housinaux, K. M. L. (2003). *The Consumption Reader*. London: Routledge.

Clayton, J. L. (2000). *The Global Debt Bomb*. New York: M.E Sharpe.

Bibliography

Clowes, M. J. (2000). *The Money Flood: How Pension Funds Revolutionized Investing*. New York: John Wiley & Sons.

Coggan, P. and Chung, J. (2006). 'Gilts Crisis Hits Pension Funds', *Financial Times*, 19 January, 1.

Coles, A. and Hardt, J. (2000). 'Mortgage Markets: Why US and EU Markets Are So Different', *Housing Studies*, 15(5): 775–84.

Collard, S. and Kempson, E. (2005). *Affordable Credit: The Way Forward*. Bristol, UK: The Policy Press for the Joseph Rowntree Foundation.

Combs, A. L. (2004). 'Remarks of Assistant Secretary Ann L. Combs at the 57th National Conference of the Profit Sharing/401(k) Council', 30 September. Available at: http://www.dol.gov/ebsa/newsroom/sp09004.html

Connolly, W. E. (2002). *Identity\Difference: Democratic Negotiations of Political Paradox*. Minneapolis, MN: University of Minnesota Press.

Costello, M. (2006). 'Personal Insolvencies Soar', *The Times*, 4 August, online edition.

Cowan, A. M. and Cowan, C. D. (2004). 'Default Correlation: An Empirical Investigation of a Subprime Lender', *Journal of Banking and Finance*, 28(4): 753–71.

Creswell, J. (2007). 'Shaky Markets Prompt Rumors of Who's in Trouble', *New York Times*, 10 August, online edition.

Crews Cutts, A. and Van Order, R. (2003). *On the Economics of Subprime Lending*. Washington, DC: Office of the Chief Economist.

Crook, S. (1999). 'Ordering Risks', in D. Lupton (ed.), *Risk and Sociocultural Theory: New Directions and Perspectives*. Cambridge: Cambridge University Press, pp. 160–85.

CUNA (2005). *The Credit Union Movement: A History of People Helping People*, Credit Union National Association. Available at: http://www.creditunion.coop/download/CUHistory.ppt

Cutler, T. and Waine, B. (2001). 'Social Insecurity and the Retreat from Social Democracy: Occupational Welfare in the Long Boom and Financialization', *Review of International Political Economy*, 8(1): 96–117.

——and Whiting, M. (2002). 'Risk and Return: The "Crisis" of the Final Salary Pension Scheme, its Causes and Implications', paper presented at the British International Studies Association 27th Annual Conference, London School of Economics, 17 December.

Darlin, D. (2006a). 'Keep Eyes Fixed on Your Variable Rate Mortgage', *New York Times*, 15 July, online edition.

——(2006b). 'On Making Enrollment in a 401(k) Automatic', *New York Times*, 19 August, online edition.

Dash, E. (2005). 'Debtors Throng to Bankruptcy as Clock Ticks', *New York Times*, 15 October, online edition.

——(2006). 'Health Savings Accounts Attract Wall Street', *New York Times*, 27 January, online edition.

—— (2007). 'Fannie Mae's Offer to Help Ease Credit Squeeze Is Rejected, as Critics Complain of Opportunism', *New York Times*, 11 August, online edition.

Davey, J. (2006). 'Barclays Shines in Spite of Huge Rise in Bad Debt', *The Times*, 4 August, online edition.

Davies, M. (2006a). 'Everyday Life and the Global Political Economy', in M. de Goede (ed.), *International Political Economy and Poststructural Politics*. Basingstoke, UK: Palgrave MacMillan, pp. 219–37.

Davies, P. J. (2006b). 'European RMBS Volumes Surge', *Financial Times*, 12 May, 40.

—— and Scholtes, S. (2007). 'Big Deals in Trouble Over Debt Take Up', *Financial Times*, 26 July, 1.

Dean, M. (1999). *Governmentality: Power and Rule in Modern Society*. London: Sage.

de Certeau, M. (1988). *The Practice of Everyday Life*. Trans. Steven Rendall, Berkeley, CA: University of California Press.

Defert, D. (1991). '"Popular Life" and Insurance Technology', in G. Burchell, C. Gordon, and P. Miller (eds.), *The Foucault Effect: Studies in Governmentality*. Hemel Hempstead, UK: Harvester Press, pp. 211–26.

de Goede, M. (2004). 'Repoliticizing Financial Risk', *Economy and Society*, 33(2): 197–217.

—— (2005a). 'Carnival of Money: Politics of Dissent in an Era of Globalizing Finance', in L. Amoore (ed.), *The Global Resistance Reader*. London: Routledge, pp. 379–91.

—— (2005b). *Virtue, Fortune, and Faith: A Genealogy of Finance*. Minneapolis, MN: University of Minnesota.

Desai, M. and Said, Y. (2001). 'The New Anti-Capitalist Movement: Money and Global Civil Society', in H. Anheier, M. Glasius, and M. Kaldor (eds.), *Global Civil Society Yearbook 2001*. Oxford, UK: Oxford University Press, pp. 51–78.

Dodd, C. J. (2007). 'Statement of Christopher J. Dodd at Mortgage Market Turmoil: Causes and Consequences', Hearing of US Senate Committee on Banking, Housing, and Urban Affairs, 22 March. Available at: http://banking.senate.gov/index.cfm?Fuseaction = Hearings.Detail&HearingID = 254

Dodd, N. (1994). *The Sociology of Money: Economics, Reason and Contemporary Society*. Cambridge: Polity Press.

DoL (2002). *Delegate Resources: The 2002 National Summit on Retirement Savings, February 27th – March 1st, 2002*. Washington, DC: International Foundation of Employee Benefit Plans Inc.

—— (2004a). *A Look at 401(k) Plan Fees for Employees*. Washington, DC: Department of Labor.

—— (2004b). *Saving Fitness: A Guide to Your Money and Your Financial Future*. Washington, DC: Department of Labor.

—— (2004c). *Women and Retirement Savings*. Washington, DC: Department of Labor.

Donnelly, R. and Haggett, A. (1997). *Credit Unions in Britain: A Decade of Growth*. London: The Plunkett Foundation.

Donovan, K. (2005). 'Legal Reform Turns a Steward into an Activist', *New York Times*, 16 April, online edition.

Dreblow, J. (2005). 'The Different Ethical and SRI Investment Models', in J. Hancock (ed.), *An Investors Guide to Ethical and Socially Responsible Investment Funds*. London: Kogan, pp. 17–24.

Drucker, P. F. (1976/1995). *The Unseen Revolution/The Pension Fund Revolution*. New Brunswick: Transaction Publishers.

DSS (1998). *A New Contract for Welfare: Partnership in Pensions*. Green Paper, London: Department of Social Security.

DTI (2005). *Over-Indebtedness in Britain: A DTI Report on the MORI Financial Services Survey 2004*. London: Department of Trade and Industry. Available at: http://www.dti.gov.uk/files/file18550.pdf

——and DWP (2004). *Tackling Over-indebtedness—Action Plan 2004*. London: Department of Trade and Industry and Department of Work and Pensions. Available at: http://www.dti.gov.uk/files/file18547.pdf

————(2005). *Tackling Over-indebtedness—Annual Report 2005*. London: Department of Trade and Industry and Department of Work and Pensions. Available at: http://www.dti.gov.uk/files/file18547.pdf

du Gay, P. (1996). *Consumption and Identity at Work*. London: Sage.

Duncan, R. (2003). *The Dollar Crisis: Causes, Consequences and Cure*. London: John Wiley & Sons.

DWP (2006). *Security in Retirement: Towards a New Pension System*. London: Department of Work and Pensions. Available at: http://www.dwp.gov.uk/pensionsreform/pdfs/white_paper_complete.pdf

Dymski, G. A. (2005*a*). 'Discrimination in the Credit and Housing markets: Findings and Challenges', in W. M. Rodgers, III (ed.), *Handbook on the Economics of Discrimination*. Cheltenham, UK: Edward Elgar, pp. 245–69.

——(2005*b*). 'Financial Globalization, Social Exclusion and Financial Crisis', *International Review of Applied Economics*, 19(4): 439–57.

——and Veitch, J. M. (1996). 'Financial Transformation and the Metropolis: Booms, Busts, and Banking in Los Angeles', *Environment and Planning A*, 28(7): 1233–60.

Egan, T. (2005). 'Debtors Rush to Bankruptcy as Change Nears', *New York Times*, 21 August, online edition.

Eggert, K. (2007). 'Testimony at Subprime Mortgage Market Turmoil: Examining the Role of Securitization', Senate Banking, Housing and Urban Affairs Committee's Subcommittee on Securities, Insurance, and Investments, 17 April, Available at: http://banking.senate.gov/index.cfm?Fuseaction = Hearings.Detail&HearingID = 256

Elliott, L. (2007). 'We Have Nothing to Fear But Wall Street', *The Guardian*, 26 March, online edition.

Engelen, E. (2003). 'The Logic of Funding European Pension Restructuring and the Dangers of Financialisation', *Environment and Planning A*, 35(8): 1357–72.

Erturk, I., Froud, J., Sukhdev, J., Leaver, A., and Williams, K. (2007). 'The Democratization of Finance? Promise, Outcomes and Conditions', *Review of International Political Economy*, 14(4): 553–76.

European Commission (1999). *Towards a Single Market for Supplementary Pensions.* Commission Communication: COM(1999)134, 11 May 1999.

Ewald, F. (1991). 'Insurance and Risk', in G. Burchell, C. Gordon, and P. Miller (eds.), *The Foucault Effect: Studies in Governmentality*. Hemel Hempstead, UK: Harvester Press, pp. 197–210.

Fannie Mae (2005). *Housing Solutions: Working With Our Partners to Meet America's Toughest Housing Needs*. Available at: http://www.fanniemae.com/iniatives/pdf/housing/housingsolutionsreport.pdf

Featherstone, M. (1992). 'The Heroic Life and Everyday Life', in M. Featherstone (ed.), *Cultural Theory and Cultural Change*. London: Sage, pp. 159–82.

Federal Trade Commission (2006). *The Fair Credit Reporting Act*. Available at: http://www.ftc.gov/os/statutes/fcradoc.pdf

Feng, H., Froud, J., Johal, S., Haslam, C., and Williams, K. (2001). 'A New Business Model? The Capital Market and the New Economy', *Economy and Society*, 30(4): 467–503.

Fligstein, N. (2001). *The Architecture of Markets: A Economic Sociology of Twenty-First Century Capitalist Societies*. Princeton, NJ: Princeton University Press.

Flint, J. (2003). 'Housing and Ethopolitics: Constructing Identities of Active Consumption and Responsible Community', *Economy and Society*, 32(4): 611–29.

Foucault, M. (1976). *The Will to Knowledge, The History of Sexuality, Volume 1.* London: Penguin.

—— (1977). *Discipline and Punish: The Birth of the Prison.* London: Allen Lane.

—— (1979). 'On Governmentality', *Ideology and Consciousness*, 6: 5–22.

—— (1980). *Power/Knowledge: Selected Interviews and Other Writings, 1972–1977*, edited by Colin Gordon, Brighton, UK: Harvester Press.

—— (1984). *The History of Sexuality, Volume 3: The Care of the Self.* Harmondsworth, UK: Penguin.

Francis, C. (2006a). 'Fears over Spiraling Home Loans', *Sunday Times*, 5 November, Money section, 3.

—— (2006b). 'Investors Dump Shares to Buy Property', *Sunday Times*, 4 June, Money section, 1.

Frank, R. H. (1999). *Luxury Fever: Money and Happiness in an Era of Excess*. Princeton, NJ: Princeton University Press.

Frank, T. (2000). *One Market Under God: Extreme Capitalism, Economic Populism and the End of Economic Democracy*. New York: Doubleday.

Fraser, S. (2005). *Wall Street: A Cultural History*. London: Faber & Faber.

Freddie Mac (2005). *Just The Facts: How We Make Home Possible*. Available at: http://www.freddiemac.com/news/pdf/Just_the_Facts3.pdf

French, S. and Leyshon, A. (2004). 'The New, New Financial system? Towards a Conceptualization of Financial Reintermediation', *Review of International Political Economy*, 11(2): 263–88.

Friedman, T. (2000). *The Lexus and the Olive Tree*. London: HarperCollins.

Froud, J., Johal, S., Haslam, C., and Williams, K. (2001). 'Accumulation Under Conditions of Inequality', *Review of International Political Economy*, 8(1): 66–95.

—— —— and Williams, K. (2002). 'Financialisation and the Coupon Pool', *Capital and Class*, 78: 119–51.

—— —— Leaver, A., and Williams, K. (2006). *Financialization and Strategy: Narrative and Numbers*, London: Routledge.

FSA (2002*a*). *FSA Guide to Saving for Retirement—Reviewing Your Plans*. London: Financial Services Authority.

—— (2002*b*). *FSA Guide to Saving for Retirement—Starting to Save*. London: Financial Services Authority.

—— (2004*a*). *Building Financial Capability in the UK*. London: Financial Services Authority. Available at: http://www.fsa.go.uk/pubs/other/financial_capability_uk.pdf

—— (2004*b*). *FSA Factsheet: Stakeholder Pensions and Decision trees*. London: Financial Services Authority.

—— (2005). *Financial Risk Outlook*. London: Financial Services Authority. Available at: http://fsa.gov.uk/pubs/plan/financial_risk_outlook_2005.pdf

—— (2006). *Financial Capability in the UK: Establishing a Baseline*. London: Financial Services Authority. Available at: http://www.fsa.gov.uk/pubs/other/fincap_baseline.pdf

Fuerbringer, J. (2004). 'Americans Pour Money into Stock Funds in Near Record Amounts', *New York Times*, 13 February, online edition.

Fuller, D. and Jonas, A. E. G. (2003). 'Alternative Financial Spaces', in A. Leyshon, R. Lee, and C. Williams (eds.), *Alternative Economic Spaces*. London: Sage, pp. 55–73.

Fusaro, P. and Miller, D. (2002). *What Went Wrong at Enron*. Hoboken, NJ: John Wiley & Sons.

Gamble, A. (2003). *Between Europe and America: the Future of British Politics*. Aldershot, UK: Palgrave MacMillan.

Gardiner, M. E. (2004). 'Everyday Utopianism: Lefebvre and his Critics', *Cultural Studies*, 18(2–3): 228–54.

Gerard, L. W. (2001). 'Foreword', in A. Fung, T. Hebb, and J. Rogers (eds.), *Working Capital: The Power of Labor's Pensions*. Ithaca, NY: Cornell University Press, pp. vii–viii.

Germain, R. D. (1997). *The International Organization of Credit: States and Global Finance in the World-Economy*. Cambridge: Cambridge University Press.

Ghilarducci, T. (1992). *Labor's Capital: The Economics and Politics of Private Pensions*. Cambridge, MA: MIT Press.

Gibson-Graham, J. K. (1996). *The End of Capitalism (As We Knew It): A Feminist Critique of Political Economy*. Oxford: Blackwell.

——(2006). *A Postcapitalist Politics*. Minneapolis, MN: University of Minnesota.

Giddens, A. (1998). *The Third Way: The Renewal of Social Democracy*. Cambridge: Polity Press.

Gill, S. (2003). *Power and Resistance in the New World Order*. Basingstoke, UK: Palgrave MacMillan.

Gilmore, G. (2006). 'Silence is Golden for Secretive Lenders', *The Times*, 15 July, online edition.

Gotham, K. F. (2006). 'The Secondary Circuit of Capital Reconsidered: Globalization and the U.S. Real Estate Sector', *American Journal of Sociology*, 112(1): 231–75.

Gourevitch, P. A. and Shinn, J. J. (2005). *Political Power and Corporate Control: The New Global Politics of Corporate Governance*. Princeton, NJ: Princeton University Press.

Grant, J. (1992). *Money of the Mind: Borrowing and Lending in America from the Civil War to Michael Milken*. New York: Farrar Straus Giroux.

Greenspan, A. (1996). 'The Challenge of Central Banking in a Democratic Society', Remarks at the American Enterprise Institute for Public Policy Research. Washington, DC, 5 December. Available at: http://www.federalreserve.gov/BoardDocs/speeches/19961205.htm

——(2004). 'Understanding Household Debt Obligations', Remarks at the Credit Union National Association 2004 Governmental Affairs Conference. Washington, DC, 23 February. Available at: http://www.federalreserve.gov/boardDocs/speeches/2004/20040223/default.htm

Greider, W. (2005). 'The New Colossus', *The Nation*, 28 February, online edition. Available at: http://www.thenation.com/doc/20050228/greider

Grey, C. (1997). 'Suburban Subjects: Financial Services and the New Right', in D. Knights and T. Tinker (eds.), *Financial Institutions and Social Transformations*. Basingstoke, UK: MacMillan, pp. 47–67.

Gross, D. (2000). *Bull Run: Wall Street, the Democrats, and the New Politics of Personal Finance*. New York: Public Affairs.

Guseva, A. and Rona-Tas, A. (2001). 'Uncertainty, Risk, and Trust: Russian and American Credit Card Markets Compared', *American Sociological Review*, 66(5): 623–46.

Hakim, D. and Fuerbringer, J. (2003). 'G.M. to Raise $10 billion for Pension Gap', *New York Times*, 21 June 21, online edition.

Hall, S. (1996). 'Introduction: Who Needs "Identity"?' in S. Hall (ed.), *Questions of Cultural Identity*. London: Sage, pp. 1–17.

Halligan, L. (2005). 'The Debt Pandemic', *New Statesman*, 24 October, 12–5.

——(2006). 'One More Push Will Do the Trick', *Sunday Telegraph*, 12 November, B4.

Hancock, J. (2005). 'The Advantages of Ethical Investment', in J. Hancock (ed.), *An Investors Guide to Ethical and Socially Responsible Investment Funds*. London: Kogan Page, pp. 121–31.

Hannah, L. (1986). *Inventing Retirement: The Development of Occupational Pensions in Britain*. Cambridge: Cambridge University Press.

Hannan, M. E., West, E., and Baron, D. (1994). *Dynamics of Populations of Credit Unions, Madison*. Madison, WI: Filene Research Institute.

Hardie, I. and MacKenzie, D. (2006). 'Assembling an Economic Actor: The Agencement of a Hedge Fund', paper presented to 'New Actors in a Financialised Economy and Implications for Varieties of Capitalism', Institute of Commonwealth Studies, London, 11–12 May.

Harmes, A. (1998). 'Institutional Investors and the Reproduction of Neoliberalism', *Review of International Political Economy*, 5(1): 92–121.

——(2001*a*). 'Mass Investment Culture', *New Left Review*, 9: 103–24.

——(2001*b*). *Unseen Power: How Mutual Funds Threaten the Political and Economic Wealth of Nations*. Toronto: Stoddart Publishing Co.

Harrower, G. (2002). 'Tax Aspects of Securitisation', in J. Borrows (ed.), *Current Issues in Securitisation*. London: Sweet & Maxwell, pp. 95–117.

Harvey, D. (1999). *The Limits to Capital*. New edition, London: Verso.

Hebb, T. (2001). 'Introduction: The Challenge of Labor's Capital Strategy', in A. Fung, T. Hebb, and J. Rogers (eds.), *Working Capital: The Power of Labor's Pensions*. Ithaca, NY: Cornell University Press, pp. 1–12.

——and Wójcik, D. (2005). 'Global Standards and Emerging Markets: The Institutional-Investment Value Chain and the CalPERS Investment Strategy', *Environment and Planning A*, 37(11): 1955–74.

Helleiner, E. (1994). *States and the Re-emergence of Global Finance*. Ithaca, NY: Cornell University Press.

Helman, R. and Paladino, A. (2004). 'Will Americans Ever Become Savers? The 14th Retirement Confidence Survey, 2004', *Employee Benefit Research Institute Issue Brief*, 268: 1–20.

Henwood, D. (1997). *Wall Street: How it Works and For Whom*. London: Verso.

——(2003). *After the New Economy*. New York: The New Press.

Higgins, V. (2001). 'Assembling Restructuring: Governmentality, Economic Regulation and the Historical Emergence of the 'Enterprising Farmer' in Australian Agricultural Policy', *Review of International Political Economy*, 8(2): 311–28.

Highmore, B. (2002). 'Introduction: Questioning Everyday Life', in B. Highmore (ed.), *The Everyday Life Reader*. London; Routledge, pp. 1–36.

Hilferding, R. (2005). *Finance Capital: A Study of the Latest Phase of Capitalist Development*. London: Routledge.

Hill, R. P., Ainscough, T., Shank, T., and Manullang, D. (2007). 'Corporate Social Responsibility and Socially Responsible Investment: A Global Perspective', *Journal of Business Ethics*, 70(2): 165–74.

Hinz, R. (2000). 'Overview of the United States Private Pension System', in OECD (eds.), *Private Pensions Systems and Policy Issues: No. 1*. Paris: OECD, pp. 23–42.

HM Treasury (1999). *Access to Financial Services*, Report by Policy Action Team (14) of the Social Exclusion Unit. London: HM Treasury. Available at: http://www.hm-treasury.gov.uk/media/D6E/61/pat14.pdf

——(2004). *Promoting Financial Inclusion*. London: HM Treasury. Available at: http://www.hm-treasury.gov.uk./media/8F9/37/pbr04_profininc_complete_394. pdf

——(2005). Budget 2005. *Investing For Our Future: Fairness and Opportunity for Britain's Hard Working Families*. London: HM Treasury. Available at: http:// www.hm-treasury.gov.uk/budget/budget_o5/budget_report/bud_bud05_ report.cfm

Hobson, J. A. (1988). *Imperialism: A Study*, 3rd edn., introduction by J. A. Townsend London: Unwin Hyman.

Hochschild, A. R. (2003). *The Commercialisation of Intimate Life: Notes from Home and Work*. Berkeley, CA: University of California Press.

Hodgson, G. M. (1988). *Economics and Institutions: A Manifesto for a Modern Institutional Economics*. Cambridge: Polity Press.

Holden, S., Ireland, K., Leonard-Chambers, V., and Bogdan, M. (2005). 'The Individual Retirement Account at Age 30: A Retrospective', *Investment Company Institute Perspective*, 11(1): 1–24.

Hosking, P. (2006). 'Banks Told to Predict Effects of a 40% Crash in House Prices', *The Times*, 16 November, online edition.

House of Commons Treasury Select Committee (2003). *Transparency of Credit Card Charges*, First Report of the Session 2003–04. Available at: http:// www.parliament.the-stationery-office.co.uk/pa/cm200304/cmselect/ cmtreasy/125/125.pdf

——(2004a). *Restoring Confidence in Long-Term Savings*, Eighth Report of the Session 2003–04. Available at: http://www.publications.parliament.uk/ pa/cm200304/cmselect/cmtreasy/71/71.pdf

——(2004b). *Restoring Confidence in Long-Term Savings: Endowment Mortgages*, Fifth Report of the Session 2003–04. Available at: http://www. publications.parliament.uk/pa/cm200304/cmselect/cmtreasy/394/394.pdf

——(2005). *Credit Card Charges and Marketing*, Second Report of the Session 2004–05. Available at: http://www.parliament.the-stationery-office.co.uk/pa/cm200405/cmselect/cmtreasy/274/274.pdf

ICI (2004). *Profile of Mutual Fund Shareholders*, ICI Research Series. Washington, DC: Investment Company Institute. Available at: http:// www.ici.org/statements/res/arc-rpt/rpt_profile04.pdf

ICI and SIA (2005). *Equity Ownership in America, 2005*. Washington, DC: Investment Company Institute. Available at: http://www.ici.org/pdf/ rpt_05_equity_owners.pdf

IMF (1995). *International Capital Markets: Developments, Prospects, and Policy Issues.* Washington, DC: International Monetary Fund.

——(2004). *Global Financial Stability Report: Market Developments and Issues.* Washington, DC: International Monetary Fund. Available at: http://www.imf.org/External/Pubs/FT/GFSR/2004/02/index.htm

Ingham, G. (2004). *The Nature of Money*, Cambridge: Polity Press.

Inman, P. (2001). 'Donations Save Credit Union', *The Guardian*, 24 August, 27.

Jameson, F. (1998). *The Cultural Turn: Selected Writings on the Postmodern, 1983–1998.* New York: Verso.

Jeacle, I. and Walsh, E. J. (2002). 'From Moral Evaluation to Rationalization: Accounting and the Shifting Technologies of Credit', *Accounting, Organizations and Society*, 27(8): 737–61.

Jerving, J. (2007). 'Will Only the Big Dogs Survive? An Analysis of What Economies of Scale Enjoyed by Larger Credit Unions Mean for the Movements Future', *Credit Union Journal*, 18 July, online edition.

Joint Economic Committee (2004). *Household Debt and the Economy.* Washington, DC: Joint Economic Committee. Available at: http://jec.senate.gov/_files/HouseholdDebt.pdf

Jolliffe, A. (2003). 'Hopes of Savings Boost are Shot Down', *Financial Times Weekend*, 30–31 August, M22.

Jones, P. A. (2005). 'Philanthropy and Enterprise in the British Credit Union Movement', *Economic Affairs*, 25(2): 13–9.

Kemshall, H. (2002). *Risk, Social Policy and Welfare.* Buckingham, UK: Open University Press.

Kendall, G. (2004). 'Global Networks, International Networks, Actor Networks', in W. Larner and W. Walters (eds.), *Global Governmentality: Governing International Spaces.* London: Routledge, pp. 59–75.

Kennickell, A. B., Starr-McCluer, M., and Surette, B. J. (2000). 'Recent Changes in U.S. Family Finances: Results from the 1998 Survey of Consumer Finances', *Federal Reserve Bulletin*, January, 1–29.

Kerkvliet, B. J. T. (2005). *The Power of Everyday Politics: How Vietnamese Peasants Transformed National Policy.* Ithaca, NY: Cornell University Press.

Keynes, J. M. (1961). *The General Theory of Employment, Interest and Money.* London: MacMillan.

Kiff, J. and Mills, P. (2007). *Money For Nothing and Checks for Free: Recent Developments in U.S. Subprime Mortgage Markets*, IMF working paper, WP/07/188, July. Washington, DC, International Monetary Fund.

Kindleberger, C. P. (1978). *Manias, Panics, and Crashes: A History of Financial Crises.* London: MacMillan.

——(1997). 'Manias and How to Prevent Them: Interview with Charles P. Kindleberger', *Challenge*, 40(6): 21–31.

Kingson, J. A. (2005). 'Wireless Moves the Cash Register Where You Are', *New York Times*, 26 November, online edition.

Kirchhoff, S. and Block, S. (2004). 'Subprime Loan Market Grows Despite Troubles', *USA Today*, 12 July, online edition.

Klein, L. (1999). *It's in the Cards: Consumer Credit and the American Experience*. Westport, CT: Praeger Publishers.

Knight, F. (1921). *Risk, Uncertainty and Profit*. New York: A.M. Kelley.

Knights, D. (1997*a*). 'An Industry in Transition: Regulation, Restructuring and Renewal', in D. Knights and T. Tinker (eds.), *Financial Institutions and Social Transformations*. Basingstoke, UK: MacMillan, pp. 1–27.

—— (1997*b*). 'Governmentality and Financial Services: Welfare Crises and the Financially Self-Disciplined Subject', in G. Morgan and D. Knights (eds.), *Regulation and Deregulation in European Financial Services*. Basingstoke, UK: MacMillan, pp. 216–36.

—— and Vurdubakis, T. (1993). 'Calculations of Risk: Towards an Understanding of Insurance as a Moral and Political Technology', *Accounting, Organizations and Society*, 18(7/8): 729–64.

Knorr Cetina, K. and Bruegger, U. (2004). ' "Traders" Engagement with Markets: A Postsocial Relationship', in A. Amin and N. Thrift (eds.), *Cultural Economy Reader*. Oxford: Blackwell, pp. 121–42.

—— and Preda, A. (2005). 'Introduction', in K. Knorr Cetina and A. Preda (eds.), *The Sociology of Financial Markets*. Oxford: Oxford University Press, pp. 1–16.

Kochan, N. (2001). 'Turning Bad Credits Into Profits', *The Banker*, 1 August, 3–6.

Krippner, G. R. (2005). 'Financialization and the American Economy', *Socio-Economic Review*, 3(2): 173–208.

—— (2007). ' "The Rentiers" Return? The Social Politics of U.S. Financial Deregulation', unpublished manuscript, Sociology Department, University of Michigan.

Kruger, B. (2005). *Money Talks*. New York: Skarstedt Fine Art.

Laclau, E. and Mouffe, C. (1985). *Hegemony and Socialist Strategy: Towards a Radical Democratic Politics*. London: Verso.

Lane, Clark and Peacock (2006). *Accounting for Pensions UK and Europe, Annual Survey*. London: Lane, Clark and Peacock. Available at: http://www.lcp.com/information/documents/AFPSurvey2006.pdf

Langley, P. (2002). *World Financial Orders: An Historical International Political Economy*. London: Routledge.

—— (2004). '(Re)politicising Global Financial Governance: What's "New" About the "New International Financial Architecture"?' *Global Networks: A Journal of Transnational Affairs*, 4(1): 69–88.

Larner, W. and Le Heron, R. (2002). 'The Spaces and Subjects of a Globalising Economy: A Situated Exploration of Method', *Environment and Planning D*, 20(6): 753–74.

Lash, S. (2001). 'Forward by Scott Lash: Individualization in a Non-linear Mode', in U. Beck and E. Beck-Gernsheim (eds.), *Individualization*. London: Sage, pp. vii–xiii.

Latour, B. (1987). *Science in Action: How to Follow Scientists and Engineers Through Society*. Milton Keynes, UK: Open University Press.

—— (1993). *We Have Never Been Modern*, Trans. Catherine Porter. London: Harvester Wheatsheaf.

—— (1999). 'On recalling ANT', in J. Law and J. Hassard (eds.), *Actor Network Theory and After*. Oxford: Blackwell, pp. 15–25.

Law, J. (1999). 'After ANT: Complexity, Naming and Topology', in J. Law and J. Hassard (eds.), *Actor Network Theory and After*. Oxford: Blackwell, pp. 1–14.

Lazonick, W. and O'Sullivan, M. (2000). 'Maximizing Shareholder Value: A New Ideology for Corporate Governance', *Economy and Society*, 29(1): 1–35.

Lee, R. (1999). 'Local Money: Geographies of Autonomy and Resistance?' in R. Martin (ed.), *Money and the Space Economy*. Chichester, UK: John Wiley & Sons, pp. 207–24.

Lefebvre, H. (1991). *Critique of Everyday Life: Volume 1*, Trans. John Moore. London: Verso.

Lehtonen, T. K. and Pantzar, M. (2002). 'The Ethos of Thrift: The Promotion of Bank Saving in Finland During the 1950s', *Journal of Material Culture*, 7(2): 211–31.

Lemke, T. (2001). '"The birth of bio-politics": Michel Foucault's Lecture at the Collège de France on Neo-liberal Governmentality', *Economy and Society*, 30(2): 190–207.

Leonhardt, D. (2003). 'House Passes Bill to Loosen 401(k) Rules', *New York Times*, 15 May, online edition.

Leyshon, A. (2000). 'Money and Finance', in E. Sheppard and T. S. Barnes (eds.), *A Companion to Economic Geography*. Oxford: Blackwell, pp. 432–49.

—— and Lee, R. (2003). 'Introduction: Alternative Economic Geographies', in A. Leyshon, R. Lee, and C. Williams (eds.), *Alternative Economic Spaces*. London: Sage, pp. 1–26.

—— and Thrift, N. (1995). 'Geographies of Financial Exclusion: Financial Abandonment in Britain and the United States', *Transactions of the Institute of British Geographers*, 20(2): 312–41.

———— (1996). 'Financial Exclusion and the Shifting Boundaries of the Financial System', *Environment and Planning A*, 28(7): 1150–6.

———— (1997). *Money/Space: Geographies of Monetary Transformation*. London: Routledge.

———— (1999). 'Lists Come Alive: Electronic Systems of Knowledge and the Rise of Credit Scoring in Retail Banking', *Economy and Society*, 28(3): 434–66.

———— (2007). 'The Capitalisation of Almost Everything: The Future of Finance and Capitalism', paper presented at the International Working Group on Financialization (IWGF) Inaugural Workshop, London, 12–13 February.

———— and Pratt, J. (1998). 'Reading Financial Services: Texts, Consumers, and Financial Literacy', *Environment and Planning D*, 16(1): 29–55.

—— Burton, D., Knights, D., Alferoff, C., and Signoretta, P. (2004). 'Towards an Ecology of Retail Financial Services: Understanding the Persistence of Door-to-door Credit and Insurance Providers', *Environment and Planning A*, 36(4): 625–45.

LiPuma, E. and Lee, B. (2004). *Financial Derivatives and the Globalization of Risk*. Durham, NC: Duke University Press.

Lui, A. (2004). *The Laws of Cool: Knowledge Work and the Culture of Information*. Chicago, IL: University of Chicago Press.

McCulloch, A. (1990). 'A Millstone Round Your Neck? Building Societies in the 1930s and Mortgage Default', *Housing Studies*, 5(1): 43–58.

McDowell, L. (1997). *Capital Culture: Gender at Work in the City*. Oxford: Blackwell.

McGeehan, P. (2004). 'Soaring Interest Compounds Credit Card Pain for Millions', *New York Times*, 21 November, online edition.

McNay, L. (1994). *Foucault: A Critical Introduction*. Cambridge: Polity Press.

Mackenzie, C. and Sullivan, R. (2006). 'Looking Forwards', in R. Sullivan and C. Mackenzie (eds.), *Responsible Investment*. Sheffield, UK: Greenleaf Publishing, pp. 347–8.

MacKenzie, D. (2004). 'The Big, Bad Wolf and the Rational Market: Portfolio Insurance, the 1987 Crash and the Performativity of Economics', *Economy and Society*, 33(3): 303–34.

—— (2006). *An Engine, Not a Camera: How Financial Models Shape Markets*. Cambridge, MA: MIT Press.

Mandell, L. (1990). *The Credit Card Industry: A History*. Boston, MA: Twayne Publishers.

Manning, R. D. (2000). *Credit Card Nation: The Consequences of America's Addiction to Credit*. New York: Basic Books.

Marens, R. (2004). 'Waiting for the North to Rise: Revisiting Barber and Rifkin after a Generation of Union Financial Activism in the U.S.', *Journal of Business Ethics*, 52(1): 109–23.

Markowitz, H. M. (1959). *Portfolio Selection: Efficient Diversification of Investments*. New York: John Wiley and Sons.

Martin, R. (1999). 'Selling Off the State: Privatisation, the Equity Market and the Geographies of Private Shareholding', in R. Martin (ed.), *Money and the Space Economy*, London: Wiley, pp. 260–83.

—— (2002). *Financialization of Daily Life*. Philadelphia, PA: Temple University Press.

Maurer, B. (1999). 'Forget Locke? From Proprietor to Risk-Bearer in the New Logics of Finance', *Public Culture*, 11(2): 47–67.

—— (2003). 'Uncanny Exchanges: The Possibilities and Failures of "Making Change" With Alternative Monetary Forms', *Environment and Planning D*, 21(3): 317–40.

Medoff, J. and Harless, A. (1996). *The Indebted Society: Anatomy of an Ongoing Disaster*. New York: Little, Brown & Company.

Meyer, H. (2005). ' "Rate Tarts" Fall into Card Trap', *The Telegraph*, 5 January, online edition.

Miller, P. (1987). *Domination and Power*. London: Routledge.

——(1998). 'The Margins of Accounting', in M. Callon (ed.), *The Laws of Markets*. Oxford: Basil Blackwell, pp. 174–93.

——(2004). 'Governing By Numbers: Why Calculative Practices Matter', in A. Amin and N. Thrift (eds.), *Cultural Economy Reader*. Oxford: Blackwell, pp. 179–90.

——and Napier, C. (1993). 'Genealogies of Calculation', *Accounting, Organizations and Society*, 18(7/8): 631–47.

——and Rose, N. (1990). 'Governing Economic Life', *Economy and Society*, 19(1): 1–31.

————(1997). 'Mobilizing the Consumer: Assembling the Subject of Consumption', *Theory, Culture and Society*, 14(1): 1–36.

Minns, R. (1996). 'The Social Ownership of Capital', *New Left Review*, 219: 42–61.

——(2001). *The Cold War in Welfare: Stock Markets versus Pensions*. London: Verso.

Mitchell, O. S. and Schieber, S. J. (1998). 'Defined Contribution Pensions: New Opportunities, New Risks', in O. S. Mitchell and S. J. Schieber (eds.), *Living With Defined Contribution Pensions: Remaking Responsibility for Retirement*. Philadelphia, PA: University of Pennsylvania Press, pp. 1–14.

Mitchell, T. (2002). *Rule of Experts: Egypt, Techno-Politics, Modernity*. Berkeley, CA: University of California Press.

Montgomerie, J. (2006). 'The Financialization of the American Credit Card Industry', *Competition and Change*, 10(3): 301–19.

Moore, J. (1992). 'British Privatization: Taking Capitalism to the People', *Harvard Business Review*, 70(1): 115–24.

Morgan, G. and Sturdy, A. (2000). *Beyond Organizational Change: Structure, Discourse and Power in UK Financial Services*. Basingstoke, UK: MacMillan.

Morgenson, G. (2007*a*). 'Mortgage Maze May Increase Foreclosures', *New York Times*, 6 August, online edition.

——(2007*b*). 'Mutual Funds at Some Risk on Mortgages', *New York Times*, 14 March, online edition.

Mosley, L. (2003). *Global Capital and National Governments*. Cambridge: Cambridge University Press.

Moss, M. (2004). 'Erase Debt Now (Lose Your House Later)', *New York Times*, 10 October, online edition.

Munnell, A. H. and Sundén, A. (2004). *Coming Up Short: The Challenge of 401(k) Plans*. Washington, DC: The Brookings Institution.

Munro, M., Ford, J., Leishman, C., and Karley, N. K. (2005). *Lending to Higher Risk Borrowers: Sub-Prime Credit and Sustainable Home Ownership*. York, UK: Joseph Rowntree Foundation. Available at: http://www.jrf.org.uk/bookshop/eBooks/1859353355.pdf

Mutual Advisers, Inc. (2006). *Vice Fund Prospectus*, 31 July 2006. Available at: http://www.vicefund.com/docs/ViceProspectus.pdf

Myners, P. (2001). *Institutional Investment in the United Kingdom: A Review*. London: HM Treasury. Available at: http://www.hm-treasury.gov.uk/media//843FO/31.pdf

Napier, C. (2006). 'Accounts of Change: 30 Years of Historical Accounting Research', *Accounting, Organizations and Society*, 31(4/5): 445–507.

Newman, K. and Wyly, E. K. (2004). 'Geographies of Mortgage Market Segmentation: The Case of Essex County, New Jersey', *Housing Studies*, 19(1): 53–83.

Nocera, J. (1994). *A Piece of the Action: How the Middle Class Joined the Money Class*. New York: Simon & Schuster.

North, D. C. (1990). *Institutions, Institutional Change and Economic Performance*. Cambridge: Cambridge University Press.

North, P. (2007). *Money and Liberation: The Micropolitics of Alternative Currency Movements*. Minneapolis, MN: University of Minnesota Press.

NYSE (2000). *Shareownership 2000*. New York: New York Stock Exchange.

O'Brien, R., Goetz, A. M., Scholte, J. A., and Williams, M. (2000). *Contesting Global Governance: Multilateral Economic Institutions and Global Social Movements*. Cambridge: Cambridge University Press.

O'Connor, M. (2001). 'Labor's Role in the Shareholder Revolution', in A. Fung, T. Hebb, and J. Rogers (eds.), *Working Capital: The Power of Labor's Pensions*. Ithaca, NY: Cornell University Press, pp. 67–92.

Odih, P. and Knights, D. (1999). '"Disciple Needs Time": Education For Citizenship and the Financially Disciplined Subject', *The School Field*, X(3/4): 127–52.

OECD (1998). *Maintaining Prosperity in an Ageing Society*. Paris: OECD.

Olney, M. (1991). *Buy Now, Pay Later: Advertising, Credit, and Consumer Durables in the 1920s*. London: University of North Carolina Press.

O'Malley, P. (2000). 'Uncertain Subjects: Risk, Liberalism and Contract', *Economy and Society*, 29(4): 460–84.

——(2004). *Risk, Uncertainty and Government*. London: Glass House.

Palmer, H. and Conaty, P. (2002). *Profiting from Poverty: Why Debt is Big Business in Britain*. London: New Economics Foundation. Available at: http://www.neweconomics.org/gen/uploads/Profiting%20from%20Poverty.pdf

Parliamentary and Health Service Ombudsman (2006). *Trusting in the Pensions Promise: Government Bodies and the Security of Final Salary Occupational Pensions*. London: The Stationery Office.

Partnoy, F. (2004). *Infectious Greed: How Deceit and Risk Corrupted the Financial Markets*. London: Profile Books.

Pauly, L. (1997). *Who Elected the Bankers? Surveillance and Control in the World Economy*. Ithaca, NY: Cornell University Press.

Pear, R. (2005). 'Social Security Agency is Enlisted to Push Its Own Revision', *New York Times*, 16 January, online edition.

Peck, J. (2001). *Workfare States*. London: Guilford Press.

Pensions Commission (2004). *Pensions: Challenges and Choices.* London: Pensions Commission. Available at: http://www.pensionscommission.org.uk/publications/2004/annrep/index.asp

——(2005). *A New Pension Settlement for the Twenty-First Century: The Second Report of the Pensions Commission.* London: Pensions Commission. Available at: http://www.pensionscommission.org.uk/publications/2005/annrep/main-report.pdf

Pensions Service (2004*a*). *A Guide to Your Pension Options* [PM1]. London: The Pensions Service.

——(2004*b*). *Pensions for Women—Your Guide* [PM6]. London: The Pension Service.

Peters, J. W. and Andrews, E. L. (2007). 'Manageable Threats Seen by Fed Chief', *New York Times*, 29 March, online edition.

Peters, M. A. (2001). *Poststructuralism, Marxism and Neoliberalism: Between Theory and Politics.* Oxford: Rowman & Littlefield.

Pettifor, A. (1998). 'The Economic Bondage of Debt—and the Birth of a New Movement', *New Left Review*, 230: 115–22.

——(2006). *The Coming First World Debt Crisis.* Basingstoke, UK: Palgrave MacMillan.

Pollard, J. (2001). 'The Global Financial System: Worlds of Monies', in P. Daniels, M. Bradshaw, D. Shaw, and J. Sidaway (eds.), *Human Geography: Issues for the 21st Century.* Essex, UK: Pearson Education, pp. 374–98.

Pollin, R. (1995). 'Financial Structures and Egalitarian Economic Policy', *New Left Review*, 214: 26–61.

Porter, E. and Williams Walsh, M. (2006). 'Benefits Go the Way of Pensions, *New York Times*, 9 February, online edition.

Porter, T. (2005). *Globalization and Finance.* Cambridge: Polity Press.

Power, M. (2005). 'Enterprise Risk Management and the Organization of Uncertainty in Financial Institutions', in K. Knorr Cetina and A. Preda (eds.), *The Sociology of Financial Markets.* Oxford: Oxford University Press, pp. 250–68.

Preda, A. (2001). 'The Rise of the Popular Investor: Financial Knowledge and Investing in England and France, 1840–1880', *The Sociological Quarterly*, 42(2): 205–32.

——(2005). 'The Investor as a Cultural Figure in Global Capitalism', in K. Knorr Cetina and A. Preda (eds.), *The Sociology of Financial Markets.* Oxford: Oxford University Press, pp. 141–62.

President's Commission to Strengthen Social Security (2001). *Strengthening Social Security and Creating Personal Wealth for All Americans.* Washington, DC: Commission to Strengthen Social Security. Available at: http://www.csss.gov/reports/Final_report.pdf

Pryke, M. and Whitehead, C. (1994). 'An Overview of Mortgage-backed Securitisation in the UK', *Housing Studies*, 9(1): 75–102.

Reddy, S. (1996). 'Claims to Expert Knowledge and the Subversion of Democracy: The Triumph of Risk over Uncertainty', *Economy and Society*, 25(2): 222–54.

Reuters (2003). 'For First Time, More Than 50% of U.S. Households Own Stock', *New York Times*, 22 January, online edition.

Richards, T. (1987). *Unit Trusts: A Practical Guide for the First-Time Investor*. London: Telegraph Publications.

Rifkin, J. and Barber, R. (1978). *The North Will Rise Again: Pensions, Politics and Power in the 1980s*, Boston: Beacon Press.

Ring, P. (2002). 'The Implications of the "New Insurance Contract" for UK Pension Provision: Rights, Responsibilities and Risks', *Critical Social Policy*, 22(4): 551–71.

Ringshaw, G. (2006). 'Lloyds Hits at "Cavalier Debtors" ', *The Telegraph*, 4 August, online edition.

Ritzer, G. (1995). *Expressing America: A Critique of the Global Credit Card Society*. Thousand Oaks, CA: Pine Forge Press.

—— (2001). *Explorations in the Sociology of Consumption: Fast Food, Credit Cards, and Casinos*. London: Sage.

Roberts, S. M. (1998). 'Geo-governance in Trade and Finance and Political Geographies of Dissent', in A. Herod, G. O'Tuathail, and S. M. Roberts (eds.), *Unruly World? Globalization, Governance and Geography*. London: Routledge, pp. 116–34.

Rose, I. (1997). *The DIY Credit Repair Manual*. Totton, UK: Rosy Publications.

Rose, N. (1990). *Governing the Soul: The Shaping of the Private Self*. London: Routledge.

—— (1991). 'Governing by Numbers: Figuring out Democracy', *Accounting, Organizations and Society*, 16(7): 673–92.

—— (1999). *Powers of Freedom: Reframing Political Thought*. Cambridge: Cambridge University Press.

Rosenbaum, D. E. (2005). 'Bush Return to "Ownership Society" Theme in Push for Social Security Changes', *New York Times*, 16 January, online edition.

Rushton, E. W. (2007). Testimony of Emory W. Rushton, Senior Deputy Comptroller and Chief National Bank Examiner, Office of the Comptroller of the Currency, at Mortgage Market Turmoil: Causes and Consequences, Hearing of Senate Committee on Banking, Housing, and Urban Affairs, 22nd March. Available at: http://banking.senate.gov/index.cfm?Fuseaction = Hearings.Detail&HearingID = 254

Russell Research (2006). *The 2005–2006 Russell Survey on Alternative Investing: A Survey of Organizations in North America, Europe, Australia, and Japan*. New York: Russell Research.

Samuels, S. (2007). Testimony of Sandor Samuels, Executive Managing Director, Countrywide Financial Corporation, at Mortgage Market Turmoil: Causes and Consequences, Hearing of Senate Committee on Banking, Housing, and

Urban Affairs, 22nd March. Available at: http://banking.senate.gov/index.cfm? Fuseaction = Hearings.Detail&HearingID = 254

Sandler, R. (2002). *Medium and long-term retail savings in the UK*. London: HM Treasury. Available at: http://www.hm-treasury.go.uk/Documents/Financial_Services/Savings/fin_sav_sand.cfm

Sassen, S. (1999). 'Global Financial Centres', *Foreign Affairs*, 78(1): 75–87.

Saunders, P. and Harris, C. (1994). *Privatization and Popular Capitalism*. Buckingham, UK: Open University Press.

Scanion, K. and Whitehead, C. (2005). *The Profile and Intentions of Buy-to-Let Investors*. London, Council of Mortgage Lenders.

Schenk, M. (2006). *Commercial Banks and Credit Unions: Facts, Fallacies, and Recent Trends*. Madison, WI: Credit Union National Association. Available at: http://advice.cuna.org/download/combanks_cus.pdf

Schiffin, M. (1996). 'Sub-Prime Stocks', *Forbes*, 158(1): 56–7.

Scholte, J. A. and Schnabel, A. (2002). *Civil Society and Global Finance*. London: Routledge.

Scholtens, B. (2006). 'Finance as a Driver of Corporate Social Responsibility', *Journal of Business Ethics*, 68(1): 19–34.

Scholtes, S. (2007). 'Cure for Subprime Ills Will Take Protracted Effort', *Financial Times*, 18 May, online edition.

Schor, J. (1998). *The Overspent American: Upscaling, Downshifting, and the New Consumer*. New York: Basic Books.

Schumpeter, J. A. (1983). *The Theory of Economic Development: An Inquiry into Profits, Capital, Credit, Interest and the Business Cycle*, Trans. R. Opie, introduction by J. E. Elliott. London: Transaction Books.

Scott, J. C. (1985). *Weapons of the Weak: Everyday Forms of Peasant Resistance*. New Haven, CT: Yale University Press.

Scurlock, J. D. (2007). *Maxed Out: Hard Times, Easy Credit, and the Era of Predatory Lenders*. New York: Scribner.

Seabrooke, L. (2001). *U.S. Power and International Finance: Victory of the Dividends*. Basingstoke, UK: Palgrave.

—— (2006). *The Social Sources of Financial Power: Domestic Legitimacy and International Financial Orders*. Ithaca, NY: Cornell University Press.

Securities Industry and Financial Markets Association (2006). 'Asset Backed Securities Outstanding By Major Types of Credit', 1995–2006:Q3'. Available at: http://bondmarkets.com/story.asp?id = 84

Sennett, R. (2005). *The Culture of the New Capitalism*. New Haven, CT: Yale University Press.

Shaoul, M. (1997). 'The Acrobat of Desire: Consumer Credit and its Linkages to Modern Consumerism', in D. Knights and T. Tinker (eds.), *Financial Institutions and Social Transformations*. Basingstoke, UK: MacMillan, pp. 68–91.

Sharp, J. P., Routledge, P., Philo, C., and Paddison, C. (2000). 'Entanglements of Power: Geographies of Domination/Resistance', in J. P. Sharp, P. Routledge,

C. Philo, and R. Paddison (eds.), *Entanglements of Power: Geographies of Domination/Resistance*. London: Routledge, pp. 1–42.

Shell, M. (1995). *Art & Money*. Chicago, IL: University of Chicago Press.

Shiller, R. J. (2001). *Irrational Exuberance*. Princeton, NJ: Princeton University Press.

—— (2003). *The New Financial Order: Risk in the 21st Century*. Princeton, NJ: Princeton University Press.

Shlay, A. B. (2006). 'Low-income Homeownership: American Dream or Delusion', *Urban Studies*, 43(3): 511–31.

Simmel, G. (1990). In T. Bottomore and D. Frisby, trans (ed.), *The Philosophy of Money*, 2nd enlarged edn. London: Routledge.

Sinclair, T. J. (1994). 'Passing Judgement: Credit Rating Processes as Regulatory Mechanisms of Governance in the Emerging World Order', *Review of International Political Economy*, 1(1): 133–60.

—— (2005). *The New Masters of Capital: American Bond Rating Agencies and the Politics of Creditworthiness*. Ithaca, NY: Cornell University Press.

Smith, S. J. (2006). 'Owner Occupation: At Home with a Hybrid of Money and Materials', mimeo, forthcoming in *Environment and Planning A*.

Social Investment Forum (2005). *Mutual Funds, Proxy Voting, and Fiduciary Responsibility: How Do Funds Rate on Voting Their Proxies and Disclosure Practices?* Washington, DC: Social Investment Forum. Available at: http://www.socialinvest.org/areas/research/votingpractices/SRIBooklet.v8.pdf

—— (2006). *2005 Report on Socially Responsible Investment Trends in the United States: 10 Year Review*. Washington, DC: Social Investment Forum. Available at: http://www.socialinvest.org/areas/research/trends/sri_trends_report_2005.pdf

—— (2007). *Defined Contribution Plans and Socially Responsible Investing in the United States: A Survey of Plan Sponsors, Administrators and Consultants*. Washington, DC: Social Investment Forum. Available at: http://www.socialinvest.org/areas/research/other/ContributionPlansandSRIinUS.pdf

Soederberg, S. (2004). *The Politics of the New International Financial Architecture: Reimposing Neoliberal Domination in the Global South*. London: Zed Books.

—— (2006*a*). 'Demystifying US Equity Financing in Emerging Markets: The Paradox of Socially Responsible Investing and the Creation of New Spaces of Capital', paper presented to the International Studies Association annual convention, San Diego, CA, March.

—— (2006*b*). *Global Governance in Question: Empire, Class and the New Common Sense in Managing North-South Relations*. London: Pluto Press.

Sparkes, R. (2006). 'A Historical Perspective on the Growth of Socially Responsible Investment', in R. Sullivan and C. Mackenzie (eds.), *Responsible Investment*. Sheffield, UK: Greenleaf Publishing, pp. 39–54.

Squires, G. D. (2003). 'Introduction: The Rough Road to Reinvestment', in G. D. Squires (ed.), *Organizing Access to Capital: Advocacy and the Democratization of Financial Institutions*. Philadelphia, PA: Temple University Press.

SSA (2004). *The Future of Social Security*, SSA Publication No. 05–10055. Washington, DC: Social Security Administration. Available at: http://www.ssa.gov/pubs/10055.html

Stiglitz, J. (2003). *The Roaring Nineties: Seeds of Destruction*. London: Allen Lane.

Strange, S. (1986). *Casino Capitalism*. Oxford: Basil Blackwell.

——(1998). *Mad Money*. Manchester, UK: Manchester University Press.

Stuart, G. (2003). *Discriminating Risk: The U.S. Mortgage Lending Industry in the Twentieth Century*. Ithaca, NY: Cornell University Press.

Sullivan, T. A., Warren, E., and Westbrook, J. L. (2000). *The Fragile Middle Class: Americans in Debt*. New Haven, CT: Yale University Press.

Tawney, R. H. (1982). *The Acquisitive Society*. Brighton, UK: Wheatsheaf Books.

Taylor, M. C. (2004). *Confidence Games: Money and Markets in a World Without Redemption*. Chicago, IL: The University of Chicago Press.

Tett, G., Davies, P. J., and Cohen, N. (2007). 'Age-old Risk is the Big New Threat to Stability', *Financial Times*, 13 August, online edition.

Tharp, P. (2007). 'Vice Fund$ Nice', *New York Post*, 1 May. Available at: http://www.nypost.com/seven/05012007/business/vice_fund_nice_business_paul_tharp.htm

The Economist (2002*a*). 'Special report: World economy, Dicing with Debt', 26 January, 23–5.

——(2002*b*). 'Time to Grow Up: A Survey of Pensions', 16 February.

——(2003*a*). 'A Survey of Asset Management: Pension Pain', 5 July.

——(2003*b*). 'Flying on One Engine: A Survey of the World Economy', 20 September.

——(2004). 'Insecurities', 13 November, 96–9.

——(2005*a*). 'Sub-Prime Time: Credit Cards', 19 February, online edition.

——(2005*b*). 'The Global Housing Boom: In Come the Waves', 16 June, 35–9.

——(2005*c*). 'The Great Thrift Shift: A Survey of the World Economy', 24 September.

——(2006*a*). 'Battling For Corporate Democracy: Special Report on Shareholder Democracy', 11 March, 75–7.

——(2006*b*). 'Special Report: Hedge Funds, Growing Pains', 4 March, 77–9.

——(2006*c*). 'Subprime Subsidence', 13 December, online edition.

——(2007*a*). 'Bearish Turns', 21 June, online edition.

——(2007*b*). 'Bleak Houses', 15 February, online edition.

——(2007*c*). 'Cracks in the Façade', 22 March, online edition.

——(2007*d*). 'Credit Derivatives: At the Risky End of Finance', 19 April, online edition.

——(2007*e*). 'Rethinking Risk', 28 February, online edition.

——(2007 *f*). 'Rising Damp', 10 March, 93–4.

——(2007*g*). 'What Keeps Bankers Awake at Night?' 1 February, online edition.

Thomas, L., Jr. (2006). 'The Fever for Exotic Stocks', *New York Times*, 18 May, online edition.

Thrift, N. (2001). ' "It's the Romance, Not the Finance, That Makes the Business Worth Pursuing": Disclosing a New Market Culture', *Economy and Society*, 30(4): 412–32.

—— and Leyshon, A. (1999). 'Moral Geographies of Money', in E. Gilbert and E. Helleiner (eds.), *Nation-States and Money: The Past, Present and Future of National Currencies*. London: Routledge, pp. 159–81.

Tickell, A. (2000). 'Finance and Localities', in G. L. Clark, M. P. Feldman, and M. S. Gertler (eds.), *The Oxford Handbook of Economic Geography*. Oxford: Oxford University Press, pp. 230–47.

—— (2003). 'Cultures of Money', in K. Anderson, M. Domosh, S. Pile, and N. Thrift (eds.), *Handbook of Cultural Geography*. London: Sage, pp. 116–30.

Timmins, N. (2003). 'Pension Policy Attacked from Many Sides', *Financial Times*, 28 March, 10.

Toner, R. (2005). 'It's "Private" vs. "Personal" in Social Security Debate', *New York Times*, 22 March, online edition.

Toporowski, J. (2000). *The End of Finance: Capital Market Inflation, Financial Derivatives and Pension Fund Capitalism*. London: Routledge.

Tudela, M. and Young, G. (2003). 'The Distribution of Unsecured Debt in the United Kingdom: Survey Evidence', *Bank of England Quarterly Bulletin Winter*, 417–27.

UBS Global Asset Management (2003). *Pension Fund Indicators 2003: A Long-term Perspective on Pension Fund Investment*. London: UBS Global Asset Management.

UBS Warburg (2001). *UK Pensions Following FRS17*. London: UBS Warburg.

UK Social Investment Forum (2006). *Review of Activities, 1st July 2005 – 30th June 2006*. London: UK Social Investment Forum. Available at: http://www.uksif.org/cmsfiles/uksif/UKSIF%20REVIEW%200F%20ACTIVITIES%202006.pdf

Useem, M. (1996). *Investor Capitalism: How Money Managers are Changing the Face of Corporate America*. New York: Basic Books.

Velthuis, O. (2005). *Imaginary Economics: Contemporary Artists and the World of Big Money*. Rotterdam: NAi Publishers.

Verdier, D. (2002). *Moving Money: Banking and Finance in the Industrialized World*. Cambridge: Cambridge University Press.

Vogel, S. K. (1996). *Freer Markets, More Rules: Regulatory Reform in Advanced Industrial Countries*. Ithaca, NY: Cornell University Press.

Waine, B. (2006). 'Ownership and Security: Individualised Pensions and Pension Policy in the United Kingdom and the United States', *Competition and Change*, 10(3): 321–37.

Walker, R. (2006). 'Buyer Beware', *New York Times*, 19 November, online edition.

Wander, N. and Malone, R. E. (2007). 'Keeping Public Institutions Invested in Tobacco', *Journal of Business Ethics*, 73(2): 161–76.

Warren, E. and Warren Tyagi, A. (2004). *The Two Income Trap: Why Middle-Class Parents Are Going Broke*. New York: Basic Books.

Watkins, J. P. (2000). 'Corporate Power and the Evolution of Consumer Credit', *Journal of Economic Issues*, 34(4): 909–35.

Watson, M. (2007). *The Political Economy of International Capital Mobility*. Basingstoke, UK: Palgrave MacMillan.

Watson Wyatt (2003). *Pension Plan Design Survey: 2003 Update*. London: Watson Wyatt.

Weber, M. (1978). In G. Roth and C. Wittich (eds.), *Economy and Society: An Outline of Interpretive Sociology*. Berkeley, CA: University of California Press.

Wharf, B. (1994). 'Vicious Circle: Financial Markets and Commercial Real Estate in the United States', in S. Corbridge, R. Martin, and N. Thrift (eds.), *Money, Power and Space*. Oxford: Basil Blackwell, pp. 309–26.

White, B., Knight, R., Callan, E., Beales, R., Scholtes, S., and MacKenzie, M. (2007). 'How a Fiasco of Easy Home Loans Has Tipped Up America', *Financial Times*, 15 March, online edition.

Whitehouse, E. (2000). *Pension Reform, Financial Literacy and Public Information: A Case Study of the United Kingdom*, Social Protection Discussion Paper Series. Washington, DC: The World Bank.

Whitford, D. (1997). 'Why Risk Matters', *Fortune*, 29 December, 147–52.

Williams, C., Aldridge, T., and Tooke, J. (2003). 'Alternative Exchange Spaces', in A. Leyshon, R. Lee, and C. Williams (eds.), *Alternative Economic Spaces*. London: Sage, pp. 151–67.

Williams Walsh, M. (2003*a*). 'A Plan to Recalculate Pensions', *New York Times*, 11 April, online edition.

——(2003*b*). 'Discord over Efforts at Valuing Pensions', *New York Times*, 1 May, online edition.

——(2003*c*). 'New Rules Urged to Avert Looming Pension Crisis', *New York Times*, 28 July, online edition.

——(2003*d*). 'White House Seeks Revised Pension Rules', *New York Times*, 8 July, online edition.

——(2006*a*). 'More Companies Ending Promises for Retirement', *New York Times*, 9 January, online edition.

——(2006*b*). 'Pension Overhaul Gives, and Later Takes Away', *New York Times*, 5 August, online edition.

World Bank (1994). *Averting the Old Age Crisis: Policies to Protect the Old and Promote Growth*. New York: Oxford University Press.

Wyderko, S. F. (2004). 'Statement to the Senate Committee on Governmental Affairs—The Federal Government's Role in Empowering Americans to Make Informed Financial Decisions', March 30th. Available at: http://www.senate.gov/~govt-aff/index.cfm?Fuseaction = Hearings.Testimony& HearingID = 163&WitnessID = 589

Wyly, E. K., Atia, M., Foxcroft, H., Hammel, D. J., and Phillips-Watts, K. (2006). 'American Home: Predatory Mortgage Capital and Neighbourhood Spaces of Race and Class Exploitation in the United States', *Geografiska Annaler*, 88(2): 105–32.

Zelizer, V. A. (1994). *The Social Meaning of Money: Pin Money, Paychecks, Poor Relief, and Other Currencies*. New York: Basic Books.

Zysman, J. (1983). Governments, Markets and Growth: Finance and the Politics of Industrial Change. Ithaca, NY: Cornell University Press.

Index